THE WELL-BEING
OF CHILDREN IN THE UK
Fourth Edition

Edited by Jonathan Bradshaw

First published in Great Britain in 2016 by

Policy Press
University of Bristol
1-9 Old Park Hill
Bristol
BS2 8BB
UK
+44 (0)117 954 5940
pp-info@bristol.ac.uk
www.policypress.co.uk

North America office:
Policy Press
c/o The University of Chicago Press
1427 East 60th Street
Chicago, IL 60637, USA
t: +1 773 702 7700
f: +1 773 702 9756
sales@press.uchicago.edu
www.press.uchicago.edu

© Policy Press 2016

British Library Cataloguing in Publication Data
A catalogue record for this book is available from the British Library

Library of Congress Cataloging-in-Publication Data
A catalog record for this book has been requested

ISBN 978 1 44732 562 8 hardcover
ISBN 978 1 44732 563 5 paperback
ISBN 978 1 44732 567 3 ePub
ISBN 978 1 44732 566 6 Mobi

Cover design by Policy Press
Front cover image: Shutterstock
Printed and bound in Great Britain by CMP, Poole
Policy Press uses environmentally responsible print partners

Contents

List of figures and tables

Figures

Tables

List of abbreviations

AHC	after housing costs
BHC	before housing costs
BHPS	British Household Panel Survey
CDS	Child Deprivation Scale
CHIMAT	Child and Maternity Public Health Observatory
CSEW	Crime Survey for England and Wales
CYPU	Children and Young People's Unit
DCSF	Department for Children, Schools and Families
DfE	Department for Education
DfES	Department for Education and Skills
DTO	Detention and Training Order
DWP	Department for Work and Pensions
EEAD	European Alliance Against Depression
ESRC	Economic and Social Research Council
EU	European Union
HMRC	Her Majesty's Revenue and Customs
HSE	Health Survey for England
IDAC	Income Deprivation Affecting Children Index
LSOA	lower layer super output area
OECD	Organisation for Economic Co-operation and Development
OLS	Overall Life Satisfaction
ONS	Office for National Statistics
PSA	Public Service Agreement
PWI-SC	Personal Well-being Index – School Children
RPI	Restrictive Physical Intervention
SLSS	Student's Life Satisfaction Scale
YRO	Youth Rehabilitation Order

Notes on contributors

Karen Bloor is Professor of Health Economics and Policy in the Department of Health Sciences at the University of York, and the University's Research Champion for Health and Wellbeing. As part of a broader research portfolio she is involved in various projects relating to child health, including a cohort study of children 'Born in Bradford'. She also constructed the health domain of the Local Index of Child Well-being.

Jonathan Bradshaw CBE, FBA is Emeritus Professor of Social Policy at the University of York and Associate Director of the Social Policy Research Unit. In recent years his research has focused on child poverty, child benefit packages, child well-being and comparative social policy. He has also written about family policy. He is UK coordinator of the European Social Policy Network, is a member of the board of the Child Poverty Action Group (CPAG) and the editorial board of the journal *Child Indicators Research*. See http://php.york.ac.uk/inst/spru/profiles/jrb.php for more information.

Veronica Dale is a statistician and Research Fellow in the Department of Health Sciences at the University of York. She has worked on a variety of clinical trials and other statistical analyses, particularly in the fields of addiction and cardiac rehabilitation. She is now part of a 'fast response analytical facility' providing research and analysis for the Department of Health.

Antonia Keung is Associate Lecturer in the Department of Social Policy and Social Work at the University of York. Her research interest primarily focuses on the well-being of children and young people, particularly the links between children's homes, school context and their well-being and future outcomes. Previously she was a Research Fellow at the department and completed a number of collaborative research projects for organisations such as the Cabinet Office, The Children's Society and the former Audit Commission.

Gill Main is a University Academic Fellow in the School of Education at the University of Leeds. She was formerly a Research Fellow at the University of York. Her research focuses on child and youth poverty, social exclusion and well-being. She has investigated the links between child poverty and subjective well-being, and how incorporating children's own perspectives of their needs can elucidate these links. She has recently worked on the 2012 UK Poverty and Social Exclusion Study and the Children's Worlds study. She is currently working on a study of child poverty and social exclusion in Australia.

Rachel Morris is a Lecturer in the Department of Social Policy and Social Work, University of York. Her research interests focus on the relationship between youth justice policy and practice and the criminal careers of young people, in particular, looked-after children and girls. She also teaches undergraduate students, focusing on criminal justice, youth justice and qualitative research methods.

Lisa O'Malley is a Lecturer in the Department of Social Policy and Social Work, University of York. Her research interests focus on the links between crime, risk and place. She also teaches undergraduate students, specialising in criminal justice, policing and punishment.

Deborah Quilgars is a Senior Research Fellow at the Centre for Housing Policy, University of York. She has 25 years' experience in housing research, with particular expertise in homelessness and housing and support services. Deborah has undertaken a number of studies on youth homelessness and evaluations of services for homeless people and other excluded groups including teenage parents. See www.york. ac.uk/chp/people/quilgars/ for more information.

Gwyther Rees is an Honorary Research Fellow at the Social Policy Research Unit, University of York. Gwyther was formerly Research Director at The Children's Society where his research focused primarily on young runaways, child protection and safeguarding, and children's subjective well-being. Gwyther is also currently studying for a doctorate at Cardiff University and is a member of the core group of researchers leading the Children's Worlds research project, an international study of children's lives and well-being.

Christine Skinner is Reader in Social Policy at the University of York. Childcare and early education is a key aspect of her research work on children and families, the other being child support policy nationally and comparatively. Her research projects have included exploring how parents manage to coordinate childcare and education arrangements to fit with paid work, and also an evaluation of free early years services for vulnerable two-year-olds for a local authority in England. Christine also teaches.

Mike Stein is Emeritus Professor in the Social Policy Research Unit at the University of York. During the last 30 years he has been researching the problems and challenges faced by vulnerable teenagers including young people leaving care and maltreated and neglected adolescents. He is a joint coordinator of the Transitions from Care to Adulthood International Research Group (INTRAC) and a consultant to The Children's Society Adolescent Neglect Research programme. See http://php.york.ac.uk/inst/spru/profiles/ms.php for more details.

Acknowledgements

This is the fourth edition of *The well-being of children in the UK*, but actually the fifth book on the subject that we have produced from the University of York, and each builds on the one that went before. We are grateful for the sponsors of the earlier volumes. The first volume (Bradshaw, 2001) was supported by the Economic and Social Research Council (ESRC, Children 5-16 programme) and was published by the Family Policy Studies Centre. The second and third volumes (Bradshaw, 2002 and Bradshaw and Mayhew, 2005) were sponsored and published by Save the Children (UK), and the last volume (Bradshaw, 2011) was sponsored by CHIMAT (Child and Maternal Health Observatory, now the National Child and Maternal Health Intelligence Network, see www.chimat.org.uk/).

We are also grateful to our colleagues who worked on earlier volumes, but for various reasons did not contribute to this volume. From the last volume they include Carol-Ann Hooper and Sharon Grace.

We are grateful for the funding that we have received over the years, which has supported the research that has contributed to this book. This includes support from ESRC, UNICEF (the UK office, Office for Research [Innocenti Centre] and the Central and Eastern Europe [CEE]/Commonwealth of Independent States [CIS] Regional Office), The Children's Society, European Commission, International Labour Office, Joseph Rowntree Foundation, Jacobs Foundation, Social Exclusion Task Force of the Cabinet Office, and the Department for Communities and Local Government.

Many thanks also to Teresa Frank and Emese Mayhew, for their contributions in preparing the typescript.

ONE

Introduction

Jonathan Bradshaw

> The true measure of a nation's standing is how well it attends to its children – their health and safety, their material security, their education and socialization, and their sense of being loved, valued, and included in the families and societies into which they were born. (UNICEF, 2007, p 1)

In the UK we have no official means of establishing how our children are doing, no 'State of UK children' report. This book is an attempt to fill that gap. It is the fifth in a series of volumes that has been produced out of the University of York stable since Bradshaw (2001). That book emerged from the Economic and Social Research Council (ESRC) Children 5-16 research programme, and was motivated by anxiety about the impact that the doubling of relative child poverty rates under the Thatcher government might be having on the well-being of children in the UK. It concluded by recommending that the UK should produce a regular review of the well-being of its children, and that perhaps responsibility for it could be taken by the Office for National Statistics (ONS). When this looked unlikely, Save the Children (UK) stepped in and supported the publication of two further volumes – Bradshaw (2002) and Bradshaw and Mayhew (2005). The last volume was produced with the support of the Child and Maternity Public Health Observatory (CHIMAT) in Bradshaw (2011).

The 2011 volume reported the situation of children around 2009/10, and focused on the years of the Labour government during 1997-2010. It really covered a period before the global financial crisis in 2008, and certainly before the impact of the austerity measures introduced by the coalition government (elected in 2010) could be felt. Time has passed on, and another cohort of children has gone through infancy, primary and secondary schools, and much that might affect children has changed since the last volume.

Up until 2008 the UK had experienced an unprecedented period of economic growth, with employment rates reaching record levels, and unemployment had never been so low. During this period, there were substantial increases in public expenditure on education, health, transport and cash and tax benefits for families with children. Other significant developments for children were the establishment of *Sure Start*, the extension of nursery education to three- and four-year-olds and substantial investment in pre-school childcare. In schools, the standards agenda had sought to improve literacy and numeracy, and to improve performance at key stages and at GCSE (General Certificate of Secondary Education) level. Efforts had been made to increase staying on rates at school and to expand opportunities for tertiary education. During this period the government had been pursuing the child poverty strategy announced by the Prime Minister in 1999, which aimed to eradicate child poverty by 2020 and to halve it by 2010. The apotheosis of this was the Child Poverty Act, passed with all-party support in 2010, with explicit child poverty targets to be reached by 2021.

There had also been an institutional transformation. In England the Children and Young People's Unit (CYPU) had been absorbed into the Department for Education and Skills (DfES) and a Minister for Children appointed. Later, it became the Department for *Children*, Schools and Families (DCSF), and acquired a new strategy in *The children's plan* (DCSF, 2007a). Commissioners for Children were established in all countries of the UK. There had also been a transformation of children's services locally, with the establishment (in England) of Children's Trusts and Partnerships.

After the formation of the coalition government, following the 2010 General Election, the situation for children began to change. Perhaps the first signal was that the DCSF reverted to the Department for Education (DfE). The coalition government decided to tackle the deficit by cuts in benefits and services. Working-age benefits were most affected by the reforms to social security spending, and some benefits were abolished altogether – including the Health in Pregnancy Grant and Educational Maintenance Allowances (in England). However, most of the savings were achieved by not uprating cash benefits. Child benefit was frozen for four years, and Child Tax Credits uprated by only 1%. Council Tax Benefit and the Social Fund were localised, which meant cuts for households with children in most areas. These cuts, rising unemployment and falling real wages meant that real incomes fell for six successive years. At the same time the number of unemployed reached over 2 million.

A number of attempts have now been made to evaluate the distributional consequences of these austerity measures (Cribb et al,

2013; Office of the Children's Commissioner, 2013; Reed and Portes, 2014; Lupton et al, 2015). They all show that it is the poorest families with children who have suffered the biggest losses in income, and it is families with children who have suffered the largest cuts in services. The cuts have not only been regressive and hit families with children hardest, they have also been spatially regressive, with the largest cuts in central government grants falling most heavily on local authority areas with the highest levels of child poverty (Beatty and Fothergill, 2013).

As a result of the election of a Conservative government in 2015 we can expect further austerity measures, with £12 billion of cuts to come from working-age benefits, which will inevitably entail further cuts to cash benefits and tax credits for families with children.

Efforts to monitor child well-being

Although there is already a great deal of material available on children's well-being in the UK (and we shall be drawing on it), the objective of this book is to bring the evidence together in one place in a critical discursive review, which has not, as yet, been done elsewhere.

One welcome development since the last volume has been that the Office for National Statistics (ONS), as part of its efforts to measure national happiness, has begun to produce an index of children's well-being. A report published in October 2014 (ONS, 2014a) presents estimates for 22 of 31 measures of children's well-being, covering:

- personal well-being
- relationships
- health
- what we do
- where we live
- personal finance
- education and skills.

The ONS says that these estimates can be thought of as a baseline for children's well-being, and intends to update them annually.

One source that the ONS index uses for this data is the surveys of children undertaken since 2010 by The Children's Society in England in collaboration with some of the authors of this volume. These have formed the basis of *The good childhood reports* (The Children's Society, 2011, 2012, 2013, 2014, 2015). The 2015 survey funded by the Jacobs Foundation also forms the England contribution to the Children's Worlds[1] comparative survey of child well-being in 16 countries.

In 2009 the DCSF let a contract for a new Childhood Well-being Research Centre.[2] The Centre has now produced a number of fast reviews and scoping reviews for the DfE, but its funding ran out in 2015.

What does child well-being mean?

McAuley and Rose (2010) identified four major influences on the concept of child well-being:

- *Children's rights* as set out in the United Nations (UN) Convention on the Rights of the Child (UN General Assembly, 1989) and also in the European Human Rights Charter. Included in the UN Convention is the clause that says that 'the primary consideration in all actions concerning children must be in their best interests *and their views must be taken into account*' (emphasis added).

- The so-called *new sociology of childhood*, which argued that childhood should be treated as a stage in life with its own value and not just as a passage towards adulthood. Thus the well-being of children in childhood should be the main focus of attention, not just how successful as adults they become – well-becoming – indeed, well-becoming could be in conflict with well-being.

- The *ecological perspective* on child development, which located the child in the context of the family, friendship networks, school, neighbourhood and the family's place within the community. Well-being is influenced by many dimensions – it is multidimensional. What matters to children is not just how well they do at school, or what their health is like, or how they get on with friends, but all of these things and more.

- The new *science of happiness* has been mainly applied to adults, and has its roots in hedonic psychology and self-assessed evaluations of quality of life. Economists such as Layard (2005) have argued that increasing wealth beyond a point does not necessarily result in improved happiness, that happiness or life satisfaction should be the focus of endeavour in our societies – not just increasing wealth – and that inequity associated with market competition does not enhance society. In *The spirit level* Wilkinson and Pickett (2009) argued that inequality in society is actually harmful. These ideas have spread to children and to an increasing preoccupation with what makes for a good childhood (The Children's Society, 2006).

This book has been influenced by these developments and also by the so-called *child indicators movement*. The study of child well-being is not new. Ben-Arieh (2010) finds that 'State of the child' reports were being published as early as the 1940s, but more recently, in the 1960s, the child indicators movement was influenced by the social indicators movement. It was believed that well-measured and consistently collected social indicators could provide a way to social progress. The child indicators movement developed towards the end of the last century, with UNICEF publishing the first *State of the world's children* report in 1979. The movement was facilitated in a series of meetings organised by Ben-Arieh under the umbrella of the so-called Jerusalem Project, and this eventually developed into the Multinational Indicators Project that sought to develop indicators for monitoring and measuring child well-being. This, is turn, developed into the International Society for Child Indicators that publishes a journal, *Child Indicators Research*, and newsletter, and organises seminars and conferences.[3]

Ben-Arieh (2010) lists nine major developments in the child indicators movement:

- A shift from a preoccupation with physical survival and basic needs to development and well-being.
- A shift from negative indicators of problems and failure to positive indicators that hold societies accountable for more than the warehousing of children.
- Incorporating child rights perspectives that focus on the child.
- A shift from well-becoming to well-being.
- A shift from traditional domains such as education and health to new domains such as life skills and civic involvement.
- A shift from an adult to a child perspective – focusing on children's lives.
- A new focus on data at the local level.
- The development of more policy-oriented indicators.

He also discusses a trend towards producing single composite indices, the use of the child as the unit of observation, and the emerging importance of subjective measures.

Comparative indices of child well-being

UNICEF was the pioneer of well-being indices. Professor Andrea Cornia, working at the UNICEF Innocenti Centre in Florence (now the UNICEF Office for Research), became concerned about what was happening to children in rich countries, and commissioned a series of national case studies, including one for the UK (Bradshaw, 1990, updated by Kumar, 1995). UNICEF eventually published a book on the well-being of children in industrialised countries in 1997 (Cornia and Danziger, 1997). This work led, in turn, to a series of *Innocenti Report Cards* comparing aspects of child well-being in OECD (Organisation for Economic Co-operation and Development) countries. However, the first overall comparative index of child well-being was a comparison of European Union (EU) countries (Bradshaw et al, 2007a), which showed the UK placed 21 out of 25 EU countries. Bradshaw, Hoelscher and Richardson (2007b) then did the work for the UNICEF (2007) Innocenti Report Card no 7, which caused a great stir in the UK, because the UK found itself at the bottom of the league table of 21 OECD countries. Bradshaw and Richardson (2009) updated the EU comparisons for the 29 EU countries. The UK came 24th out of the 29 countries. Then the OECD (2009) itself undertook a similar analysis, but cut the domains rather differently and excluded subjective well-being and children's relationships. Although the OECD did not produce a league table, it is easy to estimate one. The UK came 20th out of 30 OECD countries. Innocenti Report Card no 11 (UNICEF, 2013) updated Report Card no 7 using very similar indicators but a slightly wider range of countries. The UK had moved from the bottom of the child well-being league table to the middle, coming 16th out of 29 countries, or 17th if subjective well-being was included.

This improvement in the well-being of children in the UK echoes the findings of our previous volume. In its concluding chapter we collected 48 indicators of child well-being using all the domains covered in the book, and found that between 1997 and 2010, 40 of the indicators had got better or stayed the same. Only four indicators had got worse. We shall be repeating this exercise in the conclusion of this volume (see Chapter Thirteen).

Spending on children

This book is about outcomes. Spending on children is about inputs. Nevertheless, the comparative studies of child well-being have found an association between spending on children and child outcomes. This is illustrated in Figure 1.1, which shows that the percentage of GDP spent on family cash benefits, services and tax breaks in 2011 explains 20% of the variation in overall well-being from UNICEF Innocenti Report Card no 11 (UNICEF, 2013). The UK is one of the outliers, achieving lower levels of child well-being than the general relationship might suggest that it should do. The spending data excludes health and education expenditure. Also there may be a lag between spending and well-being.

Unfortunately UK national accounts do not monitor expenditure on children. Although Sefton (2004) demonstrated how it could be done, his work has not been updated, so we have to rely on international sources, which are not very up to date. Figure 1.2 shows a league table of education and family spending as a percentage of GDP in OECD countries in 2011, with the UK coming fifth. Health spending

Figure 1.1: Spending on family cash benefits, services and tax breaks as a percentage of GDP by overall child well-being, 2011

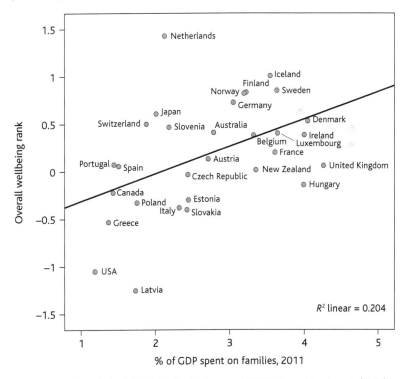

Source: Author's analysis of OECD Family database and UNICEF Report Card no 11 (2013)

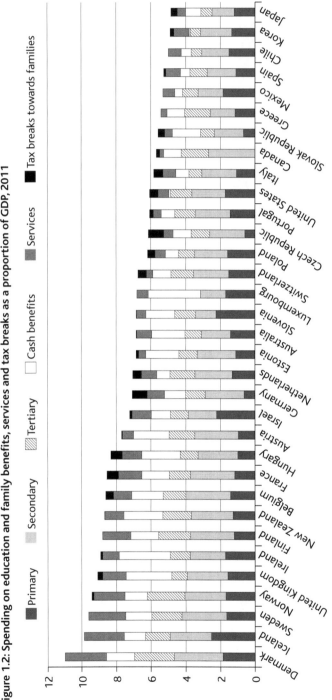

Figure 1.2: Spending on education and family benefits, services and tax breaks as a proportion of GDP, 2011

Source: OECD Family database

is an obvious missing domain but it is very difficult to isolate health spending on children.

Figure 1.3 shows trends in social spending in the UK as a percentage of GDP since 1991-92. It shows the big increase in health and education spending after 1999. Between 2009/10 and 2014/15 real spending on education has fallen and health spending has changed very little. During this period the education system has had to cope with rising school rolls on a falling budget, and the health service has had to cope with an increase in the very old elderly and increased pressures because of cuts in social care funding. Spending on employment policies and housing have fallen. Within the education budget there was a very small real terms increase in spending on the under-fives and a very large fall in the post-secondary non-tertiary sector. The social housing budget also took a big hit, but spending on social protection had increased.

However, Figure 1.4 shows that this increase in social protection expenditure is attributable to increases in spending on pensions, housing benefit and disability benefits. Spending on family benefits has taken the biggest hit.

Figure 1.3: Social spending as a proportion of GDP, 1991-92 to 2014-15

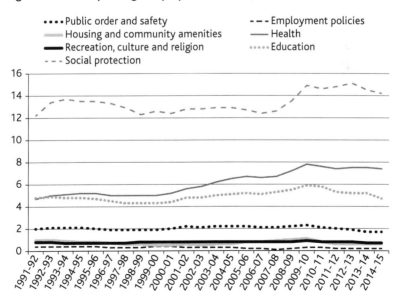

Source: HM Treasury (2015, Chapter 4)

Figure 1.4: Social protection expenditure, real terms (£ billion)

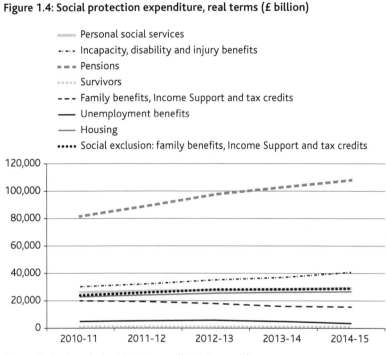

Source: Author's analysis of HM Treasury (2015, Chapter 5)

Structure of the book

Chapter Two contextualises child well-being by describing the recent demographic trends affecting children. This includes trends in fertility, trends in the number of children within families, and their distribution and ethnicity across UK countries. It also illustrates recent developments in family formation and dissolution, and the proliferation of modern family types that children live in today. Subsequent chapters deal with the different domains of child well-being. The conclusion brings together the findings, and attempts to develop an index of child well-being for the UK.

In tackling this subject matter chapter by chapter, the book tries to sustain a framework of questions:

- What is the current trend in child well-being? Are things getting better or worse over time, with a special effort to assess change over the period since the start of the recession in 2008 and since austerity began in 2010?

- How do the countries of the UK compare? While it is not always possible to do this on a consistent basis – indeed, one of the outcomes of the establishment of the devolved governments and administrations is a decline in the comparability of the data available – the institutional framework is also different and becoming more different, and it is inevitable that the review tends to fall back on England, where 84% of children in the UK live.

- What are the associates of the outcomes that are being reviewed and how do they vary by age, gender, class, ethnicity, family structure and poverty?

- How does the UK compare with other industrialised countries? International comparisons are fraught with difficulties, but without them we cannot establish how well we are doing for our children. We can say whether things are getting better or worse, but we cannot say how well or badly we are doing, or whether we are doing as well as we could be.

Conclusion

Children are our future. Children are tomorrow's workforce, parents and citizens. Investment (or the lack of it) in their well-being will shape the future of the country. As such, their well-being matters to us all.

As a nation we pay enormous attention to the well-being of our economy, the state of the weather, sporting league tables, the City and the Stock Market. Indicators of these take up pages of the media every day.

We need to make more effort to monitor the well-being of our children, and we need to devote more resources to understanding how they are doing and to ensuring that their childhood is as good as it can be. This book is a small contribution to that end.

Notes

[1] See www.isciweb.org

[2] See www.cwrc.ac.uk/

[3] See http://isci.chapinhall.org/

TWO

Demography of childhood

Jonathan Bradshaw

Key statistics

- In 2013 there were 10.44 million children under the age of 16 in the UK.
- The majority of children are White (84%). The largest group of ethnic children are Asian, forming 8% of the child population.
- In 2014 23% of children were living in a lone-parent family.
- The UK has the highest proportion of children living in lone-parent families in the European Union (EU).

Key trends

- The number and proportion of children has been declining, especially in Scotland. Children made up 16.4% of the UK population in 2013.
- There is projected to be a sharp rise in the number of young adolescents (aged 10-19) in the next 10 years.
- Rates of childlessness have increased, from 10% for women born in 1945 to 20% for women born in 1965. Average family size is falling, and there are more one-child families.
- Fertility increased after 2003, mainly as a result of migration, but the increase stopped in 2009 and has not reached replacement level.
- The proportion of households with children has fallen, from 39% in 1977 to 30% in 2013.
- There has been a persistent, sharp fall in births to unmarried teenage mothers since 1976.
- The number of births within marriage/civil partnerships has undergone a steady decline, which was mirrored by an increase in the number of births within cohabiting relationships.
- The proportion of children living with parents in cohabiting partnerships has doubled over the last 18 years.
- Compared to 1977, there are now 7% fewer homes containing a couple and two or more children.

Key sources
- Office for National Statistics (ONS)
- Family Resources Survey
- Labour Force Survey
- Millennium Cohort Survey
- European Union Statistics on Income and Living Conditions (EU-SILC)

Introduction

This chapter reviews recent developments in the demography of childhood in the UK as well as children's changing social relationships within the family. It describes the demographic characteristics of children – their numbers, gender, age, ethnicity, geographical location and family composition. It presents comparisons of UK children with those of other countries, and reviews evidence of the impact of family structure on child well-being.

Child population

In 2013 there were 10.44 million children under the age of 16 in the UK. Of these, 6.17 million were boys and 5.88 million girls. Table 2.1 shows how the numbers and proportion of children under 16 have changed between 1971 and 2013 in each country of the UK. The number of children under 16 in the UK has fallen by 3.8 million, and the overall proportion of children under 16 in the population has fallen, from 25.5% in 1971 to 16.4% in 2013. The largest reduction in the proportion of children has been in Scotland, and the distribution of children in the UK has shifted towards England, which, in 2013, contained 84.6% of all children in the UK.

Age composition of the child population

Table 2.2 shows how the age composition of children in the UK has changed between 1971 and 2013. The number of pre-school-age children decreased after 1971, interrupted by a brief recuperation during the late 1980s and early 1990s. However, in 2003, the number of births began to increase again, and with it, the pre-school population. The number of school-age children declined after 1976, and there were more than 2 million fewer children aged 5-14 in the UK in 2009 than there had been in 1976. Since the late 1990s the number of school-age children has started rising gradually again.

Table 2.1: Trends in the child population, 1971-2013

	England	Wales	Scotland	Northern Ireland	UK
1971					
000s	11,648	686	1,440	483	14,257
% of children in the population	25.1	25	27.5	31.4	25.5
% of children in the UK	81.7	4.8	10.1	3.4	100
1981					
000s	10,285	626	1,188	444	12,543
% of children in the population	21.9	22.3	22.9	28.7	22.3
% of children in the UK	82	5	9.5	3.5	100
1991					
000s	9,658	589	1,021	417	11,685
% of children in the population	20.2	20.5	20.1	25.9	20.3
% of children in the UK	82.7	5	8.7	3.6	100
2001					
000s	9,908	587	970	397	11,863
% of children in the population	20	20.2	19.2	23.5	20.1
% of children in the UK	83.5	4.9	8.2	3.3	100
2013					
000s	8,830	483	795	332	10,440
% of children in the population	16.4	15.6	15	18.4	16.4
% of children in the UK	84.6	4.6	7.6	3.2	100

Source: ONS (2014b)

Table 2.2: Trends in the number of children by age, UK (000s)

	1971	1976	1981	1986	1991	1996	2001	2009	2013
Under 1	899	677	730	748	790	719	663	784	793
1-4	3,654	3,043	2,726	2,886	3,077	3,018	2,819	2,994	3,321
5-14	8,916	9,176	8,147	7,143	7,141	7,544	7,624	7,017	7,293

Source: ONS (2014b)

Figure 2.1 shows the projected numbers of children in different age groups in the UK, based on the latest (2012) national population projections. The projections estimate a slight rise and fall in the number of pre-school children in the 20-year period between 2012 and 2032. The 5-9 age group, after undergoing a sharp increase until 2017, shall rise only slightly and level out in the following two decades. After a three-year dip, the 10-14 age group is just beginning to increase rapidly until 2021, when the trend slows down but continues. The

Figure 2.1: Projected numbers of children in different age groups, UK (000s)

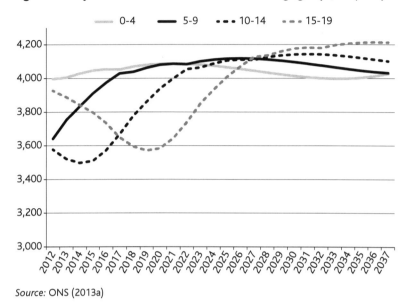

Source: ONS (2013a)

15-19 age group follows a very similar path to the 10-14 age group, only with a five-year delay.

Fertility

These fluctuations in the number and age composition of children reflect changes in fertility and birth rates. The total period fertility rate is the number of children that would be born to a woman if current patterns of fertility persisted throughout her childbearing life. Figure 2.2 shows that it reached a post-war high point in 1964 at 2.93, and then declined rapidly to a low point of 1.66 in 1977. Thereafter, it was remarkably stable and below replacement level (2.1), until in 2003 fertility began to rise again, increasing every year and reaching 1.96 in 2008. By 2013 it was 1.85 (for England and Wales), which may indicate that the recuperation has run its course. Scotland's fertility rate has been below that of England and Wales since 1981, and in 2012 it was 1.67. The fertility rate in Northern Ireland was above the replacement rate until the early 1990s, but fell rapidly and was 2.03 in 2012.

The fertility rate is influenced by changes in the number of children women will have, the timing of births and migration patterns. Age-specific fertility rates are shown in Figure 2.3, and it is apparent

Figure 2.2: Total period fertility rate, UK

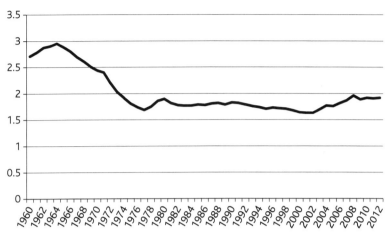

Source: Vital statistics: Population and health reference tables, ONS (nd)

that they have been declining for younger women (under 30) and increasing for older women (over 30). However, one of the main reasons for the increase in fertility has been a recovery of the age-specific fertility of women aged 25-29 as well as a rise in the rate for women aged 20-24. Tromans et al (2009) explored the reasons for the increase in births between 2001 and 2007, and concluded that two-thirds of the increase could be attributed to the increase in the number of foreign-born women in the UK who have higher fertility rates. In 2014, 27% of live births were to non-UK-born mothers, an increase from 12.4% in 1994.

Average family size

Table 2.3 shows that the rates of childlessness among women increased dramatically towards the end of the 20th century. Only 10% of the 1945 cohort of women was childless as opposed to 20% of those born in 1965. While some women are voluntarily childless, others may be unable to have children as a result of fertility problems. The postponement of motherhood to later in life can lead to difficulties in conceiving. The increased rate of childlessness has been exacerbated by decreases in the number of children mothers will have, especially those having three or more children, which was 33% in the 1945 cohort and 29% in 1965. As a result, the average completed family size is getting smaller. The predictions for the future have been revised upwards as a result of the fertility recuperation.

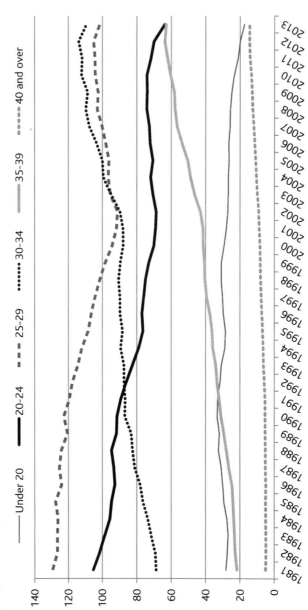

Figure 2.3: Age-specific fertility rates – births per 1,000 women in the age group, England and Wales

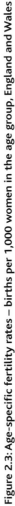

Source: Birth summary tables, England and Wales, 2013 (Final), ONS (nd)

Table 2.3: Percentage of women by number of children and average completed family size by woman's year of birth, England and Wales

	Actual completed family size					Predicted when completed				
	1945	1950	1955	1960	1965	1970	1980	1990	2000	2010
Childless	10	14	16	19	20	17	16	17	18	18
1 child	14	13	13	12	13	18	17	17	18	18
2 children	43	44	41	38	38	37	38	36	37	37
3 children	21	19	19	20	19	18	18	18	17	17
4+ children	12	10	10	11	10	10	11	12	11	10
Average family size	2.19	2.07	2.02	1.98	1.91	1.91	1.97	2	1.91	1.9

Source: Cohort fertility, ONS (2014c, nd)

Ethnicity

The vast majority of children living in the UK are of White ethnic origin. Table 2.4 shows the distribution of ethnicities. The best source of this data would be the population Census, but the 2011 Census is too out of date for estimates of ethnicity, especially because of the very substantial inward migration over the last 10 years. This data is derived from a large sample survey, the Family Resources Survey. In 2012/13, 84% of UK children were White. The largest ethnic group were Asian (9%), and within this group Pakistanis and Bangladeshis. Only 4% of all children are Black.

Table 2.4: Ethnicity of children in the UK, 2012/13 (three-year average)

	% of children
White	84
Mixed/multiple ethnic groups	1
Asian/Asian British	9
Indian	3
Pakistani	3
Bangladeshi	1
Chinese	–
Any other Asian background	1
Black/African/Caribbean/Black British	4
Other ethnic group	2
All children (millions = 13.4)	100

Source: DWP (2014, Table 4.3db)

Marriage, cohabitation and lone parenthood

One of the main precursors of late childbearing is the postponement of marriage. The mean age of first marriage for women rose from 23.1 in 1981 to 30.2 in 2011 (in England and Wales). The majority of births (52.5% in 2014) still occur within marriage, so the postponement of marriage leads to later fertility.

However, marriage rates are continuing to fall. In England and Wales, the rate of men marrying per 1,000 unmarried men in 2011 was 22.1 compared to 78.4 per 1,000 in 1972. The rate of unmarried women marrying was 19.9 per 1,000 in 2011 compared to 60.5 per 1,000 in 1972. Figure 2.4 gives the proportion of live births to unmarried mothers for all ages and the percentage of live births under 20 outside marriage. The percentage of births outside marriage increased from 8.4% in 1971 to 47.5% in 2014. In 1976, 36.8% of live births outside marriage were to women under 20, but by 2013 that proportion had declined to 8.4%. Having births inside marriage is most likely in the 30–34 age group, but 30.0% of births to this age group were outside marriage (see Table 2.5).

The marriage rate in itself reveals increasingly little about household composition because of the substantial increases in the levels of cohabitation. While in the 1970s over 50% of unmarried mothers were lone parents, today, this is by no means the case. Now most births outside marriage are registered by both parents living at the same address (65.9% in 2013), and only 11.9% of births to unmarried

Figure 2.4: Live birth rates outside marriage, England and Wales

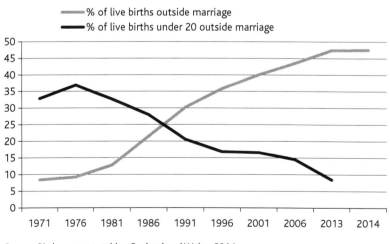

Source: Birth summary tables, England and Wales, 2014

mothers are sole registrations by the mother. The trends are shown in Figure 2.5.

Table 2.5 shows that the proportion of births to married parents increases with the age of the mother and the proportion with cohabiting or lone mothers decreases with the mother's age.

Divorce and remarriage

In 2012, the divorce rate in England and Wales was 10.8 per 1,000 marriages, slightly lower than the rate in the 1990s. However, with fewer parents marrying, divorce statistics only provide an ever-narrowing view into parental break-up. The breakdowns of other

Figure 2.5: Registration of live births outside marriage, England and Wales

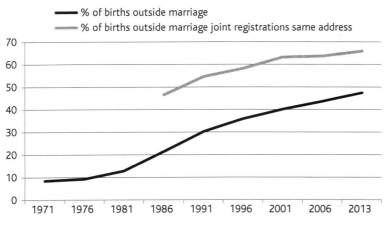

Source: Birth summary tables, England and Wales, 2014

Table 2.5: Mother's age and partnership at birth of child, England and Wales, 2013

	Under 20	20- 24	25- 29	30- 34	35- 39	40- 44	45 and over	All
Within marriage/civil partnership	4.4	21.5	51.9	68.0	68.2	61.8	61.7	52.6
Outside marriage/civil partnership	95.6	78.5	48.1	32.0	31.8	38.2	38.3	47.4
Joint registrations same address	38.5	47.4	33.6	23.5	23.5	26.8	24.0	31.2
Joint registrations different address	36.5	21.2	9.6	5.3	4.9	6.4	7.0	10.5
Sole registrations	20.6	9.8	4.9	3.2	3.3	5.0	7.3	5.6

Source: Live births by age of mother and registration type

forms of parental relationships are not recorded in official statistics. There is also a dearth of data on re-partnering. We know that the re-marriage rate (per 1,000 widowed or divorced people aged 16 and over in England and Wales) was 24.4 for men and 12.2 for women in 2011, and that it has declined even more rapidly than the marriage rate – less than one-fifth of their levels in the 1970s. But there is a gap in the official statistics on re-partnering after parental break-up. Wilson and Stuchbury (2010) used the longitudinal census data to explore what happened to partnerships between 1991 and 2001. They found that 82% of marriages were still intact but only 61% of cohabitations. They found that being older, male, better qualified and not unemployed increased the odds of partnerships surviving. Having a dependent child also increased the odds by 7%, all other things being equal.

Another insight comes from the Millennium Cohort Survey. At the most recent sweep, when the cohort members were 11 years old, the pattern of parent/carers had become quite complicated. Table 2.6

Table 2.6: Parent/carers in the household of children aged 11

	%
Both natural parents	66.0
Natural mother and stepparent	8.0
Natural mother and other parent/carer	1.1
Natural mother and adoptive parent	0.1
Natural father and stepparent	0.5
Natural father and other parent/carer	0.0
Two adoptive parents	0.1
Two foster parents	0.1
Two grandparents	0.2
Grandmother and other parent/carer	0.1
Two other parents	0.1
Natural mother only	22.1
Natural father only	1.3
Adoptive mother only	0.0
Adoptive father only	0.0
Stepmother only	0.0
Grandmother only	0.2
Other parent/carer only (foster/sibling/relative)	0.1
Stepfather only	0.0
Grandfather only	0.0
Adoptive mother and stepparent	0.0
Total *n* = 13,469	100.0

Source: Own analysis of Millenium Cohort Survey, fifth wave

shows that 66% of the cohort members had both natural parents living with them, 22.1% had their natural mother alone, and 8% had their natural mother and a stepparent. In all, 97.3% of 11-year-old children were living with their natural mother. Very few were living only with their natural father – only 1.5%. Further analyses of the same dataset showed that of those children living in households with both natural parents, 14.8% were still cohabiting, and of all the households with two parents/grandparents, 10% were cohabiting. Moreover, 32.2% of the cohort members were not living with their natural father but 62.3% of them had contact with their natural father.

In the absence of better indicators, two types of data have become very important: data on lone parents and that on stepparents.

Lone parents

A more reliable indication of what is happening to the families that children live in is the composition of families with children. Perhaps the best indication of all is trends in lone-parent families. Table 2.7 provides one picture of this. It shows a breakdown of household types in the UK over time. The proportion of households with children has fallen from 39% in 1977 to 30% by 2013. The proportion with one

Table 2.7: Household composition, UK

Household type	1977	1987	1997	2007	2013
Retired					
1 adult	12	14	14	14	14
1 adult man		3	4	4	4
1 adult woman		11	10	10	10
2 or more adults	10	12	11	12	13
Non-retired					
1 adult without children	8	11	15	14	14
1 adult man		6	10	8	8
1 adult woman		5	6	6	6
2 adults without children	22	20	20	23	21
3 or more adults without children	9	9	9	8	8
1 adult with children	3	4	6	6	5
2 adults with 1 child	9	8	8	7	9
2 adults with 2 children	13	12	9	9	8
2 adults with 3 or more children	6	5	4	3	4
3 or more adults with children	8	5	4	4	4
Households with children as % of all households	39	34	31	29	30

Source: Own analysis of ONS household characteristics by quintile group

adult and children has risen from 3% to 5% over that period, and the proportion made up of couples and two or more children has fallen from 19% to 12%.

Table 2.8 gives a slightly different picture. The proportion of children living in lone-parent families has remained fairly stable between 1996 and 2014 when it was 23%. However, the proportion of children living in married couple families has declined over the period, from 73% to 63%. The big increase has been in the proportion of children living in cohabiting couple families that has increased from 7% to 14%. The proportion of children in large three or more child families has fallen from 32% to 28%.

Lone-parent families are predominantly headed by women, and in 2014, 13.1% were headed by a man. Male lone parents tend to be older, with older children, and they include more widowers.

Figure 2.6 compares the proportion of children living in lone-parent families in the EU using SILC data. It is actually quite difficult to identify lone-parent families in EU-SILC. This is mainly because in some countries many lone parents are hidden in multi-unit households and are not classified as lone parents, but Bradshaw and Chzhen (2009) manipulated the data using the links in the household grid between

Table 2.8: Dependent children in families by family type (Labour Force Survey)

	1996	2000	2004	2008	2014
Married couple family	73	69	66	64	63
One child	15	13	13	14	14
Two children	34	33	32	30	31
Three or more children	24	23	20	20	18
Civil partner couple family	na	na	na	0	0
Opposite sex cohabiting couple family	7	9	11	13	14
One child	2	3	3	4	4
Two children	3	4	5	5	6
Three or more children	2	3	3	3	4
Same-sex cohabiting couple family	0	0	0	0	0
Lone-parent family	21	22	23	23	23
One child	6	7	8	8	8
Two children	8	8	9	9	9
Three or more children	6	7	6	6	6
All families	100	100	100	100	100
One child	23	23	24	26	26
Two children	45	45	46	45	46
Three or more children	32	32	29	29	28

Source: ONS (2015c)

Figure 2.6: Percentage of children living in lone-parent families in the EU, 2008

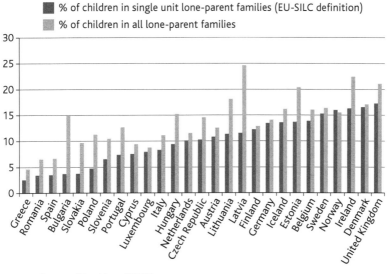

Source: Chzen and Bradshaw (2012)

adults and children. Both definitions are shown in Figure 2.6. The problem with the revised estimate is that parents with one partner working abroad are classified as lone parents, and it is arguable whether this is socially equivalent for a child. However, the main point from Figure 2.6 is that the UK has one of the highest, if not *the* highest, prevalence of children in lone-parent families in the EU.

Stepparents

Changes in the timing and manner of family formation and increased rates of family dissolution and reformation have increased the complexity of family forms, as seen in Table 2.6. Consecutive separations and re-partnerings result in a complex web of family types. Children can become part of a large network of relationships, including natural parents, grandparents and siblings, but now more often stepparents and other step-relationships, half-siblings, visiting children from parents' previous relationships. These patterns of relationships are extremely difficult to summarise, and official statistics have yet to get to grips with the issues. One estimate for 2007 suggest that 86% of stepfamilies with dependent children have children from the woman's previous marriage/cohabitation, 10% from the man's previous marriage/cohabitation, and 4% from both partners' previous marriages/cohabitation. There will be a great deal more complexity than this suggests, with children increasingly splitting their time between their resident and non-resident parent. Indeed, it is becoming increasingly difficult to establish the main carer.

For aggregate families, the separation of parents is often only one major event in a life already full of fluctuation and change (Wade and Smart, 2002). Re-partnering often results in the improvement of household finances but may create new sources of tension between children and their stepparents. Many children find it difficult to take discipline from a stepparent and feel insecure about their position in the family with regard to their step- and/or half-siblings (Dunn and Deater-Deckard, 2001). Becoming part of a stepfamily seems to be helpful for younger children but harder for older children to adapt to (Hawthorne et al, 2003). Older children have a higher risk of adverse outcomes, especially in areas of educational achievement, family relationships, sexual activity, early partnership formation and young parenthood (Rodgers and Pryor, 1998). In their review, Rodgers and Pryor (1998) concluded that for the child, parental separation resulted in short-term unhappiness, low self-esteem, behavioural difficulties, problems with friendships and loss of contact with extended family. They also found that these effects could be mitigated by communication and contact between parents, and that distress faded over time. Mooney et al (2009) also found a small but significant difference in outcomes for children who experience parental divorce or separation compared to those children who grow up with both parents. Many of these differences are primarily evident during the initial crisis of separation, and diminish over time.

It is also important to remember that the source of most of these findings is the long-term follow-up of the of the 1958 and 1970 birth cohorts. Parental separation was much less common then, at least for the children of the 1958 cohort. Although analysts make brave attempts to control for the effects of other variables, including poverty, which is more or less inevitably associated with lone parenthood in the UK, the data is not very comprehensive. Most important of all, this research can never pinpoint whether it is the separation that is the cause of these outcomes or the parental conflict that preceded the separation.

These points should be borne in mind when claims are made that the children of lone parents do worse in various ways. When UNICEF (2007) published Innocenti Report Card no 7, which showed the UK at the bottom of the league table of child well-being, the popular press claimed that it was the result of family breakdown. When the analysis was updated for EU countries, Bradshaw and Richardson (2009) looked at the relationship between the proportion of children living in 'broken' families – lone-parent and stepparent families – and overall well-being. The results are re-presented in Figure 2.7. There is no relationship between family structure and child well-being at an international level. Indeed, the Nordic countries have high proportions of children in 'broken families' and very high levels of child well-being. This suggests that what matters is how society responds to new family forms, and in particular, whether it protects lone parents and children from poverty. As we shall see in the next chapter, the UK does not do well in this regard.

There is also some comfort from The Children's Society surveys of child well-being in England (Rees et al, 2010). Children living with both parents in the same household had higher well-being than those living with lone parents, but not higher than those living with stepparents. The difference remained significant after controlling for age, gender, employment and ethnicity. But the difference was very small – family structure only explained about 2% of the variation in

Figure 2.7: The relationship between overall well-being and the proportion of children living in lone and stepparent families, EU

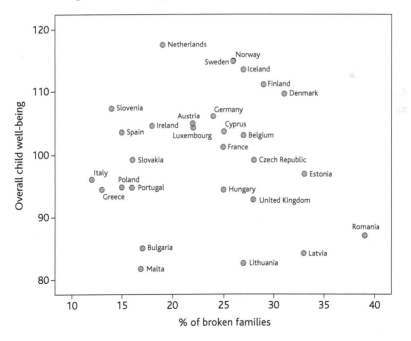

Source: Bradshaw and Richardson (2009)

overall subjective well-being. When the *quality* of family relationships ('my family gets along well together') and *changes* in family structure in the last year were taken into account, the influence of family structure was even more limited. By far the most important determinant of subjective well-being is the quality of family relationships.

Only children

The reduction in the number of siblings, and especially the growth in the population of only children, raises the question of whether 'only childhood' affects children's social development. The positive aspects of growing up in a small family are associated with reduced risks of experiencing poverty, greater physical space and increased parental attention devoted to the only child, although there are some possible drawbacks. Siblings can play a critical role in child socialisation (Parke and Buriel, 1998). Research shows that children with siblings have better conflict resolution skills (Patterson, 1986) and form closer friendships with peers (Stocker and Dunn, 1990) than only children. Children with siblings can learn through observing parent–sibling interactions, and are exposed to experiences that provide the opportunity to learn to deal with differential treatment, rivalry and jealousy (Dunn et al, 1994). Inter-sibling interactions also provide important practice for similar exchanges with peers and help children gain practice with affective perspective taking and consideration of others' feelings (Youngblade and Dunn, 1995). Having a sibling can also be a source of support in periods of stress (such as parental divorce) (Caya and Liem, 1998). The social benefits of being a sibling have a bigger role in childhood than in adulthood. Self-report studies of adults have not found differences between adults with or without siblings in terms of social skills and social competence (Riggio, 1999).

Conclusion

Delayed fertility, falling birth rates and the relative instability of new family forms is giving rise to very different experiences of childhood, both within and between peer groups. Children of the 21st century have a higher probability of experiencing parental separation, lone-parenting, stepfamilies, visiting families, half-siblings and being an only child than children of any previous period of time. In 2014, 26.4% of children lived in a household without other siblings, 22.8% lived in a lone-parent family, and 14.2% lived in a cohabiting couple family. More than 10% lived in stepfamilies. Family disruption and its correlates are associated with increased risk of poverty, academic under-achievement, behavioural problems, early partnership formation and early parenthood. At the same time, the quality of relationships within the family and the extent to which society accommodates changes in family formation has the potential to protect children from the negative consequences of family break-up. Recent demographic changes challenge the well-being of children in the UK, and the outcomes depend on children's and their families' ability to develop strategies that help to adapt successfully to changing circumstances. But they also present a considerable challenge to social policy-makers who need to take into account the increasing complexity of modern family life.

THREE

Child poverty and deprivation

Jonathan Bradshaw and Gill Main

Key statistics

- In 2013/14, 17% of children were living in income poverty in the UK.
- Two-thirds of children in poverty live in households with someone in employment.
- Three-quarters of children in poverty live in couple households.
- In 2013, the UK child poverty rate was 17th out of 33 European countries.
- The UK has the second highest proportion in the European Union (EU) of child poverty generated by low work intensity.
- In the countries of the UK, Wales has the highest child poverty rate before and after housing costs. Among the regions, Inner London has by far the highest child poverty rate both before and after housing costs.
- Child poverty is very spatially concentrated.
- Child poverty cost the UK government £29 billion in 2013.

Key trends

- The child poverty rate began to fall after 1998/99 until 2004/05.
- The UK had the largest reduction in child poverty between the mid-1990s and 2010.
- There has been no reduction in the Child Poverty Act measures since 2010.
- The child poverty rate anchored at 2010/11 prices has risen since 2010 both before and after housing costs.
- The low income and material deprivation rate is also up since 2011.

Key sources

- Households Below Average Income (HBAI)
- European Union Statistics on Income and Living Conditions (EU-SILC)
- Poverty and Social Exclusion (PSE) Survey
- Luxembourg Income Study (LIS)

Introduction

This book is about all children, not just poor children. However, the well-being of children is affected if they are poor, and, as we shall see, most domains of child well-being are affected by poverty or its proxies.

A vast literature on the impact of poverty on outcomes has been reviewed by Griggs and Walker (2008), and their review covered:

- *Health.* The impact of poverty on health during the antenatal period, birth and infancy is profound. This is the period of foetal development which has great significance for later health, cognitive development, educational attainment and thus, employment and earnings potential. There is evidence that poverty is associated with lower rates of breastfeeding, earlier births, low birth weight, higher rates of mortality and morbidity and maternal depression. These have knock-on effects in childhood health with poverty associated with school absences due to infectious illnesses, obesity, anaemia, diabetes, asthma, poor dental health, higher rates of accidents and accidental deaths, and physical abuse. Poor children also have less access to health services. Poverty is associated with poor and overcrowded housing conditions, with poor health outcomes. It is also associated with poor health behaviours, especially higher rates of maternal smoking, and is strongly associated with poor mental health. These health experiences in childhood lead to poor health outcomes in adulthood and old age including worse cardiovascular health, diabetes and heart disease. Hirsch (2013) has estimated the health costs of child poverty to be £500 million per year.

- *Education.* There is a large body of evidence linking poverty to poor educational outcomes, much of it associated with difficulties in cognitive developments in infancy. Deprived areas act as localised 'pockets' of educational disadvantage where limited access to high-quality pre-school provision leads to poor quality schooling and constraints on in-school and extra-curricular activities. Children receiving free school meals are less likely to meet Key Stage standards and achieve five or more good GCSEs, to stay on at school and enter tertiary education. Low skill sets have a knock-on effect in employment, with high levels of young people who are not in education, employment or training (NEET), and long-term unemployment, which, in turn, is associated with crime and substance abuse. The lifetime costs of NEET have been estimated at £15 billion (£7 billion in resource costs and £8.1 billion in public finance costs; Godfrey et al, 2002). Special educational provision resulting from disadvantage and neglect also costs £3.6 billion per year.

- *Employment.* There is a strong relationship between growing up in poverty, labour market participation and progress in a career. The relationship between poverty and worklessness persists even if education is controlled for. Lower educational attainment is associated with low skills and thus lower paid jobs. Unemployment arising from poverty is an inefficient use of human resources and results in lost productivity in the labour market as well as decreased tax contributions. Moreover, it puts a strain on the welfare state in the form of benefit payments.

One way the outcomes of poverty can be measured is by estimating their economic costs. Blanden et al (2010) used the 1970 British Birth Cohort survey to estimate the earnings loss at ages 26, 29/30 and 34. They estimated that growing up in child poverty reduced earnings by between 15% and 28%, and the chances of being in employment by 4-7%. Most of the penalty was due to low skills. If child poverty had been abolished, it would have generated an extra 1-1.8% of GDP from increased productivity, increased tax revenue and reduced benefit payments.

As part of the same research programme for the Joseph Rowntree Foundation, Bramley and Watkins (2008) estimated the public service costs of child poverty including personal social services, health services, education, police and criminal justice, housing, fire and safety, area-based programmes and local environmental services. Their total estimate for 2006/07 was between £11.6 billion and £20.7 billion.

Hirsch (2008) concluded that child poverty costs the UK at least £25 billion a year, including £17 billion that could accrue to the Exchequer if child poverty were eradicated. He uprated those estimates in Hirsch (2013), concluding that:

- Spending on services to deal with the consequences of child poverty rose from £12 billion to £15 billion.
- Tax receipts lost to government as a result of people earning less, having grown up in poverty, rose from £3.3 billion to £3.5 billion due to a small increase in average earnings.
- Benefits spent on people who are out of work primarily as a result of growing up in poverty rose from £2 billion to £2.4 billion, due to benefit uprating.

- Loss in private post-tax earnings by adults who have grown up in poverty rose from £8 billion to £8.5 billion.

This raised the total cost of child poverty from £25 billion in 2008 to £29 billion in 2013. Moving all families above the poverty line would not instantly produce this sum, but in the long term, huge amounts would be saved from not having to pick up the pieces of child poverty and associated social ills:

> The moral case for eradicating child poverty rests on the immense human cost of allowing children to grow up suffering physical and psychological deprivations and unable to participate fully in society. But child poverty is also costly to everyone in Britain, not just those who experience it directly. (Hirsch, 2008, p 1)

Policy context

In 1999 former Prime Minister Tony Blair made the historic commitment to eradicate child poverty in the next 20 years and, as a result, child poverty began to be at the heart of the domestic agenda in the UK. The highpoint was the Child Poverty Act passed with all-party support in 2010. It established four targets that had to be met, and a fifth was added later. These were:

1. The so-called relative measure: the percentage of children in households with incomes less than 60% of the contemporary median. The target was to reduce this to 10% by 2021.

2. The so-called absolute (I prefer 'anchored') measure: the percentage of children in households with incomes less than 60% of the median, held constant at 2010-11 prices. The target was to reduce this to 5% by 2021.

3. The low income and deprivation measure: the percentage of children in households with less than 70% of contemporary median income and lacking 'necessities' because they cannot afford them. There is a list of 12 necessities covering essential household and personal items, adequate personal space as well as access to leisure activities to achieve a reasonable standard of living. For example, a washing machine in the household, a bedroom for each child of the opposite sex aged more than 10, school trips, a warm winter coat, a hobby and celebrations on special occasions. The target for

2021 was for only 5% of children to live in a household that was missing some of these necessities.

4. Persistent low income is a measure of deprivation over time: the percentage of children in households with incomes less than 60% of contemporary median in three out of four years. The 2021 target was 7%.

5. Severe low income and material deprivation: the percentage of children in households with incomes less than 50% of the median and lacking necessities because they cannot afford them. The 2021 target was 0%.

The Act also established a Social Mobility and Child Poverty Commission to advise on and monitor progress towards meeting the targets.

The coalition government launched a consultation on the relative child poverty measures in 2012, arguing that it was absurd that the child poverty rate should fall just because median incomes fall. After the consultation they backed off, partly because of considerable scientific criticisms from many quarters (for an example, see Bradshaw, 2013).

After the election in 2010 the new Conservative government again raised the same issue, but for the opposite reason – that if median incomes rise, so, too, would child poverty. The government said that it would like to take account of the causes of child poverty, and mentioned: indebtedness, family breakdown, addiction, housing problems, educational attainment and worklessness. All these may be associated with child poverty, but they are not measures of child poverty – rich families also break down. What ministers were clumsily trying to do was to get the measures to focus on individual behaviours rather than most of the structural causes of poverty. These, as we shall see, are unemployment, low pay (67% of poor children live in households with someone in work), high childcare costs, high rents and cuts in benefits and tax credits.

The government has now published a Welfare Reform and Work Bill[1] which will, among other things, amend the Child Poverty Act 2010. The Bill also renamed the Social Mobility and Child Poverty Commission the Social Mobility Commission. They are seeking to abolish the Child Poverty Act targets. So the Child Poverty Act 2010 is to become the Life Chances Act, and will:

- introduce new measures to improve the life chances of children;
- create a statutory duty on the Secretary of State to lay before Parliament an annual report containing data on children living in

workless households in England and the educational attainment of children in England at the end of Key Stage 4.

These two new statutory measures will each contain two measures, so there are four measures in total:

- children in workless families
- children in long-term workless families
- educational attainment for all children
- educational attainment for disadvantaged children.

This chapter ignores these developments and examines the progress that has been made on child poverty using the conventional measures of child poverty employed by the Child Poverty Act 2010, the EU, the Organisation for Economic Co-operation and Development (OECD), UNICEF, and most international agencies and governments throughout the world.

Child poverty

Figure 3.1 shows that in 1961 Great Britain had a child poverty rate (using the conventional threshold of 60% of median income) of only 13%. That rate more than doubled while Mrs Thatcher was in power during the 1980s, fluctuated in the 1990s, reaching 27% before housing costs (BHC) and 34% after housing costs (AHC), when the Labour government came to power in 1997.

Figure 3.2 shows the trends after 1994/95 (when the series switched from the Family Expenditure Survey to the Family Resources Survey – for Great Britain until 2001/02 and then for the UK) up to the latest year available, 2013/14. Following the former Prime Minister's announcement in 1999 that poverty would be eradicated in 20 years, the government set targets to reduce child poverty by 25% in five years by 2004-05 and by 50% by 2010-11. Neither target was reached, but the child poverty rate did come down, and during a period when median incomes were rising. The child poverty rate continued to fall after the start of the economic crisis in 2008. After 2010 median incomes fell, and from 2011 they remained constant. If median income falls, the contemporary poverty threshold will fall. For this reason it is probably best to trace child poverty after 2010/11 using the fixed (or anchored) 2010/11 threshold. This shows that child poverty rates began to rise after 2010-11.

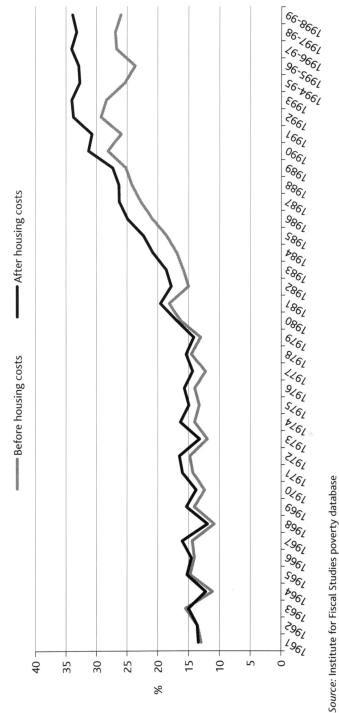

Figure 3.1: Percentage of children falling below 60% of the contemporary median, 1961-98/99

—— Before housing costs —— After housing costs

Source: Institute for Fiscal Studies poverty database

Figure 3.2: Percentage of children falling below 60% of the contemporary median and 2010/11 median, 1994/95-2013/14

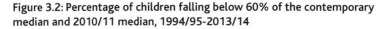
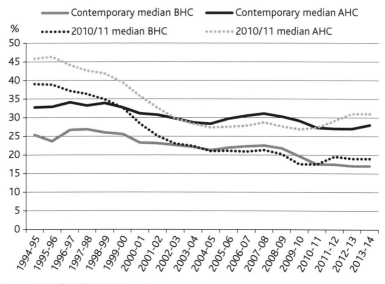

Source: DWP (2015), Table 4 trends

Table 3.1 summarises changes in the Child Poverty Act target rates since the aspiration to eradicate child poverty was announced. We only have data on the low income and deprivation measure and the severe low income and deprivation measure since 2004/05, and the switch from the British Household Panel Survey (BHPS) to the Understanding Society Survey has created a hiatus in the persistent poverty data while we wait for the new survey to mature. However, steady progress can be observed up to 2010, but there is really no evidence of progress since then.

When the child poverty strategy was announced after 1999, the Department for Work and Pensions (DWP) set up a process to monitor progress. This was a set of statistics called *Opportunity for all* (DWP, 2007), published annually after 1999. This series covered not only income poverty, but also examined children living in workless households, health, education and housing. In all, there were 24 indicators covering children and young people. Unfortunately, the series was abandoned after 2007. By then the indicators had all become Public Service Agreement (PSA) targets, and many were incorporated into the UK National Action Plan for Social Inclusion reports that the UK had to produce every two years for the EU (DWP, 2008). This was unfortunate, because the National Action Plan process was abandoned

Table 3.1: Trends in Child Poverty Act targets (% of children in the UK)

	<60% contemporary median BHC	<60% 2010/11 median income BHC	Low income and material deprivation	Persistent poverty BHC	Severe low income and material deprivation
1998/99	26	35		17	
1999/00	26	33		17	
2000/01	23	29		17	
2001/02	23	25		17	
2002/03	23	23		16	
2003/04	22	22		14	
2004/05	21	21	17	12	6
2005/06	22	21	16	11	6
2006/07	22	21	16	10	6
2007/08	23	21	17	10	6
2008/09	22	20	17	12	6
2009/10	20	18	16		5
2010/11	18	18	13		4
2011/12	17	20	12		3
2012/13	17	19	13		4
2013/14	17	19	13		4
Target 2020/21	10	5	5	7	0

Source: DWP (2015)

by the EU soon after. However, many of the indicators are used in the chapters of this book.

Country, regional and area variations in child poverty

The child poverty rates for the countries and regions of the UK are presented in Table 3.2. Scotland has a lower rate of child poverty than the other countries in the UK; Wales and Northern Ireland have the highest rates before housing costs. After housing costs, Northern Ireland has a lower child poverty rate than England. In the English regions, Inner London has the highest child poverty rate before and after housing costs.

There are two sources of data on the spatial distribution of children in poverty. First, the DWP publishes data on the numbers of children living in households receiving out-of-work benefits. The benefits include Income Support, Jobseeker's Allowance, Incapacity Benefit, Severe Disablement Allowance and Pension Credit. This

Table 3.2: Child poverty rates (<60% contemporary median) by country and region, three-year average, 2011/12-2013/14

	Before housing costs	After housing costs
England	17	28
North East	18	26
North West	21	30
Yorkshire and the Humber	21	28
East Midlands	16	25
West Midlands	20	29
East of England	14	24
London	18	37
Inner	24	46
Outer	15	33
South East	13	23
South West	15	24
Wales	22	31
Scotland	16	21
Northern Ireland	22	25

Source: DWP (2015, Table 4.6db)

includes children in families receiving non-income tested Jobseeker's Allowance, Incapacity Benefit and Severe Disablement Allowance, and who therefore may not be poor. It also excludes children in households with a working parent, which now represents two-thirds of children in poverty. So it is not a particularly sensitive index of child poverty.

Second, there is the Income Deprivation Affecting Children Index (IDACI). This shows, by area, the proportion of children under 15 receiving the following means-tested benefits:

- children aged 0-15 in households claiming Income Support
- children aged 0-15 in households claiming income-based Jobseeker's Allowance
- children aged 0-15 in households claiming Pension Credit (Guarantee)
- children aged 0-15 in households claiming Working Tax Credit in receipt of Child Tax Credit whose equivalised income (excluding housing benefits) is below 60% of the median before housing costs
- children aged 0-15 in households claiming Child Tax Credit (but not eligible for Income Support, income-based Jobseeker's Allowance, Pension Credit or Working Tax Credit) whose equivalised income (excluding housing benefits) is below 60% of the median before housing costs.

The IDACI is an improvement on the DWP area-based benefit data because it includes Her Majesty's Revenue and Customs (HMRC) data on children in poor working families – families receiving Child Tax Credit with incomes less than 60% of the median.

A new edition of the index was published in 2015.[2] However, the 2010 version of the index has been updated to October 2013 by Hirsch on behalf of End Child Poverty that took the HMRC IDACI estimates and updated them using data from the Labour Force Survey on changes in the proportion of children in employed and non-employed families at local authority level. In a recent paper, Hirsch and Valadez (2014) have introduced further adjustments to their methods. The latest estimates for October 2013 produced using this method have been published at ward, local authority and parliamentary constituency level.

Tables 3.3 and 3.4 list the 20 local authority districts with the lowest and highest child poverty rates (after housing costs). The districts with the lowest rates are Wokingham and the Shetland Isles, with only 10% of their children in poverty. The district with highest child poverty rate by some margin is Tower Hamlets in Inner London, with 49% of its children in poverty.

Hirsch and Valadez (2014) have also produced their child poverty data at lower layer super output areas (LSOA)[3] for an analysis for the North East Child Poverty Commission (Bradshaw and Mayhew, 2015). One LSOA in Newcastle had a child poverty rate of 59% after housing costs.

The IDACI spatial child poverty data can also be used to explore the correlates of child poverty. For a project linked to the Index of Deprivation 2007, Bradshaw et al (2009) developed an index of child well-being at small area level (local authority district and LSOAs). The index was created from, mainly, administrative data covering six domains: material (the IDACI index), health, education, crime, housing and the environment.

Table 3.5 shows the strength of the association between child poverty and the other domains at LSOA level. The strongest association between income poverty was with education (attainment and participation), but all the domains are associated with poverty, so small areas with high poverty rates also have the worst housing conditions, the poorest child health and the highest crime rates. The lowest correlation, as one would expect, is with the environment, which was made up of two sub-domains, quality and access. Rural environments are better in terms of quality – air quality, green space, woodland, richness of bird species and lower numbers of road traffic accidents – but they do much less well in terms of access to facilities and services.

Table 3.3: Top 20 local authorities with lowest levels of child poverty across the UK

Local authority	% of children in poverty 2013 (AHC)
1 Shetland Islands	10
2 Wokingham	10
3 Hart	11
4 Isles of Scilly	12
5 South Northamptonshire	12
6 South Oxfordshire	12
7 Harborough	13
8 Rushcliffe	13
9 Mole Valley	13
10 Ribble Valley	13
11 South Cambridgeshire	13
12 Mid Sussex	13
13 East Dunbartonshire	13
14 Waverley	13
15 West Oxfordshire	13
16 Vale of White Horse	13
17 Elmbridge	13
18 South Bucks	13
19 Fareham	14
20 Aberdeenshire	14

Source: www.endchildpoverty.org.uk/images/ecp/Report_on_child_poverty_map_2014.pdf

Characteristics of children in poverty

Table 3.6 provides a summary of the characteristics of children in poverty in the UK – both the rate and the composition, and using the less than 60% median threshold before housing costs and the low income and deprivation measure:

- Sixty-seven per cent of income-poor children live in households with someone in employment, but the risk of child poverty is much higher in workless households: 37% of workless families have income less than the 60% median as opposed to only 13% of those families where at least one adult is in work; 43% of deprived children live with lone parents, and 24% of children living with lone parents are deprived, but only 9% of children of lone parents are deprived if the parents work full time.

- In couple families, children are very unlikely to be income-poor or deprived if both parents are in full-time employment – only 1%

Table 3.4: Top 20 local authorities with highest levels of child poverty across the UK

Local authority	% of children in poverty 2013 (AHC)
1 Tower Hamlets	49
2 Hackney	41
3 Newham	41
4 Manchester	39
5 Westminster	39
6 Islington	38
7 Enfield	37
8 Birmingham	37
9 Leicester	37
10 Barking and Dagenham	37
11 Haringey	36
12 Camden	36
13 Nottingham	36
14 Brent	35
15 Waltham Forest	35
16 Middlesbrough	35
17 Lambeth	34
18 Lewisham	34
19 Southwark	34
20 Oldham	34

Source: www.endchildpoverty.org.uk/images/ecp/Report_on_child_poverty_map_2014.pdf

Table 3.5: Spatial association between poverty and other domains of well-being at LSOA level (Spearman rank correlations – all coefficients statistically significant at the <0.01 level)

Domains	Correlation coefficient
Education	0.80
Housing	0.63
Health	0.56
Crime	0.55
Environment	0.07

Source: Bradshaw et al (2009, Table 4)

are deprived. If neither parent is employed, 46% of children are deprived.

- Thirty-seven per cent of income-poor and 41% of deprived children are living in workless households.

Table 3.6: Percentage of children in income poverty or deprivation by various family and household characteristics, UK, 2013/14

	Income <60% contemporary median BHC		Material deprivation and low income	
	Rate	Composition	Rate	Composition
Economic status of the family				
At least one adult in work	13	64	8	49
Workless families	37	36	41	51
Economic status of the family and family type				
Lone parent:	19	26	24	43
In full-time work	9	3	9	4
In part-time work	16	7	15	8
Not working	27	17	38	31
Couple with children:	16	74	10	57
Self-employed	22	16	6	5
Both in full-time work	3	3	1	1
One in full-time work, one in part-time work	5	6	2	4
One in full-time work, one not working	20	19	13	16
One or more in part-time work	41	10	30	10
Both not in work	57	19	46	20
Economic status of household				
All adults in work	8	27	4	18
At least one adult in work, but not all	25	40	16	34
Workless households	38	33	42	48
Marital status				
Couple	16	74	10	57
Married or civil partnered	15	55	8	39
Cohabiting	21	19	15	18
Single	19	26	24	43
Number of children in family				
One child	15	26	10	24
Two children	15	40	10	35
Three or more children	22	35	20	42
Disability and receipt of disability benefits				
Those living in families where no one is disabled	15	64	10	54
Those living in families where someone is disabled	22	36	22	46
One or more disabled adult, no disabled child	26	24	25	30

(continued)

Table 3.6: Percentage of children in income poverty or deprivation by various family and household characteristics, UK, 2013/14 (continued)

	Income <60% contemporary median BHC		Material deprivation and low income	
	Rate	Composition	Rate	Composition
Disability and receipt of disability benefits				
Those living in families with disabled children	18	12	17	16
With no disabled adult	15	6	12	7
With one or more disabled adult	22	6	26	10
In receipt of disability benefits	14	6	17	10
Not in receipt of disability benefits	26	30	24	36
Ethnic group of head (three-year average)				
White	15	74	11	72
Mixed/multiple ethnic groups	23	2	21	2
Asian/Asian British	31	16	20	13
Indian	19	3	8	2
Pakistani	42	7	26	6
Bangladeshi	42	3	33	3
Chinese	33	1	11	–
Any other Asian background	24	2	21	2
Black/African/Caribbean/Black British	26	7	27	9
Other ethnic group	22	2	22	3
State support received by family				
Disability Living Allowance	13	6	16	10
Personal Independence Payment	...	–	...	–
Jobseeker's Allowance	52	12	49	14
Incapacity Benefit	...	1	...	1
Employment and Support Allowance	30	6	45	11
Child Tax Credit	23	67	22	84
Working Tax Credit	19	24	15	24
Income Support	26	13	36	23
Housing Benefit	28	39	35	64
Not in receipt of any state support listed above	9	26	2	8
Age of youngest child in family				
0-4	18	46	14	47
5-10	15	27	12	28
11-15	18	19	12	17
16-19	20	8	14	8

(continued)

Table 3.6: Percentage of children in income poverty or deprivation by various family and household characteristics, UK, 2013/14 (continued)

	Income <60% contemporary median BHC		Material deprivation and low income	
	Rate	Composition	Rate	Composition
Tenure				
Owners	11	37	4	17
Owned outright	20	10	4	3
Buying with mortgage	10	27	4	14
Social rented sector tenants	29	38	33	55
All rented privately	20	25	16	27
Savings and investments				
No savings	23	71	23	90
Less than £1,500	15	12	6	7
£1,500 but less than £3,000	14	4	2	1
£3,000 but less than £8,000	7	4	1	1
£8,000 but less than £10,000	8	1	2	–
£10,000 but less than £16,000	9	2	1	–
£16,000 but less than £20,000	3	–	–	–
£20,000 or more	8	5	1	–
Household bills in arrears				
No bills in arrears	15	71	8	49
One or more bills in arrears	28	28	39	50
Total	17	100	**13**	100

Source: DWP (2015, Table 4db)

- The risk of poverty is higher if there are three or more children in the family, but most children in poverty are in small families – 66% of income-poor households contain only one or two children.

- Having a disabled adult or a disabled child in the household increases the risk of poverty, but that risk is mitigated if the child is receiving a disability benefit.

- Seventy-four per cent of income-poor children are in White families, but there is a much higher risk of poverty for children in Pakistani and Bangladeshi families, and indeed, all ethnic groups except Indian and Chinese in the case of deprivation.

- Fifty-two per cent of recipients of Jobseeker's Allowance and 30% of recipients of Employment and Support Allowance are income-poor, but only 12% of income-poor children are receiving either

Jobseeker's Allowance or Employment and Support Allowance; 84% of deprived children are receiving Child Tax Credits.

- Children are more likely to be poor if the youngest child is under five and 46% of all poor children live in households with a child under five.

- The risk of deprivation is much higher among children living in the social rented sector, but 17% of deprived children are living in owner-occupied accommodation.

- Seventy-one per cent of income-poor children live in households with no savings, and households with poor children are much more likely to be in arrears with household bills.

The 2012 UK Poverty and Social Exclusion (PSE) Survey was the largest-scale survey of poverty in the UK to date, and is an important source of data on child poverty. It covers 5,193 households in the UK, containing 12,097 individuals, 3,101 dependent children (defined as such according to the Households Below Average Income [HBAI] definition). An adult in their household collects data on children. The study draws on the consensual approach to poverty measurement – that is, in a preliminary survey, adults are asked to identify which of a list of adult-, child- and household-related items and activities are necessities, and which are not. Those deemed necessities by 50% or more of the population are termed *socially perceived necessities*, and items and activities meeting these criteria are then used as indicators of deprivation, independently and alongside income measures. Three objective poverty measures can be discerned from the data:

- low income, defined as living in a household with an equivalised income below 60% of the national median
- deprivation, defined as lacking three or more socially perceived necessities
- PSE poverty (combined low income and deprivation), defined as lacking three or more necessities and living in a low-income household.

For more details on the calculation of these measures, see Gordon and Nandy (2012) and Main and Bradshaw (2014).

Table 3.7 shows the associations between sociodemographic characteristics and the odds of children experiencing these different kinds of poverty.

Table 3.7: Odds of children experiencing different types of poverty by sociodemographic factors

	Deprivation				Low income				PSE poverty				Total composition
	Rate	Composition	Odds	Sig	Rate	Composition	Odds	Sig	Rate	Composition	Odds	Sig	
Household employment status													
All adults work full-time	15	18	1.0		11	8	1.0		13	12	1.0		23
Some full- and some part-time work	11	8	0.7	NS	25	12	2.6	*	21	12	1.7	NS	15
Some full-time work, no part-time work	12	19	0.8	NS	27	27	3.0	*	16	19	1.3	NS	30
All adults work part-time, no full-time work	37	11	3.2	*	43	9	5.9	*	43	11	5.0	*	6
Some adults work part-time, no full-time work	17	7	1.1	NS	35	9	4.3	*	18	6	1.5	NS	8
Primarily unemployed (no work)	42	7	4.0	*	77	8	27.1	*	47	6	5.8	*	3
Primarily inactive (no work)	42	30	4.1	*	57	27	10.5	*	60	34	9.8	*	14
Family type													
One adult, one child	36	9	1.0		51	9	1.0		44	9	1.0		6
One adult, two children	32	12	0.8	NS	45	10	0.8	NS	39	11	0.8	NS	7
One adult, 3+ children	49	17	1.7	NS	67	14	2.0	NS	80	20	5.1	*	7
Two adults, one child	8	6	0.2	*	24	12	0.3	*	18	10	0.3	*	16
Two adults, two children	18	28	0.4	*	24	23	0.3	*	18	22	0.3	*	32
Two adults, 3+ children	24	24	0.5	NS	40	25	0.6	NS	30	22	0.5	NS	21
Other	8	4	0.2	*	21	7	0.3	*	15	6	0.2	*	11

(continued)

Table 3.7: Odds of children experiencing different types of poverty by sociodemographic factors (continued)

	Deprivation				Low income				PSE poverty				Total composition
	Rate	Composition	Odds	Sig	Rate	Composition	Odds	Sig	Rate	Composition	Odds	Sig	
Age of child													
0-1	10	5	1.0		31	10	1.0		22	9	1.0		11
2-4	15	13	1.7	NS	36	20	1.2	NS	28	18	1.4	NS	18
5-10	25	39	3.1	*	36	35	1.3	NS	30	36	1.6	NS	32
11-15	26	34	3.3	*	32	27	1.0	NS	29	29	1.4	NS	28
16-17	19	9	2.1	NS	23	8	0.7	NS	19	7	0.8	NS	11
Ethnicity													
White British	19	77	1.0		31	75	1.0		27	78	1.0		80
White other	19	4	1.0	NS	27	3	0.8	NS	30	5	1.2	NS	4
Black Caribbean/mixed	45	4	3.4	*	45	3	1.9	NS	44	3	2.1	*	2
Black African/mixed	51	6	4.4	*	52	4	2.4	*	44	5	2.1	*	3
Asian Indian	4	0	0.2	*	38	3	1.4	NS	9	1	0.3	*	3
Pakistani/Bangladeshi	37	5	2.5	*	54	6	2.7	*	43	5	2.1	NS	3
Asian other	16	2	0.8	NS	34	3	1.2	NS	16	2	0.5	NS	3
Other	26	2	1.5	NS	48	2	2.1	NS	28	2	1.0	NS	2
Tenure													
Owner	10	26	1.0		17	30	1.0		10	22	1.0		58
Social renter	43	55	7.2	*	59	47	6.9	*	57	55	11.7	*	26
Private renter	25	18	3.2	*	49	23	4.7	*	42	23	6.2	*	15
Other	11	0	1.1	NS	4	0	0.2	NS	10	0	1.0	NS	1
Total rate	21				33				27				

Source: Main and Bradshaw (2014)

Household employment status

Deprivation rates were significantly higher among children in households where all adults work part time (37%), and those where no adults work and the majority are either unemployed (42%) or inactive (42%). All household employment statuses other than all adults working full time represent a greater risk of low income, with the highest rates among children in households where no adults work and the majority are unemployed (77%) or inactive (57%). Household employment status is associated with similar poverty rates on the combined (PSE) measure of poverty as on the deprivation measure of poverty. Households where all adults are in full-time work experience the lowest poverty rate (13%) on this measure, while households containing inactive adults have the highest (60%) poverty rate. Households where adults' employment status is predominantly part-time work also have high poverty rates of around 45% on average.

In terms of poverty rates, statistically significant associations exist between household worklessness and the chances of experiencing poverty, and between part-time working and poverty. Looking at the composition of poor children, however, on all measures the majority of children in poverty live in households with at least some paid work (63% of deprived children, 65% of children in households on a low income, and 60% of children in PSE poverty). Between two-fifths and a half of children living in poverty live in households with at least one adult in full-time work – 45% of deprived children, 47% of children in low-income households, and 43% of PSE poor children.

Family type

Deprivation rates according to family types vary depending on the number of adults and children in the household. Generally, the more adults and the fewer children there are in a household, the lower the deprivation rate. This principle does not entirely seem to hold in single-parent households where lone parents with one child have higher deprivation rates than lone parents with two children (although the difference is not significant). Households containing two adults with one child (8%) and two adults with two children (18%) have significantly lower deprivation rates than a lone-parent household with one child (36%). The same groups were at lower risk of low income – with rates of 24% among children in households with two adults and one child, 24% in households with two adults and two children, and

21% in 'other' household types. While trends were similar for PSE poverty (statistically significant associations and rates of 18% for two adults and one child, 18% for two adults and two children, and 15% for 'other' household type), lone parents with three or more children were at a greater risk of PSE poverty, with a poverty rate of 80%.

The above findings indicate that children in lone-parent families are at higher risk of poverty, and evidence based on the PSE poverty measure suggests that children in lone-parent families with larger numbers of children (three or more) are at higher risk. However, the majority of poor children by all measures of poverty live in households containing two or more adults (62% of the deprived, 67% of those in low-income households, and 60% of those in PSE poor households), and the majority live in households containing only one or two children (at least 55% of deprived children, 54% of children in low-income households, and 52% of children in PSE poor households; children in 'other' household types excluded from these calculations).

Child's age

Children aged 5-10 (rate of 25%) and 11-15 (26%) face a significantly higher risk of deprivation than children aged 0-1. Age is not significantly associated with low income or PSE poverty.

Ethnicity

Children of Black Caribbean (rate of 45%), Black African (47%) and Pakistani/Bangladeshi (37%) ethnic origins were more likely than White British children to be deprived (19%). Those from Asian Indian ethnic backgrounds (4%) were less likely. Black African children (52%) and Pakistani/Bangladeshi children (54%) were more likely to be in low-income households. Black Caribbean (44%) and Black African (44%) children were more likely to be in PSE poverty, and Asian Indian children (9%) were less likely.

Across all poverty measures, White British children formed the bulk of poor children – 77% of the deprived, 75% of those in low-income households and 78% of those in PSE poverty.

Tenure

Across the poverty measures, children living in socially (43% deprivation rate; 59% low income rate; 57% PSE poverty rate) or privately (25% deprivation rate; 49% low income rate; 42% PSE poverty rate) rented accommodation were at higher risk than those in owner-occupied housing.

The majority of deprived children (55%) and PSE poor children (55%) lived in socially rented accommodation, as did nearly half of children in low-income households (47%).

Child poverty dynamics

It is arguable that a brief experience of living in poverty is less likely to be harmful to children than a long episode. It can be seen in Table 3.1 that in 2008/09, 12% of children (BHC) had been living in poverty in at least three out of the last four years (the definition of persistent poverty). It also shows that there had been a welcome decline in the prevalence of persistent poverty between 1998/99 and 2008/09.

Barnes et al (2015) produced an analysis of child poverty transitions between 2009 and 2012 using Understanding Society and Millennium Cohort Survey data. Transitions were recorded if the child moved at least 10% above or below the less than 60% median income threshold. Around 7% of children initially not in poverty had moved into poverty in the next year, and 38% of poor children had moved out of poverty by the following year. The key events leading to entry into poverty in order of importance were: part-time work to workless, full-time work to workless, three to four children, part-time work to fall in earnings, two to three children, full-time to part-time work and couple to lone parent. The key events leading to exit from poverty in order of importance were: part-time to full-time work, workless to full-time work, full-time to increase in earnings, workless to part-time work, three to two children, part-time to increased earnings and two to one child.

Intergenerational transmission of poverty

There is really no satisfactory data on intergenerational transmission of child poverty in the UK, although there is evidence from the analysis of cohort studies by Blanden and Machin (2007), shown in Table 3.8, that the links between the relative incomes of children and their parents appear to have strengthened between those born in 1958 and 1970.

The links between the income of parents and the educational attainment level of their children shown in Table 3.9 may also have widened (Blanden and Machin, 2007).

Table 3.8: Links between parents' income group and son's earnings, 1958 and 1970

		Parents' income group	
Son's earnings at 33/34 (%)		Bottom 25%	Top 25%
In bottom 25%	Born 1958	30	18
	Born 1970	37	13
In top 25%	Born 1958	18	35
	Born 1970	13	45

Table 3.9: Links between parents' income and educational attainment

	Parent's income group	
Degree by age 23 (%)	Bottom 20%	Top 20%
Born 1958	5	20
Born 1970	7	37
Born around 1975	11	40
Born around 1979	10	44

The views of children

Children's own views of their material needs and their experiences of poverty are often absent from research on child poverty. This absence may explain why measures of child poverty (which rely on adult conceptions of children's needs, and on adult reports of children's access to resources) tend to have no or minimal association with children's subjective well-being. This is surprising given that Ridge's (2002) qualitative research with children living in households dependent on Income Support indicates that children:

- experience stress and distress as a result of poverty
- go to efforts to protect parents from realising the full extent of the impact of poverty on their lives and
- have creative strategies including employment and tapping the resources of relatives external to their households.

Main (2013, 2014), Main and Bradshaw (2012) and Main and Pople (2011) have attempted to understand the relationship between child poverty and children's subjective well-being through the development of a Child Deprivation Scale (CDS), based on children's own perceptions of their needs. Focus groups were conducted with children (aged 8-16) to identify items and activities perceived as necessities, in line with the consensual approach to poverty measurement detailed above. These were followed by a representative survey of over 5,000 school children. Items included in the CDS comprise:

- clothes to fit in with other people their age
- shoes or footwear to fit in with other people their age
- an annual family holiday
- monthly day trips with family
- pocket money
- money to save
- a garden or safe place nearby to spend time
- an iPod or other MP3 player
- cable or satellite TV
- access to a family car.

Many of these items – such as having a garden and an annual holiday – are in line with adult perceptions of children's needs; others – such as clothes and shoes to fit in with peers – are far from in accordance with adult perspectives (see Main and Bradshaw, 2014). Main (2013) notes, however, that the importance of items and activities was often symbolic and social rather than materialistic – children in the focus groups discussed the importance of items to their ability to join in with peer group discussions and activities, and to avoid being singled out and/or bullied. Using the CDS as a whole, a significant association was found with subjective well-being, explaining about 7-10% of the variation once demographic characteristics were controlled for. This compares to 0-1% of variation explained by household income or adult-defined indices of children's needs (Knies, 2011; Rees et al, 2011). Having clothes to fit in with others of their age was the single item with the strongest association to children's subjective well-being, stressing the importance of having the need to fit in to children's happiness.

Child poverty and the financial crisis

It is now established that the global recession, and subsequent austerity measures in the UK, have hit children harder than other groups (Reed and Portes, 2014; UNICEF, 2014). As part of their ongoing well-being research programme, The Children's Society asked 14-year-olds a series of questions about their experiences of the recession and their material living conditions (including the CDS described above). In line with previous research into children's experience of poverty (see, for example Ridge, 2002), findings indicate that children are aware of their family's material well-being, and in this instance, of the financial crisis. They do appear to be able report on their perceptions of its impact on their own family – 36% of children reported the impact of the crisis on their family to be either 'a fair amount' or 'a great deal', as shown in Figure 3.3.

In addition to the impact of austerity measures on children as a whole, Reed and Portes (2014) found that poorer families suffered a greater impact than non-poor families. To examine this, using children's perspectives on poverty, Figure 3.4 shows the mean number of items on the CDS that children lack, according to their assessment of the impact of the financial crisis on their family. Poorer children reported a greater impact of the crisis than their better-off counterparts. It may be the case that children living in poverty would be more likely to respond positively to all questions about material and financial deprivation, but the evidence suggests that children were able to discriminate between poverty and the impact of the crisis – 23% of children surveyed reported a medium or strong impact of the financial crisis and were not materially deprived, while 18% were deprived but reported no or just a little impact. This suggests that the data picks up on something different to just the experience of or entry into poverty which may happen irrespective of the financial crisis.

Children were asked three questions relating to increasing financial stress in their families – how much money their family had compared to a year ago (ranging from a lot less to a lot more); how much money

Figure 3.3: Children's perceptions of the impact of the economic crisis on their families

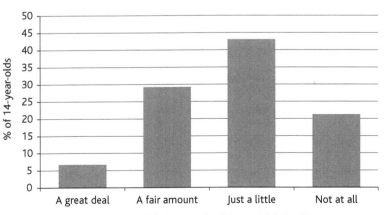

Source: UNICEF (2014)

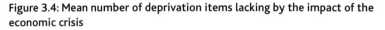

Figure 3.4: Mean number of deprivation items lacking by the impact of the economic crisis

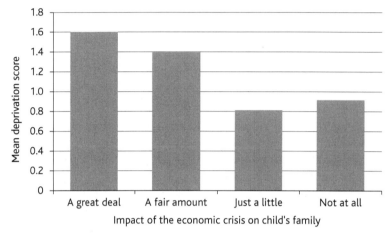

Source: UNICEF (2014)

their parents spent on them compared to a year ago; and how often they heard adults in their families discussing money worries. In Figure 3.5 we see that for all of these questions, children reporting a greater impact of the crisis were more likely to report more strain – that is, their family having less money, their parents spending less on them, and hearing more discussions about money worries.

As we would expect, children's reports of poverty and of the impact of austerity are related but not identical. Turning to the impact of austerity on children, The Children's Society data includes a measure of subjective well-being. Controlling for gender and family type, we were able to examine the relative impact of poverty and the impact of the economic crisis on children's subjective well-being, shown in Table 3.10. The strongest association was for children who were both poor and had felt a strong impact of the crisis – these children suffered a deficit of almost 4 points on the 21-point scale compared to non-poor children reporting no or low impact of the economic crisis. They were also four times as likely to report low subjective well-being (that is, below the mid-point of the scale). However, it is worth noting that experiencing an impact of the economic crisis alone (that is, in the absence of poverty) was sufficient to have a significant negative impact on children's subjective well-being. Children in this category scored on average just over one point less than those who were neither poor nor reported a substantial impact of the crisis.

Figure 3.5: Children reporting a worsening of their family economic situation by the impact of the financial crisis

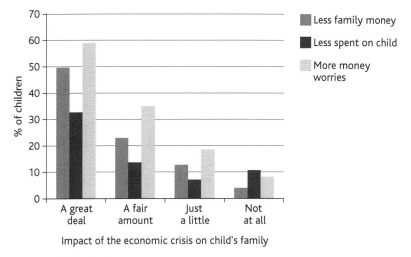

Source: UNICEF (2014)

Table 3.10: Regression of children's subjective well-being (SWB) by poverty and the economic crisis

		B	t	p	Odds of low SWB	p
Gender (boys as reference)		1.4	4.7	<0.001	0.5	<0.001
Family type (both parents as reference)	Lone parent	−1.3	−3.6	<0.001	2.1	0.001
	Stepfamily	−1.2	−2.7	0.006	1.9	0.012
Poverty and impact (not poor, not strong impact as reference)	Poor, strong impact	−3.8	−8.0	<0.001	4.0	<0.001
	Not poor, strong impact	−1.2	−3.0	0.003	1.6	0.078
	Poor, not strong impact	−2.3	−5.0	<0.001	2.0	0.014

International comparisons of child poverty

There are three main sources of comparative data on child poverty: the OECD collects data from national governments, and their Income Distribution and Poverty database provides child poverty rates up to 2012[4]; the Luxembourg Income Study (LIS) collects together national micro-social data and makes them available for analysts and they also publish their own summary statistics in LIS Key Figures[5] – their most recent data is for mid-2010; and for European countries, the Statistics on Income and Living Conditions (SILC) has replaced the European Household Panel Survey, and become a major resource with data published on the Eurostat database and available for secondary analysis.

The most current data available is from EU–SILC 2013 (2012 income data), and most of the analysis in this section is based on this. However, because EU–SILC was only developed after 2005, we turn first for a historical picture, to the LIS data in Figure 3.6. Between the mid-1990s and mid-2010 most countries for which there is data at both points experienced an increase in their child poverty rates. The UK was the country where child poverty decreased most, although this reduction was from a comparatively high level.

Figure 3.7 uses the latest available EU–SILC data to compare the child poverty rates in the EU countries with the pensioner and population poverty rates. The UK is middling in its child poverty. Like most other countries, the UK child poverty rate is higher than the population and pensioner poverty rates.

This analysis is based on the conventional 60% of median income poverty threshold, but leaves a lot to be desired, especially in a comparative analysis, because:

Figure 3.6: Percentage point change in child poverty rate between the mid-1990s (LIS wave IV) and 2010 LIS wave VIII (% of children living in households with equivalent income less than 60% median)

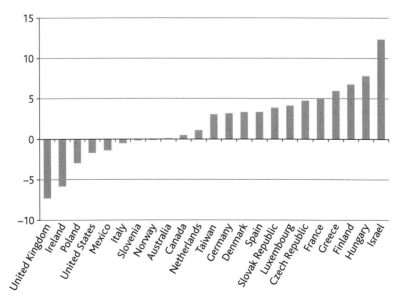

Source: LIS key figures, see http://www.lisdatacenter.org/data-access/key-figures/download-key-figures/

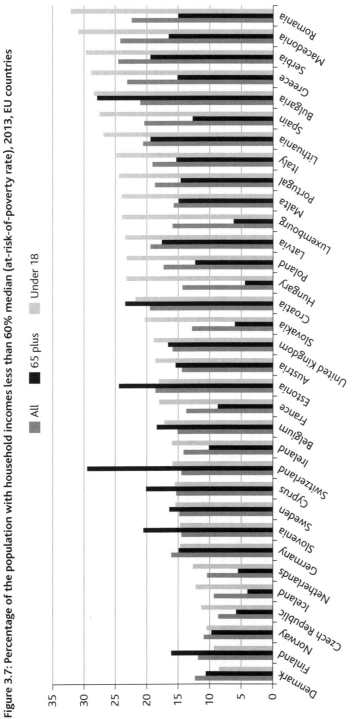

Figure 3.7: Percentage of the population with household incomes less than 60% median (at-risk-of-poverty rate), 2013, EU countries

Source: Eurostat database, http://ec.europa.eu/eurostat/data/database, 23 July 2015

- It is hard for non-experts to understand what is meant by 'X% of the population live in households with disposable income less than 60% of the national median equivalised household income.' It does not resonate with persuasive power or credibility.

- Income is only an indirect indicator of living standards.

- It is probably not as good an indicator of command over resources as expenditure, not least because it does not take account of the capacity to borrow, dissavings, gifts and the value of home production.

- The 60% of the median (and any other) income threshold is arbitrary. It is not related to any understanding of need, but is merely a line drawn on the income distribution.

- The equivalence scale that is used to adjust income to household need adopted – the modified OECD scale – has no basis in science (and has been abandoned by the OECD, that now uses the square root of the number of people in the household).

There are limitations of a relative income measure in a comparative context:

- The EU publishes estimates of the monetary value of the poverty threshold in Euro purchasing power parity. This reveals that we are not comparing like with like when we compare poverty rates between countries using this threshold. So, for example, the relative poverty threshold for a couple with two children in Estonia in 2013 was €10,845 per year and in the UK €21,201 per year. The child at-risk-of-poverty rate was 18.1% in Estonia and 18.9% in the UK. Yet the poor in Estonia were living at much lower levels, even when taking into account equivalent purchasing powers.

- In many of the countries, including many using 60% of the median as their poverty threshold, the cash value of the threshold is very low. The threshold for a couple with two children in 2013 in purchasing power parity terms per person per day was €2.72 in Romania.

It is for some of these reasons that the European Commission has developed a variety of measures of poverty, including:

- at-risk-of-poverty rates at different thresholds (40, 50, 60 and 70% of the national median equivalised household income)

- an at-risk-of-poverty gap
- an at-risk-of-poverty rate 'anchored' at a point in time
- a persistent at-risk-of-poverty rate
- a material deprivation indicator.

More recently, in 2010, the European Council adopted an EU target (so-called AROPE) to lift at least 20 million people out of poverty by 2020. Three poverty thresholds are being prioritised here:

- at-risk-of-poverty – the population living in households with equivalent income less than 60% of the median, or
- material deprivation – the population living in households lacking four or more out of nine indicators,[6] or
- people living in jobless households – no one working or work intensity of household is below 0.2.

Figure 3.8 gives the breakdown of the AROPE child poverty indicator for 2013. It can be seen that one reason why the UK has a comparatively high child poverty rate is that it has a comparatively high proportion of children living in households with low work intensity. The countries are ranked by the levels of child poverty generated by low work intensity, and the UK comes second to Ireland.

It is arguable that of equal importance to the poverty rate is the poverty gap, that is, how far below the poverty threshold poor children are living. Figure 3.9 compares the mean child poverty gap across EU countries. The UK does rather better in the league table of the gap measure, at 16.3%. This is considerably better than Bulgaria, where poor children live 41.7% below their (very low) poverty threshold, but it is not as good as the Netherlands, where the mean poverty gap is only 12.1% of the poverty threshold.

In comparisons there is a strong case for moderating the relative income measure with deprivation. In the richer EU countries there are many households with incomes below 60% of the median that are not lacking any deprivation indicator (and also say they do not have any difficulty making ends meet). Figure 3.10 presents a child poverty rate based on the overlap between the at-risk-of-poverty rate and severe deprivation. The UK is still towards the middle of the EU league table with a considerably higher child poverty (1.9%) rate than Denmark (0.2%) but much lower than Romania (15.7%).

Another criticism of the at-risk-of-poverty threshold is that if it falls, it may appear that child poverty falls without there being any real reduction. This is a problem for analysis over time and in particular

Figure 3.8: EU 2020 at risk of child poverty rates (AROPE), 2013

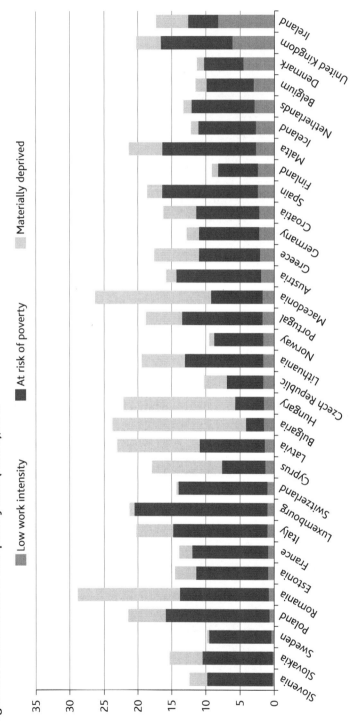

Source: Eurostat database, http://ec.europa.eu/eurostat/data/database, 23 July 2015

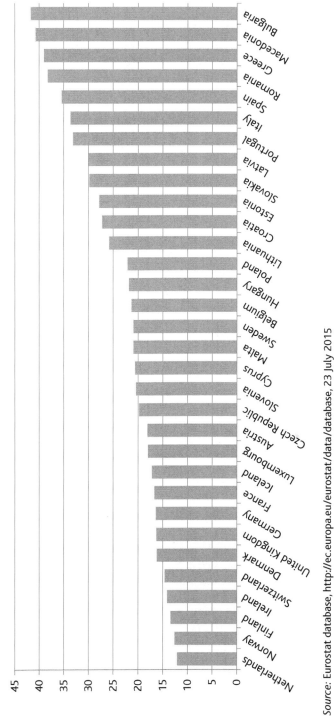

Figure 3.9: Child poverty gap, 2013

Source: Eurostat database, http://ec.europa.eu/eurostat/data/database, 23 July 2015

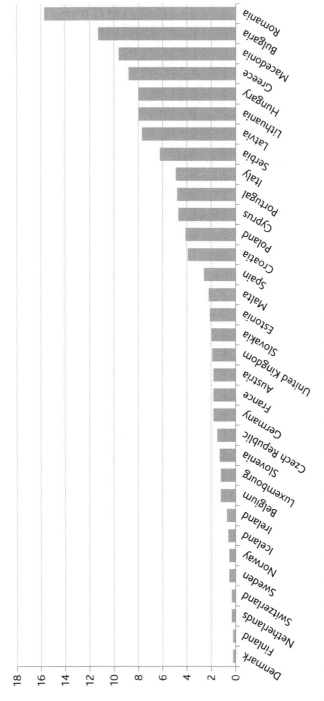

Figure 3.10: At risk of poverty and severe material deprivation, 2013 (% of children under 18)

Source: Eurostat database, http://ec.europa.eu/eurostat/data/database, 23 July 2015

during the recent recession when the child poverty threshold fell in many countries, including the UK. A way to deal with this is to use a poverty threshold anchored at a point in time (like the so-called absolute poverty threshold in the UK). In Figure 3.11 we show the changes in child poverty between 2008 and 2013 using the 2008 60% median income threshold for 2008. It can be seen that child poverty increased in most EU countries over that period, including in the UK (by 9.6%).

Comparisons of material well-being and other domains of well-being at an international level

In a follow-up analysis of data collected for UNICEF Innocenti Report Card no 11, Bradshaw (2015) found a strong association between a composite indicator of material well-being and all the other domains of well-being. The associations were strongest for housing satisfaction and subjective well-being (see Table 3.11). Also, despite the criticisms of the relative child poverty rate, it was strongly associated with the other domains of child well-being – indeed, it correlated higher with many of the domains than the composite material well-being indicator.

Figure 3.12 presents the association between overall well-being less the material domain and the relative child poverty rate. The relative child income poverty rate explains 62% of the variation in overall child well-being. The countries to the right of the diagonal line have higher child well-being than you would expect given their child poverty (including the US, Spain and Japan). The countries to the left have lower well-being than you would expect given their child poverty rates (including Finland, Hungary, Malta and Bulgaria). Clearly, relative income poverty is not the sole determinant of well-being, but it is still quite strongly and, given it is a relative measure, surprisingly associated with overall well-being.

Conclusion

Child poverty had declined after the Labour government came to power in 1997. Nevertheless, by 2010 child poverty was still double the level it was in 1979, and the government had missed its targets to reduce child poverty by a quarter in five years and by a half in ten years. Child poverty was still comparatively high in the UK compared to other countries in the EU. The proportion of children living in workless families was also comparatively high and had not changed much since 1997, despite the fact that until 2009 unemployment was

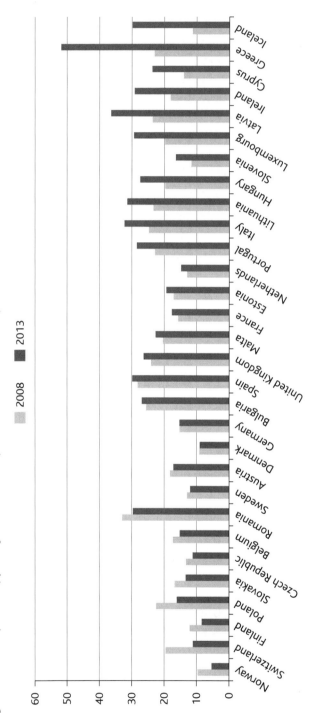

Figure 3.11: Child (under 18) poverty rates, 2008-13 (threshold anchored at 2008)

Source: Eurostat database, http://ec.europa.eu/eurostat/data/database, 23 July 2015

Table 3.11: Correlation coefficients of material well-being and all the other domains

	Material well-being	Relative child poverty rate
Health	0.630**	−0.592**
Education	0.540**	−0.650**
Subjective	0.664**	−0.713**
Behaviour	0.588**	−0.648**
Housing	0.664**	−0.545**
Overall well-being	0.823**	−0.826**
Overall excluding material	0.719**	0.780**

Figure 3.12: Relative child income poverty rate by overall child well-being excluding material well-being

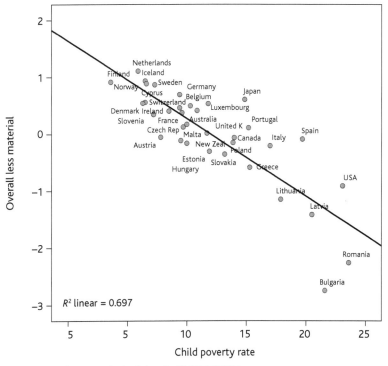

Source: Author's own analysis of data for UNICEF (2013)

at the lowest level for decades and the employment rates at record levels.

The coalition government endorsed the Child Poverty Act targets and established the Social Mobility and Child Poverty Commission, but the real living standards of families with children have fallen as price inflation has exceeded income growth in every year for the six years up to 2014. The cuts in spending on working-age benefits and tax credits resulted in low-income families with children carrying the main burdens of austerity. This is partly the result of the freeze in child benefits and the uprating of working-age benefits and tax credits by only 1% over three years (offset in part by real increases in the personal tax allowance). In contrast, since 2010, the triple lock has protected pensioner incomes.

The Social Mobility and Child Poverty Commission (2014) said:

> ... plans to cut in-work support in real terms in the next Parliament will make the working poor worse off, not better off. Similarly, further increases in the personal income tax allowances are not the best use of resources if the aim is to tackle poverty and promote mobility. Finally our analysis suggests that if pensioner benefits continue to be protected, that will require a 13% reduction in tax credits and benefits for children and working-age adults over and above the big cuts in working-age benefits during this Parliament. It is difficult to see how this is deliverable without child poverty rising further over and above existing projections. (p viii)

During the election campaign in 2015 the Conservative Party committed itself to £12 billion further cuts in social security spending. These have now been revealed in the summer 2015 budget. The Welfare Reform and Work Bill proposes to emasculate the Child Poverty Act and abolish the child poverty targets and replace them with a duty to report an annual report on children in workless households in England and on the educational attainment of children in England at the end of Key Stage 4. In addition:

- The benefit cap is to be lowered, which is expected[7] to reduce the household incomes of 333,000 children by a median of £50 per week, comprising two-thirds of lone-mother families.

- Working-age benefits are to be frozen for four years from 2016.

- The child element of tax credits is to be limited to two children, affecting 640,000 families by 2020/21.

- The family element in tax credit is to be abolished, affecting 1.18 million families by 2020/21.[8]

These cuts are to be partially offset by the introduction of a new increased National Minimum Wage (wrongly named as a National Living Wage). This will add a premium to the existing and prospective national minimum wage for those over 25 of £7.20 from April 2016 rising to £9 by 2020, pegged to 60% median earnings.

The impacts of the budget are still being considered, but there is a useful analysis by the Institute for Fiscal Studies (see Hood, 2015), which shows that it is highly regressive. Child poverty is bound to increase again.

Notes

[1] See www.gov.uk/government/uploads/system/uploads/attachment_data/file/444371/welfare-reform-and-work-bill-2015-delegated-powers-july-2015.pdf

[2] See https://www.gov.uk/government/statistics/english-indices-of-deprivation-2015

[3] Which are 32,482 geographical, spatially contiguous areas with a mean population of 1,500 and minimum of 1,000, which are designed, using the 2001 Census outputs, to be relatively socially homogeneous and constrained to 2003 ward boundaries.

[4] See http://stats.oecd.org/Index.aspx?DataSetCode=IDD

[5] See www.lisdatacenter.org/data-access/key-figures/download-key-figures/

[6] The EU uses the so-called Guio index containing nine items – cannot afford: to pay rent or utility bills; to keep home adequately warm; to pay unexpected expenses; to eat meat, fish or equivalent every second day; a week's holiday away from home once a year; a car; washing machine; colour TV; telephone.

[7] See www.parliament.uk/documents/impact-assessments/IA15-006.pdf

[8] See www.parliament.uk/documents/impact-assessments/IA15-006E.pdf

FOUR

Physical health

Jonathan Bradshaw, Veronica Dale and Karen Bloor

Key statistics
- Infant mortality rates in the UK remain relatively high compared to other rich countries. Northern Ireland has a higher infant mortality rate than the rest of the UK.
- Low birth weight births are also higher than in comparable countries, and this appears static over time.
- The child mortality and child accidental death rates are comparatively low and similar across the constituent countries of the UK.
- Immunisation rates for infectious diseases are slightly lower than in other rich countries, particularly for measles, mumps and rubella.
- Breastfeeding rates remain low.
- With the exception of physical exercise, most health behaviour is comparatively poor.
- Rates of sexually transmitted diseases are high, but this may be affected by recent campaigns to increase the take-up of screening.
- The UK failed to meet its target on teenage pregnancy, but the rate has been falling rapidly since 2008.
- Self-assessed health is comparatively poor.

Key trends
- The long-term downward trend in infant and child mortality continues, and the infant mortality rate for 2013 is the lowest ever recorded.
- The social class gap in infant mortality has been increasing over the last decade.
- Cancer has overtaken accidents as the main cause of child deaths.
- Immunisation rates are recovering, but there have been epidemics of measles and mumps.
- Breastfeeding rates have improved very slightly.
- The incidence of deaths and serious injuries on the roads has continued to decline.
- Health behaviour has been improving. The exception is early sexual activity, although teenage conceptions have fallen rapidly since 2008.

- The upwards trend in sexually transmitted diseases may be levelling off.
- There is tentative evidence that obesity rates may be falling.
- Self-assessed health has been improving.

Key sources
- Office for National Statistics (ONS)
- Health and Social Care Information Centre (HSCIC)
- Health Survey for England (HSE)
- OECD Health database
- Health Behaviour of School-aged Children (HBSC) study
- Department for Transport (DfT)
- Child and Maternal Health Observatory (CHIMAT)

Introduction

This chapter focuses on the physical health of children and their health behaviour (subjective well-being and mental health are covered in Chapter Five). Topics covered relating to physical health include infant and child mortality, birth weight, immunisations, self-reported health, longstanding illnesses and chronic conditions, non-intentional accidents and injuries (also covered from a different perspective in Chapter Ten), HIV/AIDS, sexual health and teenage conceptions. Under health behaviours smoking and alcohol consumption, diet, obesity, physical activity and illicit drug use are covered. Analysis is generally restricted to children aged 16 or under, although in respect of sexual health we also report data on young people aged 16-19.

The purpose of this book is to monitor and reflect on changes in indicators of child well-being for children living in the UK, but in order to know how well we are doing, where possible, comparisons are made with other countries. We also review the association between child health and social, demographic and economic characteristics.

Infant and child mortality

Official mortality statistics distinguish between six types of mortality in childhood:

- early neonatal: deaths during the first six completed days of life
- late neonatal: deaths between 7 and 27 completed days of life
- perinatal: stillbirths plus neonatal deaths (deaths during the first 28 days of life)

- post–neonatal: deaths at 28 days and over but under one year
- infant: deaths aged under one year
- child: deaths aged 1-14.

Early and late neonatal deaths are usually presented together as neonatal deaths, and stillbirths are often presented separately. Child mortality is commonly presented in three age groups: 1-4, 5-9 and 10-14.

A number of detailed analyses of factors related to mortality have been carried out, particularly by staff at the ONS, but many of these analyses only cover figures for England and Wales or the whole of the UK, without disaggregation by country or region. One of the reasons for this is that when disaggregated, the numbers for each country are small, making it difficult to conduct reliable analyses.

Trends in mortality

Mortality rates are highest just after birth. They then fall in the post-neonatal period and during childhood, with the lowest rates between the ages of five and nine. Figure 4.1 shows a general downward trend in mortality. The rate of decline has been slower since the 1990s than the 1980s. The exception is the stillbirth rate that increased in 1993 and again in 2002 and 2011. The former increase is due to a change in definition – up to 1992, stillbirths were foetal deaths at or over 28 weeks gestation, and from 1993 at or over 24 weeks gestation. The increase in 2002 occurred in all countries except Scotland. An investigation (ONS, 2003) found this was due to a sharp increase in stillbirths to sole registration births outside marriage, but the reasons for this are not known.

A similar trend is observed in Figure 4.2 for child mortality – a downward trend with smaller rates of reduction since the mid-1990s.

Table 4.1 compares the stillbirth, infant mortality and child mortality rates in the countries of the UK for the latest available year (2013). England had a slightly higher rate of stillbirths and Northern Ireland a higher rate of infant deaths, but these rates fluctuate from year to year and are not consistently different.

The latest comparative data on child mortality is also for 2013. Figure 4.3 shows that the UK has an infant mortality rate in the middle of the European Union (EU) distribution and over twice the level of Iceland and Luxembourg, which have the lowest rate by some margin. Some of this variation in infant mortality could be the result of differences in the quality of antenatal and perinatal care and in the rates of smoking during pregnancy and other health behaviours

Figure 4.1: Stillbirths and mortality rates, England/Wales

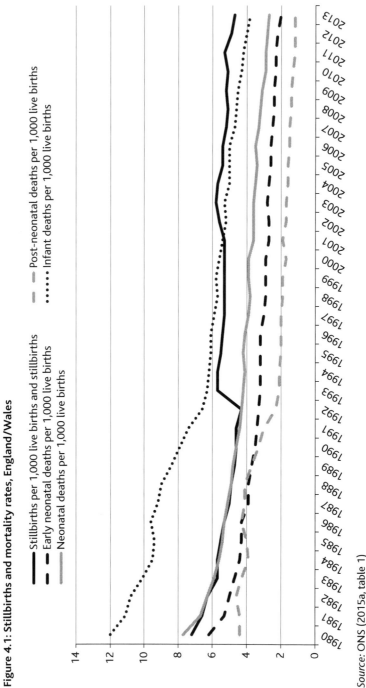

— Stillbirths per 1,000 live births and stillbirths
- - Early neonatal deaths per 1,000 live births
〰 Neonatal deaths per 1,000 live births
- - Post-neonatal deaths per 1,000 live births
•••• Infant deaths per 1,000 live births

Source: ONS (2015a, table 1)

Figure 4.2: Child mortality per 100,000 of the same age, England/Wales

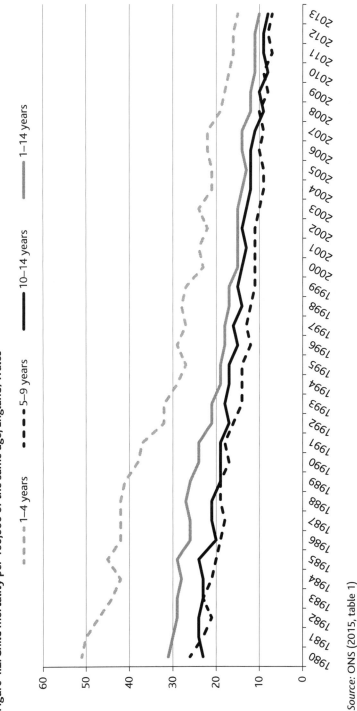

- - - - 1–4 years   ■ ■ ■ 5–9 years   —— 10–14 years   —— 1–14 years

Source: ONS (2015, table 1)

Table 4.1: Stillbirths, infant and childhood death rates, 2013

	Stillbirths per 1,000 live births and stillbirths	Infant deaths per 1,000 live births	Child mortality (age 1-14) per 100,000 population of the same age
UK	4.6	3.8	10
England	4.6	3.8	10
Wales	4.5	3.6	11
Scotland	4.2	3.3	10
Northern Ireland	4.5	4.6	11

Source: ONS (2015a, Table 2)

(Richardus et al, 2003). There may also be differences in the rate of pre-term birth and survival rates. MacDorman et al (2014) found, for example, that over a third of the difference in infant mortality rates between the US and Sweden could be explained by higher rates of pre-term births in the US.

Child deaths are comparatively low in the UK (Figure 4.4), which is probably attributable to relatively low rates of road traffic accidents (see below).

There is a strong association at an international level between poverty and infant mortality. Figure 4.5 shows the association between the infant mortality rate and poverty in the EU countries using, as an indicator of poverty, the proportion of households lacking three or more deprivation items.

Causes of infant and child mortality

The main causes of infant deaths (under one year) are conditions in the perinatal period (related to immaturity and/or low birth weight) and congenital malformations. Sudden infant deaths have declined substantially, particularly since changes in the recommended sleep position for babies (Kinney and Thatch, 2009), and were only 5.6% of all infant deaths in England and Wales in 2013 (ONS, 2015a, Table 8).

For children aged 1-14 the most common causes of death in 2008 were cancers. These have overtaken external causes (including injuries and poisonings) as the main cause of death, although both have been declining. The next most important cause is congenital malformations (ONS, 2015a, Table 4).

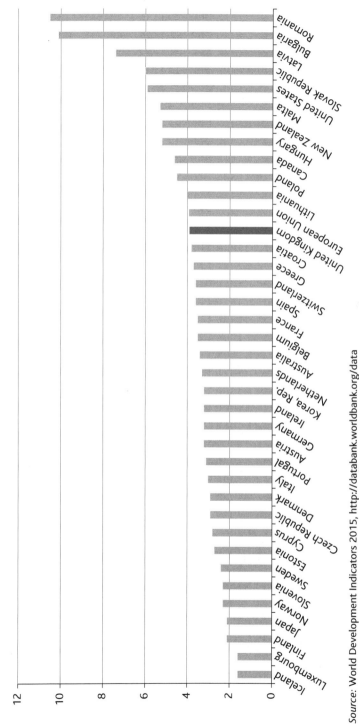

Figure 4.3: Infant mortality rates (deaths before the age of 12 months per 1,000 births), EU and selected rich countries, 2013

Source: World Development Indicators 2015, http://databank.worldbank.org/data

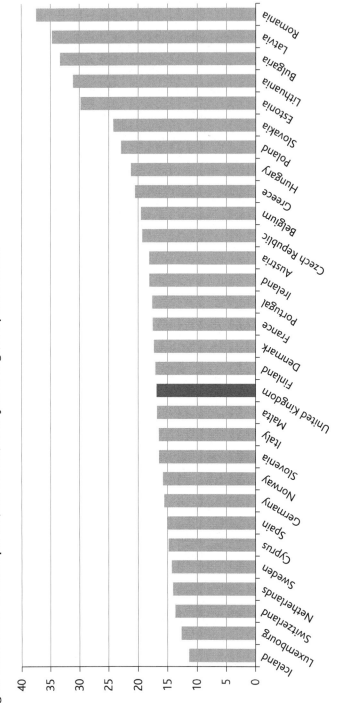

Figure 4.4: All under-19 deaths per 100,000 children, three-year average, European countries

Source: WHO mortality database in UNICEF (2013)

Figure 4.5: Association between infant mortality rate and the percentage of households lacking three or more deprivation items

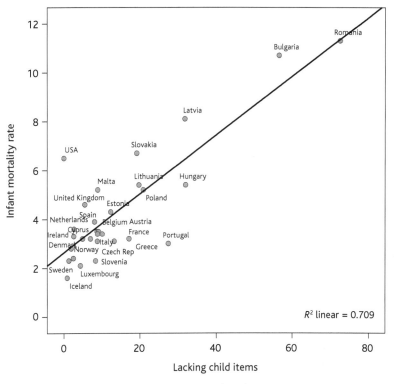

Source: Authors' own analysis of data from UNICEF (2013)

Key factors associated with child mortality

- *Parity.* Overall infant mortality was 3.5 per 1,000 in 2013 for all births inside marriage or joint registration at the same address. It was higher for fourth and subsequent births, at 4.8 per 1,000 (ONS, 2010b, Table 13).

- *Gender.* Boys have higher mortality rates than girls at all ages. In 2013, the UK infant mortality rates were 4.2 per 1,000 for boys compared with 3.5 per 1,000 for girls. The child mortality rates (per 100,000 for ages 1–14) were 11 for boys compared to 9 for girls (ONS, 2015a, Table 2). All countries and regions of the UK show the same pattern except in Wales, where the boys' infant mortality rate was 3.5 and the girls' 3.7 in 2013.

- *Occupational group.* Despite the decline in infant mortality, there is still a class gradient (Weightman et al, 2012). Among births inside marriage the infant mortality rate in socioeconomic group 1.1[1] was 1.6 per 1,000 compared with 7.9 per 1,000 in socioeconomic groups 7 and 8[2] (ONS, 2015a, Table 12). One of the *Opportunity for all* indicators was the differential in the infant mortality rate between routine and manual social groups and all other groups. The differential was falling up until 1996-98 but increased after that, and the last ratio for 2003-05 was 1.18 – that is, the infant mortality for routine and manual was 18% higher than for all. Figure 4.6 shows changes in the infant mortality rate by socioeconomic group over the period 2005-13. Unfortunately there were two breaks in the series. From 2011 the ONS switched the socioeconomic classification of occupations that underpin the National Statistics-Socioeconomic Classes (NS-SEC) from SOC2000 to SOC2010, and we cannot be certain that the jump in infant mortality in NS-SEC groups 4, 5, 7 and 8 is not a consequence of this definition change. From 2012 there was also a switch from classifying births by the occupational status of fathers to classifying births by the status of mothers or fathers, whichever was highest. This may have increased the mortality rates of groups 3 and unclassified. There is a series that corrects for this change for 2008, 2009 and 2010 (but not 2011) (see Figure 4.7). Overall, there is little evidence here that inequalities in infant mortality have diminished since 2005.

- *Age of mother.* Infant mortality rates vary by mother's age and are highest for mothers aged under 20 (6.1 per 1,000 live births) in England and Wales in 2013. The next highest rates are births to mothers over 40 (4.7 per 1,000), and the lowest are to mothers aged 25-29 (3.4 per 1,000) (ONS, 2015a, Table 10).

- *Marital status.* Infant mortality rates are higher for births jointly registered at different addresses (5.6 per 1,000) or sole registered (5.2 per 1,000) compared to births inside marriage or jointly registered at the same address (3.5 per 1,000) (ONS, 2015a, Table 12).

- *Country of birth.* Table 4.1 has already compared mortality by country in the UK, but it also varies by country of birth of the mother. The highest rates of infant mortality are found in births to mothers born in the Caribbean (9.0 per 1,000), Central Africa, (8.3 per 1,000), Pakistan (7.2 per 1,000) and West Africa (7.2 per 1,000). The overall rate for mothers born outside the UK is 4.2 per

Figure 4.6: Infant mortality by socioeconomic classification[1]

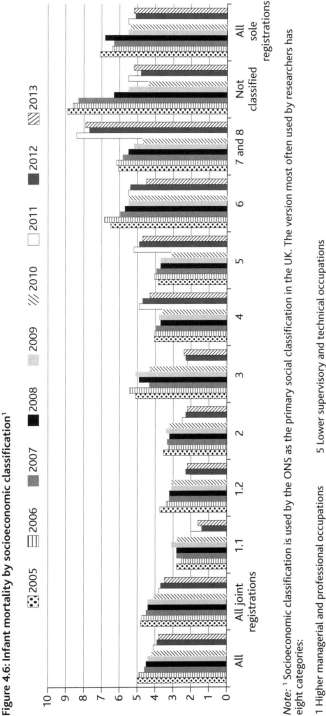

Note: [1] Socioeconomic classification is used by the ONS as the primary social classification in the UK. The version most often used by researchers has eight categories:

1 Higher managerial and professional occupations
2 Lower managerial and professional occupations
3 Intermediate occupations (clerical, sales, service)
4 Small employers and own account workers

5 Lower supervisory and technical occupations
6 Semi-routine occupations
7 Routine occupations
8 Never worked and long-term unemployed

Source: Authors' own analysis of ONS child mortality statistics

Figure 4.7: Ratio of infant mortality in socioeconomic groups 7/8 to all groups

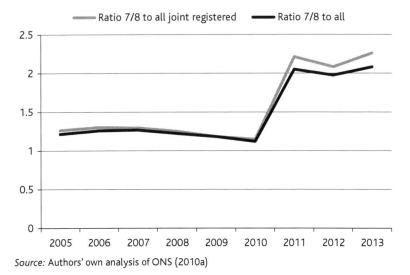

Source: Authors' own analysis of ONS (2010a)

1,000 compared with 3.6 per 1,000 for mothers born in England and Wales (ONS, 2015a, Table 11).

Birth weight

Birth weight is one of the main indicators of the outcome of pregnancy, and low birth weight is a well-established risk factor for immediate and long-term health problems (Macfarlane et al, 2004). The World Health Organization (WHO) defines a birth weight of less than 2500g as a low birth weight. Births under 2500g made up 66% of all stillbirths and 60% of all infant deaths in England and Wales in 2012 (ONS, 2015a, Table 14). Figure 4.8 shows that there has been very little change in low birth rates in England and Wales since 2005.

Compared with other countries, the UK has a comparatively high rate of low birth weight (see Figure 4.9). There is generally an increasing proportion of babies being born with low birth weight in most other countries. One factor contributing to this new trend is likely to be the increasing survival rates of pre-term infants. However, as the gestational age of live births is not recorded, it is not possible to explore whether this hypothesis is true.

Figure 4.8: Low birth weight rates in England and Wales

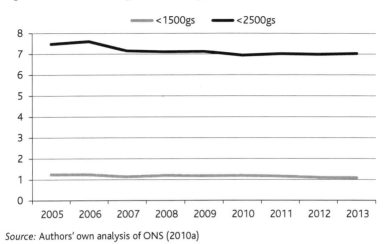

Source: Authors' own analysis of ONS (2010a)

Factors associated with low birth weight

Unsurprisingly, given the association between low birth weight and stillbirth and infant mortality, the factors associated with low birth weight are very similar. Overall 7.0% of live births were under 2,500g in 2013 (ONS, 2015a). But there were certain risk groups where the proportion of low birth rate was higher:

- births to mothers under 20 (8.3%) and over 40 (9.9%) (ONS, 2015a);
- births to mothers born outside the UK (7.5%) in Africa the Caribbean (10.1%), Pakistan (9.2%) and Bangladesh (11.1%);
- births to mothers of lower socioeconomic groups: for jointly registered births with a socioeconomic classification of 1.1, the percentage of low birth weight is 6.1, the proportion rises for each social group and is 8.7% for socioeconomic groups 7 and 8; it is 9.1% for sole registrations.

Analysis of the Millennium Cohort Survey on birth weight is in line with these findings. Bradshaw and Mayhew (2005) found that after controlling for other factors, the risk of low birth weight was higher for mothers in poverty, underweight mothers, mothers who smoked in pregnancy, first births and mothers from minority ethnic groups. However, having controlled for these factors, marital status and where they lived in the UK were not associated with low birth weight.

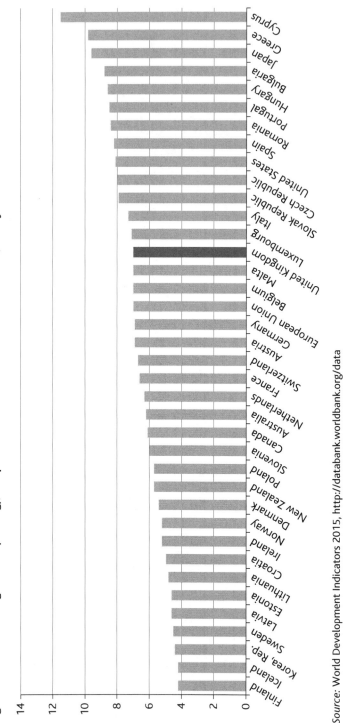

Figure 4.9: Low birth weight births (<2500g), European and selected rich countries latest data, mainly 2011 or 2012

Source: World Development Indicators 2015, http://databank.worldbank.org/data

Infant feeding

The benefits of breastfeeding to a baby's health are well documented and include increased immunity to infection and hence lower susceptibility to illness, which in turn results in reduced mortality. Breastfed babies are less likely to suffer from conditions such as gastroenteritis, chest infections, ear infections, diabetes in childhood and childhood obesity (Ip et al, 2007; Quigley et al, 2007). In addition, breastfeeding offers protection against chronic conditions such as atopic disease, inflammatory bowel disease and childhood leukaemia (Ip et al, 2007), and there is increasing evidence of improved cognitive and behavioural outcomes (see, for example, Kramer et al, 2008; Belfort et al, 2013). The current policy on breastfeeding is that breast milk is the best form of nutrition for infants; exclusive breastfeeding is recommended for the first six months of life and breastfeeding should continue beyond the first six months of life (WHO, 2002).

There have been slight improvements in the initiation of breastfeeding (any breastfeeding at birth) in the UK since 1990. The latest Infant Feeding Survey for 2010 (HSCIC, 2012) found initial breastfeeding rates were 83% in England, 74% in Scotland, 71% in Wales and 64% in Northern Ireland. Breastfeeding rates were higher among mothers from higher socioeconomic groups, those aged over 30 and first-time mothers.

But breastfeeding rates drop off rapidly in the early weeks of life. In the UK 55% of all mothers were breastfeeding at six weeks and 34% at six months. This applies even more to exclusive breastfeeding – only 46% of UK mothers were exclusively breastfeeding at one week and 23% at six weeks (see Table 4.2 and Figure 4.10).

Analysis of the Millennium Cohort Survey in which low-income families were over-sampled (Mayhew and Bradshaw, 2005) found that 71% of mothers had ever tried to breastfeed their babies and that, controlling for other factors, the odds of breastfeeding were higher for married mothers, older mothers, home owners, only children,

Table 4.2: Infant feeding

		UK				England		Wales		Scotland		Northern Ireland	
	1990	1995	2000	2005	2010	2005/10		2005/10		2005/10		2005/10	
Birth	62	66	69	76	81	78	83	68	71	71	74	62	64
6 weeks	na	42	42	48	55	50	57	37	40	44	50	32	33
6 months	na	21	21	25	34	26	36	18	23	24	32	14	16

Note: na – data not available.

Figure 4.10: Infant feeding in the UK

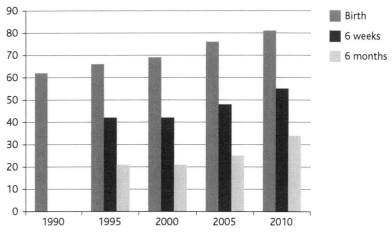

Source: HSCIC (2012), www.hscic.gov.uk/catalogue/PUB08694/ifs-uk-2010-chap1-tab.xls

mothers of minority ethnic groups and mothers in England. Poor mothers were less likely to breastfeed, but this association disappeared when controlling for other factors such as marital status, mother's ethnicity, paid work status, number of siblings of the baby, tenure, country or region (within the UK) and mother's age at birth.

International comparative data is probably not very reliable as data are not consistently collected. Figure 4.11 presents some breastfeeding initiation rates from the OECD that show that the UK has a comparatively low proportion of mothers who have ever breastfed. They also publish data showing the proportion of mothers exclusively breastfeeding at three, four and six months, and the UK comes at the bottom of this league table of 20 countries (OECD, 2015a, Chart CO1.5.B).

Immunisations

Routine immunisation of babies and young children benefits the health of children and their communities where immunisation rates are high – so-called herd immunity (Nicoll et al, 1989). In 1997, almost all two-year-old children in the UK had been immunised against diphtheria, tetanus and polio (96%), whooping cough (94%) and measles, mumps and rubella (MMR) (91%). However, following the publication of a flawed study in *The Lancet* in 1998 (since retracted by the journal) that associated the MMR vaccine with bowel disease and autism, immunisation rates began to fall. Rates of MMR vaccination fell from

Figure 4.11: Proportion of mothers who have ever breastfed, around 2005

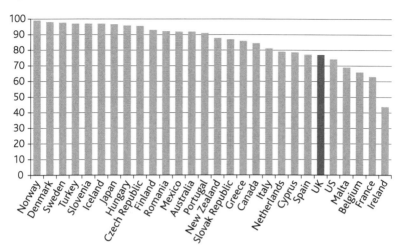

Source: OECD Family database (2015a, Chart CO1.5.a)

91.8% in 1995/96 to 79.9% in 2003/04. They have since recovered, and Table 4.3 summarises the immunisation rates for children in the countries of the UK, which all exceed 90%. Immunisation rates in England are slightly lower than the other countries, particularly for MMR (92.7% compared with over 95% in the other three countries).

Figure 4.12 shows international comparative immunisation rates for measles in 2000, 2005 and 2010. In 2000 the UK was in the middle of the international league table. By 2005 it had fallen back, and in

Table 4.3: Percentage of children immunised by their 2nd birthday, 2013-14

	Diphtheria Tetanus Polio Pertussis Hib (DTaP/IPV/Hib) primary (%)	MMR 1st dose (%)	Hib/Men C booster (%)	PCV booster (%)
UK	96.4	93.1	93.0	92.9
England	96.1	92.7	92.5	92.4
Northern Ireland	98.6	96.2	96.2	96.0
Scotland	98.2	95.6	95.7	95.5
Wales	97.7	96.5	95.3	95.5

Source: HSCIC (2014a, table 5b), www.hscic.gov.uk/catalogue/PUB14949/nhs-immu-stat-eng-2013-14-tab-exc.xlsx

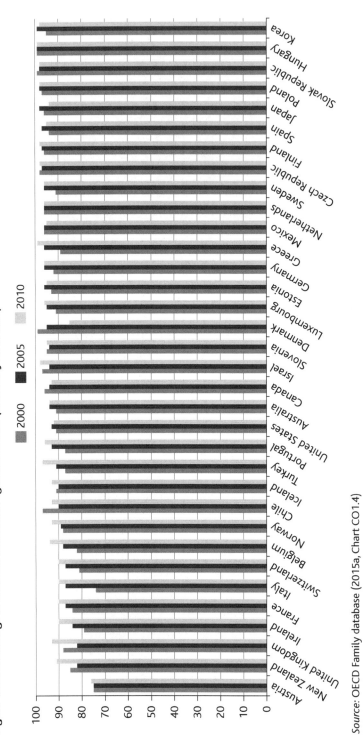

Figure 4.12: Percentage of children vaccinated against measles (ranked by 2005 rate)

■ 2000   ■ 2005   ░ 2010

Source: OECD Family database (2015a, Chart CO1.4)

2008 the UK had the third lowest rates in the countries for which we have data. By 2010 the rate had recovered and the UK returned to its mid-table position.

The introduction of the MMR vaccination programme in the late 1980s resulted in a significant decrease in notifications of cases of measles, mumps and rubella among children. However, the difficulty of consistently achieving very high levels of vaccination coverage (Nicoll et al, 1989), in addition to the impact of the vaccine scare, led to a decrease in coverage, and herd immunity of children against these three infectious diseases has been threatened. In England and Wales there was an epidemic of mumps around 2005 and very high levels of measles in 2008 and 2009 (NOIDS; see HPA, 2010a). To achieve herd immunity for these highly contagious diseases, vaccination levels should ideally exceed 95%, which is challenging, particularly (and ironically) given the success of immunisation, which means that infectious childhood diseases are perceived as much less problematic than in the past (Cockman et al, 2011). The challenge of achieving herd immunity is not just a UK problem – outbreaks of measles have also been reported in Germany and the US, again apparently linked to 'anti-vaccination' scaremongering (*New Scientist*, 2015).

Self-assessed health

The Health Survey for England (HSE) indicates that the vast majority of children rate their health as good or very good, and the proportion has increased from 91% in 1995 to 96% in 2013. The proportion reporting longstanding illness has fallen from 21% in 1995 to 13% in 2013, and the proportion reporting a limiting longstanding illness has fallen from 9% in 1996 to 7% in 2012, but with a very small possible upturn for girls in 2013 (see Figure 4.13).

The British Household Panel Survey (BHPS) youth panel (of 11- to 15-year-olds) has included a subjective health question since 1994. Unfortunately, there was a break in the series between 1998 and 2004 as well as a change to the question, and now there is a hiatus resulting from the switch to the Understanding Society study.

Table 4.4 is from the Health Behaviour of School-aged Children (HBSC) study (Currie et al, 2012), and compares the percentage of young people reporting good or excellent health by age and gender in the different countries of Great Britain and Ireland (Northern Ireland is not in the HBSC study). Overall, the vast majority report good or excellent health. The proportion is highest in Ireland and lowest in Wales. In all countries and at all ages the proportion is lower for girls

Figure 4.13: Percentage of all children aged 0-15 with general health good or very good, longstanding illness and limited longstanding illness

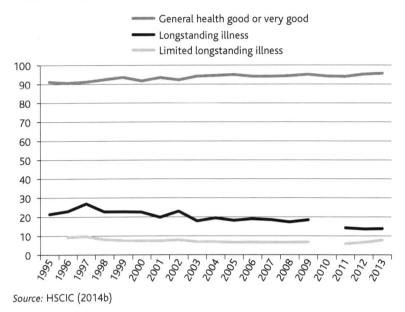

Source: HSCIC (2014b)

Table 4.4: Percentage of young people who reported good or excellent self-rated health by gender, age and country, 2009/10

	Males			Females			Both genders			
Age	11	13	15	11	13	15	11	13	15	All
Wales	86	80	79	82	72	66	84	76	73	78
Scotland	86	84	77	88	76	66	87	80	71	79
England	87	84	84	87	83	77	87	83	80	84
Ireland	93	90	88	93	88	79	93	89	84	88

Source: Authors' own analysis of HBSC study (2009/10)

than boys, and in all countries and for both genders it declines with age.

The Children's Society has conducted a number of Good Childhood surveys since 2010 using both regular online household surveys and school-based surveys of children aged 8-17. These have resulted in the publication of a Good Childhood Index that includes a question on satisfaction with health. The 2014 school-based survey of 3,000 8-, 10- and 12-year-olds (Rees et al, 2015) found the 10- and 12-year-olds scoring an average of 8.8 on an 11-point Likert scale. Scores were slightly higher for boys than girls, and for 10-year-olds than for 12-year-olds (see Table 4.5).

Comparative studies of self-assessed child health

The Children's Society 2014 school-based survey of children in England (Pople et al, 2015) was part of the international Children's Worlds survey of child well-being for 8-, 10- and 12-year-olds in 15 countries. Table 4.6 compares the satisfaction with health of the 10- and 12-year-olds. Children in England score in the bottom half of this league table.

Table 4.5: Satisfaction with health in England, 2014

	Mean score out of 11
Boys	8.9
Girls	8.7
10-year-olds	8.9
12-year-olds	8.6
All *n* = 2000	8.8

Source: Rees et al (2015)

Table 4.6: Satisfaction with health, 10- and 12-year-olds, 2014

	Mean satisfaction with health out of 10	% with low satisfaction
Romania	9.6	1.3
Colombia	9.5	1.9
Turkey	9.4	3.2
Israel	9.3	3.1
Spain	9.3	1.5
Algeria	9.0	4.2
Norway	9.0	2.2
Germany	9.0	2.7
Poland	9.0	3.8
Ethiopia	8.9	4.0
South Africa	8.8	5.8
Estonia	8.8	4.9
England	8.8	5.4
Nepal	8.6	5.7
South Korea	8.4	5.0

Source: Rees and Main (2015)

The best source of comparative data on child health is the HBSC study, which is carried out every four years on a large school-based sample of children. Figure 4.14 compares the proportion of children in EU countries (and some others) who describe their health as only fair or poor. Wales, Scotland and England all have comparatively high proportions rating their health as only fair or poor.

Common chronic conditions with increasing prevalence

Successful prevention and treatment of infectious diseases means that childhood illness tends to be chronic and non-communicable. Severe problems such as cancer and cardiac problems need specialist care, but common long-term illnesses, such as asthma, diabetes and mental health problems, are treated in primary and community care, sometimes with variable quality (Wolfe et al, 2013). (Mental health is covered in a Chapter Five of this book.) The reported prevalence of diabetes and asthma has increased substantially over recent years.

Diabetes

Type 1 or insulin-dependent diabetes is one of the most common chronic conditions to emerge in childhood. It is a condition that requires daily management, and poor management threatens both current and future health. The cause of type 1 diabetes is not fully understood, but it is thought to be due to a genetic predisposition coupled with exposure to 'environmental risk factors' including perinatal infection and rapid growth rate in early life, although these have yet to be definitely identified. The incidence of type 1 diabetes is growing across Europe by around 3-4% per year, although this increase is not uniform across countries or over time (Patterson et al, 2012). The prevalence of type 1 diabetes is not associated with disadvantage, and some research suggests that there is a higher prevalence of type 1 diabetes among the least deprived groups (ONS, 1998).

There was insufficient data on type 1 diabetes until the National Paediatric Diabetes Report audit was launched in 1999. The most recent report for 2013/14 (see Table 4.7) indicates that the highest rates are for children aged 10-14 and that the total rate for the under-25s is 15.2 per 1,000 for boys and 13.6 per 1,000 for girls.

Type 2 diabetes usually occurs in adults, but it is now beginning to be diagnosed in children and adolescents. Ehtisham et al (2000) published the first case report of the incidence of type 2 diabetes in UK children at the same time as reports of its occurrence in children

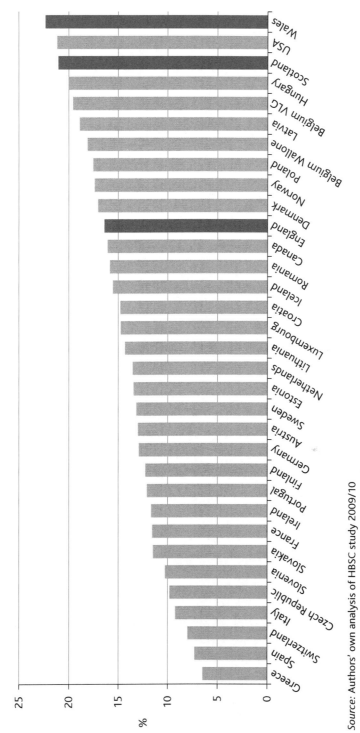

Figure 4.14: Proportion of children who rate their health as fair or poor

Source: Authors' own analysis of HBSC study 2009/10

Table 4.7: Type 1 diabetes incidence rates per 100,000 people by age group and sex, 2011-12

Age group	England Boys	England Girls	Wales Boys	Wales Girls	England and Wales Boys	England and Wales Girls
0-4	12.5	13.8	9.8	11.5	12.4	13.6
5-9	24.8	20.6	17.9	31.5	24.5	23.5
10-14	35.5	28.3	40.6	40.4	35.8	29.0
15-19	6.6	5.4	5.9	4.1	6.5	5.4
20-24	0.1	0.0	0.9	0.0	0.2	0.0
Total under 25	15.2	13.4	14.3	16.3	15.2	13.6

Source: RCPCH (2015, table 6)

in North America emerged. The onset of type 2 diabetes in children appears to be linked to obesity and a family history of the condition, and certain minority ethnic groups are particularly at risk. The increase in obesity among children is being ascribed as the cause for the emergence of type 2 diabetes in children.

Type 2 diabetes accounts for 2.6% of girls' diabetes diagnoses and 1.1% of boys'. The proportion of type 2 diabetes varies with ethnicity – 1% of White children are diagnosed with type 2 diabetes compared to 2.1% of Asian and 8.7% of Black children (RCPCH, 2015, Tables 4 and 5)

Type 2 diabetes is of concern, as it is a new chronic condition for children, and as it is thought to be associated with obesity, there is an expectation that the prevalence rate will rise. Diabetes affects children's quality of life, disrupts their activities and carries a risk of substantial and severe complications in later life.

The UK has a high prevalence of diabetes in children compared with a selection of other countries (see Figure 4.15, from IDF, 2014).

Asthma

Asthma is one of the most common non-communicable childhood illnesses around the world (Lai et al, 2009). From the International Study of Asthma and Allergies in Childhood (ISAAC), the UK has a high prevalence of asthma symptoms compared with other countries, with reported asthma symptom prevalence of 20.9% in the 6-7 year age group and 24.7% in the 13-14 year age group (Asher et al, 2006). This compares with global prevalence of reported symptoms of 9.4% in the 6-7 year age group and 12.6% in the 13-14 year age group (Lai et al, 2009). In the UK, asthma symptoms increased over a five-year period in the 6-7 year age group but decreased in the 13-14 year

Figure 4.15: Incidence of type 1 diabetes in children aged 0-14 per 100,000, 2013

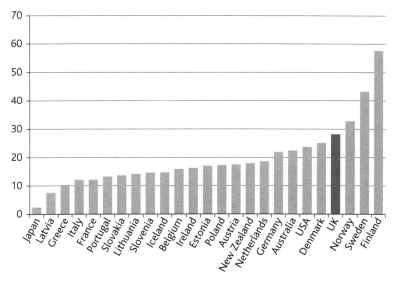

Source: IDF (2014)

age group (Asher et al, 2006). In general, asthma symptoms tend to be more prevalent in more affluent countries, like the UK, but they also appear to be less severe in affluent countries (Lai et al, 2009), presumably reflecting better treatment and symptom control.

Trends in the prevalence and incidence of childhood asthma over time were summarised over 50 years (1955-2004) by Ross Anderson et al (2007). Using data from surveys and routine data from primary care, hospital admissions and mortality, the authors found that the prevalence of asthma in children increased two- to three-fold, but it has flattened or even decreased slightly more recently.

Earlier analysis of the HSE 2002 explored the association between asthma and a number of factors thought to be associated with its presence. The findings were that, overall, doctor-diagnosed asthma was 23% for 0- to 15-year-old boys and 18% for girls in the same age range. Doctor-diagnosed asthma varies by:

- Social class: the prevalence of asthma was higher for boys and girls from households where the reference person was in a semi-routine or routine occupation.
- Income: the prevalence of doctor-diagnosed asthma decreased as income increased.

- Region: the North East was the region with the highest rates and there were generally higher rates in the North than the South.
- Indoor risk factors: the prevalence of doctor-diagnosed asthma in children aged 0-15 was significantly higher in children exposed to cigarette smoke than those not exposed (boys: 28% vs 21%; girls: 22% vs 16%). However, the use of domestic gas appliances and keeping household pets did not show a significant association with doctor-diagnosed asthma.
- Degree of urbanisation: there was no significant tendency for doctor-diagnosed asthma to be more common among children living in urban areas.

The HSE 2004 explored the health of minority ethnic groups including children (HSCIC, 2006), and found 33% higher rates of doctor-diagnosed asthma among Black Caribbean children, but the other ethnic groups had lower rates than the general population in 2001-02.

In general, prevalence of asthma in the UK and elsewhere rose over the 1980s and 1990s, particularly in younger age groups, and has since flattened or even fallen. Various explanations for the trends have been proposed, including air pollution, smoking, diet and infections in early life, but none of these explanations cover both the rise and flattening or decrease, and the changes in prevalence cannot be accounted for adequately on the basis of current epidemiological knowledge (Anderson, 2005).

Injuries and accidents

As we have seen above, injury is the second main cause of deaths in childhood (ages 1-15) in the UK (ONS, 2015a). In England and Wales, in 2013 there were 169 deaths of children aged between one month and 15 years resulting from external causes (accidents, injuries, poisoning, drowning and assault) (ONS, 2015a). Table 4.8 shows that boys are more likely than girls to die from accidental injuries and other external causes.

The most common cause of accidental death in children is transport accidents, which account for around half of the deaths in 5- to 14-year-olds in England and Wales (12 deaths per million boys aged 5-14 and 8 deaths per million girls aged 5-14). In 2013, there were 83 deaths and 2,877 serious injuries of road users aged 0-17 in Great Britain. There is a downward trend of fatal and serious injuries of children in road traffic accidents over time (see Figure 4.16).

Table 4.8: Post-neonatal (one month to one year) and childhood (1-14 years) deaths from external causes (accidents, injuries and assault) by gender, England and Wales, 2013

	<1 year	1-4 years	5-9 years	10-14 years	1 month-14 years
Boys	11	27	11	34	102
Girls	9	17	7	20	67

Source: ONS (2015a, Table 4), www.ons.gov.uk/ons/taxonomy/index.html?nscl=Child+Mortality#tab-data-tables

Figure 4.16: Child (0-15) casualties in reported road accidents in Great Britain

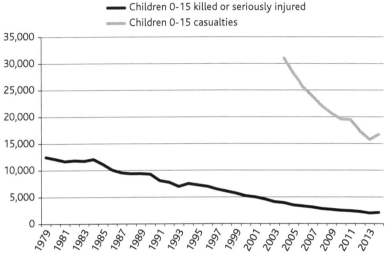

Source: DfT (2013)

Internationally, Great Britain's fatality rate from road traffic accidents (aged 0-14) per 100,000 of the population is relatively low (see Figure 4.17).

While childhood deaths from injuries and accidents are highly unusual, it has been estimated that for every death due to injury, there are numerous non-fatal accidents, including 5,000-6,000 minor injuries, 630 consultations with a doctor and 45 hospital admissions (Conway and Morgan, 2001). In 2013/14, in England there were 133,203 in-patient hospital episodes of children aged under 15, including around 8,300 episodes related to transport accidents, over 47,600 falls and over 6,900 accidental poisonings (for example, involving medicines) (HSCIC, 2015a). In 2013/14 there were estimated to be over 4.5 million attendances at accident and

Figure 4.17: Road user fatalities aged 0-14, international comparison, 2012

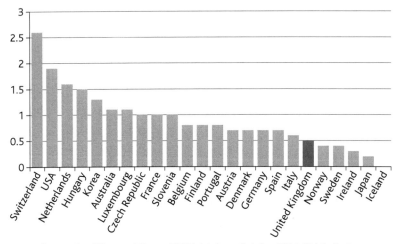

Source: International Transport Forum IRTAD database, October 2014, Risk Indicators (http://internationaltransportforum.org/irtadpublic/pdf/risk.pdf)

emergency of children and young people aged 0-19 (around 60% of these aged 0-9 and 40% aged 10-19) (HSCIC, 2015a).

Childhood deaths from injury declined in all countries of the UK between 1980 and 2010, and England has consistently held the lowest mortality rate (Hardelid et al, 2013). Children from disadvantaged backgrounds are more likely to experience unintentional injury (Pearce et al, 2012), and injuries and accidents in children remain a major area of socioeconomic inequality in the UK. Where fire was the cause of death, the death rate for children has been estimated at 15 times higher in the lowest socioeconomic group compared with the highest, and for child pedestrian deaths, the mortality rate in the lowest socioeconomic group is five times that of the highest (Towner, 2002).

Dental health

Oral health affects the health and well-being of older children and their families. The latest Children's Dental Health Survey (HSCIC, 2015b) found that 22% of 12-year-olds reported experiencing difficulty eating in the past three months; 35% of 12-year-olds reported being embarrassed to smile or laugh due to the condition of their teeth; 58% of 12-year-olds reported that their daily life had been affected by problems with their teeth and mouth in the past three months; 35% of the parents of 15-year-olds reported that their child's oral health had impacted on family life in the last six months; and 23% of the parents had taken time off work because of their child's oral health in that period.

There were reductions in the extent and severity of tooth decay present in the permanent teeth of 12- and 15-year-olds overall in England, Wales and Northern Ireland between 2003 and 2013. In 2013, 46% of 15-year-olds and 34% of 12-year-olds had 'obvious decay experience' in their permanent teeth. This was a reduction from 2003, when the comparable figures were 56% and 43% respectively. The proportions of children with some untreated decay in permanent teeth also reduced, from 32% to 21% of 15-year-olds and from 29% to 19% of 12-year-olds. However, there was no improvement in the proportion of older children with untreated dentine cavities (generally more advanced decay) in permanent teeth.

Table 4.9 shows that dental health is better in England than in Wales and Northern Ireland. Children eligible for free schools meals have worse dental health and girls have slightly worse dental health than boys.

Table 4.9: Percentage of children with no obvious experience of tooth decay, England, Wales and Northern Ireland, 2013

		5 years	8 years	12 years	15 years	Total
Overall		68	50	61	54	58
By country	England	69	51	63	56	60
	Wales	59	41	44	37	45
	Northern Ireland	60	38	41	27	41
By eligibility for free school meals	Eligible	58	38	49	41	47
	Not eligible	70	52	65	57	61
By gender	Male	67	50	64	57	60
	Female	69	51	58	50	57

Source: HSCIC (2015b)

There does not appear to be any source comparing child dental health between countries, but the HBSC asks about brushing teeth, and Figure 4.18 shows that England, Scotland and Wales have a comparatively high proportion brushing their teeth more than once a day.

Health behaviours in children

Obesity, diet and exercise

There is widespread concern over childhood obesity, and increasing evidence that it can be linked with long-term and immediate health

Figure 4.18: Proportion of 11-, 13- and 15-year-olds brushing their teeth more than once a day

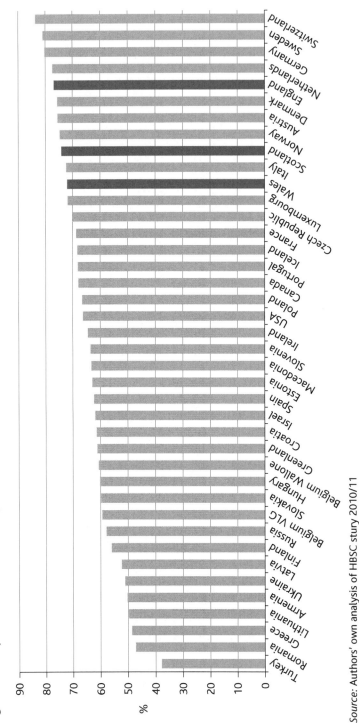

Source: Authors' own analysis of HBSC stury 2010/11

risks (HSCIC, 2009). This has led to numerous national, regional and local initiatives to improve the diet of children and to increase levels of exercise. A Public Service Agreement (PSA) target was created to 'reduce the proportion of overweight and obese children to 2000 levels by 2020 in the context of tackling obesity across the population'. Strategies to achieve this target include the 'change4life' campaign.[3] Children who are overweight and obese have an increased risk of becoming overweight and obese adults, with the associated implications for health risks (including increased risks of heart attack, stroke, type 2 diabetes, bowel cancer and hypertension). Being an overweight child can also be associated with psychological stress and lack of confidence and self-esteem (Young-Hyman et al, 2006).

Reports of obesity in the HSE 2013 were 15.2% of boys and 15.7% of girls, and around 30% were classified as overweight or obese (see Figures 4.19 and 4.20). Although this data source showed substantial increases from 1995 to 2004, since then the trend appears to have flattened and even slightly reduced, at least until 2012.

The HBSC study includes questions on self-reported height and weight, from which body mass index can be calculated to determine overweight and obesity prevalence in the constituent countries of the UK (see Table 4.10). There was a high proportion of missing data,

Figure 4.19: Percentage of children aged 2-15 overweight and obese

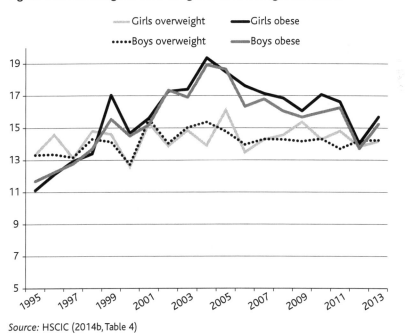

Source: HSCIC (2014b, Table 4)

Figure 4.20: Obesity rates

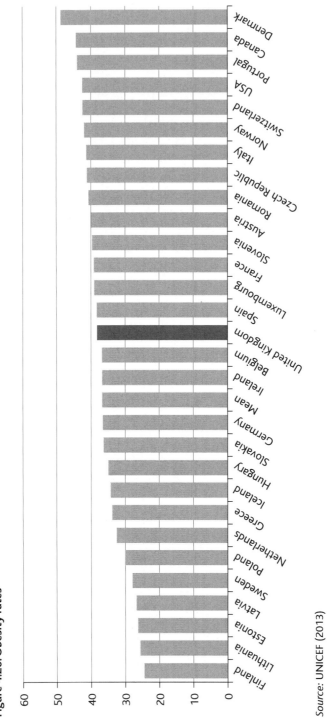

Source: UNICEF (2013)

Table 4.10: Percentage of young people who reported being overweight by gender, age and country

	Boys			Girls		
Age	11	13	15	11	13	15
England	13	9	11	14	14	11
Ireland	25	12	16	18	9	12
Scotland	16	16	16	15	6	11
Wales	21	19	22	16	14	15

Source: HBSC study 2009/10

but of those who answered, the highest percentage of young people who reported that they were overweight was found in Wales and the lowest in England. In Wales, the percentages of young people who reported being overweight were found to be significantly higher than elsewhere. In addition, England was found to have significantly fewer children who reported being overweight compared with Scotland. Across all four countries, young people with low family affluence were significantly less likely to report that they were overweight compared to those with medium and high family affluence.

The HBSC study is undertaken in a large number of countries around the world. Using this methodology, the UK's rate of self-reported childhood obesity is in the middle of the international distribution (see Figure 4.20).

The HBSC also asked children if they were 'on a diet or doing something else to lose weight.' In all four countries of the UK, a positive response was significantly more likely from girls aged 15 compared with younger ages, and from girls compared with boys. Children were also asked about their rates of consumption of fruit, vegetables, sweets, soft drinks and crisps. In general, girls were more likely than boys, and children in more affluent families more likely than those in less affluent families, to report at least daily consumption of fruit and vegetables.

Fruit and vegetable consumption has been increasing over time, at least in England, until 2009 (see Figure 4.21). Patterns were slightly less clear in reports of daily consumption of soft drinks – boys were more likely than girls to have soft drinks every day and the rate in England was the highest of all HBSC study countries. Children in less affluent families were more likely to report daily consumption of soft drinks in Wales and Scotland, but not England.

Figure 4.21: Trends in fruit and vegetable consumption by children aged 5-15 (mean portions per day)

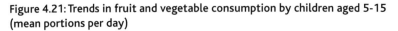

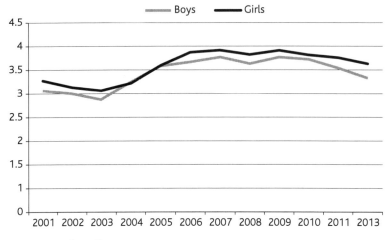

Source: HSCIC (2014b)

Physical activity

According to the HSE 2013, only 18% of children aged 5-15 reached the recommended level of physical activity. The proportion was higher from boys (21%) than girls (16%), and the proportion reaching the recommended level has declined from 24% in 2008.

The HBSC study also found that boys are significantly more likely than girls to report undertaking vigorous activity for two or more hours a week (see Table 4.11). Physical activity declines with age. Ireland has the highest self-reported rates of physical activity for both boys and girls and Scotland the lowest. Across the four countries, children living in more affluent families were not significantly more likely than those in less affluent families to engage in vigorous physical activity.

Table 4.11: Percentage of young people who reported vigorous activity for two or more hours per week

	Boys			Girls		
Age	11	13	15	11	13	15
England	33	27	25	20	15	12
Ireland	43	36	28	31	20	12
Scotland	24	19	13	16	10	8
Wales	29	23	21	19	13	9

Source: HBSC study 2009/10

Smoking

The prevalence of smoking in children appears to be declining over time, at least in England (Scholes, 2014). The percentage of children who have ever smoked in 2013 (6%) is the lowest since the HSE began in 1997. Figure 4.22 from the HSE shows the percentage of 8- to 15-year-old pupils who have ever smoked. In an analysis of children's smoking for the HSE 2013, Scholes (2014) found girls were more likely than boys to smoke regularly and less likely to never have smoked at age 15. There were large regional differences with the highest rates of boys smoking in the North East and the highest rates of girls smoking in the West Midlands and East of England.

In 2007/08, 74% of boys aged 0-15 had not been exposed to other people's smoking. By 2011/13 this had increased to 84% and there were similar improvements for girls. In a regression analysis of the factors associated with objectively measured second-hand smoke exposure in cotinine-validated non-smokers aged 4-15, the following factors were key influences on exposure to second-hand smoke, and were more strongly associated with high exposure:

- living in the most deprived quintile of the IMD (Index of Multiple Deprivation)
- whether anyone smoked in the home on most days
- reported hours of exposure to other people's smoke
- parental smoking behaviour

Figure 4.22: Children's self-reported cigarette smoking status

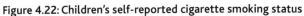

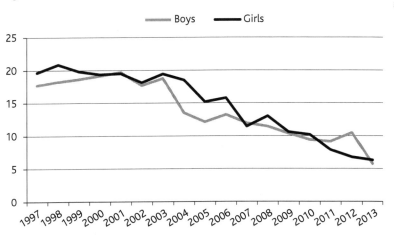

Source: HSCIC (2014b)

- whether or not the child had smoked in the past.

Fuller and Sanchez (2010) found that pupils who received free school meals (as a proxy for household income) had an increased risk of being regular smokers compared with those who did not (odds ratio 1.61). Social class, as proxied by number of books at home, was not significantly linked with the odds of being a regular smoker. Other factors that predicted regular smoking included ethnicity (Black pupils and those of mixed ethnicity were less likely to smoke than White pupils) and use of alcohol and drugs, which was strongly linked with likelihood of smoking. Young people classified as regular smokers smoked an average of 38 cigarettes a week (about 5-6 per day).

The HBSC permits comparisons between the constituent countries of the UK with regard to daily smoking. Fifteen-year-old girls in England and Wales (but not Scotland are more likely than boys to smoke at least once per week. Less affluent girls are more likely to smoke in Wales and Scotland (but not in England). Overall smoking is lower in England than Wales and Scotland but all three countries are well below the HBSC study average (see Figure 4.23).

Alcohol

Prevalence of children ever drinking has been declining in England since 2004 (see Figure 4.24). According to the HSE 2013 the mean consumption by pupils who had drunk alcohol in the last week was 9.8 units per week (median 5.5 units). There is no significant difference in the amount consumed by boys (mean = 10.6, median=5) and girls (mean = 9.0, median=5), and mean and median consumption of alcohol increases with age (mean 5.5, median 3 units per week for 11- to 13-year-olds, mean 10.0, median 6.5 units per week for 15-year-olds).

Factors associated with having drunk alcohol in the last week included age (odds ratio 1.64 for each additional year), and ethnicity (other ethnic backgrounds were more likely to have drunk alcohol in the last week compared to White children (odd ratios 7.69). Those pupils in schools where there were higher numbers of those eligible for free school meals were likely to drink *less* (odds ratio 0.98).

The HBSC permits comparisons between the constituent countries of the UK with regard to drunkenness (having been drunk more than once in the last 30 days). Boys were significantly more likely than girls to report that they had been drunk four or more times. The highest percentage of young people who have been drunk at least four times

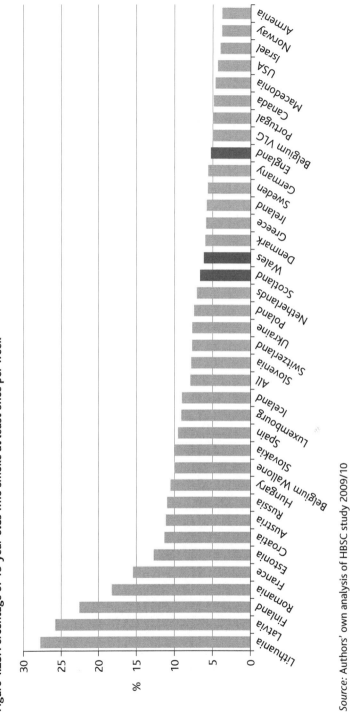

Figure 4.23: Percentage of 15-year-olds who smoke at least once per week

Source: Authors' own analysis of HBSC study 2009/10

Figure 4.24: Percentage of children aged 8-15 who have ever had a proper alcoholic drink

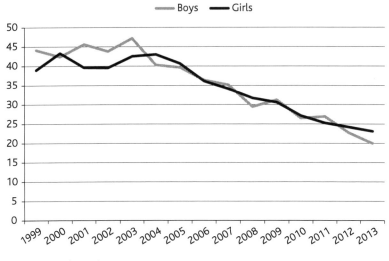

Source: HSCIC (2014b)

was found in Wales and Scotland, followed by England and Ireland. Young people with low family affluence were more likely to report being drunk at least four times, followed by those with high and medium family affluence. Wales and Scotland have a higher percentage of 11-, 13- and 15-year-olds reporting that they had drunk alcohol in the last 30 days than England (see Figure 4.25).

Drug use

The Crime Survey for England and Wales provides data on drug taking by young people aged 16-24. Figure 4.26 indicates that 15.1% had ever taken a Class A drug during their lifetime and 3.2% had taken a class A drug in the last month. Drug taking appears to have fallen since the 1990s, although not consistently in the last few years.

The National Survey of Smoking, Drinking and Drug Use among 11- to 15-year-olds shows that there is not much difference in drug taking between the genders, but it has general fallen since 2001 (Figure 4.27). The same survey shows that the proportion that had ever taken drugs increases from 6% at 11 years old to 24% at 15. The most common drug taken by 11- to 15-year-olds was cannabis, but cannabis taking fell from 13.4% in 2001 to 6.7% in 2014. The proportion taking all other drugs fell over the same period except for amphetamines.

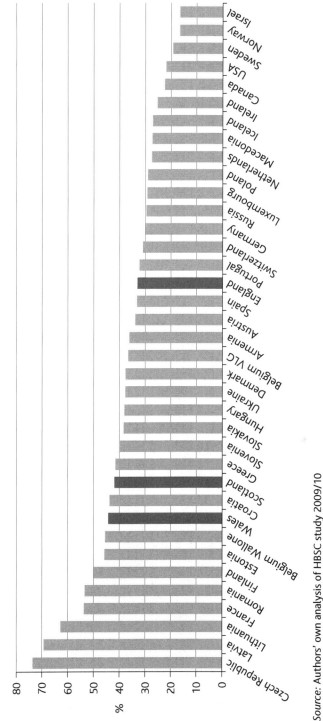

Figure 4.25: Drunk alcohol in the last 30 days

Source: Authors' own analysis of HBSC study 2009/10

Figure 4.26: Percentage of 16- to 24-year-olds taking drugs

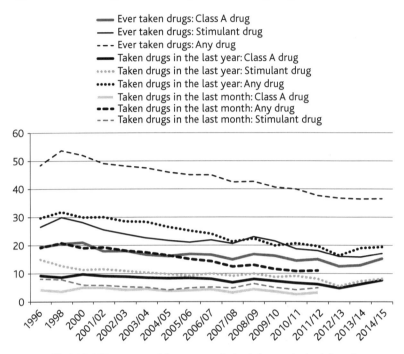

Source: Table 1.05-1.07, www.gov.uk/government/uploads/system/uploads/attachment_data/file/448083/drug-misuse-1415-tabs.xls

Figure 4.28 shows the proportion of 15-year-olds who had never taken cannabis. The proportion in England and Wales was 78% and in Scotland it was 81%. England and Wales had comparatively fairly high rates of cannabis use and Scotland was in the middle of the distribution.

Sexual health and health behaviours

While adolescence is a time when physical sexual maturity is acquired, some features of adolescence, such as social immaturity, spontaneity and risk-taking, generate risks in terms of sexual and general health. For adolescents, two of the key health issues are teenage pregnancy and sexually transmitted infections (STIs). We deal with both these issues here. Data on adolescent sexual health are typically reported for young people under 16 and those aged 16-19. Thus, while in much of this chapter we have restricted our data reported to children aged 15/16 and under, in this section we have extended the upper age limit for

Figure 4.27: Lifetime, last year and last month drug use from 2001 to 2014 among 11- to 15-year-olds (%)

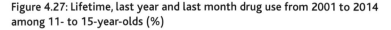

▬▬ Ever taken drugs: boys	‒ ‒ ‒ Ever taken drugs: girls
••••• Ever taken drugs: total	▬▬ Taken drugs in the last year: boys
‒ ‒ ‒ Taken drugs in the last year: girls	••••• Taken drugs in the last year: total
••••• Taken drugs in the last month: boys	‒ ‒ ‒ Taken drugs in the last month: girls
▬▬ Taken drugs in the last month: total	

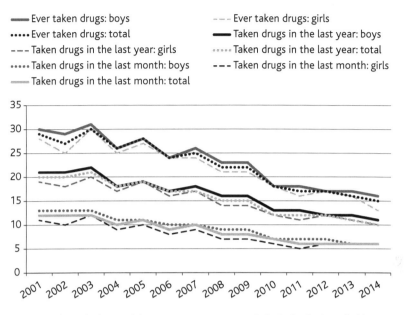

Source: Smoking, drinking and drug use among young people in England – 2014 (Tables 8.1, 8.2 and 8.3), www.hscic.gov.uk/catalogue/PUB17879/smok-drin-drugs-youn-peop-eng-2014 -chap8tab.xlsx

data to 19 so as to give as complete a picture as possible of adolescent sexual health in the UK today.

There are a number of ways to look at sexual health behaviours – including age at first sexual intercourse, use of condoms/contraception and number of sexual partners. Collecting such data from children and young people is ethically fraught, and researchers often rely on retrospective accounts of adolescent sexual activity. The National Survey of Sexual Attitudes and Lifestyles (Natsal) takes place every 10 years and is currently in process. The most recent survey, Natsal3 (2010/12), found 24.4% of all men and 17.4% of all women and 30.9% of men and 29.2% of women aged 16-24 reported first heterosexual intercourse at younger than 16 (Mercer et al, 2013).

The HBSC study asked 15-year-olds if they had ever had sexual intercourse, and if so, their age at first sexual intercourse. Girls were significantly more likely to report having had sex by age 15 than boys in England, Scotland and Wales. Boys in England and boys and girls in Scotland were more likely to have had sexual intercourse if they had lower family affluence. In terms of international comparisons,

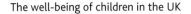

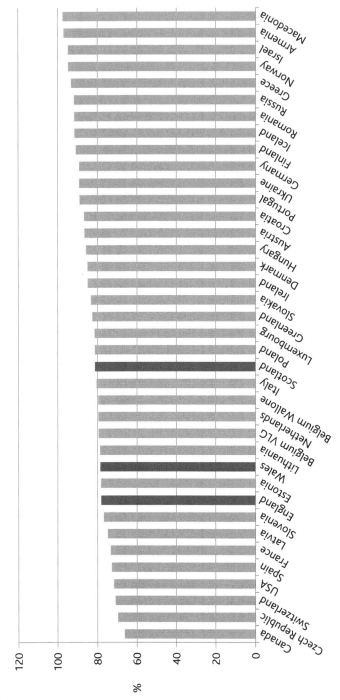

Figure 4.28: Proportion of 15-year-olds who have never taken cannabis

Source: Authors' own analysis of HBSC study 2009/10

experience of sexual intercourse at age 15 varies considerably, from 12% in the Netherlands to 52% in Greenland (see Figure 4.29). The highest rate in Britain was in Wales, but all three countries in Britain had rates above average.

Having multiple partners and not using contraceptives and/or condoms increase the risk of early pregnancy and contracting an STI. The HBSC study questions 15-year-olds about condom use and contraception. Sexually active 15-year-old boys (77.9%) were more likely to report that they used a condom during their last sexual intercourse than sexually active 15-year-old girls (70.7%). There were no significant differences between countries, but those with high family affluence were more likely to report condom use at last intercourse than those with low family affluence. Condom use was lower in Scotland than in England and Wales (see Figure 4.30).

Young people are vulnerable to acquiring STIs as they tend to have more sexual partners and to change partners more frequently than older age groups. The increasing incidence of STIs in the population as a whole (Public Health England, 2015) only serves to increase this risk for adolescents. Table 4.12 shows the diagnoses rates of five of the most commonly occurring STIs among adolescents in the UK. The most commonly occurring STI among adolescents is genital chlamydia, and after a period of substantial increase, following the (imperfect) (House of Commons Committee of Public Accounts, 2010) roll-out of the national chlamydia screening programme, the number of diagnoses appears to have fallen since 2010. This is despite a media campaign to encourage young people to take up screening, which was launched in January 2010 (Gobin et al, 2013). Chlamydia can result in pelvic inflammatory disease, with associated reproductive health concerns, and can increase the risk of ectopic pregnancy. The rate of genital warts among adolescents has been falling, but the rates of gonorrhoea have been increasing. The rates of genital herpes and syphilis are lower and relatively stable.

Teenage conceptions and abortions

Teenage conception is discussed in this chapter because of evidence that teenage births are associated with poor outcomes for the teenager and her child, including health outcomes, both in the short and long term. This evidence was reviewed in *Teenage pregnancy* (Social Exclusion Unit, 1999) and in a previous edition of this book (Tabberer, 2002) in more detail than is included here. Teenage pregnancies are more likely to result in low birth weight babies, infant and child

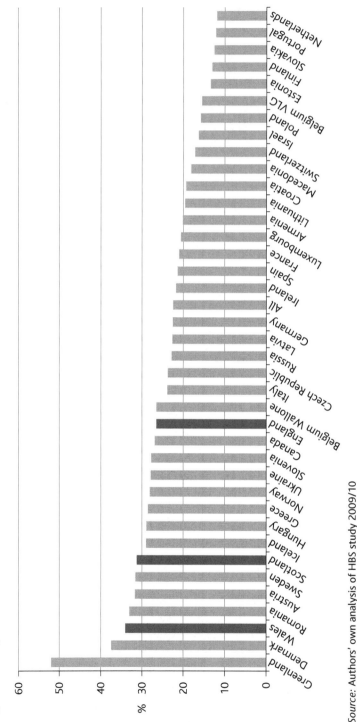

Figure 4.29: 15-year-olds who have had sexual intercourse

Source: Authors' own analysis of HBS study 2009/10

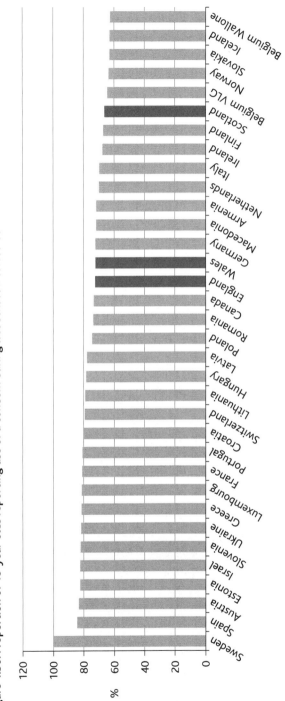

Figure 4.30: Proportion of 15-year-olds reporting use of a condom during last sexual intercourse

Source: Authors' own analysis of HBS study 2009/10

Table 4.12: STI diagnoses rates per 100,000 by gender, England

			2010	2011	2012	2013	2014
Chlamydia	Males	13-14	3.1	3.7	14.4	16.2	8.9
		15-19	1,111.0	1,035.1	945.5	958.5	881.3
	Females	13-14	40.5	41.9	149.8	161.3	136.4
		15-19	3,169.0	2,973.8	2,776.6	2,780.2	2,651.1
Gonorrhoea	Males	13-14	0.5	0.3	0.8	1.4	1.1
		15-19	67.1	76.4	81.9	93.3	101.3
	Females	13-14	6.3	7.0	8.0	8.7	10.0
		15-19	114.3	118.8	135.2	152.3	166.0
Anogenital herpes	Males	13-14	0.2	0.8	1.1	0.5	0.2
		15-19	44.8	44.8	44.8	41.1	40.2
	Females	13-14	7.2	8.9	7.1	8.3	7.5
		15-19	207.4	217.7	218.8	211.2	216.1
Syphilis	Males	13-14	0.0	0.0	0.0	0.0	0.0
		15-19	3.1	3.9	3.3	3.7	3.7
	Females	13-14	0.0	0.2	0.2	0.3	0.0
		15-19	1.9	1.2	1.4	2.1	2.0
Anogenital warts	Males	13-14	1.7	1.4	2.0	1.1	1.1
		15-19	254.4	252.1	229.8	232.2	208.1
	Females	13-14	15.4	14.4	10.0	12.9	3.5
		15-19	622.2	608.4	547.8	518.4	475.7

Source: Public Health England 2015, www.gov.uk/government/statistics/sexually-transmitted-infections-stis-annual-data-tables

mortality, hospital admissions of children, post-natal depression and low rates of breastfeeding. Bradshaw and Mayhew (2005), using the Millennium Cohort Survey, found that:

• teenage mothers were over three times more likely to be poor
• the odds of a low birth weight baby were 40% higher for teenage conceptions
• teenage mothers were 50% more likely to be depressed
• 100% were less likely to breastfeed.

We also know that teenage mothers are less likely to complete their education and are more likely to be out of employment and live in poverty, and their children are more likely to experience these disadvantages and twice as likely to become teenage parents in their turn (Rendall, 2003).

UNICEF published an Innocenti Report Card (UNICEF, 2001) on teenage births, and found that the under-20 birth rate in the UK was the second highest out of 28 OECD countries, only less than the US, and even in affluent areas the teenage birth rate in the UK was higher than the average for the Netherlands or France. Figure 4.31 shows that in 2011 the UK had the seventh from highest teenage fertility rate in the OECD.

The Labour government's Teenage Pregnancy Strategy targets were to:

- halve the under-18 conception rate by 2010, taking 1998 as a baseline year
- increase the proportion of teenage parents in education, training or employment to reduce their risk of long-term social exclusion.

The strategy is monitored by statistics on teenage conceptions produced by combining birth registrations and notifications of legal abortions, and so excludes miscarriages and illegal abortions. The 2010-15 coalition government included the under-18 teenage conception rate as one of its three sexual health indicators in its Public Health Outcomes Framework (2013-16). This ensures a continued focus on preventing teenage conceptions as well as the social impact on teenage mothers.

The latest data in Figure 4.32 shows that teenage conceptions have declined since 1998 and much more rapidly since 2008. In 2013 the under-18 conception rate was 24.5 per 1,000, the lowest rate since records began in 1965. The rapid decline since 2008 is surprising because this was a period of rising youth unemployment, and there is a strong association between unemployment and teenage pregnancy. The ONS (2013b) found that the unemployment rate accounted for 67% of the variation in the under-18 conception rate in local authorities across England and Wales. The target to reduce teenage conceptions by a half by 2010 was not met, but by 2013 the conception rate had fallen by 47.9% since 1998.

The number of teenage births is a function of conception rate and the proportion of conceptions that end in abortion. It can be seen that the proportion of conceptions aborted has risen slightly between 1998 and 2013, and in 2013 over half (50.7%) of under-18 conceptions ended in abortion; the proportion is higher for under-16 conceptions (61.6%) and lower for under-20 conceptions (44.2%). The decline in the conception rate and the increase in the abortion rate have resulted in the maternity rate declining from 27.4 per 1,000 in 1998 to 12.1 per 1,000 in 2013, a fall of 55.8%.

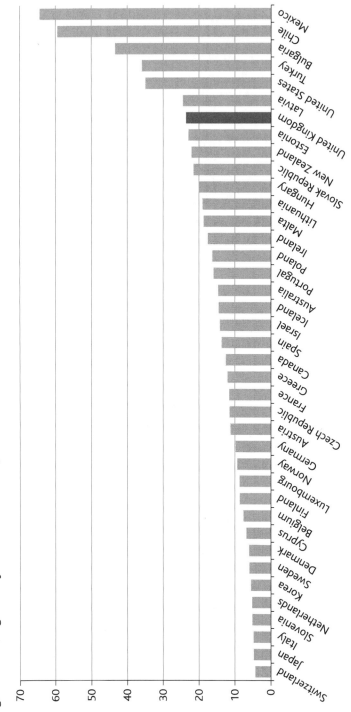

Figure 4.31:Teenage fertility rate across the OECD, 2011

Source: OECD (2015a) Family database Sf2.4D

Figure 4.32: Under-18 conception rate and percentage leading to abortion in England and Wales

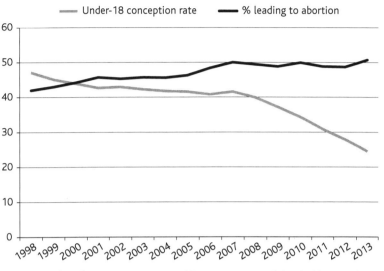

Source: ONS (2015) Conception statistics Table 6, www.ons.gov.uk/ons/publications/re-reference-tables.html?edition=tcm%3A77-348338

International comparisons of overall child health

In the health domain of the 2013 international index of child well-being (UNICEF, 2013), the UK came 16th out of 29 countries, and a similar index produced by the OECD (2009a) showed the UK 20 out of 29 in their health domain. The UNICEF (2013) health domain index was made up of health at birth (infant mortality and low birth weight), immunisation rates and child and youth mortality. The UK was in the bottom third of distribution on infant mortality, and in the middle third of the distribution on low birth weight, immunisation rates and child mortality rates. The subjective well-being domain contained the HBSC study data on self-defined health and an index of health complaints, and the UK came in the bottom third, 23rd out of 28 countries. In the behaviours and risk domain that included health behaviours (being overweight, eating breakfast, eating fruit, taking exercise, teenage fertility and smoking), risk behaviours (smoking, drinking and drugs) and exposure to violence (being bullied and fighting), the UK came in the middle of the distribution, 15th out of 29 countries. Out of all these indicators the UK was ranked highest (7th) on smoking and lowest on teenage fertility (27th out of 29).

Conclusion

There is a fairly consistent pattern to these results on health and health behaviour. The health of UK children is comparatively poor and so is their health behaviour. However, on most indicators, the health of children and their health behaviour has been improving.

A report by the Cabinet Office Horizon Scanning Team (Cabinet Office, 2014) found that 'risky behaviours' by young people, such as drinking, smoking, taking drugs, other youth crime and teenage pregnancy, are all declining. On average, they found that children's happiness scores are increasing slightly over time. But this report identifies possible emerging risk behaviours and negative findings, including self-harm, social isolation, loneliness, anxiety and body appearance issues. Some of these problems relate to the increasing use of social and other digital media (Cabinet Office, 2014).

The NHS received substantial increases in national resources during the period 2000-10, and has been protected from real cuts since 2010. Investments included many child-related initiatives: Sure Start, the reintroduction of nutritional standards in school meals, the free school fruit scheme, investment in children's sports, smoking and drinking campaigns, Healthy Start, Health in Pregnancy Grants, Sure Start Maternity Grants and child benefit paid to pregnant mothers. During the 2010-15 coalition government other policy initiatives emerged, perhaps most notably the free school meals scheme, but large and inexplicable variations remain in healthcare for children (Cheung, 2012), alongside substantial inequalities in health outcomes (Wolfe et al, 2014).

It could be argued that child health is impervious to the activities of health professionals, although the remarkable reduction in teenage pregnancy demonstrates that much can be achieved by concerted effort. At the same time, child health outcomes are about poverty and inequality, parental and child behaviour, some of which may be influenced by popular culture and advertising. Perhaps there is not much that the NHS can achieve for children. This was one conclusion that could have been drawn from the *Statement on child health* that was preoccupied with ensuring 'support for families in securing world class health and well-being outcomes for their children' (DH and DCSF, 2009, p 8).

A more structural interpretation was presented by The Marmot Review, *Fair society, healthy lives* (2010), which concluded:

> Disadvantage starts before birth and accumulates throughout life. Action to reduce health inequalities must start before birth and be followed through the life of the child. Only then can the close links between early disadvantage and poor outcomes throughout life be broken. That is our ambition for children born in 2010. For this reason, giving every child the best start in life is our highest priority recommendation. (p 20)

Notes

[1] Higher managerial and professional occupations.

[2] Routine occupations and never worked and long-term unemployed.

[3] See www.nhs.uk/change4life

FIVE

Subjective well-being and mental health

Gwyther Rees and Gill Main

Key statistics

- Children in the UK fare poorly (ranked between 11th and 14th in a sample of 15 countries) in international comparisons of children's overall subjective well-being.
- Children's happiness with their material living standards and friends are relatively high in the UK; their happiness with their appearance is very low.
- Around 1 in 10 children aged 5-16 had a clinically diagnosed mental disorder in 2004.
- Conduct disorders (5.8%) and emotional disorders (3.7%) are the two most common forms of disorder.
- Boys are more likely than girls to have a mental disorder.
- Rates of most mental disorders tend to increase with age through childhood, adolescence and into adulthood, but exceptions are separation anxiety disorder and attention deficit hyperactivity disorder (ADHD) that decrease.
- There were 188 suicides and undetermined deaths of 10- to 19-year-olds in the UK in 2012/13, a rate of around 25 per million of the population.
- Rates of suicides and undetermined deaths are lowest in England/Wales and highest in Northern Ireland.
- Males in this age group are more than four times more likely to die as a result of suicide or undetermined death than females.

Key trends

- Happiness with schoolwork appears to have increased from 2009/10-2012/13, while happiness with friends appears to have decreased across this time frame.
- Older children tend to report lower levels of subjective well-being than younger children.

- The picture of long-term trends in mental ill-health is complex and varies according to age group, gender and category of mental health problem.
- Within England and Wales, the suicide rates either declined slightly or remained relatively stable between 1985 and 2012. Rates for Scotland are higher but have seen some decreases in recent years. The suicide rate among young people in Northern Ireland has seen an increase up to 2012.
- In 2008 the suicide rate of young people aged 15 to 19 in the UK was 3.1 per 100,000 which is much lower than the OECD average of 6.5

Key sources
- The Children's Society well-being research programme
- Understanding Society survey
- Millennium Cohort Survey
- Health Behaviours in School-aged Children (HBSC) study
- Programme of International Student Assessment (PISA)
- Office for National Statistics (ONS) surveys of mental health of children and young people
- Official statistics on suicide rates for England/Wales, Scotland and Northern Ireland

Introduction: Subjective well-being

A great deal of research is concerned with the well-*becoming* of children, that is, the factors that help and hinder children's transitions to a healthy and productive life as an adult. There is also a wealth of evidence around the objective facets of children's well-being, and their links with future outcomes – many of which are detailed in other chapters of this volume. But there is an increasing acknowledgement that we should also be concerned with children and childhood as a life stage in its own right (Ben-Arieh, 2007). This concern with childhood as a distinct and important phase of life has coincided with a growing appreciation that children are active participants in their lives, making sense of the world and affected by life events in ways that adults are not always privy to or able to report on. As a result, increasing attention has been paid within research to children's perspectives of issues that affect them (Christensen and James, 2008), and children's right to participation, as well as to protection and provision, is enshrined in the United Nations (UN) Convention on the Rights of the Child (UN General Assembly, 1989). Alongside these shifts in perceptions of children – from 'becomings' to simultaneous 'becomings' and 'beings' (see Uprichard, 2008), and from objects of study and passive recipients of adult intervention to active participants in their own lives – there has been a movement towards concern with the subjective well-being of children.

Defining and measuring subjective well-being

Subjective well-being can be understood as an individual's own evaluations and feelings about their life. It is common, in the research literature on subjective well-being, to consider it as consisting of two distinct components – cognitive and affective (Diener, 1984). The cognitive component refers to people's evaluations of their lives as a whole and particular aspects (or domains) of their lives. The affective component refers to people's moods and emotions (positive and negative affect). Substantial conceptual and empirical work has been done on frameworks of subjective well-being. Initially this field of research tended to focus primarily on adult populations, but in recent years there has been a growing interest in children's subjective well-being.

An important recent development in the UK has been the ONS' Measuring National Well-Being programme. This programme has developed sets of national indicators relating to objective and subjective well-being, both in relation to adults (Beaumont, 2011; Evans et al, 2015) and children (Beardsmore and Siegler, 2014).

Different approaches to measuring subjective well-being vary in relation to whether their concern is with global life satisfaction or with sub-domains, and in relation to whether single or multiple survey items are used to assess satisfaction. Some examples of different measures that have been used in relation to children are as follows:

- Overall Life Satisfaction (OLS) and Cantril's Ladder represent global, single-measure approaches to measuring life satisfaction. These ask respondents to choose on a scale (often of 0-10) the point that best represents their level of happiness or satisfaction with their life as a whole.
- Huebner's Student's Life Satisfaction Scale (SLSS) represents a global, multi-item approach. Respondents are asked to rate the extent of their agreement with a range of statements relating to life satisfaction (including, for example, 'my life is going well' and 'my life is just right'), and responses are summed or otherwise combined to produce an overall score.

- The Personal Well-being Index – School Children (PWI-SC), and the Good Childhood Index, represent a domain-based, multi-item approach. Respondents are asked to rate their satisfaction in a range of domains (in the PWI-SC, this includes, for example, 'how happy are you with your health?' and 'how happy are you about how safe you feel?'). As above, these items are then combined to form a scale.

These different approaches to measurement have different strengths and weaknesses, and are suited to different types of question. For example, single-item tools are simple to understand and administer, while multi-item tools are more complex but tend to produce more nuanced data with a more normal distribution that facilitates better analysis. Similarly, global assessments are conceptually independent from other factors that researchers may be interested in, facilitating multivariate analysis, while domain-specific measures allow an exploration of the relative importance of different domains in assessing overall subjective well-being, and of the relationships between such domains.

In the UK, data has been gathered on children's subjective well-being for some time. The British Household Panel Survey (BHPS) began using a small number of measures of happiness with life and some aspects of life in 1994, and the same measures have been used more recently in the Understanding Society survey and Millennium Cohort Study. Recent waves of the Millennium Cohort Study have also gathered some child self-report data on affective subjective well-being. These are valuable data sources, but there are limitations in the measures used – in particular, the aspects of life included (family, friends, appearance, school and school work) do not represent a comprehensive set of domains relevant to children's lives (see later). A second important source of UK data is the ongoing research programme on children's subjective well-being being undertaken jointly by The Children's Society and the University of York that was initiated in 2005. We make use of all these data sources in the discussion below.

Levels of children's subjective well-being

The ONS, as part of its Measuring National Well-being programme, has developed four overall measures of personal well-being (life satisfaction, feeling life is worthwhile, recent feelings of happiness and of anxiety) and three[1] of these four measures have been measured for children over the last few years by The Children's Society. The most recent figures are shown in Figure 5.1 for children and young people aged 10-17 in England, Wales and Scotland.

Mean scores out of 10 for recent feelings of happiness, life satisfaction and finding life is worthwhile were all at a similar level, close to 7.5 out 10. The proportion of children with low subjective well-being varies somewhat according to the component being measured, and was highest for recent feelings of happiness (8.7%). These patterns, with most children being relatively happy with their lives, are fairly typical for findings on subjective well-being, both in relation to children and adults.

Variations in subjective well-being

Bradshaw (2015) notes that to improve subjective well-being, we must first understand which factors of children's lives are associated with variations in it. To date, research has mainly focused on explaining variations in overall cognitive subjective well-being (life satisfaction), although some recent work has also begun to look at variations in affective subjective well-being.

In England, Goswami (2014) found that sociodemographic factors explained about 15% of the variation in life satisfaction, and personality explained another 18%. These figures – that is, models explaining around 20-35% of the variation in children's subjective well-being – are fairly standard across the field. Klocke et al (2014) explained about 23% of the variation across participant countries in the HBSC study.

Below are some of the factors that researchers have found to be associated with subjective well-being.

Figure 5.1: Latest subjective well-being figures (ONS measures of overall subjective well-being)

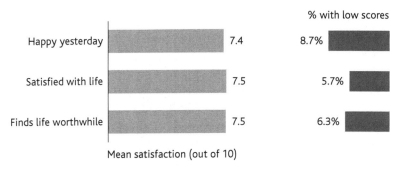

Mean satisfaction (out of 10)

Note: Children and young people aged 10-17, Great Britain.
Source: Reproduced from The Children's Society (2015)

- *Age.* Research into the association between children's age and subjective well-being consistently finds that younger children report higher levels of well-being than older children. This result has been found in repeated surveys as part of The Children's Society well-being research programme (for details, see The Children's Society, 2015), and also in Knies' (2012) analysis of Understanding Society data.

- *Gender.* The association between gender and subjective well-being is less clear than that of age. Research from The Children's Society has found mixed results, with some surveys showing slightly higher well-being among boys, and some finding no significant differences. In their analysis of Millennium Cohort Study data, Rees and Bradshaw (2016: forthcoming) find no significant associations between gender and subjective well-being. Knies' analysis of Understanding Society data found that girls were marginally less happy than boys.

- *Ethnicity.* Very limited associations have been found between ethnicity and subjective well-being. There is some evidence that children from Black African, Black Caribbean and Pakistani/Bangladeshi backgrounds have higher well-being in terms of their happiness with their appearance than White children (The Children's Society, 2015), and some evidence that White children have lower overall subjective well-being than others, while children from Indian and from Pakistani/Bangladeshi backgrounds have highest well-being (Rees and Bradshaw, 2016: forthcoming), but associations are limited and inconsistent between different studies.

- *Health and disability/learning difficulties.* Research from The Children's Society (2015) has consistently found that children with disabilities or who report difficulties with learning have substantially lower subjective well-being than their peers. Analysis of Millennium Cohort Study data produced similar results, with parental reports on children's physical health and mental health, and that they had special needs or a disability being associated with lower subjective well-being (Rees and Bradshaw, 2016: forthcoming).

- *Family structure and family relationships.* Evidence on the impact of family structure on subjective well-being is mixed. Evidence from The Children's Society (2015) finds only small associations between family structure and subjective well-being, especially when economic factors are controlled for. However, they note that children who report that they do not live with their families have substantially lower well-being than children living with families in any structure. Analysis of the Millennium Cohort Study using separate constructs of life satisfaction, happiness and sadness found that children living with both birth parents had higher levels of life satisfaction than children in any other family structure, but noted no associations between family structure and happiness or sadness (Rees and Bradshaw, 2016: forthcoming). However, Rees and Bradshaw note that family relationships and interactions may be much more important than family structure, with children whose parents reported higher engagement with the child and lower levels of conflict having higher levels of subjective well-being. Knies (2012) found that children in two-parent families were happier than children in all other family types.

- *Poverty/deprivation.* The association between poverty/deprivation and subjective well-being is explored in more detail in Chapter Three, this volume. Repeated studies (Knies, 2012; Rees and Bradshaw, 2016: forthcoming) have found limited if any association between household income, adult-defined necessities for children and children's subjective well-being. However, Main (2013) developed an index of child deprivation based on children's own perceptions of their needs, and this index has been consistently found to have a moderate and significant association with subjective well-being, adding approximately 7-10% to the explanatory power of models.

- *Recent events.* The Children's Society (2015) highlights the importance of recent events to children's subjective well-being. Bullying in particular can be a very important factor in explaining children's reports of their life satisfaction.

- *Behaviours and activities.* Children's behaviours and activities have been linked to variations in subjective well-being, although associations tend to be small in magnitude. Research by The Children's Society (Abdallah et al, 2014) explored the importance of various ways to well-being, identified as important to adults' subjective well-being, in children's lives. They found that activities including connecting with other people, being active, taking notice of surroundings and keeping learning were somewhat associated with children's well-being. However, they also found that the nature of the association varied for different activities – more participation in activities is not necessarily straightforwardly associated with better outcomes. Similarly, The Children's Society (2014) found that only one of 20 children's activities that parents were asked about in the Millennium Cohort Study – playing sports or exercising – was substantively associated with higher subjective well-being. In her analysis of Understanding Society data, Knies (2012) found that children with low fruit and vegetable consumption, high fast food consumption, and who used social media for over an hour per day had lower levels of subjective well-being, and those who reported having a religion, using the internet every day, having more close friends, and doing sport at least once a week had higher well-being.

- *Personality.* Goswami (2014) found that personality is an important predictor of subjective well-being, explaining about 18% of the variation as noted above. Openness and emotional stability were particularly important in explaining variation in subjective well-being.

- *Education.* Much of children's lives are spent in the school setting, and it is therefore not surprising that Bradshaw and Rees (2015: forthcoming) found that parental reports of children enjoying school, looking forward to seeing their teacher, and not being bored at school were associated with them reporting higher levels of subjective well-being. Knies (2012) also found that the behaviour of other children in schools is important; children reporting that other children in their class misbehaved in school had lower levels of subjective well-being.

Domains of subjective well-being

As noted above, child subjective well-being can be understood as both an overall assessment of life satisfaction, and also as an assessment of satisfaction with various domains. The Good Childhood Index, developed as part of The Children's Society well-being research programme, is the most comprehensive attempt to measure subjective well-being in the UK according to children's own conceptions of which aspects of their lives are important. The Children's Society (2015) details the development of this programme, comprising extensive qualitative and quantitative research with children conducted on an ongoing basis since 2005. Through this research, 10 domains of child well-being have been identified that draw on children's qualitative accounts of domains of their lives which are important to them, and on quantitative assessments of the statistical reliability and validity of data relating to these domains (Rees et al, 2010).

Figure 5.2 shows the latest mean scores and the percentage with low satisfaction for each of the 10 domains for children aged 10-17 in Great Britain in 2013-15. Children were happiest with their family relationships, followed by health, home and friends. They were least happy with what might happen to them in the future, and also had relatively low rankings for appearance and the amount of choice they had in life.

Trends in subjective well-being over time

The longest-standing UK data on trends in children's subjective well-being over time has been gathered through the BHPS and its

Figure 5.2: Latest figures from the Good Childhood Index

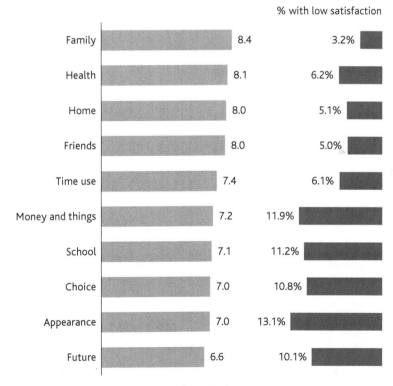

Note: Children and young people aged 10-17, Great Britain.
Source: Reproduced from The Children's Society (2015)

successor, the Understanding Society survey. The last edition of this book presented trends in the subjective well-being of children aged 11-15 in the UK up to 2008 using data from the BHPS, and this is reproduced below in Figure 5.3. There is evidence here of a long-term increase in children's happiness with life as a whole.

It is not possible to update this trend data from the Understanding Society survey due to issues of sampling structure. However, more recent trend analysis using Understanding Society data, covering the period from 2009 to 2013, has recently been published by The Children's Society (2015). Figure 5.4 shows their results. The solid line shows the mean scores for each wave. The dotted lines show approximate upper and lower 99% confidence intervals.

Variations in levels of subjective well-being are quite small, but the analysis suggests that there has been a decline in happiness with friends over the four waves, and an increase in happiness with school work. For overall life satisfaction and the other three domains no trend is evident, although satisfaction with life as a whole, while not statistically significant, has shown decreases each year. The Children's Society (2015) stress the need for caution in interpreting results as fluctuations between years are evident in the findings, but note that as more waves of data are added, it will become easier to detect trends in the levels of children's subjective well-being.

Figure 5.3: Trends in children's happiness with life as a whole, 1994-2008

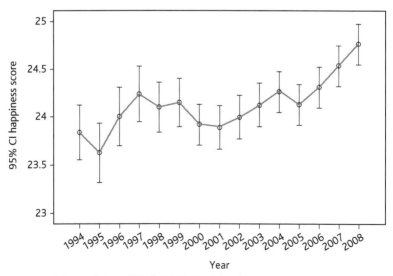

Source: Bradshaw and Keung (2011); British Youth Panel Survey

Figure 5.4: Trends in children's subjective well-being, UK, 2009-13

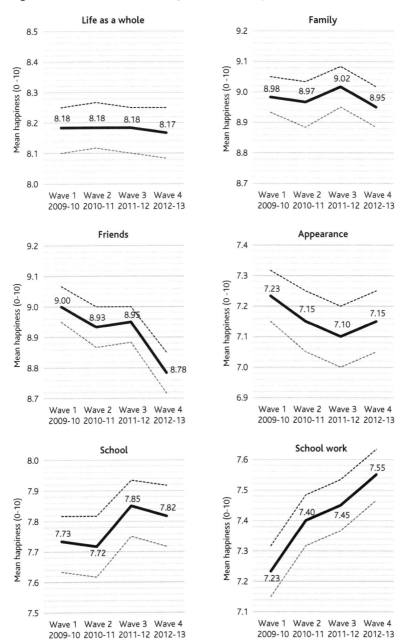

Note: Children aged 10-15, weighted (but 99% confidence intervals do not take account of design effect)

Source: The Children's Society (2015)

International comparisons

There are two main sources of international comparative data on children's subjective well-being – the Health Behaviour in School-aged Children (HBSC) study and the Children's Worlds study.

HBSC surveys children aged 11, 13 and 15 years old in a range of European and North American countries. The survey is conducted every four years, and is primarily concerned with health and health behaviours, including a focus on social contexts and links with well-being more broadly. It measures life satisfaction using Cantril's Ladder (see above). Table 5.1 shows the most recent statistics (2009/10) on life satisfaction in England, Scotland and Wales from this survey. Of the three UK countries, Scotland tended to rank highest among the 39 countries included in the survey, and Wales tended to rank lowest.

However, the relative rankings of the three countries are not confirmed by analysis of the Millennium Cohort Study (children aged 11), which suggests that, within the UK, children in Northern Ireland tend to have slightly the highest subjective well-being followed by Scotland and Wales (roughly equal), and then England with the lowest (The Children's Society, 2014).

The HBSC survey also collects data relating to children's experiences of family relationships, relationships with classmates, well-being at school and subjective health. Klocke et al's (2014) analysis of the data found children in the UK to have comparatively low subjective well-being, ranked 21st out of 28 countries. Children in the UK also fared worse than average in their satisfaction with relationships, subjective education and subjective health. Sociodemographic factors including age, gender, family structure, parental employment and family affluence were found to explain some of the variation in children's subjective well-being, but behavioural factors such as bullying were more strongly predictive of variation. In terms of international variations, large-scale

Table 5.1: Percentage of young people who reported positive life satisfaction by gender, age and country, 2009/10 (rankings out of 39 countries in Europe and North America)

	11 years old			13 years old			15 years old		
	Girls (%)	Boys (%)	Rank	Girls (%)	Boys (%)	Rank	Girls (%)	Boys (%)	Rank
England	86	88	27	83	91	13	79	89	17
Scotland	90	92	9	84	90	12	82	87	11
Wales	86	88	25	78	87	31	74	84	34

Source: Currie et al (2012)

economic factors such as GDP were found to be less important to child subjective well-being than school- and family-level factors. This indicates that efforts to improve children's subjective well-being may be best directed towards family- and school-level interventions.

Children's Worlds is the first international survey primarily concerned with measuring the subjective well-being of children. It is concerned with middle childhood (ages 8-12), and covers 15 diverse countries. In the UK, data coverage is of England only, although the survey is currently being conducted in Wales. In addition to overall subjective well-being, the survey covers subjective well-being in relation to various aspects of children's lives, including family and home, money and possessions, friends and other relationships, school, local area, self, time use and other aspects of life.

Rees and Main (2015: forthcoming) report on international findings for the 10- and 12-year-old age groups. In terms of overall subjective well-being, England ranked 14th out of 15 countries for life satisfaction, 11th for recent feelings of happiness and 11th for feeling positive about the future.

The Children's Worlds survey also asked about children's satisfaction with the domains covered in the Good Childhood Index and a range of other aspects of life. Table 5.2 shows England's ranking out of 15 countries for all these aspects of life. England ranked relatively high for satisfaction with the local police (3rd). The next highest ranking was for friends. However, children ranked lower than 8th (the mid-point in the rankings) for 24 out of the 30 aspects of life. The lowest rankings were for self-confidence (15th), body (14th) and relationships with teachers (14th).

In addition, some international comparative data on children's subjective well-being at school is available from the PISA study. PISA is a triennial OECD-run survey evaluating education systems across the world based on the performance of 15-year-old students in Reading, Maths and Science. Due to the centrality of school to the lives of children in this age group, subsidiary questions concerning children's sense of belonging in school are asked. In 2012, for the first time PISA asked children to evaluate their happiness and satisfaction with school, and the extent to which their school situation is ideal for them (OECD, 2013). While these questions focus on only one domain of children's lives — school — they nonetheless represent an increasing acknowledgement in policy circles of the importance of subjective well-being, and of viewing children as beings as well as becomings. Across participating countries, almost 80% of children 'agreed' or 'strongly agreed' that they felt happy at school and were

Table 5.2: England's ranking out of 15 countries in the Children's Worlds survey 2013/14 on mean scores for different aspects of subjective well-being

The house/flat where you live	9th
The people you live with	10th
All the other people in family	7th
Your family life	12th
All the things you have	9th
Your friends	6th
Your relationships ... in general	10th
Other children in your class	12th
Your school marks	10th
Your school experience	12th
Your life as a student	10th
Things you have learned	11th
Relationship with teachers	14th
The people in your area	11th
The local police in your area	3rd
How dealt with at doctors	11th
Outdoor areas ... in your area	8th
The area you live in general	10th
How you use your time	10th
What do in your free time	10th
Your health	13th
The way that you look	13th
Your own body	14th
Your self-confidence	15th
The freedom you have	8th
Amount of opportunities ...	8th
Listened to by adults ...	10th
How safe you feel	11th
Things you want to be good at	13th
Doing things away from home	10th

Source: The Children's Society (2015)

satisfied in their school. A substantially smaller majority – just over 60% – agreed that things in their school were ideal. Within the UK, figures for happiness in school and satisfaction with school were similar to the international average, at 83% and 84% respectively. Children in the UK appear to fare better than average on feeling that their school is ideal for them, with 71% agreeing with this.

Bradshaw and Richardson (2009), in their comparison of child well-being in Europe, compared the relationship between overall wellbeing, which was based on 43 indicators in seven domains, and the percentage of children reporting high life satisfaction. The results are shown in Figure 5.5 – high life satisfaction explains 59% of the variation in overall well-being. The UK is one of the countries with low overall well-being given its level of life satisfaction. From this we might conclude that children are happier than they should be!

Introduction: Mental health

The following sections focus primarily on clinically measured mental 'disorders'. We review the trends and prevalence of mental illness among children and young people in the UK, and summarise evidence on factors associated with the onset and persistence of mental health problems. As in the last edition, this section is mainly drawn on findings from two surveys undertaken by the ONS of the mental health of children and young people surveys in 1999 and 2004, and a follow-up to the latter survey undertaken in 2007. Since the last edition, there has been no new comparable data, but there has been more statistical exploration of these survey datasets and of longer-term trends. The last part of the section considers suicide among children

Figure 5.5: Overall well-being by life satisfaction

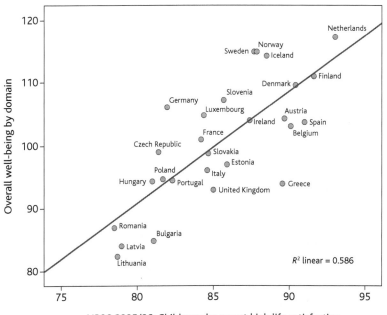

HBSC 2005/06: Children who report high life satisfaction

Source: Analysis of data from Bradshaw and Richardson (2009)

and young people, its prevalence in the UK and time trends in 15 European countries.

Prevalence of mental disorders among children and young people

Green et al (2005) estimated the prevalence rate for childhood mental disorders based on the 2004 Mental Health of Children and Young People in Great Britain survey. The overall figure suggests that one in ten children aged 5-16 has a clinically diagnosed mental disorder. It can be seen in Table 5.3 that boys are more likely than girls to have a mental disorder, although the gender ratio is greater among the younger age group than the older one. The findings also indicate that the older age group has a higher prevalence rate of any mental disorder than the younger. Based on the broad categories used by Green et al, conduct disorders (5.8%) and emotional disorders (3.7%) are the two most common form of disorder. Boys are more likely to have conduct disorders whereas girls are more likely to have emotional disorders.

There is evidence from the UK and elsewhere (reviewed in Costello et al, 2011) that between childhood and adolescence some types of mental health problems increase (depression, panic disorder, agoraphobia and substance use disorders) while others decrease (separation anxiety disorder and ADHD). These patterns mostly continue in the same direction between adolescence and early adulthood.

Profiles of children and young people with mental disorders[2]

The prevalence of mental disorders is clearly linked to children's socioeconomic backgrounds. Results from the 2004 survey report

Table 5.3: Percentage of children with each disorder by age and sex, 2004, Great Britain

	5- to 10-year-olds		11- to 16-year-olds		
	Boys	Girls	Boys	Girls	All
Emotional disorders (anxiety or depression)	2.2	2.5	4.0	6.1	3.7
Conduct disorders	6.9	2.8	8.1	5.1	5.8
Hyperkinetic disorders	2.7	0.4	2.4	0.4	1.5
Less common disorders (including autism, tics, eating disorders and selective mutism)	2.2	0.4	1.6	1.1	1.3
Any disorder	10.2	5.1	12.6	10.3	9.6

Source: Green et al (2005)

(Green et al, 2005) show that mental disorder is more common among children:

- in lone-parent families (16% versus 8% in two-parent families)
- in reconstituted families (14% versus 9% in intact families)
- whose parent had no qualifications (17% versus 4% of those who had a degree)
- in families with unemployed parents (20% versus 8% with both parents employed)
- in families with a low household income (16% versus 5% with relatively high household income)
- in households with someone receiving disability benefit (24% versus 8% with no disability benefit)
- in families from a lower social class background defined by occupational group (15% versus 4% from a higher social class group)
- living in the private/social rented sector (14–17% versus 7% in owned accommodation)
- living in a deprived area (15% versus 7% in a well-off area).

Additionally, earlier findings suggest that parental mental health, family functioning, level of family discord and stressful life events are all linked to mental illness in children. Results from the 1999 survey report (Meltzer et al, 2000) indicate that a higher rate of mental disorders is found among children:

- whose parents scored highly in GHQ-12 (General Health Questionnaire) (18% versus 6% with low GHQ-12)
- living in poorly functioning families (18% versus 7% in well-functioning families)
- living in a discordant family (35% versus 19% with a low level of family discord)
- who have experienced three or more stressful life events (31% versus 13% reported less stressful events).

Factors associated with the onset of mental disorders

The report of the 2007 survey on the emotional development and well-being of children and young people (Parry-Langdon, 2008) explored factors that are linked to emotional and conduct disorders. The survey followed a sample of almost 5,000 children and young people from the 2004 survey sample, and among those who did not have a disorder in 2004 (Time 1), around 3% developed an emotional disorder and/or conduct disorder by 2007 (Time 2). The analysis results of the 2007 survey suggest that there are a number of factors associated with the onset of the disorders, including child, family and household characteristics (Parry-Langdon, 2008).

The findings from logistic regression analysis (the odds ratio [OR] is only shown for factors that are statistically significant) give the odds of developing emotional disorder among children decreasing in families with two (OR=0.6) or more children (OR=0.8). However, it was noted that children with the following characteristics are more likely to have developed an emotional disorder by Time 2 if they:

- are older (OR=2.2)
- have a physical illness (OR=1.7)
- are girls (OR=1.6)
- live in single-parent families
- live in families that become single-parent families (OR=4.5)
- are in (persistent) workless households (OR=4.4)
- are in rented accommodation
- are in a lower-income household
- are from a lower social class background defined by the household occupational status
- have mothers who scored highly in GHQ-12 (OR=2.2)
- have mothers whose GHQ-12 'remained high' (OR=3.5)
- have mothers reporting three or more stressful life events (OR=1.5-2.7).

Next we consider factors associated with the onset of conduct disorders. The research findings suggest that being a girl reduces the odds of such an onset (OR=0.7). However, the findings show increased likelihood of developing conduct disorders among children and young people:

- with physical illnesses (OR=2.9)
- with special educational needs (SEN) (OR=3.7)
- living in reconstituted families
- whose families became single-parent families (OR=2.9)
- in families with more than one child
- whose mothers have no qualifications
- in (persistent) workless households
- (continuously) living in rented accommodation (OR=3.5)
- from a lower social class background

- whose mothers scored highly and/or remained highly scored in GHQ-12 (OR=3.5 and 2.3)
- experienced three or more stressful life events (OR=2.7).

Factors associated with persistence of mental disorders

The same research (Parry-Langdon, 2008) also shows that in a sub-sample of around 400 children and young people who have emotional disorders recorded in the last interview in 2004 (Time 1), 30% were also assessed as having an emotional disorder three years later in 2007 (Time 2). In terms of conduct disorders, around 43% of children and young people who were assessed with a disorder in 2004 were also assessed with it in 2007. Again, in the research a number of factors, including the characteristics of the children, their families and households, as well as social factors, are explored in relation to the persistence of the emotional and/or conduct disorders.

A factor identified by Parry-Langdon et al as being significantly associated with increased likelihood of a child having a persistent emotional disorder was the mental health of the child's mother, as measured by a persistently high GHQ12 score (OR=3.4).

Turning to factors related to the persistence of conduct disorder, the findings show that the odds of persistent conduct disorder decreases if the mother's GHQ score reduced. Factors associated with higher odds are found among:

- the older age group (OR=2.1)
- those who have SEN at Time 1 (OR=2.1)
- those in households being classified as of 'lower supervisory, semi-routine and routine occupations' (OR=2.3)
- those living in a household with three or more children (OR=2.54)
- those living in rented accommodation (OR=5.9)
- those living in low-income families (OR=2.2)
- those whose mothers' GHQ scores were persistently high (OR=6.9) or became high (OR=2.5).

Trends in mental health

Two studies making comparisons between the 1999 and 2004 surveys (Green et al, 2005; Maughan et al, 2008) suggest that the prevalence rates of childhood mental disorders remained largely stable between 1999 and 2004. There was no evidence of a change in conduct or hyperkinetic disorders over this period and some evidence of a slight decline in emotional disorders. Sellers et al (2015) also report a decrease in emotional, conduct and hyperactivity problems in children aged seven (parent and teacher reports) across three surveys conducted in Great Britain in 1999, 2004 and 2008.

However, several studies in the UK undertaking longer-term analysis have suggested a different picture. Collishaw et al (2004) studied time trends in adolescent mental health over a period of 25 years based on three large-scale national samples, and found overall increases in the proportions of conduct, hyperactive and emotional problems observed over the period. Sweeting et al (2009) found successive increases in psychological distress among young people aged 15 in Scotland over three surveys in 1987, 1999 and 2006. The increases were larger for females than males. Collishaw et al (2010) used two data sources that measured emotional problems among young people aged 16-17 in England in 1986 and 2006. Their analysis found an increase in emotional problems for girls (based on youth and parent reports) and for boys (based on parent reports but not youth reports). Fink et al (2015) found evidence of increases in emotional problems in girls aged 11-13 in England between 2009 and 2014.

Collishaw (2015) notes that there is also evidence of increases in adolescent emotional problems in a number of other countries – Greece, Germany, the Netherlands, Sweden, Iceland, Norway, China and New Zealand – from the 1980s onwards, although there is less evidence of similar increases for younger age groups. In relation to conduct problems, Collishaw summarises that a range of studies found increases in rates of anti-social behaviour between the 1970s and early 1990s, but that this trend has halted, and in some cases reversed, in many countries since that time. Finally, the evidence does not suggest a major change in neurodevelopmental disorders over similar time periods.

Research attention has also focused on possible explanations for these changes in adolescent mental health rates, including the potential influence of changes in individual vulnerability, family life, extrafamilial influences and broader socioeconomic and cultural factors (Collishaw, 2015; Verhulst, 2015). However, findings so far are inconclusive. Sweeting et al (2010), in a study of adolescents in Scotland, found some evidence that changes in the family and educational contexts could explain some of the increase in rates of psychological distress. On the other hand, Collishaw et al (2012) found little evidence of a decline in quality of parenting between 1986 and 2006 that might explain the pattern of increasing youth conduct problems during that period. Schepman et al (2011) found some evidence that maternal emotional problems may have contributed to increasing emotional problems in adolescents in England between 1986 and 2006

Finally, one unresolved issue identified by Collishaw (2015) is whether the long-term changes in adolescent mental health have continued over the last decade, and what effect the recent economic recession might have had in this respect. Collishaw cites a study in the US and Canada that suggested a decline in adolescent psychological distress between 1997 and 2007 but then an increase between 2008 and 2010. Clearly, reliable recent UK data is required to address this issue.

International comparisons

The HBSC study surveys children aged 11, 13 and 15 years old in a range of European and North American countries. The questionnaire includes a set of items that have been shown to be a valid and reliable measure of psychosomatic complaints (Ravens-Sieberer et al, 2008):

* headache
* stomach ache
* feeling low
* feeling irritable
* feeling bad tempered
* feeling nervous
* having difficulty getting to sleep
* feeling dizzy.

Children are asked to respond on a frequency scale. Currie et al (2012) provide statistics for each country in the 2009/10 survey. Table 5.4 shows figures for England, Scotland and Wales (data is not available for Northern Ireland). Girls had higher levels of complaints than boys across all three countries and age groups. England ranked lowest of the three UK countries for the 11- and 13-year-old age groups. Scotland ranked highest for the 11-year-old age group but lowest for the 15-year-old age group. Wales ranked highest for the 13- and 15-year-old age groups.

Suicide

Statistics on suicide and undetermined deaths are published annually by the ONS, Register General for Scotland and Register General for Northern Ireland. Table 5.5 reports the number of suicides and the rates per million for 10- to 19-year-olds in the UK by countries and

Table 5.4: Percentage of children with more than one psychosomatic complaint more than once a week, 2009/10 (rankings* out of 39 countries in Europe and North America)

	11 years old			13 years old			15 years old		
	Girls (%)	Boys (%)	Rank	Girls (%)	Boys (%)	Rank	Girls (%)	Boys (%)	Rank
England	34	26	25	37	27	22	44	23	15
Scotland	24	20	6	33	24	12	42	27	18
Wales	26	21	12	34	20	9	41	23	10

Note: A higher ranking refers to a lower percentage of children.

Source: Currie et al (2012)

Table 5.5: Numbers and rates of suicides and undetermined deaths[1] in the UK among 10- to 19-year-olds by country, sex and age group, 2013

	England/Wales	Scotland	Northern Ireland	UK
10-14 years old				
Males	10	1	1	12
Females	2	2	1	5
All	12	3	2	17
15-19 years old				
Males	113	16	11	140
Females	23	6	2	31
All	136	22	13	171
10-19 years old				
Males	123	17	12	152
Females	25	8	3	36
All	148	25	15	188
Rates per million	**22.5**	**42.3**	**63.6**	**25.3**

Note: [1] Defined as 'intentional self-harm'; and event of undetermined intent with inquest verdict 'open' (ICD10 coding).

Sources: ONS, Mortality statistics: deaths registered in England and Wales (Series DR); General Register Office for Scotland (vital events reference tables): Northern Ireland Registrar General Annual Reports

sex. It can be seen that Scotland and Northern Ireland have a much higher suicide rate among this age group than England/Wales.

Hawton et al (2012) undertook a review of international research on self-harm and suicide in young people from 2001 to 2011. They identified a set of risk factors for suicide as follows:

- sociodemographic and educational factors – being male, low socioeconomic status and restricted educational achievement

- individual negative life events and family adversity – parental separation or divorce, parental death, adverse childhood experiences, parental mental disorder, family history of suicidal behaviour and interpersonal difficulties
- psychiatric and psychological factors – mental disorder, drug and alcohol misuse and hopelessness.

Analysis of long-term trends (five-year moving averages) in national suicide rates from 1981 to 2012 is presented in Jütte et al (2014). In England and Wales the rate of suicides has remained relatively stable for the 10-14 age group and has decreased for the 15-19 age group. In Scotland the rate for the 10-14 age group reached a peak in around 1996, dropped a little between then and 2005, reached another peak in 2009 and declined a little up to 2012. For the 15-19 age group in Scotland there was a relatively steady increase from 1985 to 2002 and a reduction since then (although the rate is still above the 1985 level). Finally, in Northern Ireland the rate for 10- to 14-year-olds rose substantially between around 2002 and 2012, while the rate for 15- to 19-year-olds has also mostly shown an upward increase, and in 2012 was more than twice the rate in 1985. However, Jütte et al (2014) note that the numbers involved in Northern Ireland and Scotland are relatively small, and so a small numerical change can have a substantial impact on rates (even when smoothed using five-year averages).

International comparisons on suicide rates among young people

In Europe, suicide has been listed as the second leading cause of death among young people aged 15-29 (Blum and Nelson-Mmari, 2004). Worldwide, official statistics indicate that there are about 164,000 self-inflicted deaths of people under the age of 25 each year, and this is likely to be an under-estimate (Hawton et al, 2012).

Värnik et al (2009) analysed the trends in suicide rates among 15- to 24-year-olds during 2000-05 using data from the European Commission-funded project, European Alliance Against Depression (EAAD), which aimed to prevent and reduce suicide rates. This analysis related to a total of 4,739 suicides in this age group, of which around 80% were men and 20% were women. Värnik et al reported that England had one of the lowest rates of youth suicide both among males and females, and that there had been a statistically significant decline in the suicide rate of young men in England in this six-year period.

Comparative international data for 37 countries is also provided for long-term trends in suicide rates for the 15-19 age group in the OECD Family database. Table 5.6 shows that in 2008 the UK had the sixth lowest suicide rate for this age group among the countries included. There was also evidence of a reduction in rates between 2000 (4.1 per 100,000) and 2008 (3.1 per 100,000).

Conclusion

There have been substantial developments in recent years in our knowledge about children's subjective well-being, both in the UK and internationally. Some subjective well-being data is now available for the UK from two longitudinal studies (Understanding Society and the Millennium Cohort Study), and the research programme undertaken jointly by The Children's Society and University of York has generated a large amount of new evidence on this topic. We now know much more about variations in children's subjective well-being between sub-groups (for example, decreases in well-being between the ages of about 8 and 14) and the extent to which different factors – such as demographics, economic factors, personality and life events – are associated with variations in subjective well-being. There is also a growing body of evidence on international variations in children's subjective well-being from the HBSC survey (including England, Wales and Scotland) and the Children's Worlds survey (currently only including England). The overall picture from these two studies is that children in the UK do not appear to fare that well in a comparative context, although the challenges in making reliable cross-national comparisons in this field are substantial. One particular issue that has emerged from the recent Children's Worlds survey is the particularly low satisfaction ratings for aspects of self (appearance, body and self-confidence) among children in England.

The most recent comprehensive data on the mental health of children and young people in the UK is from surveys undertaken in the mid-2000s. These surveys suggested that, after an increase in children's mental health problems in the latter part of the last century, the trend may have levelled off in the 2000s. However, there is a lack of information for more recent years, and it is not yet known, for example, what impact the recent economic recession may have had on children's mental health.

Statistics suggest that overall, suicide rates among children and young people in the UK are relatively low in comparison with a range of other countries, and have been falling in recent years.

Table 5.6: International comparisons of suicide rates per 100,000 in the 15-19 age group, 1990-2008

	Circa 1990	Circa 2000	Circa 2008
Greece	1.4	1.8	1.0
South Africa		0.7	1.0
Spain	3.2	2.9	1.8
Italy	2.1	2.6	2.0
Portugal	3.0	1.8	2.2
United Kingdom	3.9	4.1	3.1
Slovakia	6.0	4.3	3.4
Netherlands	3.8	4.2	3.5
*Luxembourg	13.4	5.5	3.5
Denmark	4.7	5.9	3.6
Brazil	2.6	3.3	3.7
France	5.5	5.4	4.4
Germany	5.8	5.9	4.4
Israel	4.1	6.2	4.6
Mexico	2.5	4.8	5.2
Czech Republic	6.6	6.6	5.3
*Iceland	26.6	15.7	5.7
OECD-33	8.4	8.1	6.5
Hungary	9.8	7.5	6.6
Korea	5.8	6.5	6.8
Austria	11.5	12.1	6.9
United States	11.1	8.0	7.3
Australia	10.8	9.4	7.7
Slovenia	7.8	10.8	7.8
Japan	4.0	6.7	7.8
Switzerland	9.8	9.6	7.9
Belgium	5.4	8.6	8.1
Sweden	8.1	6.6	8.1
Norway	12.8	13.5	8.5
Poland	6.8	9.1	9.6
Estonia	16.4	18.3	9.9
Canada	12.9	10.9	10.0
Chile	4.8	7.4	10.2
Finland	20.1	13.4	11.3
Ireland	6.1	12.7	12.0
New Zealand	16.7	16.2	15.7
Russia	14.4	23.1	19.7
China	12.8	3.7	

Note: * Due to small population, Iceland and Luxemburg suicide rates are very sensitive to yearly reported data and thus likely to show high variability and outliers across the time series.

Source: OECD Family database, CO4.4: Teenage suicide (15-19 years old)

Notes

[1] The question on feeling 'anxious' has not so far been asked of children by The Children's Society due to concerns raised by children during piloting about the perceived sensitivity of this question.

[2] This, and the next two sections, are reproduced from a chapter in the previous edition (written by Jonathan Bradshaw and Antonia Keung) as there has been no new major study of children's mental health in the UK since the last edition.

SIX

Education

Antonia Keung

Key statistics

- Eighty-nine per cent of Key Stage 2 pupils achieved the attainment targets in Reading and 86% in Maths in 2014/15.
- Seventy-eight per cent of Key Stage 4 pupils achieved the attainment target of five good GCSEs in 2014/15.
- Over 70% of the pupils from London achieved five good GCSEs or equivalent in 2013/14 compared to only around 63% of the pupils in Yorkshire and the Humber, East Midlands and North East.
- The proportions of young people aged 19 achieving Level 2 and 3 in 2014 were 87% and 60% respectively.
- Almost 86% of all 16- to 18-year-olds in England were in education and training in 2013, which was a record high since records began, while 7.6% of them were NEET (not in education, training or employment) in the same period.
- There are some variations in the proportion of pupils with a special educational need (SEN) statement across the UK countries, ranging from less than 3% in England and Wales to 5-6% in Northern Ireland and Scotland in 2014.

Key trends

- Pupils' attainment in England has improved across all Key Stages under review, although there may be some early evidence of a decline in Key Stage 4 attainment in 2014/15.
- The reduction in attainment gap between free school meals (FSM) and non-FSM pupils remains stubbornly slow in some UK regions, but the attainment gap in London has narrowed substantially over recent years.
- UK pupils performed as well as their OECD counterparts in the Programme for International Student Assessment (PISA) 2012 assessment in Literacy and Maths and did comparatively better than the OECD average in Science. This pattern was largely similar to that observed in PISA 2006 and 2009.

- In the most recent Health Behaviour in School-aged Children (HBSC) survey (2010), fewer children said that they liked school a lot than in 2006.
- Between 2008/09 and 2013/14, overall absence rates have declined in both primary and secondary schools in all four UK countries, except for Scottish primary schools.
- The rates of fixed period and permanent exclusions declined across all schools in England between 2009/10 and 2013/14.
- A total of 2.8% of all pupils in England have a statement of SEN in 2015; this rate has remained the same for the past five years.

Key sources
- Department for Education (DfE)
- Welsh Assembly Government
- Scottish Government
- Programme for International Student Assessment (PISA) 2006, 2009, 2012
- Health Behaviour of School-aged Children (HBSC) study 2005/06, 2010/11

Introduction

This chapter provides a review on the educational attainment of children in the UK in recent years by drawing on the latest official figures. It begins with a brief overview of the major changes introduced to the education system under the Conservative and Liberal Democrat coalition government (2010-15), and explores their implications on some of the outcomes. The review then focuses on the formal qualifications achieved by pupils by the end of their compulsory schooling and up to A-level, and explores how attainment varies by age, gender, ethnicity and free school meal (FSM) eligibility.

To explore how UK children compared internationally, the review refers to the latest findings from PISA 2012 for evidence on the 'readiness' of school leavers between the ages of 15 and 16 in the UK. Additionally, the chapter also looks at children's views about their well-being at school. It then explores the prevalence of educational disaffection through reviewing the data on truancy, school exclusion and young people not in education, employment or training (NEET). This is followed by a review on the latest data and an analysis of the latest trends in education policy concerning special educational needs (SEN). In the final section, the chapter discusses the latest research findings on the links between educational attainment and social mobility and their policy implications.

Overview of key changes in education policy, 2010-15

Education policy has undergone a period of drastic and rapid change in the past five years. The previous Education Secretary, Michael Gove, had massively expanded the Academies[1] programme in 2010, which was initiated by the last Labour government in 2002. Although both the last Labour and coalition governments appeared to be pro-academies, the intentions behind their stances were arguably different. While Labour's primary aim was to replace underperforming schools with academies, the coalition government appeared to be using academies as a means to transform the entire education system. The coalition government claimed that the academies policy would allow schools the room needed to innovate which, in turn, would enable schools to drive up standards, narrow the gap between the rich and poor, and promote social mobility (DfE, 2010). As part of the academies expansion, free schools were also introduced enabling parents, teachers, the third sector and businesses to set up their own schools as and when required to meet parental demands (DfE, 2010). By the beginning of 2015, some 2,075 (61.4%) state-funded secondary and 2,440 (14.6%) state-funded primary schools in England were academies (DfE, 2015e), and over 400 free schools were approved that would offer around 230,000 new school places across the country (DfE, Cameron and Morgan, 2015).

Other areas of marked changes during the coalition's period also include reforms to the National Curriculum, assessment and performance measures affecting Key Stages 1-5, the school funding mechanism and the provision of teacher training. As a result of the latest reforms, the syllabus at all levels has been made more challenging, examinations more demanding and performance measures, although more streamlined, have also become more rigorous (Lupton and Thomson, 2015).

Education attainment of children at the end of Key Stage 2

All children in state-funded primary schools are required to take part in the National Curriculum tests at the end of Key Stage 2 (age 11) before they move on to secondary schools. The National Curriculum tests assess children's achievements against a set of attainment targets determined by the National Curriculum. By the end of Key Stage 2 pupils are expected to have achieved at least Level 4 in both English and Maths.

Major changes to Key Stage 2 assessments have already been introduced during the coalition's years (see Lupton and Thomson, 2015). Some of these changes affected English measures from 2012 onwards – for example, pupils' writing assessment is based on their teachers' evaluation instead of on that of an external examiner. In 2013, a new grammar, punctuation and spelling test was also introduced. As a result of these changes, a comparison of the overall 'English' score over time – as in the previous editions – was not possible, hence only the Key Stage 2 Reading and Maths results will be compared over time. Figure 6.1 reports the time series trend in Key Stage 2 attainments in both subjects in England, in the period from 2005/06 to 2014/15.

Figure 6.1 shows that there were overall upward trends for pupils achieving Level 4 or above in Reading and Maths between 2005 and 2015 (although there is a slight dip in reading attainment between

Figure 6.1: Percentage of pupils from all schools achieving Level 4 or above in Key Stage 2 tests for Reading and Maths, England, 2005/06-2014/15

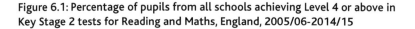

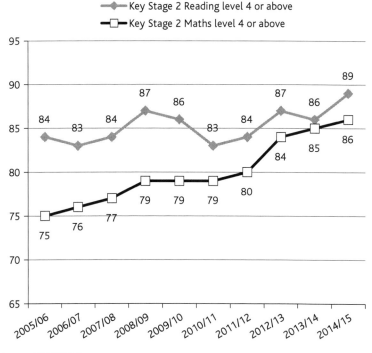

Source: DfE (2015a)

2009-11). In the 2014/15 results, 89% of the pupils achieved the expected level in Reading and 86% in Maths, which is a record high for both subjects since the coalition began in 2010. Between 2010 and 2015, the increase was 6 percentage points and 7 percentage points respectively for Reading and Maths.

Historically, girls outperform boys in Reading and Writing, and this continues to be evident in the 2014/15 data. Figure 6.2 shows that the gender gap in attainment in writing and grammar, punctuation and spelling were particularly marked – girls outperformed boys in both subjects by as much as 9 percentage points difference, whereas the attainment gap in reading was slightly smaller, but still some 4 percentage points difference. Turning to Maths, boys generally did better than girls in the past, but there is some evidence to suggest the closing of the gender gap in expected level in maths attainment has been sustained since the first record noted in 2010 (Bradshaw, 2011, p 115). However, the gender gap still exists if higher-level achievement bands are considered. For example, 44% of boys achieved Level 5 or above in Maths compared to 40% of girls (DfE, 2015a).

Some marked differences in achievement can be seen by pupils' ethnicity. Figure 6.3 shows that only 29% of children of Gypsy/Roma background and 38% of Traveller background children achieved Level 4 or above in Reading, Writing and Maths. These figures are far below

Figure 6.2: Percentage of pupils achieving Level 4 or above in Key Stage 2 tests, by subjects and sex, 2014/15

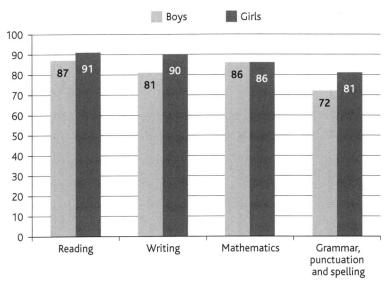

Source: DfE (2015b)

Figure 6.3: Percentage of state-funded school pupils achieving Level 4 or above in Reading, Writing and Maths by ethnicity, England, 2014/15

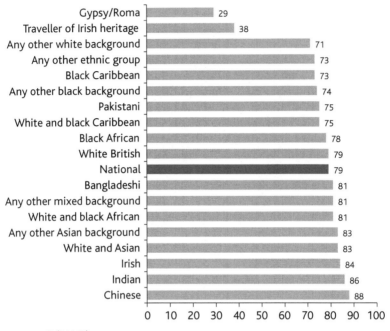

Ethnicity	Percentage
Gypsy/Roma	29
Traveller of Irish heritage	38
Any other white background	71
Any other ethnic group	73
Black Caribbean	73
Any other black background	74
Pakistani	75
White and black Caribbean	75
Black African	78
White British	79
National	79
Bangladeshi	81
Any other mixed background	81
White and black African	81
Any other Asian background	83
White and Asian	83
Irish	84
Indian	86
Chinese	88

Source: DfE (2015b)

the national average of 79%. The low level of attainment among these groups is linked to their poor attendance rate. Children of Chinese (88%), Indian (86%) or Irish (84%) ethnics topped the Level 4+ attainment table.

As we have already seen in Chapter Three of this book, children from poor backgrounds are less likely to have achieved the expected attainment level. Figure 6.4 provides a comparison of pupils' attainments in Reading, Writing and Maths between 2012/13 and 2014/15 by their FSM eligibility status. The latest statistics show that only 64% of pupils who are eligible for FSM achieved Level 4+ in Reading, Writing and Maths in 2014/15, compared to 82% who are not FSM eligible. It is also noted that the attainment rates have seen some improvement over the observed years for both groups, but the reduction in the attainment gap remained stubbornly slow. It is probably still too early to assess the effect of the Pupil Premium[2] initiative in reducing educational inequality, and the full impact of this policy might be observable in national data in the near future.

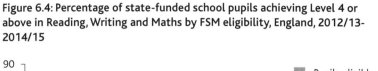

Figure 6.4: Percentage of state-funded school pupils achieving Level 4 or above in Reading, Writing and Maths by FSM eligibility, England, 2012/13-2014/15

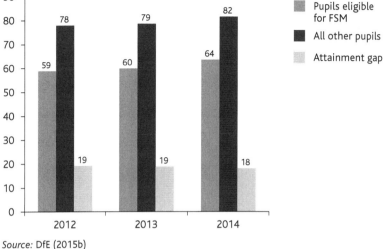

Source: DfE (2015b)

Attainment at 15+

Each year the DfE publishes Key Stage 4 and 5 pupils' attainment results, so that pupils' attainment standards can be monitored over time. Again, it is important to note that the reforms to performance measures in the league tables and to assessments and qualifications during the coalition period means that care must be taken when comparing trends over time. Of particular importance and relevance to the interpretation of the Key Stage 4 results is the government's adoption of Wolf's recommendations in 2013 (DfE and DBIS, 2014) that had led to a substantial reduction in the number of vocational qualifications that could be counted toward the school performance league tables from 2014 onwards. This has been coupled with some other major changes including the implementation of the 'early entry' policy that counts only pupils' first attempt at a qualification rather than previously the 'best result'. Adjustments had also been made on the point scores for non-GCSE qualifications so that no qualification counted as larger than one GCSE, and the total number of non-GCSE qualifications that counted towards the performance measures have also been capped at two per pupil. Furthermore, some IGCSEs[3] were no longer counted as full GCSEs but instead as approved non-GCSEs in performance tables. The latter change particularly affected several independent schools as it caused them to receive no score for the proportion of pupils obtaining five A★-C IGCSEs with English and Maths (DfE, 2015a). Finally, the changes to the English exam in particular (that is, that the speaking and listening components of the assessment were no longer to be counted towards the final grade from 2014) should be acknowledged. Figure 6.5 provides time series data on three measures: the percentage of pupils from state-funded schools attaining at least five A★-C GCSEs, the percentage attaining A★-C GCSEs including English and Maths, and the English Baccalaureate[4] (EBacc) measure which was first introduced into the performance tables in 2010. It should be noted that to allow direct comparison, the 2014/15 data reported is based on the old qualification rules.

Figure 6.5 reveals a clear upward trend in the proportion of pupils achieving five A★-C GCSEs, from 54.9% in 2005/06 to 83% in both 2012/13 and 2013/14. The latest figure in 2014/15 was 78.2%, which suggests a decline of nearly 5 percentage points from the year before. Similarly, an upward trend was observed on the proportion achieving five A★-C GCSEs including English and Maths, from 42.5%

Figure 6.5: Percentage of pupils from state-funded schools attaining Key Stage 4 performance measures, 2004/05-2013/14

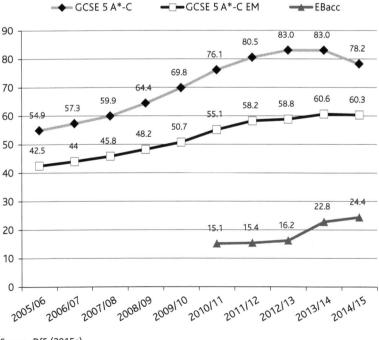

Source: DfE (2015c)

in 2005/06 to the last increase recorded in 2013/14 at 60.6%. Again, there was a slight drop in 2014/15, 0.3 percentage points less compared to the year before. Turning to the proportion of pupils attaining the EBacc, again, an upward trend could be observed between the first measure in 2010/11 (15.1%) and the latest in 2014/15 (24.4%). If the new rules in 2014 are applied to the calculation, the latest set of results would be worse: 65.5% achieved five A*-C GCSEs and 56.6% including English and Maths, and 24.2% attained EBacc (these figures are not included in Figure 6.5).

Regarding the recent rise in GCSE attainments, Lupton and Thomson (2015) argue that much of it could be attributable to 'lower attaining students gaining additional vocational qualifications or ones of higher league table value, or by having several attempts at assessment' (p 43). They further suggest that the attainment decline recorded in 2014/15 could also be partly explained by the changes in the GCSE curriculum and assessment in 2014 when previously modularised GCSE formats were replaced by the current linear approach, where students can only sit their exams at the end of the course. This implies that students taking exams only once may be achieving lower grades (Lupton and Thomson, 2015).

Next we examine the variations in GCSE performance. Figure 6.6 illustrates that there are some differences in attainment across English regions. London has the highest proportion of pupils with good GCSE qualifications (70.5%), followed by the South East (67.4%), whereas Yorkshire and the Humber (62.8%) as well as the East Midlands (63.1%) have some of the lowest proportions. Greaves et al (2014) studied the 'London effect' and concluded that the good result seen in London was largely attributable to prior attainment level. Moreover, 'London's success' can also partly be explained by the fact that more disadvantaged pupils achieved good GCSE results. Their review shows that almost half of all children who were FSM eligible in London attained good GCSE results in 2013 compared to only around 30-40% in other regions. Greaves et al (2014) concluded that the good result was unlikely to be attributable to the recent policy initiatives such as the academies programmes but instead to policies that were introduced around the late 1990s and early part of 2000s such as the National Strategies (Greaves et al 2014).

Variation in GCSE attainments can also be seen when compared across different countries in the UK. As pupils in Scotland study for the National Qualifications Standard Grades instead of the GCSEs as in the rest of the UK, its results are not included for comparison. Figure 6.7 shows the proportion of school leavers achieving five or

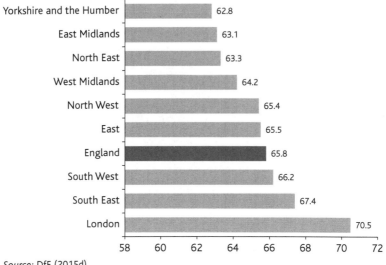

Figure 6.6: Percentage of pupils achieving 5+ A*-C grades or equivalent by English regions, 2013/14 (based on the 2014 qualification rules)

Region	Percentage
Yorkshire and the Humber	62.8
East Midlands	63.1
North East	63.3
West Midlands	64.2
North West	65.4
East	65.5
England	65.8
South West	66.2
South East	67.4
London	70.5

Source: DfE (2015d)

more GCSEs at grades A*-C or equivalent by countries and sex. It shows that girls consistently outperformed boys in attaining five good GCSEs or equivalent results in all three countries, but the gender gap appeared to be quite a bit larger in England (9.8% points) compared to Northern Ireland (7.9% points) and Wales (7.7% points). Overall, the Welsh and Northern Irish school leavers appear to do better in attainment than the English. In 2013/14, 82.3% of pupils from Wales and 81.8% from Northern Ireland achieved at least five good GCSEs or their equivalent by the end of their compulsory schooling compared to 75.8% from England.[5]

The gender gap of attainment remains the same for Level 3 qualifications but is generally much smaller compared to Level 2. Figure 6.8 shows that slightly more girls than boys achieved two or more A-levels or equivalent in all three countries. Similar to the performance in GCSE attainment, pupils in Northern Ireland (98%) and Wales (97.1%) outperformed those in England (90.5%) by quite a margin.

Turning to the time series of pupils achieving Level 2 and 3 qualifications in England, Figure 6.9 shows a steady upward trend over the period from 2004-14. In 2014/15, 87% of the 19-year-olds were qualified to at least Level 2 in England, which compares to only 66.7% in 2004/05 when the data was first published (DfE, 2015g).

Figure 6.7: Percentage of pupils in their last year of compulsory education achieving 5+ GCSEs A*-C or equivalent by country and sex, 2013/14

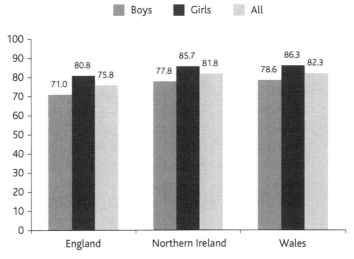

Notes: England and Wales figures were based on all schools whereas Northern Ireland excluded special and independent schools.

Source: DfE (2014a, 2015c); Department of Welsh Assembly Government (2015a)

Figure 6.8: Percentage of candidates achieving two or more A-levels or equivalent by country and sex, 2013/14

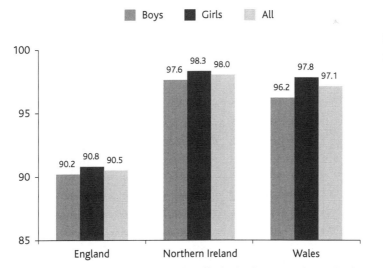

Notes: England and Wales figures were based on all schools whereas Northern Ireland excluded special and independent schools.

Source: DfE (2014a, 2015f); Welsh Assembly Government (2015b)

Figure 6.9: Percentage of candidates attaining a Level 2 or higher and Level 3 qualification or equivalent by age 19 in England, 2004-14

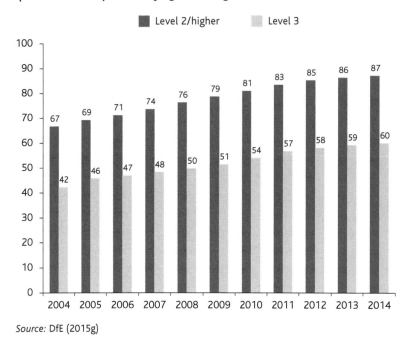

Source: DfE (2015g)

However, there are some signs of slowing down since 2012, with just 1 percentage point increase each year from then on. Similarly, a steady upward trend in Level 3 qualifications or equivalent can also be observed over the same period – 60% recorded in 2013/14 compared to 42% in 2004/05.

As a way of monitoring progress against the government's objectives of raising participation and reducing the number of young people in NEET, the DfE regularly publishes statistics on this topic, based on data from the Labour Force Survey. Figure 6.10 presents rates of all 16- to 18-year-olds in terms of participation in education and training. Statistics related to young people in NEET are examined in a later section.

There were nearly 2 million 16- to 18-year-olds in England by the end of 2013, of which 85.6% were in education or training, compared to 83.6% a year before. Figure 6.10 shows that the participation rate of 16- to 18-year-olds has been slowly but continuously rising since 2001. It should be noted that the latest increase in participation is attributable to the new legislation that extended the compulsory schooling or participation in the form of work and training beyond

Figure 6.10: Percentage of all 16- to 18-year-olds in education and training, England

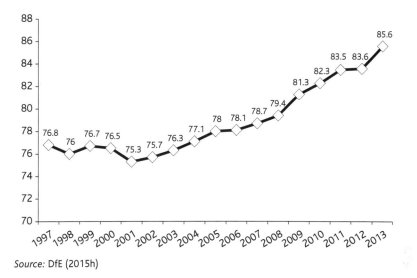

Source: DfE (2015h)

the age 16. Details of the new legislation is discussed under the NEET section, later.

Competences at the age of 15

Every three years since 2000, the OECD undertakes a comparative study known as PISA that assesses the extent to which 15-year-old students have acquired key knowledge and skills that are essential for their full participation in 21st-century societies. Each cycle of the assessment tests the competencies of students on Reading, Maths and Science, but with a specific focus on one subject at a time. Students are tested on their ability to reproduce what they have learned as well as extrapolate from what they have learned and apply that knowledge in unfamiliar settings inside and outside of school (OECD, 2014a).

So far the OECD has published five PISA survey reports. The latest report from PISA 2012 focused on Maths, with Reading and Science as minor areas of assessment. Altogether around 510,000 15-year-old school children from 65 countries and economies (of which 34 were from the OECD member states) participated in the 2012 PISA survey. In the UK, eligible schools from the main samples of all four countries took part in a two-hour assessment in PISA 2012. This involved a total of 4,185 students from 170 schools in England (Wheater et al, 2013a), 3,305 students from 137 schools in Wales (Wheater et al, 2013b),

2,224 students from 89 schools in Northern Ireland (Wheater et al, 2013c), and 2,945 students from 111 schools in Scotland (Boyling et al, 2013). The overall response rate for the UK was 89% of sampled schools and 86% of sampled pupils, representing a good response rate which fully met the PISA participation requirements (DfE, 2014b).

This section presents the performance results from PISA 2012 relating to England, Wales, Northern Ireland and Scotland. It also compares the UK results with the OECD average. Table 6.1 summarises the mean scores, variation and gender differences in student performance in Maths.

The UK achieved a mean score of 494 in Mathematics literacy, which was the same as the OECD average. However, within the UK there were some significant differences in the mean scores noted. The highest attainment for Maths was in Scotland, followed by England, and then Northern Ireland, and the lowest attainment was in Wales. However, not all the differences in scores were statistically significant; only the mean score in Northern Ireland was significantly lower than that in Scotland, and Wales also had a significantly lower score than the other constituent parts of the UK.

Table 6.1 shows some significant differences in the Maths scores between boys and girls. In all cases, boys performed better than girls and, except for Northern Ireland, these differences were statistically significant. Overall in the UK, the gender gaps in Maths attainment compared well with the OECD average and were smaller than in many other countries (DfE, 2014b). Furthermore, Table 6.1 also summarises the gap between high and low attaining pupils. This can be seen by the point score differences between pupils at the bottom 5% (low attainers) and top 5% (high attainers) of the distribution. The performance

Table 6.1: Mean score, variation and gender differences in PISA 2012 performance in Maths

| | Mathematics | | | |
| | All students | | Score difference between genders (M-F) | Score difference between bottom and top 5% |
	Mean	SD		
England	496	95	13	315
Northern Ireland	487	93	9	306
Wales	469	84	10	280
Scotland	498	86	14	282
UK	494	94	13	311
OECD average	494	92	11	301

Sources: Boyling et al (2013); DfE (2014b); OECD (2015b)

gap in maths between low and high attainers for the OECD was 301 points. The largest gap was observed in England (315 points), followed by Northern Ireland (306 points). The gaps reported for both countries were larger than the OECD average, suggesting the presence of large inequalities in Maths attainment. The gaps reported in Wales (280 points) and Scotland (282 points), however, were comparatively narrower than the OECD average.

Turing to the performance in Reading literacy, Table 6.2 shows that the UK achieved a mean score of 499, which is slightly higher than the OECD average of 496.

Comparing performance across the UK constituent countries, Table 6.2 shows that pupils in Scotland had the highest mean score in Reading, closely followed by England and Northern Ireland, although the differences were not statistically significant. While the overall mean scores in England and Northern Ireland were not significantly different from the OECD average, Scottish students performed better than their OECD peers. The lowest attainment was in Wales, where the mean score was significantly lower than the rest of the UK and the OECD average. Regarding the gender difference in Reading performance, girls had significantly outperformed boys in all the constituent countries of the UK, as well as the OECD average. The gender gaps observed across the UK in general appear to be narrower compared to the OECD average. As for the attainment gap between high and low attainers, Scotland had the best result followed by Wales. This indicates that there is generally less inequality in pupils' ability to read in both countries, and they also compared better to the OECD average. However, the attainment gaps in England and Northern Ireland were wider than the OECD average.

Table 6.2: Mean score, variation and gender differences in PISA 2012 performance in Reading

| | Reading | | | |
| | All students | | Score difference between genders (M-F) | Score difference between bottom and top 5% |
	Mean	SD		
England	500	99	−24	325
Northern Ireland	498	96	−28	319
Wales	480	90	−28	296
Scotland	506	87	−27	288
UK	499	97	−24	321
OECD average	496	94	−38	310

Sources: Boyling et al (2013); DfE (2014b); OECD (2015b)

Table 6.3 gives results on Science literacy. Overall, the UK achieved a mean score of 514, which is better than the OECD average of 501.

Table 6.3 shows that the highest attainment for Science was in England, closely followed by Scotland, and then Northern Ireland. However, the differences between these three countries were not statistically significant. The lowest attainment was in Wales, where the mean score for Science was significantly lower than in the rest of the UK. Boys generally did better than girls in Science literacy in all the four countries in the UK. The largest gender gap in Science attainment was observed in England, followed by Wales and then Scotland. As for the gender gap observed in Northern Ireland, it was not statistically significant. When looking across the other OECD countries, gender difference was not as prominent as in the UK countries in general. Comparing the attainment gaps between the top and bottom performers, the largest gaps were in England and Northern Ireland and the smallest in Scotland. The attainment gaps observed in England and Northern Ireland were also above the OECD average.

To sum up, pupils in the UK perform at around average levels in Maths and Reading, and above average in Science when compared with their OECD peers who took part in the 2012 PISA assessment. However, when assessing the inequality in educational attainment between the highest and lowest achievers, the England average was larger than the OECD average in all three subjects. Comparing the PISA 2012 results with the earlier two PISA cycles in 2006 and 2009, the performance of the UK has remained stable across all the three subjects assessed[6] (Bradshaw, 2013).

Table 6.3: Mean score, variation and gender differences in PISA 2012 performance in Science

| | Science | | | |
| | All students | | Score difference between genders (M-F) | Score difference between bottom and top 5% |
	Mean	SD		
England	516	101	14	331
Northern Ireland	507	101	5	331
Wales	491	94	11	305
Scotland	513	89	7	293
UK	514	100	13	327
OECD average	501	93	1	304

Sources: Boyling et al (2013); DfE (2014b); OECD (2015b)

Children's well-being at schools

In addition to assessing children's educational performance, PISA 2012 also surveyed how children felt about their school. According to the results, pupils in the UK are largely satisfied with their school and feel positive towards school:

> ... 79% of students feel that they belong at school, 88% make friends easily, and 89% do not feel like an outsider or feel left out of things. Some 83% of students reported that they feel happy at school, 84% are satisfied with school, and 71% believe that conditions are ideal in their school. (Bradshaw, 2013, p 5)

However, this snapshot does not really tell much about how children's feelings about school may have changed over time. The Health Behaviour of School-aged Children (HBSC) study provides some useful comparative data related to school well-being for ages 11, 13 and 15, and by comparing results over time it enables children's well-being at school to be monitored. With reference to the most recent HBSC data, there is evidence to suggest that children's school well-being in England has worsened compared to the previous survey cycle, when England compared more favourably to other countries. According to Brooks et al (2011), the proportion of children in England across all age groups surveyed who reported that they 'like school a lot' has seen a decline since the last survey in 2006. For example, among the 15-year-olds, only 16% of girls and 14% of boys reported that they like school a lot in 2010 compared to 26% of girls and 24% of boys in 2006 (Brooks et al, 2011, p 3).

Figure 6.11 presents the latest findings from the HBSC 2010 survey related to school well-being. It compares the proportions of children who said they 'like school a lot' by sex, age and countries.[7] A few points can be noted. First, girls in general are more likely to say that they like school a lot, and this is consistent across the observed age groups (except for the 15-year-olds in Scotland and Wales, where there is virtually no difference between boys and girls). Second, older age groups are less likely to say that they like school a lot compared to younger ones, and this age effect also appears to be consistent with the OECD average reported. Third, in Scotland, substantially lower proportions of 11-year-olds reported they liked school a lot compared to England and Wales as well as the OECD average. Furthermore, lower proportions of 13- and 15-year-olds in the UK countries said

Figure 6.11: Percentage of school children who reported that they 'like school a lot' by sex, age and countries

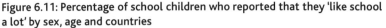

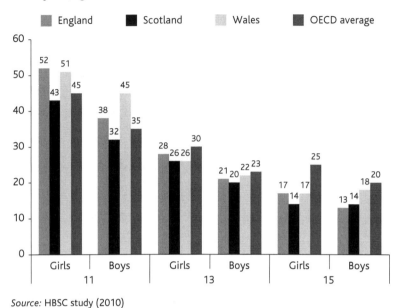

Source: HBSC study (2010)

they liked school a lot compared to the OECD average; this difference was particularly marked among 15-year-olds.

The good childhood report 2014, which accessed children's well-being on various life domains, provides more up-to-date data on children's school well-being in England. It assessed the proportion of children who might have low well-being at school, and shows that around 6% of sampled school children aged 10-13 in England were identified as having low well-being at school (Children's Society, 2014). It also indicates that slightly more girls than boys reported low well-being at school, although the difference was not statistically significant (Children's Society, 2014). There is a cause for concern over low well-being at school, as previous research suggests a potential link between school dislike, poor attainment and early drop out (Archambault et al, 2009).

Disaffection in education

Although most children in the UK are doing well and feel positive about their school, a minority of children still find themselves disengaged or have difficulty in fully engaging in education. This section reports relevant statistics in relation to disaffection in education, including truancy, school exclusions, young people NEET and those with special educational needs (SEN).

Truancy

Research highlights the educational disadvantage of absenteeism (Claes et al, 2009), and its associated risks such as engaging in risky behaviours including criminal activities, underage drinking, drug taking and smoking (Wilson et al, 2008; Henry and Thornberry, 2010; Barnes et al, 2011). The DfE collects data on pupils' attendance and absenteeism, which provide key indicators for behaviour and attendance policy. Truancy rates are calculated from absenteeism rates (the percentage of half-days of school attendance missed) collated via the School Census. A distinction is made between authorised and unauthorised absences. Truancy is defined as an unauthorised absence from school, and research evidence points to a number of risk factors that are linked to truancy, including low academic and general self-esteem of the truants, experience of stressful home environment such as poverty, domestic violence, parental drugs/alcohol abuse, and experience of bullying at school (Colechin, 2011). In addition, there is also evidence of parentally condoned absenteeism, where children are being kept away from school by their parents, for example, to provide care for a sick parent/sibling or go shopping (Wilson et al, 2008). Table 6.4 reports the absenteeism rates by primary/secondary schools and by countries. Unless otherwise specified, the data refer to the academic year 2013/14.

As shown in Table 6.4, rates for unauthorised absences in secondary schools are generally higher than that in primary schools. Northern Irish and Scottish secondary schools have the highest unauthorised absence rates in the UK. The overall absence rates reported in secondary schools are also higher than those in primary schools in all four countries. The highest overall absence rates reported for primary schools were in Wales and Scotland, both at around 5%, and for secondary schools, again, Scotland has reported the highest overall absence rate at 8%.

Compared to the 2008/09 data reported in the previous edition of this book series (Bradshaw, 2011), there are some signs of reduction in the overall absence rates in both primary and secondary schools in the UK, except for Scotland, where absence rates are on the increase. It should be noted that caution must be exercised when comparing the data across countries, owing to possible differences in the way 'absence' is being defined and recorded by schools.

Table 6.4: Percentage of total half-days absence[1] in state-funded schools in the UK, 2013/14 academic year

	Primary schools		Secondary schools	
	Unauthorised absence	Overall absence	Unauthorised absence	Overall absence
England	0.8	3.9	1.3	5.2
Wales	1.0	5.2	1.3	6.4
Northern Ireland	1.4	4.4	2.5	6.5
Scotland[2]	1.3	5.1	2.5	8.0

Notes:

[1] This is calculated by first dividing the total overall absence sessions (overall absence is the sum of authorised and unauthorised absence, and one session is equal to half a day) by the total sessions possible and then times 100 (DfE, 2015).

[2] Scotland data on attendance and absence is collected every two years and the latest available data reported here refer to the academic year 2012/13.

Source: DfE (2015a, 2015i); Welsh Assembly Government (2015c, 2015d); Scottish Government (2013)

School exclusion

Government departments in all four nations of the UK collect school exclusion data. A distinction is made between fixed period and permanent exclusion. The former refers to pupils who are excluded from school but who remain on the school register because they are expected to return when the exclusion period is completed. Permanent exclusion refers to pupils who are excluded and their names are removed from their school register. Pupils who are permanently excluded would be educated at another school, or some other type of provision made. It should be noted that the terms 'suspension' and 'expulsion' are used in Northern Ireland.

There was a change in the way the exclusion rates are calculated in England from 2013/14 release onwards. Previously the calculation was based on single registered pupils only. In order to more accurately capture the number of pupils who could be excluded, a new calculation method was introduced that includes pupils who have a single or dual registration[8] at a school at the beginning of each year (DfE, 2015j). Table 6.5 reports the numbers and rates of school exclusions in all schools in England based on the new calculation method.

The time series data summarised in Table 6.5 show a general downward trend in both fixed and permanent exclusion rates between 2009/10 and 2013/14 in England. However, the numbers of fixed and permanent exclusions across all schools have both increased slightly in

2013/14 compared to 2012/13. The DfE indicates that the increase in the number of exclusions was mainly due to the rise in the number of fixed period exclusions in primary schools (DfE, 2015j). The majority of school exclusion involves secondary students and boys in particular. The latest data provided in 2013/14 unveiled that boys are over three times more likely to receive a permanent exclusion and also nearly three times more likely to receive a fixed period exclusion than girls. This general pattern has remained stable over recent years (DfE, 2015j). Furthermore, boys are also more likely to be excluded from school at a younger age, with very few girls being excluded during primary years. Over 60% of those permanently excluded belong to the 12-14 age group. Fourteen-year-olds, in particular, have the highest fixed period exclusion rates (DfE, 2015j). The most commonly quoted reason for both fixed period and permanent exclusions was 'persistent disruptive behaviour', and this was associated with nearly 33% of all permanent exclusions and about 25% of all fixed period exclusions (DfE, 2015j).

Those with SEN are over-represented among excluded pupils. SEN pupils, including those with and without a statement, have the highest fixed period and permanent exclusion rates respectively; they are about nine times more likely to be excluded than pupils with no SEN (DfE, 2015j). Statistics also show that pupils who are FSM eligible are about four times more likely to be excluded either permanently (0.18% vs 0.04%) or over a fixed period (8.82% vs 2.46%) than those who are not eligible. Furthermore, exclusion rates also vary by ethnic group. Pupils of Gypsy/Roma (0.34%) and Traveller of Irish heritage (0.6%) ethnic groups have the highest rates of both permanent and fixed period exclusions. Pupils of Black Caribbean (0.24%) and White and Black

Table 6.5: Number of fixed period and permanent exclusion in all schools, England, 2009/10-2013/14

	2009/10	2010/11	2011/12	2012/13	2013/14
Number of fixed period exclusions	331,380	324,110	304,370	267,520	269,480
% of school population[1]	4.44	4.33	4.03	3.51	3.5
Number of permanent exclusions	5,740	5,080	5,170	4,630	4,950
% of school population[2]	0.08	0.07	0.07	0.06	0.06

Notes:

[1] The number of fixed period exclusions expressed as a percentage of the number of pupils in January each year. As pupils can receive more than one fixed period exclusion, there can be pupil duplicates in the numerator.

[2] The number of permanent exclusions expressed as a percentage of the number of pupils in January each year.

Source: DfE (2015j)

Caribbean (0.18%) ethnic groups are about three times more likely to be permanently excluded than the entire school population (0.07%).

Variations in the number and rate of exclusions across the four UK nations can be observed from Table 6.6 that provides an overview of the latest available data for each nation. Wales has the highest rate of fixed period exclusion per 1,000 pupils, followed by England and then Scotland. Regarding permanent exclusion rates, England has the highest rate per 1,000 pupils and Scotland has the lowest rate, with only about one-fifth of that recorded in England. These variations are likely to be attributable to different school policies and legislation regarding exclusion in different countries.

Not in education, employment, or training

The data reported in this section relates to England only. Figure 6.12 provides the time series of NEET percentages, and it shows that the NEET rates among the 16- to 18-year-olds has continued to decline since 2011 after a sharp increase recorded in 2010. The latest end of year figure published for 2014 suggests that the NEET rate was 7%, at its record low, and represents a sharp decrease when compared to the previous year figure of 7.6% (DfE and DBIS, 2015). This marked reduction in NEET rate despite austerity cuts under the coalition government can be explained by the rising of the participation age that has recently been legislated.

Table 6.6: School exclusions recorded at all schools in the UK, 2013/14 (unless otherwise specified)

		Permanent	Fixed period
England	Number of exclusions	4,950	269,480
	Rate per 1,000 pupils	0.6	35
Wales[1]	Number of exclusions	99	15,323
	Rate per 1,000 pupils	0.3	39
Northern Ireland[2]	Number of exclusions	29	3,677
	Rate per 1,000 pupils	0.1	13.2
Scotland[1]	Number of exclusions	21	21,934
	Rate per 1,000 pupils	0.03	32.8

Notes:

[1] The latest available data for Wales and Scotland was from the 2012/13 release.

[2] Northern Ireland reports the total pupils excluded rather than the total number of exclusions, so not directly comparable to the other countries.

Sources: DfE (2014b, 2015j); Welsh Assembly Government (2014b); Scottish Government (2014b)

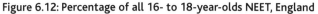

Figure 6.12: Percentage of all 16- to 18-year-olds NEET, England

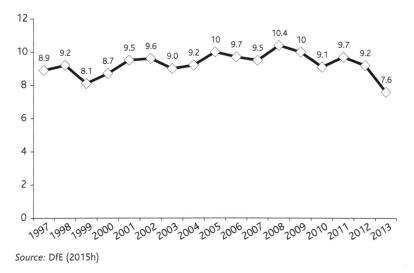

Source: DfE (2015h)

Legislation was initiated by the Labour government and was included in the Education and Skills Act 2008. It requires young people to continue in education or training beyond the age of 16. The first cohort to be affected by it would have been those leaving at Year 11 in the summer of 2013 who were required to stay on in education or training for at least a further year. Those who were leaving in the summer of 2014 would be the first group required to stay on until they turned at least 18 (House of Commons, 2015). The coalition government did not enforce this legislation, but in parallel introduced a series of other initiatives, such as the Youth Contract, study programmes, traineeships, apprenticeship reforms, the National Careers Service and the 16–19 Bursary Fund to help support young people to participate, particularly those deemed at risk of being NEET such as those with low level of attainment and/or youth offenders or care leavers (NAO, 2014). It is not sure how effective the coalition's initiatives have been in reducing young people in NEET, but there is strong evidence to suggest that the new legislation has played an important role in the decline in numbers of young people in NEET.

Figure 6.13 reports the NEET rates recorded by the end of 2014 broken down by sex and age, and shows that the proportion of young people NEET increases as they become older and boys outnumber girls in all age groups.

Despite the declining NEET rate, England continues to have one of the highest NEET rates compared to the other OECD countries. The

OECD publishes data on the proportion of young people aged 15-19 who are NEET.[9] Although the OECD data is not directly comparable to England, it provides an idea of how the UK as a whole compares internationally. In most countries, 15- to 19-year-olds are still in full-time education, although there may be small variations in terms of the age range due to various education systems in different countries. Figure 6.14 presents the percentage of these age groups NEET in the OECD countries in 2013.

Figure 6.14 shows that the NEET rate for the UK was 9% compared to the OECD average of 7%. Early experience of exclusion from education and the labour market is often linked to a series of disadvantages. Evidence from the Longitudinal Study of Young People in England shows that being NEET at 19 is associated with poor attainment, FSM status, exclusion or suspension from school, early child rearing and disability (DfE, 2011). The high rate of youth inactivity in the UK is an area of concern, as research shows that it is very costly to both the individuals as well as to society as a whole in terms of lost contribution and increased welfare expenditure (Coles et al, 2010). Although there is some sign of decline in the NEET rates in England, the latest international evidence clearly shows that more needs to be done to support young people's participation in the UK.

Special educational needs

A proportion of pupils require additional support and provisions in order to be able to fully benefit from the education system. In 2014,

Figure 6.13: Percentage of 16- to 18-year-olds NEET in England, by sex and age, end 2014

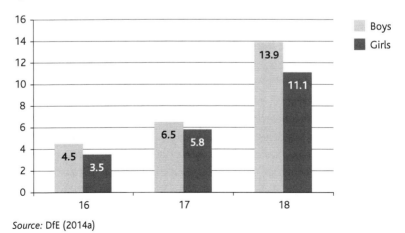

Source: DfE (2014a)

Figure 6.14: Percentage of 15- to 19-year-olds NEET in 2013

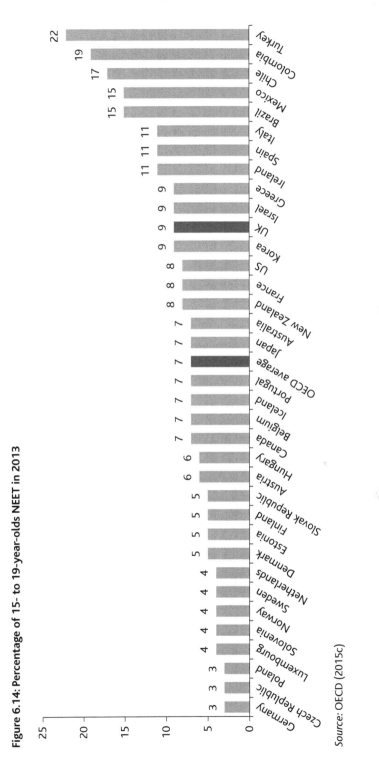

Source: OECD (2015c)

a new Education, Health and Care Plan (EHC) was introduced in England under the Special Educational Needs and Disability (SEND) reform. A pupil has a statement of SEN or an EHC plan when a formal assessment has been made and a document is provided that sets out the type of needs and extra support required. Before the reform, a statement of SEN was issued if a young person was diagnosed with any of the following conditions: visual, hearing or other physical impairments; speech, language or communication needs; cognitive disorders or learning difficulties; or behavioural, emotional or social difficulties. The latest reform has changed some of the classification of the type of needs. For example, a new category of 'social, emotional and mental health' has been added and 'behaviour, emotional and social difficulties' was removed from 2015 onwards (DfE, 2015k). According to the final set of pre-reform SEN statistics, the most common condition reported among primary school-age pupils was speech, language and communication needs, and among secondary school-age pupils, behaviour, emotional and social difficulties were the most prevalent type of SEN (DfE, 2014c). This is perhaps unsurprising as the two categories of conditions are likely to be linked. The problems with speech, language and communication needs at younger age could lead to later behaviour, emotional and social difficulties. The following review primarily focuses on pupils who have a statement of SEN.

In 2014, 232,190 pupils across all schools in England had SEN statements, representing 2.8% of all pupils; 26.2% of pupils with SEN statements were reported in state-funded primary schools and 25.7% in state-funded secondary schools. SEN is more prevalent in boys – 4% compared to 1.6% for girls (DfE, 2014c). Older age groups are more likely to have statements of SEN, for example, 3.9% of the 15-year-olds were statemented compared to 2.9% and 2% for pupils aged 9 and 6 respectively (DfE, 2014c). Pupils with SEN (29.1%) are about twice as likely to be FSM eligible compared to those who have no SEN (13.4%) (DfE, 2014c). Black pupils (3.5%) are more likely to have a statement of SEN compared to White British (3.2%) and minority ethnic pupils (2.8%). Indian (1.8%) and Chinese (2.0%) pupils have the lowest prevalence of SEN, and Black Caribbean (4.1%), Gypsy/Roma (3.6%) and Traveller of Irish heritage (4.9%) have the highest prevalence of SEN (DfE, 2014c).

Table 6.7 presents data of SEN from all four UK nations from 2010 up to 2015. There are large variations in the SEN rates within the UK, although such variations are mainly due to variations in the way SEN is defined and local government policies. Table 6.7 shows that the proportion of pupils in England with SEN remained stable at

2.8%, and for Wales a general downward trend can be noted – 2.7% in 2015 compared to 2.9% in 2010. The figures for Northern Ireland increased from 4% to 5% in 2013 and have remained stable in recent years. In Scotland, the proportion of SEN has declined from 6.9% between 2010 and 2012 to 6% in 2014.

Latest findings on educational inequality and social mobility

The coalition government considered the recent education reforms as key vehicles to improve and drive up the relatively low social mobility in the UK which has been demonstrated by international comparative research (see, for example Causa and Johansson, 2010). New research evidence provides some compelling insights into when and why the initially higher attaining poorer children fall behind their lower achieving but better-off peers (Crawford et al, 2015; Hills, 2015). Crawford et al explored the trajectories of a cohort born in 1989/90, and compared attainment progress between pupils from the most deprived and least deprived fifths of socioeconomic background. Their analysis shows that the initial higher attaining poorer children at age 11, with comparable cognitive ability to their more affluent high achieving peers, have gradually fallen behind in rankings as they progress through their secondary education. Meanwhile, the lower attainers, but from a more affluent background at age 11, manage to catch up somewhat by the age of 16 and move along the trajectory of the poorer but more able children. They explain this phenomenon

Table 6.7: Pupils with a SEN statement (or 'additional support needs' in Scotland)

		2010	2011	2012	2013	2014	2015
England	Number	223,945	224,210	226,125	229,390	232,190	236,165
	%	2.8	2.8	2.8	2.8	2.8	2.8
Wales	Number	13,767	13,407	13,098	12,738	12,530	12,437
	%	2.9	2.9	2.8	2.7	2.7	2.7
Northern Ireland	Number	12,879	12,874	12,886	16,217	16,314	16,433
	%	4.0	4.0	4.0	5.0	5.0	5.0
Scotland[1]	Number	46,736	46,436	46,295	43,368	40,768	n/a
	%	6.9	6.9	6.9	6.4	6.0	n/a

Note:

[1] Data for Scotland shows pupils with coordinated support plan and/or individualised educational programmes.

Sources: DfE (2015b, 2015c, 2015k); Welsh Government (2015e, 2015f); Scottish Government (2015a, 2015b)

as a potential result of the segregation and selective schooling system that presents in the UK, where children from poorer and richer backgrounds attend different secondary schools. Accordingly, more affluent pupils are by far more likely to be admitted to good quality secondary schools than those from a poorer background. Additionally, the different educational values, attitudes and aspirations held by poorer and richer children may also play a role in explaining why the poorer but more able children fall behind their richer but less able peers after Key Stage 4 (Crawford et al, 2015). Thus, it is suggested that to improve social mobility through education provision, equality in access to good quality secondary schools should be ensured. Targeted help should also be offered to the able but poorer children to help them achieve their full potential (Crawford et al, 2015).

Conclusion

There is evidence to suggest that pupils' level of attainment in England continued to improve during most of the coalition period. However, not enough time has passed since the recent education reforms and austerity measures to show their full impact on pupils' performance in the national statistics. To summarise, the proportions of pupils in Key Stage 2 who achieved the attainment targets in Reading and Maths had risen in the last 10 years. The rise in Key Stage 2 attainment in Maths was particularly remarkable, and the closing of the gender gap in Maths attainment has been sustained. However, girls continued to outperform boys in reading, writing and grammar, punctuation and spelling. The proportion of pupils achieving the attainment targets in Key Stages 4 and 5 had increased over the period, but there might also be some early signs of decline in the proportion obtaining five or more grade A*-C GCSEs in 2014/15. However, the latter may be the result of the changes in performance measures and assessment methods that took effect in 2014, and therefore more data would be needed to confirm this. Comparable data on pupils' education performance in England, Northern Ireland and Wales shows that Northern Irish and Welsh pupils did better than pupils from England across the board.

Internationally, the education performance of the UK remained stable in PISA 2006, 2009 and 2012. The latest findings from 2012 show that pupils in the UK performed as well as their OECD peers in reading and maths and above the OECD average in science. The quality of school life enjoyed by children in the UK was also relatively high by OECD standards, with most of them satisfied with their school and feeling positive towards school. However, comparing children's views about schools over time based on the HBSC data series, there is evidence to suggest a general decline in school experience for both boys and girls in the 2010 HBSC survey cycle.

A general reduction in the overall absence rates in both primary and secondary schools indicate that children's school engagement may have improved across most of the UK countries. There is also a decreasing trend in the exclusion rates observed in England over time. However, the latest exclusion rates in England are still comparatively higher than the other UK countries (except that Wales has the highest fixed period exclusion rate). Furthermore, in England, young people's participation in education and training has increased over time and reached its record high in 2013. The decline in NEET rate can be contributed to legislation that raised the participation age. However, comparative data shows that the proportion of young people NEET in the UK is still above the OECD average.

Finally, despite the overall improvement in pupils' education attainment, data suggests that the attainment gaps observed between those receiving free school meals and those who do not remained. An exception to this is London, where a substantial closing of the attainment gap was noted in recent years. The successful story in London suggests that with the right dose of policies and good management, reduction in the attainment gap is achievable. To improve social mobility, new research evidence points to the importance of equal opportunity in accessing good quality schooling for those coming from a poorer background. Furthermore, targeted support should also be provided to able pupils from less affluent backgrounds in order to help them reach their full potential.

Notes

[1] Academies are state-funded independent schools and do not receive money from the local authority but direct from central government. They are not required to follow the national curriculum, but they still have to follow the same rules on admissions, SEN and exclusions as other state schools (GOV. UK, 2015c).

[2] This was introduced in 2011. It is public funding provided to schools in England and Wales to reduce the attainment gap for the most disadvantaged children. For each pupil who is eligible for FSM, their school receives £1,300 (for primary school) or £935 (for secondary school). An extra top-up to £1,900 is made available to pupils who are under the local authority care or adopted from care or were in care in the past year (GOV.UK, 2015b).

[3] The International General Certificate of Secondary Education (IGCSE) is a curriculum that is being recognised as equivalent to the GCSE. It is based on GCE O-level and was developed by University of Cambridge International Examinations. They began to be counted in the five A*-C measures from 2009/10, but from 2014 onwards, IGCSEs from the AQA and WJEC examination boards were no longer counted as full GCSEs but as approved non-GSCEs.

[4] EBacc is not a qualification in itself but a term applied to the achievement of GCSEs at grades A*-C across a core of academic subjects including: English, maths, history or geography, the sciences and a language.

[5] For the purpose of comparison, the English results (2013/14) reported here are based on the 2013 methodology, that is, without applying Wolf's (DfE and DBIS, 2014) recommendations and early entry policy.

[6] The PISA 2000 and 2003 samples for the UK did not comply with the PISA response rate standards and therefore have not been included for comparison over time.

[7] The participating countries in the UK include England, Scotland and Wales. Northern Ireland did not participate.

[8] Single registration refers to pupils who are on the roll of one school only, whereas dual registration refers to pupils who are enrolled at one main school and one or more additional schools, for example, a Pupil Referral Unit (DfE, 2015m).

[9] The OECD definition of NEET: 'Education includes part-time and full-time education, but excludes non-formal education and educational activities of very short duration. Employment is defined according to the ILO guidelines and covers all those who have been in paid work for at least one hour in the reference week of the survey or were temporarily absent from such work' (OECD, 2015c).

SEVEN

Housing and the environment for children

Deborah Quilgars

Key statistics
- Children are more likely to live in overcrowded housing, but are no more likely to live in non-decent housing than the rest of the population.
- Families are more likely to be living in non-decent housing, and to be less satisfied with their housing, in the private rented sector. Children are most likely to experience overcrowding in social housing.
- Lone parents are at greater risk of experiencing homelessness and living in poor neighbourhoods.
- At the European Union (EU) level, UK households are ranked in the top half of countries on a number of measures of satisfaction with housing and living environment.

Key trends
- UK wide, housing conditions continue to improve over time, although the private rented sector continues to have a higher proportion of poor housing than other tenures.
- Problems in the local environment have also declined over time.
- Officially measured homelessness, as well as prevention of homelessness activity, has increased modestly over the period 2009-15.
- The ending of assured short-hold tenancy has increased three-fold as a reason for homelessness in England since 2009/10.

Key sources
- English Housing Survey (EHS) and other national house condition surveys
- Office for National Statistics (ONS) well-being indicators
- European Union Statistics on Income and Living Conditions (EU-SILC)
- Homelessness and prevention of homelessness statistics

Introduction

This chapter examines the extent to which children live in poor housing and environments, including experiencing homelessness, in the UK. We do not need research to know that children cannot flourish to their full potential if they live in insecure, cramped, damp or dangerous housing or live in environments characterised by noise, crime and pollution. While robust studies are few, reviews conclude that the cumulative evidence of many, often smaller, studies demonstrates a link between poor housing and poorer children's well-being, particularly in terms of impacts on health (Shaw, 2004; Quilgars, 2011; Barnes et al, 2013), as well as longer-term poorer outcomes into adulthood (Marsh et al, 1999). There is also evidence that housing circumstances (such as cost, condition and location) can mitigate the effects of poverty (Tunstall et al, 2013). This chapter begins by reviewing the nature of poor housing in the UK before examining the scale of homelessness affecting families and young people. A third section examines the evidence on poor neighbourhoods and children.

Poor housing

The overall condition of housing, including the extent of repairs, being fit for use, offering thermal comfort and having adequate facilities, is recognised as a key factor in ensuring that all households, irrespective of background, can enjoy a home. In 2000, the Labour government established a policy that aimed to ensure that all social rented homes should reach the 'Decent Homes Standard'[1] by 2010 (HM Treasury, 2000), with a target to increase the proportion of private housing in a decent condition occupied by vulnerable groups added in 2002 (HM Treasury, 2002). The coalition government continued funding for the Decent Homes programme (DCLG/Homes and Communities Agency, 2015).

The respective governments/assemblies in England, Scotland, Wales and Northern Ireland all undertake regular house condition surveys. The surveys, however, are undertaken using different measures, making precise comparisons between countries difficult.

Table 7.1 shows the proportions of houses that fall below the nationally prescribed house condition standards in the four UK nations. In England, 21% of dwellings failed the current definition of the Decent Homes Standard[2] in 2013. This differed considerably by tenure, with 30% of private rented housing failing the Decent Homes Standard compared to 19% of owner-occupied property, while social

Table 7.1: Housing failing nationally prescribed house condition standards

	Number of dwellings (1,000s)	% of dwellings failed specified standards
England	4,785	21% of properties not meeting the Decent Homes standard (2013)
Wales	57	4.1% of properties unfit (2008)
Scotland	71	3% of dwellings below tolerable standard (2013)
Northern Ireland	35	4.6% unfit dwellings (2011)
	37	4.9% lacking at least one basic amenity

Sources: Wilcox et al (2015); DCLG (2015a); Living in Wales 2008, reports on Housing Health and Safety Rating System; Scottish House Condition Survey, 2013; Northern Ireland House Condition Survey 2011 (preliminary findings).

housing had the best condition housing on these measures (16% of local authority and 14% of housing association property). In Scotland, 3% of dwellings were assessed as being 'Below Tolerable Standard'[3] (with no difference between tenures) in 2013. Scottish properties are also assessed by the Scottish Housing Quality Standard (SHQS) (which covers serious disrepair, energy efficiency, lack of modern facilities and services and whether the accommodation is healthy, safe and secure). About half (49%) of properties were measured as falling below SHQS in 2013. Table 7.1 also shows that approximately 4% of Welsh dwellings were defined as unfit in 2008 (including 11% of private rented housing, compared to 4% of owner-occupied housing and 3% of social housing). Just under 5% of Northern Irish dwellings were found to be unfit in 2011.

National surveys show that house conditions have improved considerably over the last two decades. Table 7.2 shows that over a third (35%) of dwellings did not meet the Decent Homes Standard (using the most recent definition, see earlier) in 2006, and this has improved year on year to only a fifth (21%) failing the standard in 2013. Figure 7.1, based on Table 7.2, shows that improvements have occurred in all tenures, although there have been faster improvements in social rented housing (a 49% change over the period) and slowest in the private rented sector (a 36% change over the period). In Wales, unfitness rates reduced from 13% of stock in 1993 to 4% in 2008. In Northern Ireland, the proportion of unfit properties reduced at a slower rate, from 7% in 1996 to 5% in 2011. It is not possible to compare the proportion of properties Below Tolerable Standard in Scotland over the same period due to the definition being changed in 2010 (to add thermal performance and electrical safety); however, the proportion not meeting the original standard had decreased from 1% in

Table 7.2: Decent Homes trends, 2006-13

Proportion of all dwellings that did not meet the Decent Homes standard

	2006	2007	2008	2009	2010	2011	2012	2013
Owner-occupied	34.4	34.1	32.3	29.3	25.6	22.3	20.3	19.4
Private rented	46.7	45.4	44.0	40.8	37.2	35.0	33.1	29.8
All private	**36.2**	**35.8**	**34.4**	**31.5**	**27.9**	**25.0**	**23.1**	**21.8**
Local authority	32.2	32.8	31.5	27.1	21.7	17.7	16.3	15.7
Housing association	25.0	25.8	22.8	19.7	18.3	15.9	14.3	14.0
All social	**28.8**	**29.4**	**27.2**	**23.2**	**19.9**	**16.8**	**15.2**	**14.7**
All tenures	**34.9**	**34.7**	**33.1**	**30.1**	**26.5**	**23.6**	**21.8**	**20.6**
Dwellings (000s)	**7,670**	**7,690**	**7,360**	**6,722**	**5,937**	**5,364**	**4,947**	**4,785**

Note: 2006 figures differ from those originally published following subsequent improvements to the modelling.

Sources: Table DT3101 (SST3.1), www.gov.uk/government/statistical-data-sets/dwelling-condition-and-safety

2001-07: English House Condition Survey, dwelling sample

2008 onwards: EHS, dwelling sample

Figure 7.1: Trends in the proportions of all dwellings that did not meet the Decent Homes standard by tenure type, England, 2006-13,

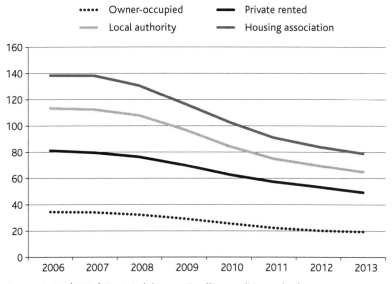

Sources: DCLG (2013a) Statistical data set: Dwelling condition and safety (Table DA3203 (SST3.4) Decent Homes – households, 2013), available at: www.gov.uk/government/statistical-data-sets/dwelling-condition-and-safety

2001-07: English House Condition Survey, dwelling sample

1996 to 0.6% in 2008, and from 3.6% to 3% using the new definition from 2010 to 2013. The proportion of properties failing the SHQS had fallen from 72% in 2003 to 49% in 2013.

Household characteristics

The English Housing Survey (EHS) 2013 (DCLG, 2013a) showed that couples with children were slightly less likely to be living in non-Decent Homes than other household types (17% compared to 21%, and 20% of lone parents) (see Table 7.3). In particular, households with children were more likely to live in homes with adequate thermal comfort.[4] Households with young children were slightly more likely to be in better condition housing than households with older children. A visual summary of the types of households living in poor housing conditions is given in Figure 7.2.

However, the EHS also showed that households living in poverty (irrespective of household type) were more likely to be in non-Decent Homes (26% compared to 19% of those not in poverty). Although the data is somewhat dated, analysis of the EHS 2008 (DCLG, 2010a) recorded that households with children living in poverty were substantially more likely to be living in homes in serious disrepair (19% compared to 12% of households with children not living in poverty), or homes with serious condensation (10% compared to 5%).[5] Lone parents (irrespective of poverty status) were the most likely type of household to live in homes in serious disrepair (17% compared to 11%).

The EHS 2013 also examined damp housing in more detail. In England, about 1 million dwellings (4%) had a problem with damp in 2013 (DCLG, 2015a), with the private rented sector having the highest incidence (8%). Crucially, households with a child under five (6%), households in poverty (7%) and minority ethnic households (9%) were more likely to have problems with damp.

The disproportionate amount of poor housing in the private rented sector is a particular concern as families with children are increasingly living in this sector: while 23% of couples and lone-parent households with dependent children lived in this type of tenure in 2003-04, this had risen to 35% in 2013-14 (DCLG, 2015b). The EHS also recorded a lower level of subjective housing satisfaction among families in the private rented sector: only 76% of couples with dependent children and 78% of lone parents were satisfied with their accommodation, compared to 85% of couples and 86% of single people (82% overall) (DCLG, 2015b).

Table 7.3: Households failing Decent Homes criteria, England, 2013

				Failed Decent Homes criteria			
	Non-decent	Minimum standard[1]	Repair	Modern facilities/ services	Thermal comfort	All households in group (1,000s)	Sample size (unweighted)
			% household within group				
Household composition							
Couple under 60	18.3	11.5	3.4	1.1	6.4	4,183	1,778
Couple 60 or over	17.6	10.1	3.3	1.2	6.0	4,006	1,787
Couple with children	17.3	11.6	3.2	0.8	4.2	4,719	2,509
Lone parent	19.6	11.7	4.5	1.4	4.2	1,635	1,373
Multi-person household	25.0	15.4	6.5	1.9	8.1	1,847	974
One person under 60	25.1	11.4	5.7	3.3	12.4	2,788	1,589
One person 60 or over	22.6	11.4	5.4	4.4	8.9	3,405	1,998
Age of youngest person							
Under 5 years	18.1	10.8	4.2	1.0	4.5	2,760	1,885
Under 16 years	18.6	12.0	3.6	1.0	4.5	6,015	3,741
16 years or more	20.7	11.4	4.5	2.2	7.8	16,568	8,267
Living in poverty							
In poverty	25.6	14.0	5.9	3.8	10.7	2,952	1,897
Not in poverty	19.3	11.2	4.0	1.6	6.4	19,631	10,111

(continued)

Table 7.3: Households failing Decent Homes criteria, England, 2013 (continued)

Ethnicity of HRP	Non-decent	Minimum standard[1]	Repair	Modern facilities/ services	Thermal comfort	All households in group (1,000s)	Sample size (unweighted)
				Failed Decent Homes criteria			
			% household within group				
White	19.7	11.4	4.1	1.8	6.9	20,191	10,691
Black	25.0	15.2	5.3	2.1	9.9	679	441
Asian	22.9	12.8	6.4	1.9	5.1	1,122	522
Other	21.9	10.9	5.2	3.7	8.1	590	354
All minority	23.3	13.0	5.8	2.4	7.2	2,392	1,317
All households	20.1	11.6	4.3	1.9	7.0	22,583	12,008

Notes: [1]Dwellings failing the minimum standard are those posing a Category 1 hazard under the Housing Health and Safety Rating System (HHSRS). From 2008 the survey is able to estimate the presence of 26 of the 29 HHSRS hazards. However to maintain consistency and avoid a break in the time series from 2006, Decent Homes estimates continue be based on 15 hazards for the 'minimum standard' criterion. Estimates for the HHSRS (SST 4.1-4.3) are based on the 26 hazards covered by the survey.

Source: Table DA3203 (SST3.4): Decent Homes – households, 2013, www.gov.uk/government/statistical-data-sets/dwelling-condition-and-safety

Figure 7.2: Distribution of households living in properties that failed the Decent Homes criteria

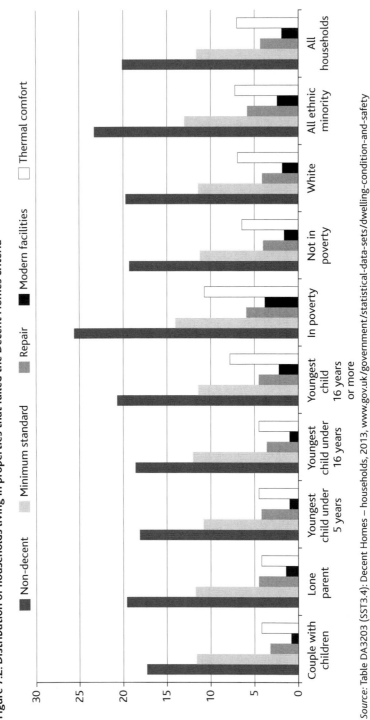

Source: Table DA3203 (SST3.4): Decent Homes – households, 2013, www.gov.uk/government/statistical-data-sets/dwelling-condition-and-safety

A recent academic study that re-analysed the EHS 2010-11 (Barnes et al, 2013) examined 'bad housing' that they defined as either a non-Decent Home *or* an overcrowded home (using the 'bedroom standard' approach[6]). They found that:

- over 975,000 children (39%) living in social rented housing are living in bad housing
- about 845,000 children (41%) living in private rented housing are living in bad housing
- over 1.7 million children (23%) living in owner-occupied housing are living in bad housing.

As reported earlier, children were most likely to be in non-Decent Homes in the private rented sector (34% of children compared to 20% in social rented and owner-occupied housing in 2010). However, children were more likely to be overcrowded in social rented housing (26% compared to 13% in private rented sector and 4% in owner-occupied; see Figure 7.3). Children were much more likely to live in overcrowded housing compared with working-age adults and pensioners (10%, 5% and 1%, respectively) (Barnes et al, 2013), with an estimated over 1.2 million children living in overcrowded housing in 2010. This highlights that overcrowding is a key aspect of housing that requires monitoring for children's well-being.

Figure 7.3: Percentage of children living in various housing conditions, England, 2010

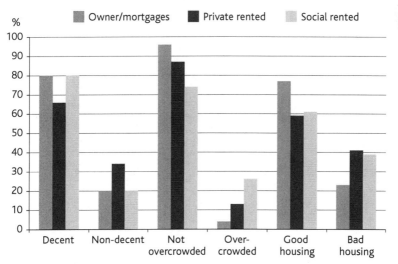

Source: EHS, 2010-11 in Barnes et al (2013)

The ONS measures of well-being include five indicators related to where children live, including the proportion of children and young people who have a relatively high level of satisfaction with their accommodation. The most recent report (ONS, 2014a), utilising data from The Children's Society *Good childhood report 2010*, recorded that approaching two-thirds (64%) of children aged 8-15 rated their happiness with their accommodation as high, while 7% rated their happiness with accommodation as very low.

European comparisons

At a European level, EU-SILC collects basic information on housing conditions and facilities on an annual basis, and periodically includes a longer housing module that includes a measure of overcrowding and an overall measure of satisfaction with the dwelling (the last module was in 2012). Analysis allows a comparison between those households at risk of poverty (defined as those with incomes under 60% of the national median) and households not at risk of poverty. Table 7.4 shows that, across Europe, households at risk of poverty are on average about twice as likely to be overcrowded (23% compared to 12%) and/ or in severe housing deprivation (9% compared to 4%) than those in total population (EC, 2014). However, Table 7.4 also shows that the UK has lower levels of poor housing on both these measures compared to the European average (12% compared to 7% overcrowding and 4% compared to 2% severe housing deprivation). Overall, levels of satisfaction with housing are also higher than the EU average (94% compared to 90%), although they fell between 2007 and 2012, whereas satisfaction rates increased Europe-wide from a lower base.

Table 7.4: Measures of housing quality, EU-SILC, 2012

(% of specified population)	Overcrowding rate, 2012		Severe housing deprivation, 2012		Share of population reporting satisfied/ very satisfied with dwelling, 2012	
	Total population	Population at-risk-of-poverty[1]	Total population	Population at-risk-of-poverty[1]	2007	2012
U-28	17	29.2	5.1	12.6	83.1	89.3
EU-28	11.7	23.3	3.5	8.6	86.8	90.0
UK	7.0	13.6	2	4.2	93.7	94.3

Note: [1] Population below 60% of median equivalised income.

Source: Figure 5, Figure 7, Figure 12, http://ec.europa.eu/eurostat/statistics-explained/index.php/Housing_conditions#Main_tables

The UNICEF Innocenti Report Card no 11 (2013), that produced an international league table of child well-being, included a 'housing and environment' dimension. This study used two measures of housing – rooms per person and multiple housing problems (as well as two measures of environmental safety – the homicide rate and air pollution, see later in this chapter). This composite score placed the UK 10th out of 29 countries on housing and environment, a slightly higher ranking than its overall rank of 16 across five domains (housing and environment was higher than all other domains: material well-being; health and safety; education; behaviours and risk).

The recent Children's Worlds survey, 2013-14 (Rees and Main, 2015), completed by over 53,000 school children in 15 countries, asked children to rate their level of satisfaction with 'the house or flat where you live'.[7] The UK was ranked joint 8th on this measure with a mean satisfaction of 8.9 out of 10 (see Figure 7.4).

Homelessness

In the UK, local authorities have a legal responsibility to rehouse (and find temporary accommodation in the meantime) for families with children who are found to be 'statutorily homeless'. Households are considered homeless if they have no accommodation, or none they can reasonably occupy (for example, without threat of violence or abuse). Under the homelessness legislation in England, Wales and Northern Ireland, homeless families with dependent children are accepted as being 'in priority need' and will therefore receive assistance with rehousing, providing they can also demonstrate a local connection (unless they are moving as a result of violence) and that they are not homeless intentionally. Following legislative change in the early 2000s, 16- and 17-year-olds and care leavers aged between 18 and 20 are now considered to be in priority need in England and Wales.[8] Other young people between 18 and 25 may be accepted as being in priority need only if they can demonstrate that they are 'vulnerable'.[9] From 31 December 2012, all people facing homelessness through no fault of their own (assessed as unintentionally homeless) have a right to settled accommodation in Scotland.[10]

Incidence of family homelessness in the UK

The main statistical sources on the incidence of family homelessness in the UK are the returns submitted quarterly by local authorities to Department of Communities and Local Government (CLG), the

Figure 7.4: Level of satisfaction with 'the house or flat where you live' by country (10- and 12-year-old surveys, all countries, equally weighted by age group)

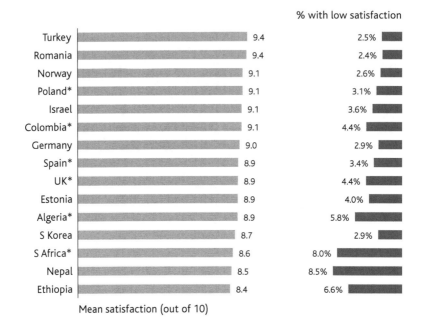

% with low satisfaction

Country	Mean satisfaction	% with low satisfaction
Turkey	9.4	2.5%
Romania	9.4	2.4%
Norway	9.1	2.6%
Poland*	9.1	3.1%
Israel	9.1	3.6%
Colombia*	9.1	4.4%
Germany	9.0	2.9%
Spain*	8.9	3.4%
UK*	8.9	4.4%
Estonia	8.9	4.0%
Algeria*	8.9	5.8%
S Korea	8.7	2.9%
S Africa*	8.6	8.0%
Nepal	8.5	8.5%
Ethiopia	8.4	6.6%

Mean satisfaction (out of 10)

Note: * Signifies countries where the sample only covers a region of the country.
Source: Figure 25 in Rees and Main (2015, p 52)

Welsh Assembly Housing Directorate, the Scottish Government and the Northern Ireland Housing Executive.

Figure 7.5 shows homelessness acceptances in England, Scotland and Wales since 2000. Following a height of 188,162 in 2003, numbers of households accepted declined steadily to half of the 2003 figure of 91,926 in 2009. Since 2010, numbers have shown modest increases to just under 100,000 households in 2013. Examining homelessness acceptances for the three countries separately, it can be seen that this trend has been driven largely by changes in the levels of homelessness acceptances in England (and to a lesser extent, Wales). The pattern is reversed in Scotland, with numbers increasing (relatively modestly) from 20,600 in 2000 to a height of 37,257 in 2009, with some reductions in numbers since this date. Unfortunately, it cannot be presumed that the incidence of homelessness has increased to a greater extent in Scotland than England and Wales, as there has been considerable policy change over the period. First, the introduction of more generous homelessness legislation, particularly the extension

Figure 7.5: Local authority homeless acceptances (all homeless acceptances)

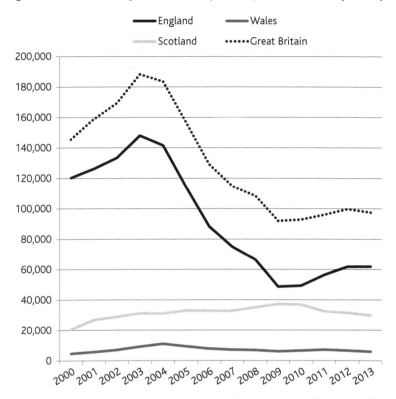

Notes: Scottish figures are for priority need homeless (until 2013 when this was abolished) and potentially homeless cases only, and figures from 2000 onwards are for financial years (i.e. 2000/01, etc).

Source: Wilcox et al (2015)

of priority need categories in the early 2000s, will have accounted for some of the rises at this time. Second, and more influentially, in England (and to a lesser extent, Wales), a prevention agenda was actively pursued from the mid-2000s onwards with local authorities attempting to assist (potentially) homeless households through a 'housing options' approach which obviates the need for a homelessness assessment to be undertaken (Fitzpatrick et al, 2009). A preventative agenda has also been adopted more recently in Scotland. Further, a 2014 survey reported that 81% of local authority respondents agreed that the emphasis on preventing homelessness 'had further increased since 2010' (Fitzpatrick et al, 2015). Qualitative analysis by the same authors also indicate that an increasing shift towards local authorities adopting new powers to discharge their statutory duty via an offer of a private tenancy has incentivised applicants to opt for 'informal' assistance rather than make a statutory application. It has therefore been suggested that statutory homelessness figures are becoming an increasingly unreliable indicator of the scale of homelessness (Fitzpatrick et al, 2015).

Figure 7.6 shows the homeless presentations and acceptances in Northern Ireland from 2000/01-2013/14.[11] As can be seen, there was a significant increase in the number of presentations in the early 2000s, from 12,694 in 2000/01 to a height of 20,121 in 2005/06, with a small decrease since then. The number of households awarded priority status also increased, but at a slower pace, from 6,457 households in 2000/01 to over 9,000 from 2005/06 onwards.

CLG homelessness statistics[12] indicate that homeless families represent a majority of homeless households accepted as in priority need in England. In 2014, 67% of households were accepted as a result of having dependent children, with a further 7% of households containing a pregnant woman. A further 3% of households were vulnerable young people (16- and 17-year-olds and 18- to 20-year-old care leavers). The proportion of families appears to have risen

Figure 7.6: Homeless presenters and acceptances, Northern Ireland, 2000/01-2009/10

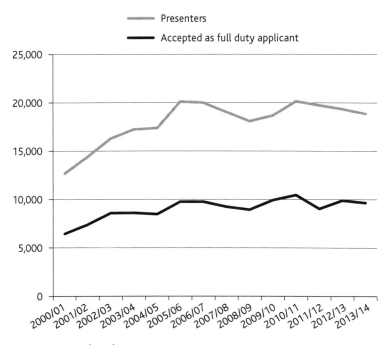

Source: Wilcox et al (2015)

recently, recorded at between 50-60% in the decade up to 2010. A higher proportion of households were young people (7-9%) in the mid-2000s, following the extension of priority need categories to include 16- and 17-year-olds but prior to the House of Lords (*R(G) v Southwark LBC* ruling in May 2009, which clarified the responsibility of children's services for accommodating homeless young people aged 16 and 17 under the Children Act 1989.

The proportion of families with children accepted as homeless is lower in other nations than in England. In Wales, in 2014/15, 36% of those households in priority need included dependent children, a further 6% included pregnant women (no other children) and 7% were vulnerable young people.[13] In Scotland, only 26% of households found homeless in 2014/15 had children (21% single parents, 5% couples with children), with 4% of homeless households being under the age of 18. This proportion has fallen since the abolition of priority need status; for example, in 2009/10, 35% of those households found priority homeless included children, with a further 6% of priority need acceptances being single people under the age of 18.[14]

In Northern Ireland, 32% of households presenting as homeless were families with children in 2014/15, with a further 2% being 16- and 17-year-olds.[15]

Homelessness prevention

CLG figures show that there were over 200,000 cases of homelessness prevention and relief in England in 2013/14 and 2014/15 (see Table 7.5), with increases in figures from 2009/10 to 2013/14. This data indicates that over three times as many households are being assisted in this way as the statutory homelessness route in England. About half of this activity involved helping households to remain in their existing accommodation, following a range of assistance including mediation, financial payments from a homeless prevention fund, debt advice, resolving housing benefit or rent problems and negotiation or legal advocacy enabling household to remain in the private sector. The other half of the activity assisted households to access alternative accommodation – this included social housing and private rented sector accommodation as well as temporary accommodation, including hostels or houses in multiple occupation (HMO), supported accommodation, and accommodation with friends or relatives. No breakdown is available by household type for England.

Prevention statistics in Scotland recorded 58,825 approaches to the housing options prevention service between April 2014 and March

Table 7.5: Outcome of homelessness prevention and relief, England, 2009/10-2014/15

	Total cases of prevention and relief	of which:				of which (prevention cases) household was:			
		Number of cases where positive action was successful in relieving homelessness	% of grand total	Number of cases where positive action was successful in preventing homelessness	% of grand total	Assisted to obtain alternative accommodation	% of prevention total	Able to remain in existing home	% of prevention total
2009/10	165,200	24,300	15	140,900	85	76,500	54	64,400	46
2010/11	188,800	24,800	13	164,100	87	82,300	50	81,800	50
2011/12	199,000	24,200	12	174,800	88	88,800	51	86,000	49
2012/13	202,900	21,000	10	181,900	90	87,200	48	94,700	52
2013/14 R	228,400	18,500	8	209,900	92	98,000	47	111,900	53
2014/15 P	220,800	15,700	7	205,100	93	95,900	47	109,200	53

Notes:

Figures reflect households where homelessness has been prevented or relieved under the Homelessness Act 2002 during the 2009/10, 2010/11, 2011/12, 2012/13, 2013/14 and 2014/15 financial years.

P = Provisional data; R = Revised data

Total figures are rounded to the nearest 100. Totals may not equal the sum of components because of rounding. Totals include estimated data to account for non-response.

Source: CLG P1E Homelessness returns (quarterly): www.gov.uk/government/collections/homelessness-statistics

2015. Here, data is collected on household type. Of these, 10,640 approaches (18% of all approaches) were from households with children, most of whom were single-parent households (13% of all approaches).

Number of children in temporary accommodation

Statistics are collected on the number of families and other households who are living in temporary accommodation while awaiting rehousing under the homelessness legislation. At the end of the first quarter of 2015 (31 March 2015), 64,710 households were recorded as in temporary accommodation in England.[16] This was a rise from 48,240 in the first quarter of 2011. This recent rise, coinciding with austerity measures, marked a change from the previous five years where numbers had fallen from 100,000 in 2004/05.

Of those in temporary accommodation on 31 March 2015, 48,880 households (76%) contained children or expected children (a total of 93,320 children or expected children). A particularly high proportion of households (44%) were lone parent households/expecting a child. The vast majority (88%) of households were in self-contained accommodation (mainly private sector leased housing). Since March 2004 English local authorities have only been able to place families in bed and breakfast (B&B) accommodation in emergency situations and for up to six weeks. Only 5% of households with children (2,570 families) were in B&B accommodation on 31 March 2015; however, 36% of these had been staying there for over six weeks. This represented an increase of over 100% from the first quarter of 2014.

In Scotland, as at 31 March 2015, 2,662 households with children were in temporary accommodation.[17] This represented 25% of the total number in temporary accommodation (10,488 households). Total numbers of households in temporary accommodation have remained fairly stable since 2010, but numbers of families have fallen from 3,714 in first quarter of 2010. Only 1% (266) families) were B&B accommodation, with the vast majority (88%) in social sector self-contained accommodation.

In Wales, there were 2,050 households in temporary accommodation on 31 March 2015.[18] Overall numbers have fallen since 2008-09 when there were 2,815 households in temporary accommodation. Private sector housing is the largest single type of accommodation used, but public sector and hostels are also used. There were only 10 families with children placed in B&B accommodation at the end of March

2015 (with no more than 30 families being in B&B accommodation at any one time since 2009).

Number of young homeless people

It was estimated that at least 78,000–80,000 young people (aged 16–24) experienced homelessness in 2008/09 (Quilgars et al, 2011; see Table 7.6). This estimate included young people accepted under the homelessness legislation (both single young people and young families), estimates of people sleeping rough, Supporting People data on those living in transitional and temporary accommodation and CORE data on social lets to homeless young people. While changes to data sources make direct comparison invalid, it was estimated that around 83,000 young people were accommodated by local authorities or homelessness services in the UK in 2013/14 (Clarke et al, 2015). There is also evidence of increased pressure on homelessness services (Homeless Link, 2014), with provision for young people at risk of homelessness (alongside other vulnerable groups) being cut back under austerity measures. Moving young people on from the sector is increasingly difficult, with fewer social tenancies and high competition for private lets (Homeless Link, 2014), leading to young people becoming stuck in expensive transitional accommodation schemes (Quilgars et al, 2011). Youth homelessness has received very little policy attention in recent years (Rugg and Quilgars, 2015), and the numbers of young people following a chaotic housing pathway is predicted to increase up to 2020 (Rugg, 2010; Clapham et al, 2012).

Table 7.6: Estimate of total youth homelessness in 2008/9

Type of homelessness	England	Scotland	Wales	Northern Ireland	UK
Statutorily homeless	21,270	12,601	2,698		39,019
Non-statutorily homeless households by social landlords	3,472	745	No data	No data	4,217
Non-statutorily homeless households using housing support services	32,900	No data	No data	No data	32,900
Young people sleeping rough	3,200	600	No data	No data	3,800
Total	60,842	13,946	2,698	2,450	79,936

Source: Table 2.5 from Quilgars et al (2011). Reported and grossed P1E statistics (England), HL1 statistics (Scotland), WHO-12 statistics (Wales), Northern Ireland Housing Executive. England, Scotland and Wales place 16- to 17-year-olds in priority need or preference groups on the basis of their age, whereas Northern Ireland does not. Partly estimated due to some data not being available at the time of writing.

Concealed family homelessness

Based on the Labour Force Survey, in 2013, there were about 4.64 million households (21%) that contained additional households who might be regarded as a potential separate household. Only a small proportion (1.2%) was couples or lone-parent families living with other households (Fitzpatrick et al, 2015).

Causes of family homelessness

Homelessness is most often understood to be an outcome of a dynamic interaction between structural factors (such as poverty, economic conditions, inadequate welfare payments or lack of affordable housing) and personal circumstances (such as relationship breakdown or domestic violence) (Pleace, 2000). Recent welfare benefit reforms have been implicated in the causation of homelessness, including the Local Housing Allowance caps in reducing access for low-income families to the private rented sector in high value areas (particularly London) and, to a lesser extent, the 'spare room subsidy limit' (widely known as the 'bedroom tax') which limits eligible rents for households in the social rented sector that have more than the 'bedroom standard' of rooms. These, along with other welfare reforms such as the introduction of Universal Credit, are not thought to have run their full course yet (Fitzpatrick et al, 2015).

Homelessness statistics in England reveal that three in ten (29%) of households accepted as homeless had lost their last settled home due to the ending of an assured shorthold tenancy with a private landlord in the first quarter of 2015 (and as high as 38% in London). This reason for homelessness has risen substantially since 2009/10 when it only accounted for 11% of all cases, and clearly points to a structural issue of short-term tenancies in the private rented sector leading to insecurity for households. The next most common reason for losing the last settled home was people no longer being able or willing to provide accommodation (parents – 14% of homeless acceptances; friends or other relatives – 12%). This was followed by relationship breakdown with a partner (17% including 5% that involved violence). Mortgage arrears only accounted for 1% of acceptances, and rent arrears for 3% of acceptances.

The Scottish government collect data on slightly different reasons for homelessness. It should be remembered that a lower proportion of homeless households are families in Scotland than in England. Here, a high proportion of applicants apply as homeless due to a dispute within the household (29% of all applications in 2014-15) or being asked to leave (25% of 2014-15 applications). Rent arrears or mortgage defaults account for around 6% of all homelessness applications in 2014-15, and other actions by landlords leading to the end of a tenancy accounted for 10%.

The last representative survey of statutorily homeless families, conducted in England in the mid-2000s (Pleace et al, 2008), found that nearly four in ten families (38%) cited relationship breakdown as the main reason for applying as homeless, with 13% citing violent relationship breakdown. Other reasons included the end of a tenancy or eviction (26%), overcrowding (24%) and 'outstaying their welcome/could no longer be accommodated' (20%). Eviction/loss of private dwelling was most commonly reported as the reason for applying as homeless in areas of highest housing stress. The same survey also included interviews with a representative sample of homeless 16- and 17-year-olds. Here, the overwhelming reason for applying as homeless (70%) was relationship breakdown, almost always with parents/stepparents. Subsequent analysis of this survey (Quilgars et al, 2008) revealed that the homeless young people had often had unstable and/or traumatic childhoods, including family disruption, witnessing or experiencing violence within the family home, living in a family that experienced financial difficulties, disrupted education and/or spending time in care.

European comparisons

The European Observatory on Homelessness has attempted to estimate the extent and profile of homelessness in European member states; however, the varying measures used across countries and lack of data mean that comparisons are difficult, if not impossible (Busch-Geertsema et al, 2014). A conceptual framework, the European Typology of Homelessness and Housing Exclusion (ETHOS), has been developed and may offer a way forward in the collection of data in the future. However, at present, few countries collect data on family homelessness, being more likely to focus on populations sleeping rough or single people living in hostels. Notwithstanding these caveats, an examination of available data across Europe found that homelessness is recorded as having increased recently in 24 out of 28 European countries (variable in three countries and down in one country, Finland) (Pleace, 2015).

Poor environments

From 2009-10 to 2011-12, the EHS provided some basic information on the types of problems in the local environment through surveyors' assessments and observations in three areas: upkeep problems, traffic and utilisation problems.[19] The 2011 report on dwellings (DCLG, 2013b) showed that problems had declined over time: 20% of dwellings had at least one of these problems in 2001 compared to 14% of dwellings in 2011; reductions had occurred across all domains, and also across all tenures (see Figure 7.7). However, improvements in some tenures had been better than others, in particular, the proportion of local authority housing with upkeep problems had reduced from 20% to 12% over 2001-11, compared to 17% to 13% in the private rented sector. In 2011, private rented housing had the highest proportion of environmental problems in all domains. Again, this is concerning given the increasing numbers of families living in the private rented sector.

The EHS 2011 showed that minority ethnic households were more likely to live in areas with environmental problems (19%), although this had fallen from 37% in 2001. Similarly, households living in poverty were more likely to live in areas with environmental problems (17%); this had also reduced, but less steeply, from 23% in 2001 (DCLG, 2013b).

Figure 7.7: Types of problems in the local environment by tenure, 2001 and 2011

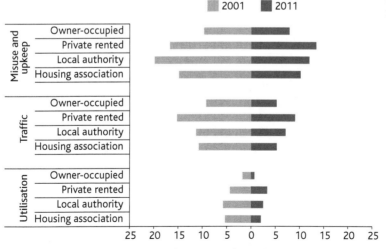

Source: Figure 2.18, EHS (dwelling sample) 2011; DCLG (2013b)

The last analysis of environmental problems by family household type appeared in the 2008-09 EHS (CLG, 2010a, 2010b). Table 7.7 shows that households with children were slightly more likely to be living in the worst neighbourhoods[20] compared to households without children (12% compared to 9%). However, lone parents were much more likely to live in the worst neighbourhoods (20%). A considerable difference was also observed between poor and non-poor households with children, with 22% of the former living in the worst neighbourhoods compared to 10% of the latter.

When households were asked to rate their satisfaction with their local area,[21] lone parents were much more likely to be dissatisfied with their local area than other household types (16% compared to 9% of all households) (CLG, 2010c) (see Table 7.8). Couples with dependent children were no more or less likely to be dissatisfied with their area than all households. A similar finding was found for reports of serious

Table 7.7: Households with children (aged 0-15) by poor living conditions

	% of group living in worst neighbourhoods	Number of households (000s)
All households		
Households with children:		
Lone parent	19.8	1,241
Couple or multi-person	10.2	4,475
All households with children	12.3	5,716
Households with no children	9.2	15,691
All households	**10.0**	**21,407**
Households in poverty		
Households with children:		
Lone parent	24.8	452
Couple or multi-person	20.7	714
All households with children	22.3	1,166
Households with no children	13.7	2,635
All households in poverty	**16.3**	**3,801**
Households not in poverty		
Households with children:		
Lone parent	16.9	790
Couple or multi-person	8.2	3,761
All households with children	9.7	4,550
Households with no children	8.3	13,056
All households not in poverty	**8.6**	**17,606**

Source: EHS 2008, household sub-sample

Table 7.8: Household type of those satisfied/dissatisfied with local area

All households[1]

Household type	Very satisfied	Fairly satisfied	All satisfied	Neither satisfied nor dissatisfied	Slightly dissatisfied	Very dissatisfied	All dissatisfied
Couple under 60	48.9	38.3	87.2	4.7	6.1	2.0	8.1
Couple aged 60 or over	60.8	30.2	91.0	2.5	4.6	1.9	6.5
Couple, dependent child(ren)	50.4	36.3	86.7	5.1	5.5	2.7	8.2
Lone parent, dependent child(ren)	40.6	36.4	77.0	6.9	8.7	7.4	16.1
Other multi-person households	48.0	36.0	83.9	6.2	6.8	3.1	9.8
One person under 60	46.2	39.2	85.4	5.6	6.3	2.7	9.0
One person aged 60 or over	60.7	29.2	89.9	3.0	5.2	1.8	7.1
Total	51.9	35.0	86.9	4.6	5.8	2.7	8.5

Note: [1] Excludes households that did not respond to question.

Source: EHS 2008-09, full household sample, reported in DCLG (2010a), Annex tables

Base: 21,530 households (100%)

issues in the local area with lone parents (and single people under 60) most likely to report issues as being a problem.

ONS (2014a, 2014b) measures of well-being include four indicators related to the local area where children live, including:

- proportion of children/young people who have been a victim of crime in the last year
- proportion of children/young people who feel safe walking alone in their neighbourhood after dark
- proportion of children who like living in their neighbourhood/ proportion of young people who agreed/agreed strongly that they belonged to their neighbourhood
- proportion of children/young people who have accessed the natural environment at least once a week in the last year.

According to the Crime Survey for England and Wales, 2013-14, around 12% of children aged 10-15 reported being a victim of crime at least once between April 2013 and March 2014, with violent crime the most common type of crime experienced (ONS, 2014a). A higher proportion, 25%, of young people aged 16-24, were victims of crime over the same period, although this had reduced from 37% in 2006-07 (ONS, 2014b).

Just over half (56%) of children aged 10-15 reported (in the UK Household Longitudinal Survey) that they felt very or fairly safe when walking alone in their area after dark. Boys were more likely to feel very or fairly safe than girls (63% and 49%, respectively) (ONS, 2014a). According to the 2013-14 Crime Survey, 70% of young people aged 16-24 felt very or fairly safe walking alone in their local area after dark (85% of men and 54% of women) (ONS, 2014b).

In 2011–12, 88% of 10- to 15-year-olds liked the neighbourhood they lived in (UK Household Longitudinal Study). In addition, of those who liked their neighbourhood, 90% were satisfied with their lives overall compared with 75% of those who did not like their neighbourhood (ONS, 2014a). Data from the same survey reported that nearly 90% of 16- to 24-year-olds reported that they liked their neighbourhood (similar to the proportion of all adults, 94%) (ONS, 2014b). A lower proportion, 49%, of 16- to 24-year-olds felt that they belonged to their neighbourhood (compared to nearly two-thirds [63%] of all adults aged 16 and over). As with those aged 10-15, those who felt they belonged to the neighbourhood were more likely to be satisfied with their life overall.

The *Monitor of Engagement with the Natural Environment*, published by Natural England (2013), reported that around 62% of 16- to 24-year-olds in England visited the natural environment at least once a week in 2012-13 (compared to about 55% of all adults during the same period).

European comparisons

At the European level, the EU-SILC collects respondent experiences of two main types of environmental problems – exposure to pollution, grime and other environmental problems (as well as recording exposure to air pollution by PM10 [particles]) and noise from neighbours or the street – as well as data on overall satisfaction with the living environment and recreational or green areas (EC, 2015). The reported incidence on both these indicators has decreased over the last decade. One in seven (14%) EU respondents reported being exposed to pollution in 2013, but this was substantially lower at 8% in the UK (ranked 8th out of 28). One in five (19%) EU respondents reported problems with noise in 2013 – a slightly lower proportion (17%) of UK respondents reported this problem (ranked 16th out of 28) (see Table 7.9). Just under one in five (19%) declared a low level of satisfaction with overall living environment – this was the case for only 11% of UK respondents (ranked 9th out of 28). In most countries,

Table 7.9: Environmental problems and satisfaction with environment in Europe

	Low satisfaction with environment	Low satisfaction with green areas	Reporting pollution, grime or other environmental problems	Reporting noise from neighbours or from the street	Average urban population exposure to air pollution by PM10[1]
	(% of the total population aged over 16)				(µg/m³)
EU-28	19.2	22.4	14.4	19.0	24.9
Netherlands	4.0	3.2	14.6	24.1	21.0
Belgium	7.5	14.7	17.5	17.5	24.8
Finland	9.0	4.4	8.4	13.4	11.0
Luxembourg	9.2	11.6	12.6	18.5	17.8
Austria	9.5	12.9	11.0	18.9	22.4
Ireland	10.1	19.6	4.6	9.4	14.0
France	10.7	19.4	12.0	16.7	23.7
Denmark	10.8	9.0	6.2	16.5	17.4
United Kingdom	11.3	16.5	8.3	17.0	18.1
Lithuania	13.0	17.8	15.6	14.1	20.6
Sweden	13.8	7.1	8.0	12.4	14.3
Romania	14.6	19.9	17.5	26.5	33.0
Germany	15.9	17.9	22.4	26.1	19.8
Spain	17.4	27.4	9.8	18.3	23.9
Slovenia	17.6	14.7	15.3	12.3	25.4
Czech Republic	17.8	19.5	15.8	14.9	27.5
Poland	18.2	19.5	11.0	14.0	36.6
Latvia	19.1	15.6	18.5	14.8	22.8
Malta	22.8	32.0	40.3	31.2	:
Slovakia	28.3	29.8	14.7	15.1	28.9
Estonia	28.5	25.7	9.7	10.8	12.7
Hungary	31.7	37.9	14.1	12.5	28.8
Italy	35.6	33.5	17.1	18.2	30.0
Croatia	36.5	40.2	26.5	24.2	:
Cyprus	37.3	39.1	15.7	26.2	36.4
Portugal	37.8	41.9	14.8	22.7	23.6
Croatia	39.7	462	6.8	10.0	:
Bulgaria	59.0	58.0	14.5	11.1	45.9
Norway	6.1	7.2	7.6	11.7	16.1
Switzerland	12.0	7.7	9.0	15.7	19.2
Iceland	14.2	10.5	9.9	11.6	8.7
Serbia	58.4	52.5	18.7	12.7	44.3

Note: [1] 2012 instead of 2013 data

Source: EC (2015, Table 1)

people at risk of poverty (defined as those with incomes under 60% of the national median) were more likely to report environmental problems than those not at risk of poverty. Environmental problems were also associated with lower subjective well-being.

The Children's Worlds survey, 2013-214 (Rees and Main, 2015) asked children a number of questions about their satisfaction with their local area (including with people in the area, police, doctors and outdoor areas) as well as an overall question on how satisfied they were with 'the area you live in general'. The UK was ranked joint 9th on this measure with a mean satisfaction of 8.4 out of 10 (see Figure 7.8).

The UNICEF (2013) league table of child well-being included two measures of environmental safety – the homicide rate (annual number of homicides per 100,000) and air pollution (annual PM10; see also Table 7.9) – within the 'housing and environment' dimension (see earlier). While recognising that these two measures are very different, and that the homicide rate can only be an approximate guide to overall levels of violence in a society, it represents a first attempt at including children's environmental well-being internationally. In terms of the

Figure 7.8: Level of satisfaction with 'the area you live in general' by country (10- and 12-year-old surveys, all countries, equally weighted by age group)

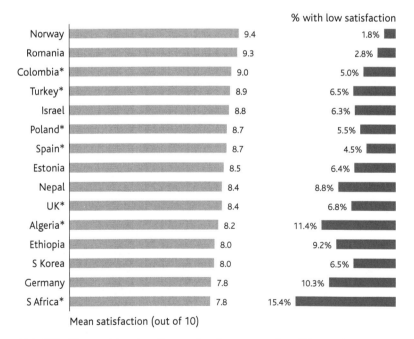

	Mean satisfaction (out of 10)	% with low satisfaction
Norway	9.4	1.8%
Romania	9.3	2.8%
Colombia*	9.0	5.0%
Turkey*	8.9	6.5%
Israel	8.8	6.3%
Poland*	8.7	5.5%
Spain*	8.7	4.5%
Estonia	8.5	6.4%
Nepal	8.4	8.8%
UK*	8.4	6.8%
Algeria*	8.2	11.4%
Ethiopia	8.0	9.2%
S Korea	8.0	6.5%
Germany	7.8	10.3%
S Africa*	7.8	15.4%

Note: * Signifies countries where the sample only covers a region of the country.

Source: Figure 61 in Rees and Main (2015, p 92)

homicide rate, the UK was 14th out of 29 countries and 10th out of 29 on air pollution.

Conclusion

Overall, housing and environmental conditions have improved over the last decade for all types of households. Families with children are no more likely to live in non-Decent Homes than other household types, but they are more likely to live in overcrowded accommodation, especially in the social rented sector. Satisfaction with housing was lowest in the private rented sector. However, in recent years, during periods of austerity, officially measured homelessness, as well as prevention of homelessness activity, has started to increase, albeit at a relatively modest level. Available evidence shows that lone parents are at greater risk of experiencing homelessness and living in poor neighbourhoods.

Notes

[1] A Decent Home is one that: (1) meets the current statutory minimum for housing, which was the 'Fitness Standard' until April 2006, which was then updated to reflect the Housing Health and Safety Rating System (HHSRS); (2) is in a reasonable state of repair – a home which fails to meet this criterion will have either one or more 'key' building components that are old and in poor condition or two or more 'other' building components that are old and in poor condition; (3) has reasonably modern facilities and services – homes that fail to meet this criterion lack three or more of a specified list of facilities; and (4) provides a reasonable degree of thermal comfort, that is, it has effective insulation and efficient heating. See CLG (2006).

[2] From 2006 onwards, the Decent Homes Standard was revised with the HHSRS replacing the Fitness Standard as one of components of the Decent Homes Standard.

[3] A house meets the Tolerable Standard if it: (a) is structurally stable; (b) is substantially free from rising or penetrating damp; (c) has satisfactory provision for natural and artificial lighting, for ventilation and for heating; (d) has an adequate piped supply of wholesome water available within the house; (e) has a sink provided with an adequate supply of both hot and cold water within the house; (f) has a water closet or waterless closet available for the exclusive use of the occupants of the house and suitably located within the house; (g) has a fixed bath or shower and a wash-hand basin, all with a satisfactory supply of hot and cold water suitably located within the house; (h) has an effective system for the drainage and disposal of foul and surface water;

(i) has satisfactory facilities for the cooking of food within the house; and (j) has satisfactory access to all external doors and outbuildings. In addition, the Housing (Scotland) Act 2006 (implemented in 2010) added additional criteria, covering thermal performance and electrical safety.

[4] These associations have not been tested for statistical significance.

[5] Although differences for 'excess cold' (7% compared to 6%) and 'falls' (14% to 12%) were small.

[6] 'Bedroom standard' allocates one bedroom to each couple, any other person aged 21 or over, each pair of adolescents aged 10-20 of the same sex, and each pair of children aged under 10. Any other adults are allocated a separate bedroom. This is then compared to the actual number of bedrooms (self-reported). Any household with a bedroom allocation higher than the actual number of bedrooms is defined as being overcrowded.

[7] This uses data from The Children's Society's *The good childhood report 2014*.

[8] England – Homelessness (Priority Need for Accommodation) (England) Order 2002) and Wales – Homeless Persons (Priority Need) (Wales) Order 2001. It should also be noted that England defines people aged 21 who are 'vulnerable as a result of having been looked after, accommodated or fostered' as a priority need group, whereas Wales and Northern Ireland do not. In Wales and Northern Ireland young people who are at risk of financial or sexual exploitation are also described as a priority need group by guidance to legislation. However, while Wales requires this group also to be aged 18-20, Northern Ireland does not specify an age limit.

[9] The Homelessness Code of Guidance for Local Authorities (ODPM, 2002) defines 'vulnerability' as whether, when homeless, 'the applicant would be less able to fend for himself than an ordinary homeless person so that he would be likely to suffer injury or detriment, in circumstances where a less vulnerable person would be able to cope without harmful effects.'

[10] Homelessness Etc (Scotland) Act 2003 and Homelessness (Abolition of Priority Need Test) (Scotland) Order 2012.

[11] These statistics are collected using different measures and are therefore presented separately to England, Wales and Scotland.

[12] See www.communities.gov.uk/housing/housingresearch/housingstatistics/housingstatisticsby/homelessnessstatistics/livetables/ (Live Table 773).

[13] See https://statswales.wales.gov.uk/Catalogue/Housing/Homelessness/Acceptances-and-Other-Decisions/

[14] See www.gov.scot/Topics/Statistics/Browse/Housing-Regeneration/ RefTables/annualreferencetables201415

[15] See www.dsdni.gov.uk/publications/northern-ireland-housing-bulletin-january-march-2015

[16] Table 782: Households in temporary accommodation, DCLG P1E homelessness returns.

[17] Table 2: Quarterly temporary accommodation reference tables, www. gov.scot/Topics/Statistics/Browse/Housing-Regeneration/RefTables/ PublicationTables2014-15.

[18] See http://gov.wales/statistics-and-research/homelessness/?lang=en

[19] 'Upkeep problems' include issues such as litter or rubbish, graffiti, dog excrement, dwelling condition, vandalism, scruffy gardens, conditions of pavements and nuisance from street parking; 'traffic' includes heavy traffic, railway/aircraft noise, air quality and intrusion from motorways or arterial roads; 'vacant sites' include vacant or boarded-up buildings, non-conforming uses and intrusive industry. Analysis on these variables does not appear in surveys post-2011/12.

[20] Professional surveyors recorded the 10% of households whose 'neighbourhoods' (defined as the public and private space/buildings in the immediate environment of the dwelling) are assessed to be the most neglected, poorly maintained and/or vandalised.

[21] The household survey asked respondents to rate the levels of satisfaction with their local area as a place to live using a five-point scale (1 = very satisfied to 5 = very dissatisfied) (CLG, 2010c). In addition, respondents were presented with a series of nine issues and asked whether these issues were 'a serious problem', 'a problem but not serious' or 'not a problem'.

EIGHT

Children's time and space

Antonia Keung

Key statistics

- A total of 3.2% of dependent children who were usually resident in England and Wales had a parental second address; 40% of them have their second parental address outside of their usual area of residence.
- Ninety-seven per cent of households with children in Great Britain have internet connection.
- One in 14 school children aged between 10 and 12 in England disagrees that there are enough places to play or have a good time in their area; as many as one in eight shows low satisfaction with their local outdoor spaces.
- In European Union (EU) countries, teenage children who go online are mainly engaged in social networking, watching online videos and online gaming.
- Four in 10 children aged 5-15 own a smartphone, and nearly one in four use their mobile phone to go online.
- One in six children aged 12-15 have had experience of potentially risky online behaviours in the past year.
- Young people from poorer backgrounds are more likely to have negative online experiences compared to their more affluent peers.
- Six per cent of young people aged 10-17 in England show a low level of satisfaction with their time use.
- The majority of children said that they watch TV/listen to music on a daily basis, while only about half participate in physical activities on a daily basis.
- Girls' employment is negatively associated with their school grades.
- The 2011 Census indicates that there were over 166,000 young carers in England. However, other research shows that the figure could be over four times this official figure.
- Young carers spend on average 15 hours per week caring for someone.

Key trends

- Children are spending less time outdoors – only 21% of children today have played in the street or neighbourhood areas every day compared to 71% of adults when they were children.
- Children are going online more, at younger ages, and in more diverse ways.
- The proportion of children using personal computers and/or laptops for accessing the internet has decreased while more children use their mobile phone/tablets for online activities.
- Children's awareness of the security risks posed by the internet underwent a decline between 2011 and 2014.

Key sources

- *The good childhood report* (The Children's Society, 2014, 2015)
- Office for National Statistics (ONS)
- EU Kids Online report 2014 (EU Kids Online, 2014)
- Office of Communications (Ofcom)
- Academic research papers and reports

Introduction

The aim of this chapter is to provide a broad picture of children's use of time and space in the UK. It provides a review of children's access to private, public and virtual spaces and factors associated with the spatial patterns. The chapter then looks into children's use of time in various activities, including paid work and provision of unpaid care.

Children's spaces

Home(s) and family

Children's home and family are the main physical and social spaces in which most children spend the majority of their time other than school. However, the UK, like many other Western developed countries, has witnessed substantial changes in the patterns of marriage, divorce and cohabitation, which means that many children today have experienced rather different home and family lives than previous generations. ONS statistics show that as many as one in four children live in a lone-parent family and more than one in ten in a stepfamily (see Chapter Two). These changes imply that many children have two homes and alternative living arrangements with their separated or divorced or never-married parents. Based on 2011 Census data, the ONS reported that as many as 3.2% (386,000) of the 12.1 million dependent children who were usually resident in England and Wales had a parental second address.

Figure 8.1 presents the proportion of these children by age, and it shows that the older age group, in particular the 10- to-14-year-olds, have the highest rate of having two homes that could be explained by the increasing chance of parental separation over time (ONS, 2014d).

There are no guidelines on the amount of time non–resident parents should spend with their children after separation or divorce. The majority of parents make their own arrangements for sharing time with their children, but some have to resort to other means, including mediated negotiation or a court order (ONS, 2008). The family life of children whose parents are separated/divorced can get very complicated at times, as their lives are no longer lived in one place but scattered between several locations. The ONS (2014d) shows that about 60% of children have a second parental address in the same local authority as their usual residence, but the other 40% have their second home outside of their local area. Data from the ONS Omnibus Survey in 2008 show that over 70% of children meet their non–resident parent at the non–resident parent's home and around one-third of these stay at their non–resident parent's home overnight at least once a week. Other common locations where contact takes place also include 'place

Figure 8.1: Percentage of dependent children with parental second address in 2011

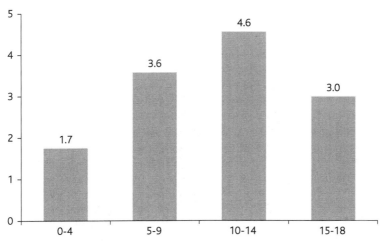

Source: ONS (2014d)

of leisure', 'at resident parent's home', 'at a relative's or friend's home', 'school' or at a 'contact centre' (ONS, 2008).

Private space at home

The child's bedroom is no longer just a space where they get rest, but to many it has become a central location of leisure and the mediation of everyday life. For older children in particular, their bedrooms provide them with much needed space, not only for individual privacy but also for the construction of personal identity, styles and tastes. Livingstone (2007) argues that 'bedroom culture' has emerged at the turn of the 21st century as part of the process of 'individualisation' and the increasing concern of children's safety in a 'risk society'. Crucially, parents consider home spaces as havens of safety for their children (Livingstone, 2007), although this view has changed somewhat, at least for parents who are more aware of the risks that their children may be exposed to when alone browsing the internet at home. There are, of course, also cases of child abuse and domestic violence, which mean home may not necessarily be safe for some children (see Chapter Ten).

Increasingly, children are spending more time indoors than outdoors, and this is implicitly linked to the perceived danger of public outside spaces by both parents and their children. Furthermore, the increasing loss of suitable outdoor space due to development is also a limiting factor for children playing outdoors, especially in urban towns and cities (Gleave and Cole-Hamilton, 2012). As a result, many parents and children are looking for indoor alternatives to spend their spare time. The convenience and the variety of entertainment that multi-media can offer mean that nowadays it is likely to be chosen as an alternative activity in many families. Children's bedrooms are now often filled with all kinds of electronic gadgets, such as personal televisions, personal computers and/or tablets, music media and so on. According to the ONS (2013c), 97% of households with children in Great Britain have an internet connection; this means that many children and young people can now easily gain access to vast amounts of information and entertainment that are available online in the comfort of their own home or bedroom. This, coupled with the proliferation of online social networking sites, has hugely transformed children's activities that can be carried out in their indoor private space.

The quality and quantity of home space is linked to socioeconomic factors. Overcrowding is endemic among poor families, and children of low-income families are likely to have to share their bedrooms with their siblings. The Poverty and Social Exclusion (PSE) survey found that 11% of households with children did not have (because they could not afford) enough bedrooms for every child of 10 or over of a different sex (Main and Bradshaw, 2015). Furthermore, hundreds of thousands of children in England are growing up in cold, damp or overcrowded homes (see Chapter Seven). These children often live in the most deprived neighbourhoods, and it is also these children who perceive the greatest risks to playing in public outdoor spaces (Farmer, 2005).

Public outdoor spaces

Despite the popularity of computer gaming and online social networking among children and young people, a recent survey found that when young people are asked about the kind of activity that they prefer to do most in their spare time, playing in public outdoor places topped the list – 54% of children aged 5-11 choose to play outdoors on a bike or some other 'wheels'. Computer gaming only comes next (52%) (Gill, 2011, p 15). There is ample research evidence that points out the importance of outdoor play for child development and keeping children active and healthy (Gleave, 2009). However, a recent Play England survey found that only 21% of children today play in the street or area near their home every day compared to 71% of adults when they were children (Lacey, 2007). There are a number of factors that limit children's outdoor play, which are common in most of the developed countries. One of these is parental anxiety about safety that restricts children's ability to play outside the home with friends (Mhonda, 2007). Gill (2007) argues that a number of social and cultural changes might have caused parents to be overprotective of their children, one of which is the danger from traffic. The increased volume of traffic has left most residential streets more dangerous and unpleasant than before. There is also a general lack of green space and open areas for children to play in as a result of increasing demand on land, especially in urban cities for house building programmes. Other factors include concerns about bullying, fear of crime and strangers, concerns about gangs, activities associated with the illegal drugs market and other less specific fears. These have made all public outdoor places feel less safe, and this is disproportionally affecting children living in very deprived or troubled estates (Matthews, 2001; Gill, 2007).

The societal expectations of good parenting also mean that children are expected to be under the active care and guidance of their parents or other responsible adults. These expectations stigmatise as irresponsible those who try to let children out to play unsupervised

(Furedi, 2001). Additionally, the excessive focus of the media on risk and stories of tragedy have also been blamed for cultivating the 'fear culture' and 'risk aversion' in Britain (Gill, 2007).

There are also a range of sociodemographic factors affecting the means and extent to which children and young people can access public outdoor places. A study conducted by Mackett et al (2007b) found that in a sample of 330 primary school children aged 8-11 from Cheshunt, Hertfordshire, 56% of the children were allowed out without an adult. Figure 8.2 presents further results, and shows that the proportion generally increases with age, and boys are more likely to be allowed out than girls.

Other research found that children from minority ethnic groups appeared to be more restricted in their use of urban space, which may be attributable to greater and stricter parental control and fear of racism (O'Brien et al, 2000). Level of income and family type are found to be associated with children's independent mobility. Mackett et al (2007b) point out that children in higher-income families seem

Figure 8.2: Percentage of children aged 8-11 allowed out without an adult

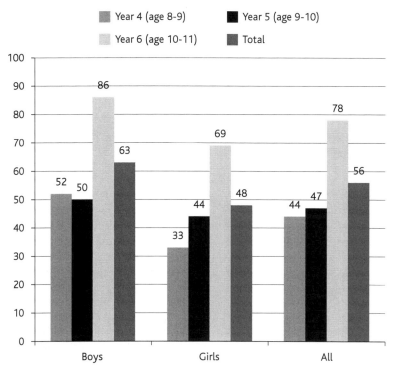

Source: Mackett et al (2007b)

to be more protected by their parents and are more likely to travel by car for safety and security reasons. It has also been suggested that children in lone-parent families are significantly more likely to be the most independent, as they do not get the same level of supervision and control as their two-parent peers.

Furthermore, Mackett et al (2007b) found that the nature of the environment and the neighbourhood's surrounding areas are also linked to whether children were allowed out alone. More specifically, their research findings suggest that children who live in urban areas, like Lewisham, are less likely to be allowed out without an adult, which is probably the result of greater perceived risk related to local traffic and street crime. On the other hand, children who live in suburban areas like Hertfordshire, with more open green space, good access to local shops and strong social support networks, are more likely to be allowed out without an adult. Schoeppe et al's (2015) research confirms the links between adults' sociodemographic background, perception of neighbourhood social cohesion and the likelihood of permitting children to have greater independent mobility for outdoor play. A sample size of approximately 1,300 Australian adults (81% were parents) interviewed in the 2013 Queensland Social Survey was analysed and the research team concluded that in general women, parents and adults with lower educational attainment and those who perceived neighbourhood social cohesion as being lower were less likely to grant children greater freedom for unsupervised outdoor play (Schoeppe et al, 2015). Other research showed that the seasons and associated weather and duration of daylight (Matthews, 2001), and the attractiveness of potential play places (Lester and Russell, 2008) could all influence the extent to which children play out in public spaces.

In a qualitative study, Sutton (2008) compared the use of free time and style of play between 'estate' and private school children, and found marked differences between the two groups. From the perspective of the estate children, street play and/or outdoor socialising are deemed important and they spend most of their free time 'hanging out' with friends at various places in their neighbourhoods. On the other hand, those private school children in the study spent more time in organised leisure activities. The study found that the estate children's preference for street play was mainly owing to financial constraint and lack of available transport to get to activity venues. Sutton (2008) illustrated that playing outside is fundamentally linked with disadvantage, as the estate children have little space at home, and few opportunities for alternative leisure activities.

Overall, research evidence from the UK and other developed countries clearly indicates that the opportunities for independent mobility and free play have significantly narrowed for many children (Lester and Russell, 2008). This trend is particularly worrying as it means that many children and young people are missing out on their outdoor unsupervised play experience and associated benefits. Further discussion of children's play its benefits are provided in a later section in this chapter.

Outdoor spaces for teenagers

The Children's Worlds survey (Rees and Main, 2015) on children's views about their lives and well-being in 15 countries in 2013/14 suggests that as many as 1 in 14 school children aged between 10 and 12 in England disagreed that there are enough places to play or have a good time in their area (see Figure 8.3), and almost 1 in 8 indicating low satisfaction when they were asked about their satisfaction regarding the outdoor spaces that they can use in their local areas. England is ranked at around the mid-table position based on the mean satisfaction score, and did less well compared to countries such as Norway, Spain,

Figure 8.3: Proportion of 10- and 12-year-olds in England who agree/disagree with the statement 'In my area there are enough places to play or to have good time'

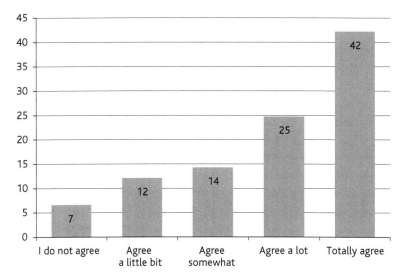

Source: The Children's Worlds survey 2013-14 data, provided by the Children's Worlds survey research team

Romania and Poland in terms of children's satisfaction with their outdoor spaces (see Table 8.1).

There is a general lack of suitable public spaces for teenagers to use for meeting and 'hanging out' with friends. It has been highlighted in a review by Lester and Russell (2008) that most of the parks and outdoor spaces and play facilities are designed for younger children, and such provisions are unattractive and do not meet the needs for the teenage groups. Thus, teenagers tend to meet on the street simply because there is a lack of alternatives. This is especially the case for those from a less affluent background, as alternatives are often unaffordable for them. Findings from a consultation with young people suggest that some young people might get themselves into trouble in public areas, and boredom is often a contributing factor (DfES, 2006).

Teenagers' activities and movement on the street are often unwelcomed by neighbours and local community members, as their group behaviours can sometimes be intimidating to others. Consequently young people may feel that they are being restricted from using much of the public realm and confronted by the intolerance

Table 8.1: Mean satisfaction score on the outdoor areas children can use in their local area by country and proportion reported with low satisfaction

Country	Mean satisfaction score[1]	% with low satisfaction[2]
Norway	8.7	5.9
Colombia	8.4	9.4
Spain	8.3	7.1
Romania	8.2	11.3
Poland	8.1	10.0
Turkey	7.8	16.5
Israel	7.7	15.6
UK	7.7	13.1
Germany	7.7	13.5
Estonia	7.5	16.4
S Korea	7.4	13.2
Nepal	7.2	17.5
Ethiopia	7.0	17.9
Algeria	6.9	23.2
S Africa	6.8	25.0

Notes:

[1] Satisfaction scale ranging from 0-10, higher score means more satisfied.

[2] Low satisfaction refers to score that is below the mid-point of an 11-point satisfaction scale.

Source: The Children's Worlds survey 2013-14 data , provided by the Children's Worlds survey research team

of local adults (Lester and Russell, 2008). Sanction and control by the police such as the use of Anti-social Behaviour Orders and Curfew Orders are some of the examples of denying some young people the use public spaces. The previous Labour government was committed to address the issue of inadequate provision of outdoor facilities and positive activities to keep children active and healthy, and away from getting into trouble, in particular children from disadvantaged backgrounds. A national 10-year play strategy was set up in 2008 that outlined the government's plan and a financial commitment of over £200 million to ensure that children and young people have more opportunities to play out of doors (DCSF, 2007c).

Ample research evidence from the UK and overseas highlights the benefits of outdoor play in parks and public open spaces and improved child health and fitness, as well as other associated positive outcomes (see further details below). However, the national play policy in England was abandoned not long after the coalition government took over in 2010. All national play contracts that were previously in place were cancelled. In the absence of a national play policy, play services and playgrounds, including facilities, are being targeted by many councils to make cuts for austerity savings, and as a result, many long-standing services and projects have been closed and the land used for redevelopment (Children's Rights Alliance for England, 2015). A survey found that overall spending by local authorities on play services and facilities between 2010/11 and 2013/14 was cut by 39%, from £67.9 million down to £41.5 million (Jozwiak, 2014, cited in Children's Rights Alliance for England, 2015). The former director of Play England, a charity organisation that promotes children and young people's right to play, warned that the abolishment of the play policy in England would bring long-term damaging consequences for children's health and well-being (Policy for Play, 2011).

Research evidence on the benefits associated with the provision of unstaffed public play facilities

Gill (2014) reviewed available evidence on the impact of public play facilities provision on children and their families, as well as on the wider community. The key benefit for children is the increased level of physical activity, and in families where children use these facilities, the parents often report higher levels of family well-being. There was also evidence to suggest that play and youth facilities in public spaces have led to reductions in levels of anti-social behaviour and vandalism. A case study was cited in Gill's (2014) report that demonstrates a significant reduction in the incidences of anti-social behaviour by young people in Halton, Merseyside. This happened after a youth-oriented play space was created that provides challenging equipment aimed at older young people. The impact of such an initiative is captured in the following response from a regeneration officer from Cosmopolitan Housing:

> In the six months before the play area was built there were 44 incidences of ASB [anti-social behaviour] by young people in this area. In the six months after the play had been built, this had reduced to four. (Taken from a Proludic video, cited in Gill, 2014, p 22)

Virtual space

As mentioned earlier, the majority of children and young people in the UK have access to the internet, and this allows them a virtual space for leisure, education and learning activities. The latest trend about children's internet use shows that they are going online more often, at younger ages, and in more diverse ways (EU Kids Online, 2014). According to Ofcom (2014), children aged 8-11 in the UK are now spending more time using the internet compared to previous years, and the latest statistics also show an increase in the proportion of three- to four-year-olds owning and using internet-connected devices, in particular, tablet computers (Ofcom, 2014). The EU Kids Online 2010 survey of 25 countries (including the UK) revealed that the types of activities that teenage children do most often while being online are: social networking (63%), watching online videos (59%), instant messaging (49%) and online gaming (28%). Using the internet for homework also accounted for 33% of internet usage (EU Kids Online, 2014). The younger age group (children aged 3-11) spend most of their time on the internet watching films or movies on TV (between 74-85%; there is more prevalence among children aged 8-11) (Ofcom, 2014, p 75). There is a clear gender difference in the UK in terms of young people's preferences of online activities. In general, more boys tend to play online games than girls, while more girls than boys prefer chatting online (Ofcom, 2014, p 4).

There is also evidence for an increased usage of mobile devices among children and young people. The latest Ofcom statistics suggest that four in ten children aged 5-15 own a smartphone and nearly one in four use their smartphone to go online (Ofcom, 2014, p 5). The use of smartphones for internet content is higher among those aged 12-15 compared to their younger peers. On the other hand, a decline in internet access via home PCs/laptops is noted, from 91% in 2013 to 88% in 2014 (Ofcom, 2014). Compared to younger children, 12- to 15-year-olds spend more time on the internet browsing than watching TV in a typical week. Among this older age group, the mobile phone is the most popular device for social and creative activities that include: "'arranging to meet friends" (71%); "messaging friends" (53%); "looking at photos posted online" (47%); and "sharing photos they have taken" (45%)' (Ofcom, 2014, p 6). Facebook is the most popular online social media site/app among teenagers in the UK (Ofcom, 2014).

The increased use of the internet is followed by an increased incidence of online risky behaviours carried out by young people. As many as one in six 12- to 15-year-olds have experienced potentially risky online behaviours in the past year. For example, 8% of the children in this age group had taken the contact details of someone they had met only online, and 4% had sent personal information to a person that they contacted online only (Ofcom, 2014, pp 119-20). A decreasing trend in awareness and experience of safe and risky measures among young people is noted between 2011 and 2014, which coincides with the trend of increased use of mobile phone and tablets and decreased use of desktop/laptop computers. It is possible that children may be less familiar with online safety measures on newer devices (Ofcom, 2014).

The EU Kids Go Online study (2014) reports that there are socioeconomic differences among young people in the types of online activities they engage in, digital skills and experience, and knowledge of safety measures for avoiding online risks. In general, young people from a poorer economic background tend to use the internet for mainly entertainment purposes only, whereas young people from more affluent backgrounds tend to be more able to make use of the internet to enhance their learning/knowledge and opportunity. It is also noted that, compared to young people from more affluent backgrounds, young people from poorer backgrounds have less digital skills and online safety knowledge, and they are also less likely to receive online safety advice from their less educated parents. Consequently, young people from poorer backgrounds are also more likely to encounter negative online experiences. This new form of digital inequality is being known as the 'second-level digital divide' (Lichy, 2011, cited in Liabo et al, 2013b). Thus, the debate around digital divides in the UK is no longer about access but the levels of digital skills and capacity to utilise technology to improve attainment and life chances.

Children's play

Article 31 of the United Nations (UN) Convention on the Rights of the Child states that children have the right to rest and leisure, to engage in play and recreational activities appropriate to their age and to participate freely in cultural life and the arts (UN General Assembly, 1989). However, as discussed earlier, children today have less opportunity and access to play compared to previous generations. This is partly due to fewer suitable outdoor spaces that are attractive and/ or safe for children to play in, as discussed earlier. The other reason is the increasing demand on children's time for other structured activities which means less free time for children to play (Play England, 2009) (a review on children's time use is provided in the next section).

The benefits of play are well researched and there is ample research evidence that supports play as important for children's physical, mental, emotional and social well-being (Lester and Russell, 2008; Gill, 2014). The value of free or unstructured play is illustrated in the research literature. Burdette and Whitaker (2005) highlighted in their literature review that unstructured free play in outdoor spaces is beneficial to child development in various ways. Cognitive benefits include concentration, self-discipline, problem-solving and creativity. Social benefits include self-awareness, flexibility and cooperation. Emotional benefits include becoming happier, reduction in mental health problems such as anxiety, depression and aggression. Burdette and Whitaker (2005) further point out that if children are given regular opportunities to engage in free and unstructured play in the outdoor environment, they can become brighter, better able to get along with others, healthier and happier.

To combat the problem of decreasing opportunity for play, a number of interventions have been introduced in the UK, each of which involves setting aside time and space for children to play. According to Gill (2014), these interventions can be grouped into the following four categories: 'playground break time initiatives', 'unstaffed public play facilities', 'supervised out-of-school play provision' and 'street play initiatives'. The existing evaluation of the evidence shows that these interventions are showing a range of positive impacts on children's well-being; in particular, the playground break time initiatives were linked to improvements in children's social skills and social relationships with others and better adjustment to school life and also improvements in academic skills, attitudes and behaviour. Unstaffed public play facilities provision is linked to increases in children's physical activity, whereas supervised play provision and street play initiatives are both linked to increased physical activity and the latter also increases interest in volunteering (Gill, 2014).

Children's time use

According to the latest *Good childhood report 2015* (The Children's Society, 2015), a sample of around 8,000 young people aged 10-17 surveyed between 2013-15 in England were asked to rate how they felt about various domains of their life. Of these children, about 6% reported low satisfaction with their time use (The Children's Society, 2015). In the same survey children were asked about how often they were engaged in various kinds of activities. Table 8.2 presents the findings on children's time use in various activities.

As shown in Table 8.2, watching TV/listening to music are the activities that the majority of children do on a daily basis. Over half also managed to spend some time on their own and to engage in physical activities. Using a computer on a regular basis was also evident – the majority of children used it at least once or twice a week if not more often. Reading for fun, participation in organised leisure activities and taking classes outside school time are some of the activities that children spent less time on. In addition to the above general activities, *The good childhood report 2015* also presents findings on how often children spend time with their family and friends on the activities presented in Table 8.3.

It is clear from Table 8.3 that the majority of children spend time talking to and/or having fun with their family most days. About half

Table 8.2: Year 6 and Year 8 children's time use in various activities (% of children)

	Rarely/ never	< Once a week	Once/twice a week	Every day/ almost
Watching TV/listening to music	2	4	13	81
Sending time by one's self	6	10	27	57
Playing sports/doing exercise	6	7	33	55
Using a computer	6	10	30	54
Helping around the house	7	10	34	49
Doing homework	6	7	41	46
Taking care of family members	18	13	29	40
Reading for fun	24	13	25	37
Organised leisure-time activities	30	11	39	20
Taking classes outside school time	48	9	28	14

Source: Data from The Children's Society (2015)

Table 8.3: Frequency of activities Year 6 and Year 8 children spend with family and friends (% of children)

	Not at all	Once/twice a week	Most days	Every day
Talking to family members	1	7	24	68
Talking to friends	5	14	27	55
Having fun with friends	7	16	31	46
Having fun with family members	3	15	44	38
Learning together with family members	13	27	39	21
Meeting friends to study	58	25	10	7

Source: Data from The Children's Society (2015)

of Year 6 and Year 8 children talk to or have fun with their friends on a daily basis. The least frequent activities reported were children and family members spending time learning together or spending time meeting their friends to study.

The good childhood report 2015 also assessed children's satisfaction with their time use. Their findings show that about 1 in 19 children from Year 6 and Year 8 cohorts reported low satisfaction[1] with how they used their time, and 1 in 20 reported low satisfaction with what they did in their free time (The Children's Society, 2015, p 49). Overall, 1 in 16 children were not satisfied with their time use, and in general girls were less satisfied with their time use and were more likely than boys to report low satisfaction (The Children's Society, 2015, p 21).

So far the review on children's time use – although providing some useful ideas about how often children engage in various common activities – has not investigated the amount of time that children spend on various activities. The last national time use survey which provided data regarding the amount of time children spend on different activities was carried out in 2000 (Ipsos-RSL & ONS, 2003). A detailed review has already been provided in the previous edition of this book series (Bradshaw, 2011). A new national time diary survey, funded by the Economic and Social Research Council (ESRC), was carried out between April 2014 and March 2015, but at the time of writing, the data was not available to be included here.[2]

Children's employment

Research into the impact of child employment on well-being and achievement remains scarce. It is, however, largely deemed as acceptable by parents and government for school-aged children to engage in part-time employment (Hobbs et al, 2007) because of the perceived potential benefits associated with the preparation of adult life. Data on child employment are very difficult to access as government employment surveys typically do not extend below people under 16. Recent figures provided by the Better Regulation Task Force (2004) suggest that work by school-aged children is widespread. Of an estimated population of 3.5 million 11- to 15-year-olds in England and Wales, around 2.3 million will have worked at some point before their school-leaving age (Better Regulation Task Force. 2004).

Research suggests that there are a number of reasons for children who do part-time work, which include gaining financial independence from parents, acquiring work experience, combating boredom, earning money to buy consumer goods (Davies, 1999), and for those who live in a poor family, contributing towards family income (Stack and McKechnie, 2002). There is a range of part-time work that children do, and the most common types of work quoted include newspaper delivery, shop floor work, waiter/waitressing, hotel and catering, agricultural work, office work and cleaning (Davies, 1999).

Present child employment legislation

In England, the rules that apply to the employment of children under the school leaving age are mainly found in the Children and Young Persons Act 1933. The Act sets out the minimum age at which children may be employed, and allows local authorities to make byelaws. Children are also protected by the terms of the European Directive on the Protection of Young People at Work, implemented into UK legislation within the Working Time Regulations. According to the present legislation, as illustrated on the GOV.UK website (2015a), children may not work:

- if under the age of 13 (except employment in areas including television, theatre and modelling, of which a performance licence would be applicable)
- without an employment permit (if this is required by local byelaws)
- in any industrial setting such as a factory or industrial site
- during school hours
- before 7am or after 7pm
- for more than one hour before school (if allowed by local byelaws)
- for more than four hours without taking a break of at least one hour
- in any occupation prohibited by local byelaws or other legislation
- in any work that may be harmful to their health, well-being or education

- without having a two-week break from any work during the school holidays in each calendar year
- for more than a maximum of 12 hours per week during term time
- for more than 25 hours per week if they are 13 to 14 years old or more than 35 hours per week for 15- to 16-year-olds during school holidays.

It is noted that children of compulsory school age are not entitled to the National Minimum Wage, but young people aged 16 and above are entitled. Employers who wish to hire a child must obtain a permit from the local education authority. Without a permit, children are working illegally. Local education authorities have powers to supervise the employment of school children in their area, and may require particulars about a child's employment. However, legislation put in place to protect working children has been criticised as ineffective as research shows that the majority of working children are unlikely to hold a permit, either because they are not aware of such requirement or they simply ignore it (Hobbs and McKechnie, 1997; Hobbs et al, 2007; McKechnie et al, 2013). Consequently, child workers in the UK are largely hidden as most are unregistered. A number of studies into the effectiveness of the current registration system have suggested that a reform is required if child employees are to be properly protected (McKechnie et al, 2013).

There are general concerns about the potential risks and danger involved in children's work, and fears that working may have a negative impact on schooling (see Hobbs et al, 2007). Although it appears that working children as a whole do not perform less well academically, this has been contradicted in research conducted by McKechnie and Hobbs (2001). They found that children performing long working hours, especially more than 10 hours per week, tend to perform less well at school than those who work five hours per week or less. Holford (2015) analysed data from the Longitudinal Study of Young People in England, and has similarly found that working part time had a negative impact on the school grades of girls. The finding suggests that 'for girls, an additional hour of paid employment per week in Year 10, reduces their final GCSE performance a year later by approximately 1 grade in one subject' (Holford, 2015). This effect could be explained by girls spending less time studying outside of lessons, and also that girls in employment may become less motivated or interested in their studies (Holford, 2015).

To sum up, existing research evidence shows that the current Working Time Regulations system does not work, and it therefore fails to protect child employees. Given that most children will have worked part time at some point before they leave school, it is important for the government to work out a system that is effective in identifying all children who work, and to look into ways to minimise any potential negative effects of work on children's education.

Children as carers

The situation of children undertaking long-term caring for their family members has been a major child welfare concern since the early 1990s. Young carers are recognised in parliamentary legislation in the Carers (Recognition and Services) Act 1995, and they have been widely accepted as meeting the definition of children in need in the Children Act 1989. Under the coalition government, two important registrations concerning young carers were implemented – the Care Act 2014 and Children and Families Act 2014, which came into effect on 1 April 2015. Accordingly, young carers include 'children and young people under 18 who provide regular or ongoing care and emotional support to a family member who is physically or mentally ill, disabled, or misuses substances' (The Children's Society, 2013b, p 6). It also stated that 'a young carer becomes vulnerable when the level of care-giving and responsibility to the person in need of care becomes excessive or inappropriate for that child, risking impact on his or her emotional or physical well-being or educational achievement and life chances' (ADASS et al, 2012, cited in The Children's Society, 2013b, p 6). Local authorities are the responsible bodies to identify young carers in their area and to assess their support needs. It is noted that all young carers under the age of 18 have a right to an assessment of their needs. This includes young adult carers in 'transition' from children's services to adult services. The assessment of this group would have a strong focus on ways that can support them to prepare for adulthood and how they might fulfil their own potential in education, employment and life. Furthermore, local authorities are also required to take an active role in preventing future need from occurring by providing services to a young carer, or the person they care for, if so doing can prevent a caring role having a negative impact on the young carers' outcomes (The Children's Society, 2015).

Numbers of young carers

Dearden and Becker (2004) point out that there may be a substantial amount of 'hidden' young carers in the UK as it is suspected that there are many young carers who are not known by the local authorities or organisations that support and provide services to them. The official figure provided by the Census 2011 suggests that there were over 166,000 young carers in England (ONS, 2013d, cited in Children's Society, 2013b); however, this figure does not include young carers who are caring for family members with mental illness and/or parental substance misuse. Additionally, some young carers might choose not to disclose their caring roles for different reasons such as 'family loyalty, stigma, bullying, or not knowing where to go for support' (Children's Society, 2013b, p 4), and their families may also fear that the children will be taken into care if they approach the authorities for help (Children's Society, 2013b). This means that it is very difficult to know how many young carers there are, and that the official figures are likely to have underestimated the number of children and young people who have a caring role. The BBC, in collaboration with the University of Nottingham, conducted a survey on young carers, and based on their survey they found that about 1 in 12 of around 4,000 schoolchildren surveyed said they had caring responsibilities such as carrying out the personal care of someone at home. This latest survey finding provides an estimation of 700,000 young carers in the UK (Howard, 2010). This means that there could be over four times as many young carers as the official Census figures indicate.

Characteristics of young carers

The Children's Society (2013b) analysed data from the Longitudinal Study of Young People in England conducted between 2004 and 2010. Young people aged 13 and 14 were asked to complete the survey questionnaires assisted by face-to-face interviews. The initial sample size was over 15,000, and by 2010 the survey sample still retained some 9,000 young people. The Children's Society (2013b) analysis indicates that young carers from the sample spend on average over 15 hours per week caring for someone. It is noted that the number of hours carers spend on caring varies substantially across the sample, from a few hours per week to over 100 hours per week in some extreme cases. In terms of ethnic background, young carers are 1.5 times more likely to be from Black, Asian or minority ethnic groups, and it is twice as likely that English is not their first language. Furthermore, young carers are also more likely to come from low-income families or workless households, or to have a mother who has no qualifications, or who live in large households with three or more other children (Children's Society, 2013b).

Earlier research carried out by researchers from Loughborough University in 2003/04, based on a large-scale national survey of young carers, found that the average age of the carers is 12, and more girls than boys act as young carers (56% girls versus 44% boys based on a sample size of over 6,000 young carers). The study shows that over half of the sampled young carers live in lone-parent families, of which 70% are caring for their mothers in need. In contrast, young carers who live in two-parent families, about half are caring for their siblings. The study also shows that young carers are more common in poor families – with unemployed parents or on a low income (Dearden and Becker, 2004). Regarding the care needs provided by young carers, the same study shows that half of all those needing care have conditions of a physical health nature, 29% with mental health problems, 17% with learning difficulties, and 3% with sensory impairments (Dearden and Becker, 2004). The study shows that young carers perform a range of caring tasks, and Table 8.4 summarises the statistics regarding the types of caring roles young carers perform. It can be seen that providing emotional support is the most common type of caring role provided by young carers (82%), followed by household chores (68%) and nursing tasks (48%).

Impacts of caring on young carers

Not all young carers consider their caring roles in a negative light or as damaging to their well-being. A number of studies cited in the Social Care Institute for Excellence (SCIE) (2005) show many young carers see 'caring gives them feelings of maturity, and a sense of closeness to both parents and family; they also value their responsibilities and consider them to be a source of practical life skills' (SCIE, 2005, p 9).

Table 8.4: Percentage of young carers providing different caring tasks in 2003

Caring tasks	%
Domestic (eg, cooking, cleaning, washing, etc)	68
Nursing-type (eg, giving medication, assisting with mobility, etc)	48
Emotional support	82
Intimate care (eg, bathing, dressing, etc)	18
Child care (ie, caring for younger siblings)	11
Other (eg, bill paying, accompanying to hospital, etc)	7

Note: Valid sample size = 5,116. Figures do not add up to 100% since most carers are doing several caring tasks.

Source: Extracted from Dearden and Becker (2004, p 7, Table 5)

However, without appropriate support, long-term demanding caring roles can have a negative impact on carers' own well-being and future outcomes.

Often young carers feel tired as a result of their caring roles, and some may experience physical problems, for instance, as a result of lifting parents with physical disabilities. Studies also show that young carers often feel concerned and worried about their parent's welfare when they are not around. Substantial numbers of young carers are stressed, feel anxious, depressed and report low self-esteem. However, it is hard to gauge the effect of caring alone on the psychological health of young carers, as it has been pointed out that many of the studies did not control for the effect of socioeconomic factors (see SCIE, 2005).

The Children's Society (2013b) also identified some of the negative impacts of caring responsibilities on young carers' educational outcomes. Around 1 in 20 miss school as a result of caring for someone. It is pointed out that young carers have significantly lower educational attainment at GCSE level, and they are also more likely to not be in education, employment or training (NEET) between the ages of 16 and 19, which is also associated with later unemployment, reduced earnings, poor health and depression (Children's Society, 2013b). Furthermore, young carers are also more likely to have a special educational need (SEN) or a disability than their peers who are not carers (Children's Society, 2013b).

Negative impacts on school life have also been reported. Young carers often experience difficulties in attending school and finding the time and energy to do homework on top of their demanding caring routines. They have also reported feeling isolated from their peers and being excluded from opportunities to socialise given their demanding caring responsibilities. Many also report being bullied or being fearful of bullying. This, in turn, has a negative impact on their social development (SCIE, 2005).

Conclusion

Children and young people nowadays spend much less time playing out and instead more time in structured activities associated with learning. Owing to urban planning and development, many green open spaces have disappeared, and the increasing volume of road traffic has also made most outdoor spaces unpleasant and unsafe to play in. Parental anxiety of the potential dangers associated with public outdoor places has also limited children's independent mobility and opportunities to play outside. Overall, children are spending more time indoors.

Home is the space where children spend most of their childhood time. And one of the most observable changes in children's home space is their bedroom. Media, telecommunications, and in particular, internet technologies, have transformed the lifestyles of many children and young people over the past decades. Personal television, internet-connected computers, tablets and video game consoles are just a few common electronic gadgets that children have in their bedrooms. The online virtual spaces also offer today's youngsters a new way of expressing themselves and a range of online activities from leisure and entertainment to education and learning. This chapter highlighted the presence of a new form of digital inequality, that is, the second-level digital divide, whereby children from poorer backgrounds are less likely to be able to utilise online resources to benefit their education/learning, and are also more vulnerable to online risks/harms.

In the UK, most school children have a part-time job at some point, and yet the majority of children's employment is unnoticed by local authorities that have statutory duties to supervise and protect children from the potential risks of labour. Some research evidence points to the need to reform the current ineffective system if young workers are to be properly protected. However, very little has been done by successive governments. It might be argued that the common perception held by parents and the government about the benefit of work experience for future adult life has outweighed concerns about the health and safety issues around child employment. Another possible reason could be that most child workers are employed by fragile small businesses, and reforms might increase the financial burdens on these, which is certainly not in the interest of the government. Furthermore, there are potentially hundreds of thousands of children who are undertaking unpaid domestic care, and many are not known to the authorities and/or to professional groups. This poses risks to young carers' rights as children, resulting in negative consequences for the young carers' own development and well-being.

Notes

[1] The satisfaction scale ranges from 0-10, and if children score less than the mid-point, this would be deemed as having low satisfaction.

[2] Interested readers can refer to the Centre for Time Use Research website at www.timeuse.org/research/resources for further updates.

NINE

Children and young people in care and leaving care

Gwyther Rees and Mike Stein

Key statistics

- In 2014, around 93,000 children and young people were being looked after by the state in the UK.
- In 2014, Scotland had the highest rate of looked-after children and England the lowest.
- During a 12-month period in 2013-14, 37,600 children and young people started to be looked after and 37,900 ceased to be looked after.
- Over 12,700 young people aged 16 and over ceased to be looked after in the UK in 2014.
- Looked-after children aged 11-15 are four to five times more likely to have mental health problems than children of the same age group living in private households.
- Looked-after children aged 10 and over in England are four times as likely to be convicted of an offence, or to be subjected to a reprimand, or final warning, than their peers.
- Looked-after children have substantially lower levels of educational attainment than other children in the population.
- Those ceasing to be looked after, compared to young people in the general population, are at substantially higher risk of not being in education, training or employment (NEET), of experiencing homelessness, and of having mental health problems as adults.

Key trends

- The numbers of children in the UK looked after at any given point has increased by almost 10,000 over the last five years. This increase has been greatest in Wales, while the numbers in Scotland remain relatively unchanged.
- There has been a decrease in the average age of children being looked after.

- There is evidence of increased educational attainment, better healthcare and lower rates of offending and substance use among looked-after children over the past five years.

Key sources
- Office for National Statistics (ONS)
- Department for Education (DfE), England
- Knowledge and Analytical Services, Welsh Government
- Education Analytical Services, Scottish Government
- Department of Health, Social Services and Public Safety (DHSSPS), Northern Ireland

Introduction

At the end of March 2014 around 93,000 children were in 'public care' in the UK. In all four countries of the UK official policy aims to improve the well-being of these children, and to help those young people who leave the care system in their often difficult transition to adulthood.

Against this background, this chapter is divided into four sections. The first section provides descriptive information about numbers, characteristics and trends. The next section covers children's experiences of care. The third section summarises research on the well-being of children in care. The final section looks at routes of care.

The evidence presented in this chapter is based on statistics that are routinely produced in all four countries of the UK, and on a growing body of research evidence about the experiences and well-being of children in care and leaving care.

Throughout this chapter we use the term 'looked-after' to describe children and young people in public care in the UK. Unless otherwise stated, all official statistics are for the most recent year available. At the time of writing this was the year ending March 2014 in England, Wales and Northern Ireland, and the year ending July 2014 in Scotland. It should also be borne in mind that comparisons between the countries are complicated by different legal frameworks, different definitions and categorisations, and different reporting periods. Further information about these issues is provided in a review of the comparability of the statistics (see Welsh Government, 2014) in a response to an initiative from the UK Statistics Authority.

Numbers, trends and characteristics of children in care

Numbers of children in care

At the end of March 2014 there were over 93,000 looked-after children in public care in the UK (see Table 9.1), amounting to a rate of 68 per 10,000 of the child population. The rate of looked-after children per 10,000 of the child population varies somewhat between the four countries of the UK. The rates are lowest in England (59), followed relatively closely by Northern Ireland (66); Wales has a higher rate (91), and Scotland has the highest rate, at 151.

However, these comparisons are distorted by the extent that Scotland counts as 'looked-after' those children who were at home on Supervision Orders,[1] who would not be counted as 'looked-after' in the rest of the UK. A more valid yardstick for comparison may be the rate of children who are looked after and not placed with parents (this happens to some extent in England, Wales and also Northern Ireland). On this basis, the approximate rates per 10,000 are 52 in England, 58 in Northern Ireland, 83 in Wales and 110 in Scotland.

Trends in the numbers of children in care

Table 9.2 shows time trends in the rates of children in care since 2000. There are quite different patterns to these trends in the four countries of the UK.

Table 9.1: Numbers and rates of looked-after children by country, 31 March 2014 (England, Wales, Northern Ireland) and 31 July 2014 (Scotland)

	Numbers	Child population[1] (thousands)	Rate per 10,000	Adjusted rate per 10,000 (see below)
England	68,840	11,591	59	52[2]
Wales	5,760	630	91	83[3]
Scotland	15,580	1,033	151	110[4]
Northern Ireland	2,860	433	66	58[5]
Total	93,040	13,688	68	62

Notes:

[1] These are ONS population estimates for mid-2014 for the 0-17 age group. Note that some looked after young people are aged 18 and over, so the rates are approximations.

[2] Excludes looked-after children in England who had a 'placement with parents'.

[3] Excludes looked-after children in Wales 'placed with own parents or other person with parental responsibility'.

[4] Excludes looked-after children in Scotland living 'at home with parents'.

[5] Excluded looked-after children in Northern Ireland who were 'placed with parent'.

Table 9.2: Trends in numbers of children in care by country, selected years, 2000-14 (rounded to nearest 10)

Year	England	Wales	Scotland	Northern Ireland	UK total
2000	58,100	(3,700)	11,310	2,420	75,530
2005	60,900	4,380	12,190	2,530	79,990
2009	60,900	4,700	15,290	2,460	83,350
2010	64,470	5,160	15,890	2,610	88,130
2011	65,500	5,410	16,230	2,510	89,650
2012	67,070	5,720	16,250	2,640	91,680
2013	68,060	5,760	16,030	2,810	92,660
2014	68,840	5,760	15,580	2,860	93,040

In England, the numbers were steady between 2005 and 2009, but then during 2009-14 they increased by 13%. In Wales, the increase over the same five-year period was over 22%. In Scotland, the increase was only around 2%, and the numbers fell from a peak in 2012 to a slightly lower level in 2014. Finally, in Northern Ireland, the numbers increased by 16% between 2009 and 2014.

The reasons that children are admitted to care

Statistics are available on broadly defined categories of need for children admitted to care in England and Wales. In England, previous editions of this book noted a long-term increase in the proportion of children looked after for reasons of abuse and neglect between 1994 and 2003, a relatively stable period from 2003 to 2009, and another increase between 2009 and 2010. The proportion of children starting to be looked after due to abuse and neglect was a little higher in 2014 (55%) than in 2010 (52%), although it has been relatively stable over the past few years. The next most common categories of need in England were family dysfunction (19% in 2014 compared to 17% in 2010), family in acute stress (10% in 2014 compared to 11% in 2010) and absent parenting (6% in 2014 from 9% in 2010). This latter decrease appears to be partly attributable to a decline in the number of unaccompanied asylum-seeking children looked after who primarily appear in this category.

For Wales, 58% of cases in 2014 were due to abuse and neglect, 15% to family dysfunction and 11% to family in acute stress. The next most common category in Wales is socially unacceptable behaviour (5%), followed by absent parenting (4%). These proportions were broadly similar to those in 2010, although there has been an increase of 2% for family in acute stress and a decrease of 2% in absent parenting.

Characteristics of children in care

Age

There is an uneven age distribution of children who are looked after (see Table 9.3). In England in 2014 there was a greater representation per year group in the under 1 year (6%), 10-15 (37%) and 16 and over (21%) age groups than in the intervening age groups – 1-4 (17%) and 5-9 (20%). In terms of trends over the last five years, there has been a further small decrease in the proportions in the 10-15 age group, and a small increase in the 5-9 age group (reversing the trend noted in the previous edition). As a result, the mean age of looked-after children in England has fallen.

Table 9.3: Age distribution of looked-after children by country, 31 March 2014 (England, Wales, Northern Ireland) and 31 July 2014 (Scotland)

	Numbers	Rate per 10,000	2014 (%)	2010 (%)
England				
Under 1	3,880	58	6	6
1-4	11,440	41	17	17
5-9	13,920	43	20	17
10-15	25,140	70	37	39
16 and over	14,460	*	21	21
Wales				
Under 1	310	92	5	6
1-4	1,120	78	19	20
5-9	1,320	75	23	21
10-15	2,030	101	35	40
16 and over	975	*	17	14
Scotland				
Under 1	434	77	3	2
1-4	2,821	120	18	19
5-11	5,818	147	37	37
12-15	4,629	208	30	32
16-17	1,647	135	11	9
18 and over	231	*	1	1
Northern Ireland				
Under 1	92	38	3	3
1-4	562	55	20	17
5-11	944	57	33	30
12-15	723	79	25	31
16 and over	537	*	19	19

In Wales the age profile in 2014 was relatively similar to that in England. There has been a recent fall in the proportion of children in the 10-15 age group (from 40% in 2010 to 35% in 2014), and increases in the 5-9 and 16 plus age groups.

In Scotland over the last decade there has been a trend for children to start to be looked after at younger ages, with an increase from 8% being aged under 1 in 2004 to 16% in 2014, and a smaller proportion increase in the 1-4 age group. There was a corresponding decrease in the 12-15 age group. Thus, the mean age of children starting to be looked after in Scotland has fallen. Scotland has a greater concentration of looked-after children between the ages of 5 and 15 (67%) than Wales (61%) and England (57%).

In Northern Ireland, there has also been some reduction in the average age of looked-after children since 2010, with increases in the 1-11 age range and decreases in the 12-15 age group.

Gender

In England, around 55% of looked-after children are male and around 45% are female. This balance has been fairly consistent over the past five years.

The proportions of males in Wales, Scotland and Northern Ireland are 54%, 53% and 51% respectively.

Disabled children

There is longstanding evidence that disabled children and young people are over-represented in the care system (Berridge, 1997). However, Hill et al (2015) draw attention to the inconsistencies and limitations of statistics on the numbers of children in the looked-after system, and argue for more robust data to be collected.

In England, for looked-after children at the end of March 2014, 2,320 (3.4%) had a need category of 'child's disability' relating to the point when they started to be looked after. However, the total number of disabled looked-after children is likely to be substantially higher than this figure.

In Wales, statistics are available for children starting to be looked after, of whom 1.2% were looked after under the 'child's disability' need category.

In Scotland, official statistics are available on the numbers of looked-after children with additional support needs. In 2014, at least 12% of looked-after children were categorised as having one or more such needs. The largest groups were social, emotional and behavioural difficulties (3.3%), multiple disabilities (3.3%) and learning disabilities (1.8%).

In Northern Ireland, in 2013/14, 12% of children looked after for more than 12 months were reported as disabled, and this is likely to be higher than for the child population as a whole. The proportion was higher for boys (14%) than girls (10%).

The above statistics, and the statistics in this section in general, exclude short-term respite care.

Ethnic origin

In England in 2014, 78% of children in care were of White origin, 8% of mixed origin, 4% Asian or Asian British, 7% Black or Black British and 3% from other ethnic groups. There was a decrease in the number and proportion of children of Asian origin, from 3,400 (5.3%) in 2005 to 2,500 (3.7%) in 2010. The largest increase over the same period was for children of White origin, up from 49,000 (76%) in 2010 to 53,400 (78%) in 2014.

In Wales, 91% of looked-after children were of White origin, 6% from Black and minority ethnic (BME) groups and the ethnicity of 3% of children was unknown.

In Scotland, 89.5% of looked-after children were of White origin, 3.1% of Asian, Black, mixed or other origins, and the ethnic origins of the remainder (7.4%) were not disclosed or not known.

Unaccompanied asylum-seeking children

The large majority of 'unaccompanied asylum-seeking children', that is, those arriving in the UK unaccompanied by a parent or responsible adult, are referred to local children's services departments for help. In some authorities their numbers represent a substantial proportion of the care population. There were 1,970 unaccompanied asylum-seeking looked-after children in England at the end of March 2014, a substantial decrease from 3,480 in 2010. In 2010, 89% of these children were male and 68% were aged 16 and over.

Young mothers

In England, there were 300 mothers aged 12 and over looked after in March 2014. This number is lower than the comparable figure of 390 in 2010. Around 44% of these young people were under 16 at the time of the birth of their first child. A recent study by Craine et al (2014) in Wales found that females in the looked-after system had a significantly higher likelihood of pregnancy at a young age.

Experiences of care

There is a huge diversity of experience of care in terms of age of entry to care, type and stability of placement(s) and length of time spent in care. A study of over 7,000 children in the English care system (Sinclair et al, 2007) identified six groups of children for whom there were different patterns of care experiences: young entrants (under the age of 11); adolescent graduates (those who entered care before the age of 11 and were still looked after aged 11 and over); abused adolescents; other adolescent entrants; young people seeking asylum; and disabled children. The study found that the first two and last of the above groups had a higher chance of achieving a stable placement (or adoption) than the other three groups. Adoption was almost exclusively reserved for those children who first entered care under the age of five.

Numbers entering care

In England, 30,430 children started to be looked after in the year ending 31 March 2014 (see Table 9.4). This is an increase of 5% on the previous year and of 8% since 2010. The corresponding numbers for Wales, Scotland and Northern Ireland were 2,005, 4,292 and 910 respectively. The numbers for Wales have been broadly constant since 2010. The figure for Scotland has decreased by around 12% since 2010. The numbers have fluctuated over the past five years in Northern Ireland, and the total in 2014 was 13% lower than in 2010.

Table 9.4: Trends in numbers of children starting to be looked after by country, 2010-14

Year	England	Wales	Scotland	Northern Ireland
2010	28,090	2,025	4,859	1,042
2011	27,510	1,890	4,746	829
2012	28,390	1,975	4,811	865
2013	28,960	2,035	4,470	995
2014	30,430	2,005	4,292	910
Change	+8%	−1%	−12%	−13%

Placement type

Statistics are available on the types of placements in which children are looked after for each of the four countries of the UK. However, each set of statistics uses slightly different categorisations, and so it is difficult to make direct comparisons. These include the different legal provisions in Scotland relating to supervision at home, which have already been discussed above. With the exception of Scotland, where the majority (53%, down from 59% in 2010) of looked-after children are placed with parents, friends or relatives in the community, most looked-after children live in foster care.

Based on the most recent available statistics, the proportion living in foster care is highest in Wales (77%), followed by England (75%, an increase from 73% in 2010) and Northern Ireland (75%, an increase from 65% in 2010).

In contrast, relatively few looked-after children are placed in children's homes and other residential settings (with the highest proportion being around 12% in England followed by Scotland, 9%, Northern Ireland, 7%, and Wales, 4%). However, in Scotland, among children not accommodated with family and others in the community, the proportion in residential placements compared to foster placements is higher than in the other three countries.

Length of time in care

Many periods of being looked after are relatively short-lived. Of the placements that ended during the year ending 31 March 2014 in England, 19% had lasted one to seven days and over 80% had lasted less than a year. The average duration of all of these placements was 284 days.

In Scotland, the most recent statistics show that 30% of children ceasing to be looked after had been looked after for less than a year (a small reduction from 33% in 2010). In the last edition we noted that in 2009 almost half (47%) of those under the age of one were looked after for less than six weeks. This pattern has changed substantially, and now around a quarter (26%) are looked after for less than six weeks, with the majority (55%) being looked after for six weeks to under six months.

In Northern Ireland, 23% of children were discharged from care within three months. This is a substantial drop from 2010 when 43% were discharged within this time frame. There was also a drop in the proportion of children being discharged within one year – down from 58% in 2010 to 45% in 2014.

Placement stability and change

Stability and continuity of care placements have been shown to be key predictors of the well-being and longer-term outcomes of looked-after children (see, for example, Biehal et al, 1995, 2010; Sinclair et al, 2007), and so statistics on these aspects of care provision have come to be seen as important indicators.

In England, 11% of looked-after children at 31 March 2014 had had three or more placements during the year – the same percentage as in 2010.

For Wales, the proportion of looked-after children having three or more placements during the same year was 8%.

In Northern Ireland, 79% of children looked after continuously for 12 months or more had not experienced a placement change in the last year, and 2% had experienced three or more changes. These figures are not comparable with those for England and Wales above, which are for all looked-after children at 31 March 2014 irrespective of length of stay.

Rock et al (2015) undertook a systematic review and narrative synthesis of correlates of stability of foster placements. Factors associated with greater stability included younger age, fewer behavioural problems, placement with siblings, greater stability of social work support, kinship care and foster carers who were older, more experienced, had stronger parenting skills and provided intellectual development opportunities.

The well-being of children in care

In this section we summarise recent evidence on the well-being of children in care across a number of domains. Overall, there are indications that, viewed as a whole group, children in care fare less well than the average for the general population of children in a number of areas including health, education and longer-term outcomes as young adults. However, there are three important overarching points to bear in mind when reviewing this evidence.

First, indicators of 'well-being' should not be seen as synonymous with 'outcomes' of being looked after. In all domains, the well-being of children in care will have been influenced by various factors that occurred before their entry into the care system. Inevitably, children who enter the care system will, by and large, have already experienced considerable adversity in their lives. For example, in early childhood many will have experienced abuse or neglect that is known to have serious consequences for mental health (see Chapters Five and Ten). They may also have been less likely to receive standard healthcare and a good start in relation to their education. It is clear, then, that comparing the well-being of these children with the general population is not particularly meaningful, and is certainly not an indicator of the 'outcomes' of the care system. The question for the care system is how well they are able to compensate children for these adverse experiences and, in this respect, it is clear that more needs to be done.

Second, many of the official statistics and research findings for looked-after children relate specifically to that group of children who were either in care at a given moment or who remained in care until after the age of 16. These findings are therefore about specific sub-groups of children who experience care at some point in their lives. They may not accurately reflect 'outcomes' for all children who have spent time in care.

Finally, research studies have highlighted the considerable diversity that exists within the care system across a range of short-term and longer-term well-being measures. Overall, a number of studies (see, for example, Sinclair et al, 2007; Jones et al, 2011) have demonstrated the importance of the quality and stability of placements for maximising the well-being of looked-after children. Jones et al (2011) also identified the presence of emotional and behavioural problems as a key mediator of outcomes. A study of adoption and long-term foster care (Biehal et al, 2010) found that stable, long-term foster care could be very successful in providing positive outcomes for children. Where this form of stability was achieved, emotional, behavioural and educational outcomes were relatively similar to those achieved through adoption. Rees (2013) found considerable heterogeneity in measures of mental health, emotional literacy, cognitive ability and literacy attainment among looked-after children, and identified parental contact and mainstream education as factors that were associated with positive outcomes.

Subjective well-being

There is relatively little evidence on the subjective, self-reported well-being of the general population of looked-after children. Some studies of specific samples have developed such measures. In one recent study of a sample of 150 young people in foster care, children's homes and residential special schools (Berridge et al, 2008), the young people were asked to rate their well-being in six areas: schooling, family relationships, friendships, staying out of trouble, achieving goals and general happiness. The study found that young people's ratings regarding schooling, friendships and general happiness were negatively associated with changes in placements.

Currently, there appears to be a significant gap in more widespread measurement of the subjective well-being of looked-after children, including comparisons with the child population as a whole. Stein (2009) argues that young people's own perspectives are 'central to identifying the quality of services that will enhance their well-being' (p 116), and Bazalgette et al (2015) argue for an emphasis on 'emotional well-being' to be embedded throughout the care system.

Mental health

A study for the ONS (Meltzer et al, 2003) found that among children looked after by local authorities, 5- to 10-year olds were five times more likely to have a mental disorder than children living in private households, and 11- to 15-year-olds were four to five times more likely. The differences in rates of conduct disorder were particularly high – for example, 40% of 11- to 15-year-olds who were looked after compared to 6% of those living in private households. Similarly, higher rates were also reported in companion studies in Wales and Scotland (Meltzer et al, 2004a, 2004b). Further analysis of these data (Ford et al, 2007) also showed significantly higher rates of disorder for looked-after children than for children living in disadvantaged private households.

The above findings relate to children already being looked after. A study by Sempik et al (2008), based on analysis of case files, highlighted the already extensive emotional and behavioural difficulties of children at the point of entry into care. Luke et al (2014) stress the need for a balanced approach, arguing that 'the increased risk of mental health and well-being problems for looked after children cannot be solely attributed to their experiences of maltreatment and neglect within their birth families' (p 19), and draw attention to the way in which different experiences of being looked after can also have an impact on children's mental health and well-being.

In the last two years, the emotional and behavioural health of looked-after children has been monitored in England through the use of the Strengths and Difficulties Questionnaire (SDQ). In 2014, just over half (50.4%) of looked-after children had an SDQ score that was considered normal, 13% had a borderline score and 37% had a score that indicated cause for concern. These latter statistics have not varied over the past three years. A higher percentage of boys (40%) had a score that indicated cause for concern than girls (33%). Analysis by Goodman and Goodman (2012) confirmed that these levels of difficulties are much higher than for the child population as a whole, and that the parental SDQ (already validated for use with general child population samples) provided accurate estimates of mental health problems for looked-after children.

Physical health

Meltzer et al (2003) found that two-thirds of all looked-after children were reported by carers to have at least one 'physical complaint'. This included a number of categories that were higher than those in the general population: eye and/or sight problems (16%); speech or language problems (14%); bed wetting (13%); difficulty with coordination (10%); and asthma (10%). A more recent analysis by Martin et al (2014) found that looked-after children had a higher prevalence of cerebral palsy, epilepsy and cystic fibrosis than other children, although they also appeared to have lower rates of asthma, eczema and hay fever. Martin et al (2014) note that placement changes may also affect continuity of healthcare.

The previous edition of this book noted a substantial increase in routine healthcare for looked-after children between 2000 and 2010. Statistics for 2014 indicate that this position has been maintained and that there have been further improvements. In the year to March 2014 (with comparable percentages for 2010 in brackets), 84% (82%) of children who had been looked after continuously for at least 12 months had had a dental check-up; 87% (77%) had up-to-date immunisations; and 88% (84%) had had their annual health assessment. Additionally, in England, 87% of looked-after children aged five or under were up to date with their developmental assessments, an increase on previous years (82% in 2012 and 85% in 2013).

In Northern Ireland, 99% of children under the age of five who had been looked after continuously for more than 12 months had up-to-date development and six monthly assessments, and 89% of children aged five and over had their annual health assessment up to date. Immunisation and dental check-up rates were 99% and 96% respectively, considerably higher than in England.

Education

Children who are looked after tend to have lower levels of educational achievement than other children. This attainment gap has been the focus of considerable policy attention in recent years. However, as with other areas of well-being discussed in this section, the educational attainment of looked-after children needs to be viewed within the overall context of their lives. Children's experiences before entering care and their experiences in care (for example, placement instability) can adversely affect their educational attainment (O'Sullivan and Westerman, 2007). In the most recent government statistics in England, around 29% of children who had been looked after continuously for a year or more had a statement of special educational needs (SEN) and a further 38% had SEN without a statement. These figures compare to 3% and 15% in the general population. Similarly in Northern Ireland 26% of looked-after children had a statement of SEN compared to 5% in the general school population.

In England, statistics are published on the educational attainment of looked-after children, and comparisons with the general population, at the end of Key Stage 1 (around the age of 7), Key Stage 2 (around the age of 11) and Key Stage 4. All statistics are for children looked after continuously for at least 12 months, and these are compared with non-looked-after children.

At Key Stage 1 the percentages of looked-after children in England achieving Level 2 or above in Reading, Writing and Maths in 2014 were 71%, 61% and 72% respectively (see Table 9.5). These percentages compare with 90%, 86% and 92% for other children. There have been improvements in all three measures for looked-after children since 2010. However, there is little evidence of a closing of the attainment gap between looked-after children and other children (although the percentage difference for Reading had fallen from 21% in 2010 to 19% in 2014).

At Key Stage 2 the percentages of looked-after children in England achieving expected levels of progress in Reading, Writing and Maths in 2014 were 75%, 81% and 82% compared to 89%, 91% and 93% for other children. There is evidence of improvements in the percentages for looked-after children over the last few years and of the attainment gap reducing. For example, the percentage gap in pupils at Level 4 or above in Maths and Reading fell from 33% and 29% respectively in 2010 to 25% and 21% respectively in 2014.

There are large attainment gaps between looked-after children and other children at Key Stage 4 (GCSEs). In 2014, 14% of looked-after children achieved A*-C grades in English and Maths and 12% achieved five A*-C grades including English and Maths. These figures compare with 54% and 52% for the population of non-looked-after children. Between 2010 and 2013, attainment gaps had increased a little. There was a change in methodology for these measures (for the population as a whole) in 2014.

Table 9.5: Educational attainment of looked-after children in England, Wales and Northern Ireland, trends and comparisons with general population

	Looked-after (%)		All (%)
	2010	2014	2014
England			
Key Stage 1			
Maths	68	72	92
Reading	64	71	90
Writing	56	61	86
Key Stage 2			
Maths	47	61	86
Reading	54	68	89
Writing	na	59	85
Key Stage 4 (GCSE)			
A*-C in English and Maths	na	14	54
5+ A*-C	na	16	62
5+ A*-C (including English and Maths)	na	12	52
Wales			
Achieved Key Stage 2 Core Subject Indicator	44	52	84
Achieved Key Stage 3 Core Subject Indicator	25	37	77
Average qualification points score at 16	152	262	501
Northern Ireland			
Key Stage 1			
Level 2 in English/Communication	na	82	91
Level 2 in Mathematics/Using Maths	na	83	92
Key Stage 2			
Level 4 in English/Communication	na	37	80
Level 4 in Mathematics/Using Maths	na	34	80
Key Stage 3			
Level 5 in English/Communication	na	27	74
Level 5 in Mathematics/Using Maths	na	22	77
GCSE			
1 or more GCSE Grades A*-G	64	73	100
5 or more GCSE Grades A*-G	42	49	98
5 or more GCSE Grades A*-C	20	29	82

Figures are also published in England on rates of school exclusions. The most recent data relates to the 2012/13 academic year. The permanent exclusion rate in 2012/13 for looked-after children was 0.11%, which is an improvement from 0.27% in 2009/10, and a closing of the gap between looked-after and other children, although the rate is still almost twice as high as for all children (0.06%). There have also been improvements in the rate of fixed term exclusions – down from 12.6% in 2009/10 to 9.8% in 2012/13, although this is still over five times as high as for all children (1.9%).

In Wales, statistics are available for the educational attainment of looked-after children at the end of Key Stages 2, 3 and 4 (see Table 9.5). The data for each year relates to the preceding school year (for example, 2014 data relates to the 2012/13 school year). The percentage of looked-after children achieving the Core Subject Indicator in the 2014 data was 52% at Key Stage 2 and 37% at Key Stage 3. These are an improvement on the 2012 figures – 44% and 25% respectively. There was also an improvement in the average qualification points score for 16-year-old children – up from 152 in 2010 to 262 in 2014. As in England, there is a large attainment gap between looked-after children and the general population. The comparable statistics for all children in Wales in 2014 were 84% at Key Stage 2, 77% at Key Stage 3 and an average points score of 501 at the age of 16.

There were similar patterns in the most recent statistics (2013/14) in Northern Ireland (see Table 9.5). The proportion of children attaining Level 2 or above at Key Stage 2 was 82% in Communication and 83% in Using Maths, compared to 91% and 92% for the general school population. At Key Stage 2, 37% of looked-after children achieved Level 4 or above in Communication and 34% in Maths, compared to 80% for both measures in the general population. At Key Stage 3, 27% of looked-after children achieved Level 5 or above in Communication and 22% in Maths, compared to 74% and 77% respectively in the general population. At GCSE level, 29% of looked-after children achieved five or more GCSEs at grades A*-C. This compares with 82% of the general school population, but is an improvement from 20% in 2009/10.

There is some evidence from research that those looked-after children who fare better educationally tend to be female, to have started to be looked after at a younger age, to have been looked after longer, most often in foster settings, to have had fairly settled care careers and active encouragement from primary caregivers, teachers and social workers (Biehal et al, 1995; Wade and Dixon, 2006; McClung and Gayle, 2010).

It remains unclear how looked-after children's educational attainment might be improved further through interventions. A systematic review of interventions to provide educational support to looked-after children (Liabo et al, 2013) found a lack of robust studies that had demonstrated evidence of effectiveness.

Offending

Young people who are looked after have a higher than average likelihood of being involved in the youth justice system. In England 1,710 children (5.6%) of looked-after children aged 10 and over were convicted or subject to a final warning or reprimand during the year ending March 2014. These numbers and percentages have fallen over the last few years, from 6.9% in 2012. The rate is substantially higher than the rate for all children of this age in the population (less than 1.5%).

In Northern Ireland 9% of looked-after children aged 10 and over had been cautioned or convicted of an offence while in care during the year ending 30 September 2014. Males (12%) were more likely to commit offences than females (7%), and children placed in foster care were the least likely (2%) to be cautioned or convicted, although differing age profiles according to placement type should be borne in mind here.

Schofield et al (2015) point out that factors in the family backgrounds of children who come into care, such as higher than average incidence of deprivation, poor parenting and maltreatment, are also factors associated with a higher risk of offending. Nevertheless, as was the case for mental health earlier, children's subsequent experiences within the care system are also linked with risk of offending. Schofield et al found that older age of entry to care, larger number of placement moves and residential placements were all associated with increased rates of offending, although in the latter case it was not clear whether being in a residential placement was the 'cause and/or the consequence of offending'. Hayden (2010) argues, using a small cohort study, that residential care 'presents a set of risks that tend to reinforce offending behaviour and that this is partly due to its "last resort" status' (p 461). As Schofield et al note, it should also be borne in mind that older children entering the care system may have already started committing offences prior to be being looked after.

Substance use

The most recent government statistics on substance misuse among looked-after children show that around 1,680 children (3.5%) who had been looked after continuously for at least 12 months in England had been identified as having a substance misuse problem during the last year. This is a reduction both numerically and proportionally compared to 2010 (2,200 children, 5%). Research has shown that compared with the general population, children in care and young people leaving care have relatively high levels of tobacco, alcohol and drug use (Meltzer et al, 2003). However, it should not be assumed that these difficulties are attributable to the care system.

Routes out of care

In the most recent years for which statistics are available, the numbers of children ceasing to be looked after in each country were as follows – 30,430 in England (an increase of over 5,000 since 2010), 2,007 in Wales (an increase of 27% since 2010), 4,676 in Scotland (a small increase of 4% since 2010) and 798 in Northern Ireland (a reduction of 12% since 2010) (see Table 9.6).

In England around two-thirds of looked-after children ceasing to be looked after were under the age of 16. Looked-after children and young people who are accommodated in foster care, residential care and other settings ceased to be looked after through four main routes – returning home to live with parents or relatives, through adoption, through special guardianship or residence orders, or to live independently (at age 16 and over).

Returning to live with parents or relatives is the most common pathway out of the looked-after system. In England it accounted for 10,300 cases in 2014. This is a slight numerical increase since 2010, but a proportional drop from 39% of cases in 2010 to 34% in 2014. In Wales, Scotland[2] and Northern Ireland the proportions leaving care through this route were 37% (down from 46% in 2010) 66% (to parents) and 68% respectively. In Scotland, in addition to this percentage, 14% of children left care to live with friends or relatives.

The number of children adopted from care in the most recent year for which statistics are available for each country was 5,050 in England (17% of children ceasing to be looked after), 345 (up from 230 in 2010) in Wales, 7% in Scotland and 9% in Northern Ireland.

Table 9.6: Trends in numbers of children ceasing to be looked after by country, 2010-14

Year	England	Wales	Scotland	Northern Ireland
2010	25,300	1,579	4,504	908
2011	27,110	1,627	4,611	837
2012	27,510	1,652	4,768	745
2013	28,640	1,967	4,731	850
2014	30,430	2,007	4,676	798
Change	+20%	+27%	+4%	−12%

In England, in the last edition we reported that there was a decrease in looked-after children being adopted over the five-year period between 2006 and 2010. This trend has now been reversed, and the number of children adopted in 2014 was much higher than in 2006, at 3,700.

The Adoption and Children Act 2002 introduced a new legal option of special guardianship for England and Wales. A Special Guardianship Order, made by a court, provides a legal status for adults (other than parents) to look after a child. Unlike adoption, the birth parents also retain legal status in relation to the child. In England in 2006, when this option first became legally available, 70 looked-after children ceased to be looked after through a Special Guardianship Order. In the last edition we reported that this number had increased substantially to over 1,200 children in 2009 and in 2010. Since 2010, the numbers leaving care with a Special Guardianship Order have continued to increase to 3,330 in 2014. This route accounts for 11% of all children ceasing to be looked after in 2014 compared to 5% in 2010. The use of Residence Orders also increased in England, from 1,010 cases in 2010 to 1,690 in 2014, accounting for 6% of children ceasing to be looked after. In Wales there has also been an increase in the use of Special Guardianship Orders, from 60 (4%) children ceasing to be looked after in 2010 to 275 (14%) children ceasing to be looked after in 2014.

The final main route of leaving care is to move into independent living from the age of 16. In England in the year ending March 2014, 12% of children leaving care moved into independent accommodation, 69% of whom moved into some form of supported accommodation. In Wales 11% of children left through this route, 78% of whom moved into supported accommodation. In Scotland, 6% of children left care to move into supported accommodation or their own tenancy. In Northern Ireland, 5% of children moved into independent living.

In Northern Ireland there are also arrangements for children aged 18-21 to live with their former foster carers to provide continuity of living arrangements. In 2014, 10% of children were discharged from care through this route. In Scotland 1.7% of children (all ages) left care to live with former foster carers.

As well as these main identified routes out of care, some children were also categorised as leaving for 'other' or unknown reasons. The percentages in this category for each country were 16% (England), 17% (Wales), 5% (Scotland) and 10% (Northern Ireland). Information is not provided for the meaning of this category for England and Wales. In Scotland it is noted to include 'residential care, homeless, in custody and other destination' and in Northern Ireland it can include 'bed and breakfasts, hostels, supported board and lodgings, prison, hospital, etc.'

Returning home from care

There has been a relative lack of research in the UK about what happens to children who return home from care ('reunification'). This is an important issue because it is common for reunification to break down and for children to return to the looked-after system. Wade et al (2010), in a comparative study of outcomes for maltreated children returning home from care and those remaining looked after, found that 35% of a sample of children who returned home had re-entered the looked-after system within six months. They also found that maltreated children who remained looked-after had better outcomes for stability and well-being than children who were reunified.

Farmer and Wijedasa (2012) studied the factors that contribute to return stability, and found a number of factors that were related to successful returns. Factors prior to return were: no previous concerns about physical abuse, 'exceptional support' by caregivers for the return, and whether the parent actively sought the return. Factors after return that were significant positively related with stability were: adequate support provided, the involvement of other agencies, a change in household composition since the child was last at home, and lack of recorded concerns about poor parenting.

Leaving care aged 16 and over

For most young people today, moving on from their families and in to their own accommodation, entering training, further or higher education, or finding employment, and achieving good health and a positive sense of well-being, represent important landmarks during their journey to adulthood.

Official data for 2014 shows that 12,761 young people aged 16 and over left care in the UK (see Table 9.7). The numbers have increased from 8,307 in 2003 to 12,761 in 2014. Between 2003 and 2014 the numbers have more than doubled in Northern Ireland (from 206 to 508) and Wales (from 327 to 665), increased in England from 6,500 to 10,310, and changed very little in Scotland (from 1,274 to 1,278).

In England and Northern Ireland there is evidence that from 2010 a greater percentage of young people were leaving care at the age of 18 and over. In 2010 two-thirds of young people in Northern Ireland remained in care until they were 18, and by 2014 nine out of ten

Table 9.7: Number of young people aged 16 and over leaving care in the UK year ending 31 March 2014 (England, Wales, Northern Ireland) and 31 July 2014 (Scotland)

	16-17 years old*		18 years old and over		
	Number	%	Number	%	Total
England	3,430	33	6,880	67	10,310
Wales					663
Scotland	1,143[1]	89	135	11	1,274
Northern Ireland	51	10	457	90	508
Total					12,761

Note: [1]Scotland includes young people aged 15-16 'who were beyond minimum school leaving age on date they cease to be looked after (on 31 July 2014).

young people left care at 18 or older. In England, from 2010, the percentage of young people leaving care at 16 and 17 has gradually reduced, from 38% to 33% for the year ending 2014. In contrast, only 11% of young people in Scotland left care at 18 and over in 2014 and just under 90% left at 16 and 17. No comparable data is available for Wales.

Young people's accommodation

There is a lack of comparable official data on accommodation in the four countries of the UK. In Scotland there is official data on 'young people eligible for aftercare services by age' between the ages of 15-16 and 19-21. In England data is only available on young people's accommodation at ages 19-21. In Northern Ireland data is available on young people aged 16-18 and at 19, and in Wales data is not currently available (see Table 9.8).

In England for the year ending March 2014, just over a third (34%) of young people were in 'independent living' accommodation at the age of 19. A further 12% were in 'semi-independent or transitional' accommodation, 8% were in supported lodgings and a further 2% were in 'ordinary lodgings'. Around one in eight (12%) 19-year-old care leavers were living with parents or relatives, and a further 5% with former foster carers. (Note that voluntary data collection on 18-year-olds in England of those eligible for care leaver support [from 120 local authorities] showed that a quarter of 18-year-olds remained with their former foster carers.)

It should also be noted that in England 1% of young people aged 19, 20 and 21 were of 'no fixed abode/homeless', and 1% were in 'bed and breakfast' accommodation at age 19 and less than 1% at age 20 and 21.

Table 9.8: Accommodation status of young people leaving care in England, Scotland and Northern Ireland, 2013-14 (%)

England	Age 19
With parents or relatives	12
Community home	4
Semi-independent, transitional accommodation	12
Supported lodgings	8
Independent living	34
With former foster carers	5
In custody	3
Other	10
Unknown	12
Scotland	**Age 19–21**
Home with (biological) parents	12
Friends/relatives	7
Own tenancy/independent living	26
Supported accommodation/semi-independent living	14
Former foster carers	3
In residential care	1
Homeless	3
In custody	2
Other destination[4]	2
Not known	6
Not receiving aftercare	22
Northern Ireland	**Age 19**
Supported lodgings	13
Foster carers	28
Parents, family or friends	22
Independent accommodation	28
Other including custody	10

[4] Home with newly adopted parents is included in 'Other destination' due to small numbers

At age 19, 83% were in 'accommodation considered suitable', at age 20, this dropped to 79% and at 21, it dropped to 71%; 6% at 19 and 20, and 5% at 21 were in 'unsuitable accommodation'.

In Scotland, just over a quarter (26%) of young people aged 19-21 were in their 'own tenancy/independent living'. A further 14% were in 'supported accommodation or semi–independent living'. Almost a fifth (19%) were either 'at home with parents' or 'with friends or relatives' and just over 3% were living with former foster carers. In Scotland 9% of 'young people eligible for aftercare services' had 'one or more spells of homelessness'.

In Northern Ireland, around 28% of care leavers aged 19 were living in independent accommodation and a further 13% were living in supported lodgings. Around 22% were living with parents, family or friends and 28% with former foster carers.

These figures illustrate the diversity of accommodation outcomes for young people leaving care across the different countries of the UK.

Leaving care and accommodation: normative context and research

In all four countries, young people leave care at a younger age than young people in the general population leave the parental home, and many feel they leave care too early (NAO, 2015). The latest ONS data (for 2013) showed that over a quarter of adults (26%) aged between 20 and 34 were living with a parent or parents, and just under half (49%) of 20- to 24-year-olds and 21% of 25- to 29-year-olds lived with their parents (ONS, 2015b).

As detailed above, most young people in the UK leave care between the ages of 16 and 18, and there is evidence of young people leaving care at an older age in England and Northern Ireland. However, normative comparisons show that only 3% of 20-year-olds and 2% of 21-year-olds in England were living with former foster carers – a very small percentage in comparison to half of 20- to 24-year-olds in the general population who were living with parents. In Northern Ireland over a quarter of young people aged 19 (28%) were living with former carers at 19, and although about half of the young people in the general population at age 20-24, this represents an upward trend. In all four countries of the UK policy changes have been introduced to give young people the right of 'staying put' in placements where they are settled (see the box below).

Research studies during the last 10 years have shown that care leavers are vulnerable to homelessness and instability after leaving care (Dixon and Stein, 2005; Stein and Morris, 2010; Dixon et al, 2015). The young people most likely to experience entrenched housing problems, including homelessness and living in 'unsuitable accommodation', include young people who leave care early, often at ages 16 and 17, who move frequently for negative reasons, who have mental health problems, emotional and behavioural difficulties, and who leave secure accommodation (Stein and Morris, 2010). In England there is evidence of an increase in 16- and 17-year-olds presenting as homeless and becoming looked after (NAO, 2105).

Evaluation of the Staying Put 18+ Family Placement pilot programme

The Staying Put 18+ Family Placement pilot programme was introduced in 11 local authorities in July 2008, giving young people who have 'established familial relationships' the opportunity to remain with their foster carers up to the age of 21. The evaluation was carried out between 2009-11 and included a mapping exercise and interviews with managers in the 11 pilot authorities, followed by peer research interviews with young people (21 staying put, 11 who did not); interviews with their carers, personal advisers; and data on time and costs of practitioners.

The benefits of 'Staying Put'

- Empowers young people and gives them greater control of the timing of their transition from care to adulthood, rather than them feeling that they are being 'kicked out' of the system.

- Young people are not penalised by virtue of their care status; they are offered the opportunity to experience transitions that are more akin to those experienced by their peers in the general population.

- Allows young people to remain in a nurturing family environment with their foster carers giving continuity and stability, and provides an environment in which young people can mature and develop, prepare for independence and receive support.

- Those staying put were more likely to be in full-time education at 19 than their counterparts who did not stay put, and a higher proportion of young people who stayed put were also pursuing higher education than those who did not.

- Those who did not stay put were more likely to be NEET (not in education, training or employment) a year after they left care.

- In-depth qualitative data on a small sample of young people also revealed that those who did not stay put were more likely to experience complex transition pathways and housing instability after they left care.

The challenges

- In most pilot authorities young people had to have an 'established familial relationship' and be in education, employment or training, potentially excluding more vulnerable young people including late entrants to care, those with a history of instability, those with emotional and behavioural difficulties and those NEET.

> • Not all young people are willing and able to stay put, and will need ongoing support services into adulthood.
>
> *Source:* Adapted from Munro et al (2012)

Education, employment and training

The educational attainment gaps between looked-after and other children up to the age of 16 have already been covered. Given these gaps, it is not surprising that care leavers had substantially lower than average levels of educational qualifications.

In Wales, over a quarter (29%) of young people leaving care aged 16 and over had no qualifications compared to just 1% of young people in the general population. In Scotland, the average tariff scores for looked-after young people was 116 compared to 407 for all school leavers, although there is evidence of improvement in outcomes between 2009/10 and 2012/13 (the most recent year). In Northern Ireland, 21% of care leavers aged 16-18 left care with five GCSEs (grades A★-C) or higher compared to more than three-quarters (79%) of all general school leavers. Just over a quarter of all care leavers (28%) left care with no qualifications compared with 1% of general school leavers.

Table 9.9 shows economic activity figures for young people aged 19 in care or leaving care. For Scotland this relates to young people eligible for aftercare, and the statistics cover a wider age range (19-21). There is apparently a wide range of proportions of young people in education, employment and training in each country, and similarly a range of proportions of young people NEET. However, there are also different categorisations in each country, as well as different legal and economic contexts, and so it is probably unwise to make comparisons.

Educational attainment, post-16 education, employment and training: normative data and research

The official data shows that in all four countries of the UK young people leaving care, aged 16-18 and over, have lower levels of educational attainment, are far less likely to go on to higher education and more likely not to be in education, employment and training than young people in the general population. There is, however, evidence of some improvement in educational attainment in recent years.

Table 9.9: Education, employment and training outcomes for care leavers at the age of 19 (%)

England	19
In higher education	6
In other education	26
In training or employment	21
NEET, illness or disability	5
NEET, pregnancy or parenting	4
NEET, other reasons	27
No information	11
Wales	**19**
In full-time education, training or employment	41
In part-time education, training or employment	10
NEET or not in touch	49
Scotland	**19-21**
In higher education	4
In other education	9
In training or employment	16
NEET, illness or disability	3
NEET, looking after family	4
NEET, other reasons	29
Not known	13
Not receiving aftercare	22
Northern Ireland	**19**
In education	26*
In training	29*
In employment	9*
Full-time parent/carer	4*
Sick or disabled	9*
Unemployed	23*

Note: * Above figures exclude care leavers not in contact with services.

Recent research in England has demonstrated the association between educational attainment and future education and employment outcomes: none of those who were *not* in education, employment or training had achieved the national indicator of attainment of five A★-C grade GCSEs. The same study showed that education engagement or success was the most prominent indication of personal achievement highlighted by young people (Dixon et al, 2015). Analysis of data from the Swedish national registers based on 10 entire birth cohorts has identified poor school performance as a major risk factor of psychosocial problems in adulthood for young people who aged out of foster care (Berlin et al, 2011).

International research has also identified the main facilitating factors and obstacles to improve post-16 educational outcomes. The former include stability, staying put in placements after the age of 18, action-orientated personal education plans, financial and practical help and support from family, friends and carers. The obstacles include multiple placements, disrupted schooling and failure to compensate for gaps in school education, problems in birth families, no emphasis on education or interest in school experience, low self-esteem and lack of aspiration, lack of basic skills (especially literacy), poor conditions for study, and not knowing any one with higher education experience (Jackson and Cameron 2014).

The National Audit Office has estimated that the lifetime cost of the 2015 cohort of 19-year-old care leavers in England being NEET would be around £240 million or £150 million more than if they had the same NEET rate as other 19-year-olds (NAO, 2015). Research has also identified what can contribute to good career outcomes, including building on educational success, encouragement by carers, stability, fewer moves after leaving care, being settled in accommodation and targeted career support (Bilson et al, 2011; Tilbury et al, 2011; Stein 2012).

Health and well-being, including offending and substance abuse

Limited official data is collected annually on the health and well-being of young people leaving care aged 16 and over. In England, the SDQ, which is used to assess the emotional and behavioural health of looked-after children, applies only to those children and young people aged 5-16. The official data for Northern Ireland, Wales and Scotland does not contain data on the emotional health and well-being of young people leaving care aged 16 and over.

Annual information on the 'health care of children who have been looked after continuously for at least 12 months' is published in England. For 2014 this showed that for young people aged 16 and over, 80% had an annual health assessment, three-quarters had a dental check-up and over three-quarters (78.9%) had up-to-date immunisations. There is no comparable data for the other three countries.

In England, for the year ending 2013, 11.1% of looked-after young people aged 16 and 17 were 'convicted or subject to a final warning or reprimand' during the year compared to 2.7% of all 16- and 17-year-olds. In 2014, 10% of looked-after young people aged 16 and 17 were 'convicted or subject to a final warning or reprimand' during the year (data for all 16- and 17-year-olds was not available). The percentage of young people aged 16 and 17 'identified as having a substance abuse problem' was 9.7% in 2012 and 9.2% in 2014. Over half (57.6%) of these young people 'received an intervention' and just over a third of young people (34%) 'were offered but refused it' in 2014. There is no comparable data for the other three countries.

In England 3% of young people were 'in custody' at ages 19, 20 and 21, and in Scotland, 2.3% for the same age group were in custody. In Wales 35 young people were sentenced to custody (13.5% of those who moved to independent living either 'supported' or 'providing no formalised support').

Health and well-being: normative data and research

There is limited research on the health and well-being of young people aged 16 and over leaving care. An analysis of four UK surveys (ONS) that included young people aged 5-17 found that the prevalence of psychosocial adversity and psychiatric disorder ranged from 45% to 49% (Ford et al, 2007). This was higher than the most socioeconomically disadvantaged children living in private households.

Their analysis also showed that fewer than one in ten looked-after children and young people demonstrated particularly good psychological adjustment, as distinct from having mental health problems. As regards 'care-related variables', they also found high rates of emotional and conduct disorder among young people living in residential care, or living independently, and associations between psychiatric disorders of looked-after children and entering the care system later, more reported changes of placement within the past year and having lived for less time in their current placement (Ford et al, 2007).

There is also research evidence that young people's physical and mental health problems may increase at the time of leaving care: those aged 16 and over are twice as likely as 13- to 15-year-olds to have mental health problems, and care leavers have a lower feeling of overall well-being than those still in care (Dixon et al, 2015). This may be associated with young people coping with the physical and psychological demands of accelerated and compressed transitions – leaving care early and coping with major changes in a short time – combined with earlier pre-care and in-care problems (Dixon, 2008).

Bullock and Gaehl (2012) undertook a longitudinal analysis over a 25 to 30-year period of children admitted to care in England and Wales in 1980. They found that, compared to the general population, all people who had been in care were at increased risk of criminality and early death, although this research is, of course, reflective of the care population in 1980.

Recent research in England has also shown that 22% of female care leavers become teenage parents – which is about three times the national average (Centre for Social Justice, 2014).

Supporting young people from care to adulthood: official data and research

There is limited official data that is comparable on the personal support and contact received by young people from children's services in the four countries of the UK. Northern Ireland provides the most information. This shows that for 2013/14, Health and Social Care (HSC) Trusts reported contact with 93% of care leavers aged 19, and this represented an increase of 21 percentage points from 2003/04 when the contact rate was just under three-quarters (72%). Social services were in contact with almost three-quarters of care leavers aged 19 at least once a month, and the data also showed that 97% of 19-year-olds with dependents were in contact with their HSC Trust compared to 93% without dependents. In relation to the last placement for care leavers, contact rates ranged between 97% for those previously in non-kinship foster care or in independent living arrangements to 90% for those whose last placement was residential care.

There is very little data on the other three countries: in England, analysis of data between 2002 and 2012 shows that local authorities were in touch with a higher number and proportion of care leavers aged 19 who were looked after aged 16. In Scotland 70% of young people 'eligible for aftercare services' aged 15-16 to 19-21 were receiving aftercare in 2014 and 89% had 'a pathway plan, and 80% 'a nominated pathway coordinator' on date of discharge. In Wales, 93% of care leavers 'on their 19th birthday' were in touch in 2014.

Research shows that young people want and value both practical and personal support in preparation for moving, at the time of moving on from care and when they have moved into their accommodation, including when they get into difficulties (Stein, 2012). A majority of young people (55%) find their pathway plans 'very' or 'quite useful', but more than four in ten answered 'not very useful' or 'not at all useful' (Dixon et al, 2015). There is also evidence from Northern

Ireland that less than half of young people surveyed over the age of 16 (44%) could 'talk to their personal advisor about what is happening in their life' (VOYPIC, 2014, p 25). Evidence from official data and research in the four countries of the UK shows wide variations between local authorities in the information and services young people receive and the way they are being supported on their journey from care to adulthood (Centre for Social Justice, 2014; Dixon et al, 2015; McGhee et al, 2014; DHSSPS, 2015; NAO, 2015).

Conclusion

The numbers of looked-after children in the UK have increased substantially over the last four or five years in England, Wales and Northern Ireland while remaining reasonably stable in Scotland. There is a trend towards children becoming looked after at a lower average age.

Research studies and official statistics have drawn attention to the higher probability of negative well-being and longer-term outcomes for looked-after children in comparison with the general population. Looked-after children as a group are more likely to have mental health problems, less likely to do well at school, and more likely to become involved in offending and substance use than the average for the population as a whole. Comparisons between looked-after children and the general population of children may not be particularly appropriate as they do not take into account the backgrounds and characteristics of children who became looked after, which often include a number of factors known to be associated with poorer well-being and outcomes.

However, we noted in the last edition that there were indications from monitoring and research that the well-being of looked-after children is improving in a number of areas. Where data is available, there appear to have been further improvements since 2010 in educational attainment and healthcare and reductions in offending and substance use. These are positive signs.

The evidence discussed above shows the vulnerability of young people leaving care. They leave care at a younger age than other young people leave the family home, and those who leave under 18 years of age are at a high risk of homelessness and instability. Opportunities for young people to 'stay put' in placements is very welcome. Looked-after children are far less likely to go onto higher education and more likely to be NEET than young people in the general population. They also have higher levels of mental health problems and involvement in risky behaviours, which may continue into adulthood.

Notes

[1] Under Section 70(1) of the Children (Scotland) Act 1995. The overall aim of these is to promote beneficial changes in the lives of children while enabling them to remain at home.

[2] In Scotland this includes children who were at home on Supervision Orders.

TEN

Child maltreatment

Gwyther Rees

Key statistics

- In March/July 2014 there were over 56,000 children on the child protection register/subject to a child protection plan in the UK*.
- There were 48 child homicides in the UK* in 2013-14.
- There were over 36,000 recorded sexual offences and 9,500 recorded offences of cruelty and neglect against children under the age of 18 in the UK* in 2013-14.
- The most recent self-report survey data (NSPCC) indicates lifetime retrospective rates of maltreatment and severe maltreatment by a parent or guardian of 25% and 15% respectively. Experience of neglect is more common than (in descending order) physical violence, emotional abuse and sexual abuse. Almost a quarter of children (24%) are exposed to domestic violence at some point in childhood.
- Many children also experience lifetime maltreatment by non-resident adults (13%), peer victimisation (63%), sibling victimisation (25%), intimate partner abuse (13%) and exposure to community violence (67%).
- Many children experience bullying at school, by siblings and online, and there is growing evidence of its negative short-term and long-term impacts.

Key trends

- Rates of child protection registration have risen substantially since 2010 in England (+20%), Wales (+17%) and Scotland (+14%), but have fallen in Northern Ireland (−20%).
- There is evidence of a long-term decline in violent death in infancy and middle childhood, while rates in adolescence have remained stable or possibly risen.
- Rates of recorded sexual offences against children have increased in all four countries since 2009-10.

- Rates of recorded offences of cruelty and neglect have increased since 2009-10 in England and Northern Ireland, have remained stable in Wales and have decreased in Scotland.
- There is some evidence of a decrease in self-reported experiences of physical abuse over the decade between 1999 and 2009

Key sources
- Child protection statistics for England, Wales, Scotland and Northern Ireland
- Crime statistics for England, Wales, Scotland and Northern Ireland
- Jütte et al (2015)
- Radford et al (2011)
- A range of other self-report surveys including Health Behaviour of School-aged Children (HBSC), Children's Worlds, EU Kids Online, Net Children Go Mobile, NSPCC Social Networking Survey, Ofcom Media Use and Attitudes Survey 2014

Note: * Legislative, definitional and reporting differences between the four countries should be borne in mind regarding the official statistics.

Introduction

This chapter focuses on child maltreatment in a broad sense. It summarises the latest available research findings and official statistics on child abuse and neglect, and covers a range of topics that may also be considered aspects of maltreatment, including child homicide, bullying and peer victimisation and harmful experiences related to new technologies.

There have been significant developments relevant to safeguarding and child protection services since the last edition of this book was published four years ago. First, the repercussions of the death of Peter Connelly in 2007 (Macleod et al, 2010) appear to have continued to have had an impact on the child protection system, not only in England, but also in the other countries of the UK. Second, the Munro Review (Munro, 2011), initiated by the new coalition government in 2010, recommended substantial changes to child protection work in England with a recalibration of the balance between central guidance and professional judgement. And third, there have been a number of high profile cases of child sexual exploitation that have been cited as putting additional pressures on the child protection and looked-after systems (NAO, 2014).

However, this is only part of the story. As Davies and Ward (2012) observe, there are definitional difficulties with concepts of maltreatment, abuse and neglect:

> One reason why it is not easy to calculate the prevalence of abuse and neglect is that definitions vary. For instance, in view of emerging evidence concerning their long-term impact on children and young people's welfare, it could be argued that greater attention should be given to bullying by peers and siblings, teenage intimate partner violence and neighbourhood violence. If the numbers of children experiencing these types of maltreatment were routinely included in calculations, the apparent prevalence would greatly increase.... (Davies and Ward, 2012, p 17)

In addition to Davies and Ward's list, concerns about the risks posed by children's use of the internet and other new technologies have also emerged and might be regarded as potential child maltreatment issues.

In line with previous editions, this chapter treats child maltreatment as an outcome of concern in its own right. However, there is also ample evidence of the negative short-term and long-term consequences of child maltreatment for other aspects of child well-being considered elsewhere in this book, including poorer physical health, mental health, life satisfaction, education and employment outcomes and higher risk of criminal involvement (in the US, see Buckingham and Daniolos, 2013; in the UK, see Bellis et al, 2014).

While recognising the limitations of existing data sources, this chapter provides an up-to-date overview of the state of knowledge about child-maltreatment in the UK first from administrative data, and then from self-report data. As well as considering overall data on maltreatment, it explores variations between the countries of the UK and according to characteristics of the child such age, gender and other factors, where available. It also considers available evidence of trends. Given the discussion above, it should be noted that it is quite possible that officially recorded child maltreatment can be increasing while the overall prevalence of maltreatment reduces.

In line with the other chapters in the book, comparisons with other countries are discussed where possible. However, there are even greater definitional and other challenges in making such comparisons, so the information is quite limited in this respect. Finally, the evidence on factors that are associated with risk of child maltreatment is briefly reviewed.

In terms of specific sources of administrative data, the chapter draws mainly on official child protection and crime statistics from the four countries of the UK. In terms of self-report data it relies heavily on the work of the NSPCC that has been responsible for conducting two waves of research that provide the most reliable and comprehensive self-report data on child maltreatment. Several other self-report sources are considered regarding the issue of maltreatment by peers, including bullying.

Definitions

There is no universally agreed definition of child maltreatment. In its narrowest form it is often used as an umbrella term to encompass abuse (emotional, physical and sexual) and neglect. However, it is also used in a broader sense to include not only abuse and neglect but also other experiences such as exposure to domestic violence, victimisation, experiences of violence and bullying. The World Health Organization (WHO) takes this broader view:

> Child abuse or maltreatment constitutes all forms of physical and/or emotional ill-treatment, sexual abuse, neglect or negligent treatment or commercial or other exploitation, resulting in actual or potential harm to the child's health, survival, development or dignity in the context of a relationship of responsibility, trust or power. (WHO, 1999)

The WHO report also goes on to provide definitions for the various components listed above – physical abuse, emotional abuse, neglect and negligent treatment, sexual abuse and exploitation. A later WHO report (Butchart et al, 2006, p 7) clarifies that maltreatment may be perpetrated by a wide range of people including: 'parents and other family members; caregivers; friends; acquaintances; strangers; others in authority – such as teachers, soldiers, police officers and clergy; employers; health care workers; and other children.'

This chapter, as far as is practical, adopts this broad conception of child maltreatment. Within this, abuse and neglect in a child protection sense is clearly a very important component. Child protection is a devolved matter in the UK, and each of the four countries has its own guidance. However, there are broad similarities in the definitions used in official guidance. As an example, the recently updated National

Guidance for Child Protection in Scotland 2014 provides the following definitions:

> Abuse and neglect are forms of maltreatment of a child. Somebody may abuse or neglect a child by inflicting, or by failing to act to prevent, significant harm to the child. Children may be abused in a family or in an institutional setting, by those known to them or, more rarely, by a stranger....
>
> Physical abuse is the causing of physical harm to a child or young person....
>
> Emotional abuse is persistent emotional neglect or ill treatment that has severe and persistent adverse effects on a child's emotional development....
>
> Sexual abuse is any act that involves the child in any activity for the sexual gratification of another person, whether or not it is claimed that the child either consented or assented....
>
> Neglect is the persistent failure to meet a child's basic physical and/or psychological needs, likely to result in the serious impairment of the child's health or development. (Scottish Government, 2014a, pp 11-12)

These extracts tend to focus both on a description of an act (of commission or omission), and also on a description of the consequences for the child or young person. The definitions have been truncated and contain much more detail about various acts that fall under each category. There are close similarities between the wording used in the above guidance and the corresponding guidance for the other three countries of the UK.

While definitions of individual categories of abuse are helpful, two points should be borne in mind. First, there may be a grey area between the categories, particularly in relation to potential overlap of emotional abuse with other categories. For example, does an instance of a parent ignoring a child count as emotional abuse or neglect, and is this dependent on whether the ignoring is intentional (an act of commission) or unintentional (an act of omission)? Second, the categories are not mutually exclusive, and many maltreated children experience more than one form of maltreatment either simultaneously or sequentially (Higgins and McCabe, 2001; Arata et al, 2007; Finkelhor et al, 2009).

Data sources

There are two main sources of data on child maltreatment in the UK – administrative and self-report. Both have their strengths and weaknesses and there are some similarities in these respects with data about crime.

Administrative data by definition only includes cases of child maltreatment that have come to the attention of agencies and have been recorded as such. Thus, first, these cases will only represent a proportion of all cases of maltreatment and, in the absence of other information, the proportion of 'hidden' cases is unknown. Second, there are various definitional challenges, and it may not always be clear whether a particular case falls within the category of child maltreatment or not. This is relevant for statutory social work with children and families in a wide range of circumstances and with diverse needs, where decisions often have to be made about the most appropriate agency response. It is also the case even with more extreme situations such as a child death, where it is still necessary for someone to make a judgement as to whether the cause of death is maltreatment, or an accident, and so on.

Self-report data on child maltreatment, by asking about people's direct experience, has the potential to overcome one of the major limitations of administrative data. It may get much closer to revealing the full extent of the issue, including cases that have never come to the attention of agencies. However, definitional difficulties still apply here, and there are also challenges that are common to this form of research (irrespective of the topic), such as issues of the reliability and validity of questions asked, about people's willingness to share sensitive information and about their ability to accurately recall past events.

Administrative data

Child protection data

Each of the four countries of the UK publishes annual data on children on the child protection register (or subject to a child protection plan in England). For example, for England, Table 10.1 summarises available data for various stages of the assessment and decision-making process.

There has been a substantial increase in children's social care activity in England related to issues of child maltreatment over the last four years.

Table 10.1: Various stages of the assessment and decision-making process, statistics and trends, England, 2013-14

Stages of assessment process		Statistics (2014)	Trends since 2010
Initial assessment of primary needs[1]	If child abuse is suspected an initial assessment is made for children in need.	'Abuse and neglect' is by far the largest category of primary need accounting for 187,710 (47%) of the cases of children in need.	Unfortunately due to missing data in previous years it is difficult to confidently identify any trends in this particular indicator.
		'Domestic violence' was identified as a factor in 65,000 initial assessments (32%) and 59,100 (41%) of continuous assessments.	
Section 47 (S47) assessment	If 'there is reasonable cause to suspect the child is suffering, or is likely to suffer significant harm', an S47 assessment determines if any actions are required.	Around 142,500 S47 enquiries were started during 2014.	This is an increase of over 50,000 since 2010. The rates of S47 enquiries per 10,000 children aged under-18 have increased by 56% from 79.5 in 2010 to 124.1 in 2014.
Child protection conference	A child protection conference is convened 'If concerns are substantiated and the child is judged to be at continuing risk of harm.'	There were 65,200 child protection conferences initiated.	This is a 45% increase since 2010, when 43,900 conferences took place (39.1 per 10,000 to 56.8 per 10,000).
Child protection plan	As result of the child protection conference, children may become subject to a child protection plan.	The number of children who became subject to a child protection plan in England was 59,800 (52.1 per 10,000).	This is also an increase from 44,300 (39.4 per 10,000) in 2010 with the rate per 10,000 increasing by 32% over that period.

Note: [1] For the first time in 2013/14, data was also recorded on other factors besides 'abuse and neglect' at assessments. This data was not available for all local authorities and only relates to around two-thirds of initial assessments conducted during the year.

In Wales and Scotland there has also been an increase in child protection registrations. In Wales at the end of March 2014, over 3,100 children were on the child protection register – an increase in the rate per 10,000 of 17% since 2010. In Scotland at the end of July 2014 almost 2,900 children were on the child protection register – an increase in the rate per 10,000 of 14% since 2010.

In Northern Ireland, on the other hand, child protection registrations per 10,000 children have fallen by 20% since 2010, and there were around 1,900 children on the register at the end of March 2014. However, it should be noted that there was a peak in child protection registrations in Northern Ireland around 2009, and that, although there has been a decrease since then, the current numbers are still higher than in 2004. This is comparable to the increase that has been seen in England and Wales over that longer-term period.

As a result of these differing trends, Wales is currently the country with the highest rates of child protection registrations (50 per 10,000), followed by Northern Ireland (44), England (42) and Scotland (28) (see Table 10.2).

Apart from overall numbers, various sources of information are available in each country regarding the reasons for children being placed on the child protection register. For England, Wales and Northern Ireland, these are recorded as a single category of abuse.

In England, for children who were the subject of a child protection plan at the end of March 2014, the largest need category was neglect (43%) followed by emotional abuse (33%), physical abuse (10%) and

Table 10.2: Numbers, rates and trends in child protection registrations/plans by country, year ending 31 March 2014 (England, Wales, Northern Ireland) and 31 July 2014 (Scotland)

	Numbers	Rate per 10,000	Rate per 10,000 2010	% change in rates 2010-14
England				
Section 47 enquiries during year	142,500	124.1	79.5	+56%
Initial child protection conferences during year	65,200	56.8	39.1	+45%
Children becoming subject to a child protection plan during year	59,800	52.1	39.4	+32%
Children subject to a child protection plan, end of year	48,300	42.1	35.0	+20%
Wales				
Children on child protection registers, end of year	3,135	50	42.9	+17%
Scotland				
Children on child protection register, end of year	2,882	28	24	+14%
Northern Ireland				
Children on child protection register, end of year	1,914	44	55	−20%

sexual abuse (5%). Finally, 9% of cases were recorded as having multiple initial categories of abuse.

In Wales, for children who were on child protection registers at 31 March 2014, the largest category of abuse was neglect only (39%) followed by emotional abuse only (38%), physical abuse only (11%) and sexual abuse only (5%). Around 6% of cases were recorded as having multiple categories of abuse.

In Northern Ireland, a slightly different categorisation is used. Of children on the child protection register at 31 March 2014, the percentages in each category were neglect only (30%), physical abuse only (28%), neglect and physical abuse (18%), emotional abuse only (12%), sexual abuse only (6%), physical and sexual abuse (2%), neglect and sexual abuse (2%), and finally, neglect, physical and sexual abuse (1%).

In Scotland, statistics are available for all concerns identified at case conferences of children who were on the child protection register. For children on the register on 31 July 2014, the average number of concerns per conference was 2.6. The most common concerns were parental substance misuse (39%), emotional abuse (39%), domestic abuse (37%), neglect (35%), parental mental health problems (26%), physical abuse (23%), non-engaging family (22%) and sexual abuse (8%).

Although there are some differences in the information recorded and the categories used, the relatively high proportion of neglect cases and the low proportion of sexual abuse cases is a consistent pattern across the four countries. Also noteworthy is the evidence in official statistics of the prevalence of domestic violence in the lives of children involved with the child protection system. There has been considerable research showing the associations between domestic violence (also termed intimate partner violence) and child maltreatment, and the detrimental effects that witnessing such violence can have on children, and there is an ongoing debate about whether this should be categorised as a form of child maltreatment (Goddard and Bedi, 2010).

Various types of other information are also available on the characteristics of children in the child protection system in each country.

In England, where gender was recorded, 51.5% of children subject to a child protection plan at 31 March 2014 were male. As there were slightly more males (51.2%) than females in the under-18 population in England, this represents a roughly equal rate per 10,000 for males and females. There were more males than females for all categories of abuse except for sexual abuse (57% female).

In Wales again there were slightly more males (51.5%) than females overall, but this is an equal rate per 10,000 children as there were more males than females in the population. Boys made up around 54% of neglect registrations. Girls made up 53% of 'sexual abuse only' registrations.

In Scotland there were a slightly larger number of boys than girls on the child protection register, but the rates per 10,000 were higher for girls (33) than boys (30).

In Northern Ireland 51% of child protection registrations were male. This is the same as the percentage of males in the population under the age of 18.

In summary, in England, Wales and Northern Ireland the gender balance of children on the child protection register is broadly in line with that of the population as a whole. In Scotland females are a little more likely to be on the register than males.

In England, there were 5,290 children aged under one subject to a child protection plan (80 per 10,000). Rates decline with age group – 51 per 10,000 for children aged 1-4; 44 per 10,000 for children aged 5-9; 33 per 10,000 for children aged 10-15; and 7 per 10,000 for the 16-18 age group. Neglect was the most common category of abuse, and emotional abuse the second most common, for all age groups.

In Wales, rates per 10,000 also declined for older age groups: under 1 (106), 1-4 (68), 5-9 (54), 10-15 (40) and 16-18 (9). Neglect was the largest category in the two youngest age groups. Neglect and emotional abuse were relatively evenly balanced for the 5-9 and 10-15 age groups.

In Scotland, the rates per 10,000 on the child protection register for the different age groups were 48 for the under–fives, 27 for children aged 5-10, 16 for children aged 11-15, and around one in 10,000 for children aged 16 and over.

In Northern Ireland data is provided on the age distributions of children on the child protection register compared to the child population as a whole. Around 11% of children on the child protection register were under 1 compared to 6% of the general population. There was a small over-representation of the 1-4 age group, a roughly proportional representation of the 5-11 age group and then lower than average representations of older age groups. Hence children on the child protection register had a younger age profile than the child population as a whole.

In summary, the data on age distributions of children on the child protection register is broadly similar in all four countries, with a decline in rates per 10,000 across the age range and a noticeable drop-off among the oldest group aged 16 and over.

Data was also available on the ethnicity of children subject to a child protection plan in England. Excluding missing data, 79% of children were White, 8% were of mixed ethnicity, 6% were Asian or Asian British, 5% were Black or Black British and 1% were from other ethnic groups. Comparable whole population figures for the 0-17 age group in the 2011 Census in England were 79% White, 5% mixed ethnicity, 10% Asian or Asian British, 5% Black or Black British and 1% other ethnic group.

Child deaths caused by maltreatment

The category of 'fatal maltreatment' covers a range of circumstances of child deaths. Sidebotham et al (2011a) argue that 'maltreatment-related fatalities can be classified into five groups: infanticide and covert homicide; severe physical assaults; extreme neglect/deprivational abuse; deliberate/overt homicide; and deaths related to but not directly caused by maltreatment' (p 299). The sections below give an overview on homicides, infanticides and deaths resulting from maltreatment in a UK and international context.

Homicides

Published data on child homicides is available jointly for England and Wales (ONS, 2015d). The number of child homicides in the most recent reporting year was 46. Seventeen of these children were under one, a further 17 were between one and four, and 12 were aged 5-15. Twenty-five of the 46 children were female; however, over the last decade, around 45% of victims of child homicide were female and 55% male. The majority of the victims knew the principal suspect of the homicide, and exactly half of the 46 homicides were children killed by a parent or stepparent. The ONS also note that proportionally fewer children are killed by a stranger than is the case for adults.

Statistics exactly comparable to the above are not available for Scotland and Northern Ireland. However, Jütte et al (2015) summarise police-recorded homicide statistics of all people under the age of 18 for each country in 2013/14. There were 62 homicides of under 18s in England, two in Northern Ireland, two in Scotland and one in Wales.

In the last edition of this book, it was noted that there was some evidence of long-term reductions in child homicides in England and Wales (Pritchard and Williams, 2010). More recently, an analysis by

Sidebotham et al (2012) of data on violent child deaths in England and Wales between 1974 and 2008 concluded that 'Rates of violent death in infancy and middle childhood have fallen over the past 30 years, while rates in adolescence have remained static or risen. Each year 5–15 infants, 15–45 children and 32–117 adolescents die violent deaths. Rates are higher in adolescent males than females' (p 193).

Infanticides

Ellonen et al (2015) provides an international comparison of trends in infanticides (under the age of one) in 28 industrialised countries between 1960 and 2009. They report an increase in rates of infanticide per 100,000 in England and Wales between 1960 and 1970, then a sharp decrease from 1975-79 to 1980-84 and a smaller decrease over the last decade. Overall, rates for the last decade (2000-09) are only around 13% of the rates in the 1960s. England and Wales has the second largest rate of decline (after Finland) over this 50-year period out of the 28 countries analysed. For Scotland and Northern Ireland the rates in 2000-09 were 56% and 85% respectively of those in 1960-69. To put these changes in to perspective, in nine of the 28 countries, the rates of infanticide had increased over the same time period.

Fatal maltreatment

An additional source of recent information about a broader range of fatal maltreatment in England has been the ongoing analysis of serious case reviews undertaken by Brandon, Sidebotham and colleagues. In the most recent analysis, Brandon et al (2012) estimate that there were around 85 violent and maltreatment-related deaths of children under the age of 18 in England in the 12-month period ending March 2010. This is considerably higher than the average number of child homicides per year discussed above, although these figures do relate to children under the age of 16.

There is a roughly equal gender split in cases of fatal maltreatment. These cases were heavily concentrated in the under one age group, followed by the 1-4 age group, but there was a slightly higher rate per 100,000 in the 15-17 age group than in the intervening age groups. There were no significant ethnic patterns compared with the general population of children. There was a disproportionally high number of cases relating to children in larger families (Sidebotham et al, 2011b).

Brandon et al (2014) focus specifically on the link between neglect and fatal maltreatment or serious injury. They find that while neglect is very rarely the primary and immediate cause of child death, it is very often a significant background factor in cases of fatal maltreatment. They draw attention, in particular, to the legacy of neglect in serious case reviews relating to young people aged 11-15.

Recorded crime statistics

In addition to child homicide there are a range of other criminal offences that can be seen as falling within the category of child maltreatment. In their annual review of child protection in the UK, the NSPCC have compiled statistics on recorded sexual offences against children and on cases of cruelty and neglect. The latest available statistics from that source are for 2013-14 (Jütte et al, 2015).

Sexual offences against children include rape, sexual assault, sexual activity, exposure to obscene material and other similar offences. There are differences in legislation, categorisation and recording between the four countries, and so figures are not directly comparable. The statistics compiled by the NSPCC show that there were over 36,000 recorded offences against children in 2013-14, and that there had been an increase in the rates of recorded offences compared to the previous year in all four countries of the UK (see Table 10.3). Jütte et al argue that this is 'likely to be due in part to increased willingness to report abuse following recent high profile sexual abuse cases in the media' (Jütte et al, p 26).

Jütte et al (2015) also summarise rates of recorded offences of cruelty and neglect of children since 2009 (see Table 10.4). Again, it should be borne in mind that statistics for the different countries are not directly comparable due to variations in legislation, categorisation and recording. Jütte et al (2015) note that figures for Scotland, in particular, have a broader scope than the other three countries.

Table 10.3: Recorded sexual offences against children under 18

	Rates per 10,000 children					Numbers
	2009-10	2010-11	2011-12	2012-13	2013-14	2013-14
England	2.0	1.9	1.9	1.9	2.6	29,792
Wales	1.9	1.9	1.9	2.0	2.3	1,446
Scotland	2.4*	2.5*	2.9	3.0	3.3	3,742
Northern Ireland	2.5	2.6	2.5	2.7	3.4	1,485

Note: *There was a change of relevant legislation in Scotland in December 2010.

Source: Jutte et al (2015)

Table 10.4: Recorded offences of cruelty and neglect against children under 18

| | Rates per 10,000 children | | | | | Numbers |
	2009-10	2010-11	2011-12	2012-13	2013-14	2013-14
England	6.4	5.8	5.8	6.0	7.6	7,726
Wales	4.9	5.0	5.2	5.2	4.9	272
Scotland	20.9	20.4	17.6	16.0	14.6	1,334
Northern Ireland	2.3	2.9	3.0	3.5	4.8	184

Source: Jutte et al (2015)

Self-report data[1]

This section considers several surveys that have aimed to estimate the prevalence of various forms of child maltreatment in the UK. Among these the primary sources are two studies undertaken by the NSPCC in 1998-99 (Cawson et al, 2000) and 2009 (Radford et al, 2011). The second of these studies contains the most comprehensive and up-to-date self-report data for the UK.

The 2009 NSPCC study drew a random sample of households in the UK. The response rate to the survey was around 60%. The survey involved: (a) 2,160 parents or guardians as proxy respondents for children aged under 11; (b) 2,275 children aged 11-17 (primary caregivers were also interviewed); and (c) 1,761 young adults aged 18-24, who reported on their experiences under the age of 18. The study yielded information on maltreatment during the past year for the under-11s and the 11-17 age group, and information on lifetime experience of maltreatment for all three age groups. Interviews used computer-assisted interviewing and included the Juvenile Victimisation Questionnaire, a validated instrument (Finkelhor et al, 2005). The methodology is described in detail in Radford et al (2011).

While the study is impressive in its scale and scope, some limitations should be noted. First, the response rate of 60% raises the question of whether adults declining to participate may have been more likely to have been the perpetrators of child maltreatment, thus leading the findings to be under-estimates. Second, the strategy of interviewing parents of younger children may be particularly likely to lead to under-reporting, although the authors argue that earlier research suggests that this strategy is satisfactory (Finkelhor et al, 2005, cited in Radford et al, 2011). Third, children and young people, particularly those still living with family, may be reluctant to disclose maltreatment or may have suppressed memories (Cameron, 2000). And fourth, respondents may find it difficult to accurately recall experiences.

We first discuss findings on child maltreatment by parents or guardians, and then go on to discuss other experiences of victimisation. Key findings are summarised in Table 10.5.

Child maltreatment by parents or guardians

The percentages of children with lifetime experiences of any form of child maltreatment (not including exposure to domestic violence) by parents or guardians were 8.9% for the under-11 age group, 21.9% for the 11-17 age group and 24.5% for the 18-24 age group. Percentages for the past year were 2.5% for the under-11s and 6.0% for the 11-17 age group. Neglect was the most common form of lifetime maltreatment for all age groups. Sexual abuse was the least common form of maltreatment.

The survey also measured exposure to domestic violence – the lifetime percentages ranged from 12% in the under-11 age group to 24% for the 18-24 age group reporting retrospectively.

There were no significant gender differences for victims in the lifetime figures for any of the forms of abuse, neglect or exposure to domestic violence, although females (17.5%) in the 18-24 age group were more likely than males (11.6%) to report lifetime experience of severe maltreatment. Past year experiences of maltreatment rose from the ages of 11 to 12, peaked between the ages of 13 and 16, and then declined (Radford et al, 2013).

In terms of the gender of the perpetrators of maltreatment, males were more frequently perpetrators than females for some specific types of maltreatment, with the largest gender differences being for severe physical abuse and contact sexual abuse.

Radford et al (2011) also make some comparisons between findings from the 1998-99 and 2009 studies. They find no significant evidence for difference in retrospective reports of neglect (absence of adequate parental care and supervision), but a decline in 'harsh emotional and physical punishment' by parents and carers and in experiences of physical violence and prolonged verbal aggression in general (in the home and elsewhere).

Child maltreatment by non-resident adults

A summary of key findings on maltreatment by non-resident adults is shown in the second section of Table 10.5. Around 2.3% of under-11s were reported to have ever been maltreated (any category) by a non-resident adult. Among the older age groups, the lifetime rates were

Table 10.5: Prevalence of lifetime and past year childhood victimisation, by victimisation type and victim age group (%)

	Under 11		11-17		18-24
	LT	PY	LT	PY	LT
Parent or guardian maltreated child	8.9	2.5	21.9	6.0	24.5
Neglect	5	–	13.3	–	16
Emotional abuse	3.6	1.8	6.8	3	6.9
Physical violence	1.3	0.7	6.9	2.4	8.4
Sexual abuse	0.1	0	0.1	0	1.0
Exposure to domestic violence	12	3.2	17.5	2.5	23.7
Severe neglect	3.7	–	9.8	–	9.0
Contact sexual abuse	0.1	–	0.1	–	0.9
Severe physical violence	0.8	–	3.7	–	5.4
All severe maltreatment	5.0	–	13.3	–	14.5
Non-resident adults maltreated child	2.3	1.2	7.8	3.1	12.8
Emotional abuse	2.1	1.2	4.3	1.9	5.3
Physical violence	0.6	0.2	3.3	1.1	5.8
Sexual abuse	0.3	0.2	1.4	0.3	5.3
Peer victimisation	28.0	20.2	59.5	35.3	63.2
Sibling victimisation	28.4	23.7	31.8	16	25.2
Intimate partner abuse	–	–	7.9	5.0	13.4
Exposure to community violence	11.3	4.8	61.4	31.2	66.5

Source: Extracted from tables in Radford et al (2011)

7.8% for the 11-17 age group and 12.8% for the 18-24 age group. Past year maltreatment rates were 1.2% for under-11s and 3.1% for the 11-17 age group.

In comparison with the statistics presented in the previous section, it can be seen from Table 10.5 that lifetime rates of emotional abuse and physical violence are higher for maltreatment within the family than maltreatment by non-resident adults. However, rates of children experiencing sexual abuse by non-resident adults are substantially higher than by parents or guardians in the 11-17 and 18-24 age groups. At the same time, it should also be noted that sexual abuse was the least common of the three forms of abuse by non-resident adults (with the exception of the lifetime rate reported by the 18-24 age group where it was approximately equal for sexual abuse and emotional abuse).

Radford et al (2011, p 70) report that non-resident males were the most frequently reported perpetrators of maltreatment in the two older age groups. They were over three times more frequently reported than females by those aged 11-17 and over six times by those aged 18-24. Looking at individual categories of abuse, there was a roughly even gender balance of perpetrators of physical violence for the under-11 age group, but male perpetrators were more common than female perpetrators for the older age groups. The most common form of sexual abuse was a male perpetrator and a female victim.

The study was also able to explore which non-resident adults are the most common perpetrators of maltreatment. For the under-11 age group, known adults (for example, relatives, neighbours, family friends and professionals) are more common perpetrators than strangers. For the older age groups, the pattern is reversed, and strangers are the most frequent non-resident adult perpetrators (Radford et al, 2011, p 72).

Child maltreatment by peers (including bullying)

Radford et al (2011) also present findings on maltreatment by siblings, peers and intimate partners. Past year and lifetime rates of sibling and peer victimisation were substantially higher than for most of the forms of maltreatment discussed in the previous two sections. For example, using a broad measure of victimisation by peers (excluding siblings), past year rates of victimisation were 20% for under-11s and 35% for the 11-17 age group. Lifetime peer victimisation rates were 28% (under-11s), 60% (11-17 age group) and 63% (18-24 age group).

One type of maltreatment by peers that has received increased international research attention (Leen et al, 2013) is violence and other victimisation experiences within teenage intimate relationships (referred to in some of the literature as 'dating violence'). This is still a relatively under-explored area. A study by Barter et al (2009) of over 1,300 young people aged 13-18 in a purposively selected sample of eight schools in England, Scotland and Wales found rates of victimisation among young people who reported having an intimate relationship as follows – physical partner violence (25% of girls and 18% of boys), severe physical force (11% of girls and 4% of boys), emotional violence (72% of girls and 51% of boys), and sexual partner violence (31% of girls and 16% of boys). Some anomalies were noted in boys' responses to questions about sexual victimisation, so the latter percentage may not be valid. The young people were also asked about the impact that victimisation had had on them. Much higher proportions of girls than boys stated that each form of victimisation had had a negative impact on their welfare. Overall, the report found that one in six girls in the study reported at least one form of severe partner violence, and it is argued that the issue of teenage partner violence should have greater recognition as a child welfare issue.

Radford et al (2011) found that 13% of young adults aged 18-24 reported experiencing intimate partner abuse under the age of 18.

An aspect of peer maltreatment that is particularly well researched is bullying by other children – at school, by siblings and via the internet. There is a growing body of evidence of the detrimental impact of bullying on children's well-being during childhood (see, for example, Klocke et al, 2014) and later in life (Wolke et al, 2013; Lereya et al, 2015).

There is a range of UK data on this issue. In terms of school bullying, international comparative data is available from two studies – the Health Behaviour of School-aged Children (HBSC) study and the Children's Worlds study.

The most recently published HBSC data was gathered in 2009/10 and covers 38 countries in Europe and North America (Currie et al, 2012). The percentages of children aged 11, 13 and 15 who reported being bullied at school at least once in the 'past couple of months' in England, Wales and Scotland are shown in Table 10.6. All three countries tended to be below the mid-point for 38 countries, with a higher ranking indicating a higher level of bullying. Of the three countries, Wales had the lowest rates of bullying for 11- and 13-year-olds and Scotland had the lowest levels for 15-year-olds.

The second wave of the Children's Worlds study was conducted in a diverse range of 15 countries around the world in 2013-14 including England, and the first international comparative results were published in Rees and Main (2015). Two questions were asked about bullying in school – regarding being hit by other children and being left out by classmates (see Tables 10.7a and 10.7b). In England, 38% of children aged 10 and 12 said that they had been hit by another child at school in the last month, including 9% who had experienced this more than

Table 10.6: Percentage of children who had been bullied in school at least twice in the past couple of months in England, Wales and Scotland by gender and age group

	11-year-olds			13-year-olds			15-year-olds		
	Girls (%)	Boys (%)	Rank*	Girls (%)	Boys (%)	Rank*	Girls (%)	Boys (%)	Rank*
England	10	12	22	12	9	19	9	7	17
Wales	10	10	27	9	10	22	6	8	22
Scotland	13	10	21	9	11	20	4	8	26

Note: * This is the ranking of the overall (both genders) percentage out of 38 countries with a higher number indicating a higher level of bullying.

Source: Currie et al (2012)

Table 10.7a: Experiences of being hit by other children in school in the past month, 15 countries, Children's Worlds survey, 2013/14

	Once (%)	2 or 3 times (%)	More than 3 times (%)	All (%)	Rank (high to low)
Turkey*	22	15	18	55	1
South Africa*	18	12	19	49	2
Estonia	18	12	14	43	3
Nepal	23	10	9	42	4
Romania	16	12	12	40	5
Israel	18	10	11	39	6
England	18	11	9	38	7
Spain*	15	9	10	34	8
Colombia*	15	8	8	32	9
Ethiopia	16	9	7	31	10
Poland*	12	8	10	31	11
Germany	13	8	6	27	12
Algeria*	16	6	5	27	13
Norway	14	6	6	25	14
South Korea	6	3	3	11	15

Source: Rees and Main (2015)

Table 10.7b: Experiences of being left out by classmates in the past month, 15 countries, Children's Worlds survey, 2013/14

	Once (%)	2 or 3 times (%)	More than 3 times (%)	All (%)	Rank (high to low)
England	21	16	14	50	1
Nepal	25	14	9	48	2
South Africa*	18	12	17	46	3
Colombia*	18	11	12	41	4
Estonia	17	11	11	38	5
Romania	12	7	19	38	6
Norway	18	9	6	34	7
Spain*	16	10	6	32	8
Algeria*	17	7	7	31	9
Turkey*	12	8	9	28	10
Poland*	13	7	8	28	11
Ethiopia	14	7	6	27	12
Germany	12	5	7	24	13
Israel	11	5	7	23	14
South Korea	2	1	1	4	15

Source: Rees and Main (2015)

three times in that period, and 50% of children said that they had been left out by classmates, including 14% who had experienced this more than three times in the past month. Children in England ranked 7th out of 15 countries for being hit by other children at school, but 1st (that is, the highest rate) for being left out by other children (although two countries had a higher frequency of this type of bullying).

These two studies therefore present a mixed picture of how children's experience of being bullied in school in the UK compares with that of children in other countries.

Sibling bullying has been measured in the Understanding Society survey. A recent analysis indicated that 46% of children aged 10-15 in the UK have experienced sibling aggression (Tippett and Wolke, 2015). Sibling bullying has been shown to be associated with poorer later mental health, controlling for a range of other factors (Bowes et al, 2014).

Risks related to new technologies

In recent years, concerns have been raised about the bullying of children through the use of mobile phones, the internet and other new technologies. However, Livingstone and Smith (2014) outline various difficulties in making reliable estimates of the extent and prevalence of 'cyberbullying' and, in relation to industrialised countries, suggest that 'it seems that occasional or one-off occurrences may be reported by over 20% of young people but serious or recent or repeated incidents are reported by only around 5%, less than for traditional bullying' (p 639).

In a European study in 2010 (Livingstone et al, 2011), 6% of internet users aged 9-16 reported having been bullied online. The UK had the sixth highest rate of online bullying (8%) out of the 25 countries covered. A comparable study in 2014 (Livingstone et al, 2014) reports that the prevalence of online bullying in the UK had increased to 12%, although it notes that this may be linked to increased opportunities to use online and mobile technologies over that period.

Further to the above discussion about cyberbullying, children's access to the internet and mobile technologies has raised concerns about the consequent potential for harm. The large majority (96%) of children aged 5-15 in the UK have access to the internet at home either through a laptop or PC or other device (Ofcom, 2014). There has recently been a substantial increase in use of tablets to go online (42% of children aged 5-15 in 2014 compared to 23% in 2013) and of accessing the internet via a mobile phone (36% in 2014 compared to 27% in 2013). Livingstone et al (2014) report that in 2014, 47% of children aged 9-16 who used the internet in the UK sometimes accessed it on their mobile phone when 'out and about', a higher rate than in the other six countries in this study (Belgium, Denmark, Ireland, Italy, Portugal and Romania).

This study of seven European countries in 2014 illustrates the prevalence of a range of potential risks that children might experience online, including having contact with someone the child had not previously met face-to-face (29% of 11- to 16-year-olds who used the internet in the sample of countries); seeing sexual images online (20%); receiving sexual messages (12%); seeing websites with material such as hate messages (20%); promotion of eating disorders (13%); and discussion of self-harm (11%) and suicide (6%). Around 13% of children said that they had met an online contact offline. The study finds only moderate increases in some risks compared to 2010. However, Livingstone and Smith (2014b), in a review of literature on this topic, note that although there is evidence of the adverse consequences of online risks, exposure to risks should not be seen as synonymous with experience of harm.

A survey in 2012 of just over 1,000 young people aged 11-16 in the UK who used social networking sites (Lilley et al, 2014) found that over a quarter (28%) experienced something that had upset them. This figure included experiences that might be categorised as cyberbullying, but also a range of other experiences such as aggressive or violent language, unwanted sexual messages and being asked for personal information. Over half of young people said that they did not know at least one of the people responsible. Girls (32%) were more likely than boys (24%) to say that they had had an upsetting experience. There were some gender differences in the types of upsetting experiences. Girls were more likely to be upset by social exclusions and pressure to look a certain way, while boys were more likely to have been upset by violent and aggressive language and unwanted sexual messages.

While the focus in this chapter is necessarily on the harm or potential harm experienced by children's use of new technologies, it is also important to acknowledge and balance this discussion with a recognition of the substantial benefits and positive experiences that children and adults gain from these technologies.

Factors associated with maltreatment

There is a vast literature on the factors associated with maltreatment, and it has become common to cite lists of 'risk and protective factors'.

For example, the Child Welfare Information Gateway[2] lists hundreds of studies and identifies the following types of factors:

- Child factors: age; health; disabilities.
- Parent or caregiver factors: individual characteristics; substance abuse; teen parenting.
- Family factors: caregiving and household structure; domestic/ intimate partner violence.
- Community and environmental factors: neighbourhood conditions; poverty and economic conditions.

It also notes the issue of co-occurring risk factors. There is an impressive body of knowledge on this issue, and space does not permit a more detailed discussion of the key findings. However, there are several risks and drawbacks to these types of lists.

Munro et al (2014) caution against viewing factors such as those listed above as adequate predictors of the likelihood of maltreatment in individual cases. They argue that the risk factors identified 'appear to be neither necessary nor sufficient conditions for maltreatment to occur' and that 'Overall, there are a complex range of factors associated with the "chances" of someone maltreating children and the truth of the matter is that largely we do not know why some people hurt children, when others in similar circumstances do not' (p 66).

A further issue is that many of the lists that are constructed of risk and protective factors treat maltreatment as a single unified concept. However, there is evidence that there are different patterns of association for different categories of maltreatment. For example, a meta-analytic review by Stith et al (2009) found many shared risk factors for physical abuse and neglect but also some differences. Family size and parent unemployment were more strongly related to neglect than to physical abuse. Similarly, Afifi et al (2015) found that being a single parent and being on a low income (themselves correlated factors) were stronger predictors of neglect than other forms of maltreatment in a Canadian Incidence Study.

There are other complicating issues in the quest to identify the most salient factors associated with child maltreatment. As Munro et al (2014) note, the occurrence of single risk factors may be relatively unimportant, and multiple risk factors may combine to create much larger associations. There is also a tendency for child maltreatment research to treat childhood as a homogeneous entity, and so far there is relatively little evidence on differential factors that may be associated with risk of maltreatment at different ages (Rees et al, 2011).

Moreover, much of the research that exists is based on samples in the US, and it is not known whether all of the factors identified are equally salient in other contexts, including the UK.

Finally, most of the evidence discussed above relates to a relatively narrow definition of child maltreatment (primarily abuse and neglect experienced within the family). There is a need for a much more detailed approach that considers the specific factors associated with the wider range of maltreatment issues discussed in this chapter, such as bullying, violence within teenage partner relationships and experiences of peer and community victimisation.

Conclusion

This chapter has given an overview of child maltreatment statistics and trends in the UK, and when possible, in an international context. Child maltreatment has been defined in its broadest sense, that is, any experience that could harm or has the potential to harm the child in any direct or indirect way. As well as the traditional concepts of maltreatment such as neglect, emotional, physical and sexual abuse, this broader definition encompasses, for example, witnessing domestic violence, exposure to (cyber)bullying as well as seeing inappropriate images or messages over the internet.

The chapter was structured around the two main types of data sources on maltreatment: administrative data and self-report data. Both these sources have their advantages and drawbacks. With administrative data there are inevitably blurred boundaries between what constitutes a genuine case of child maltreatment and what does not, which in turn affects how cases are ultimately classified in national statistics. As a result, administrative data might have serious omissions resulting from 'underdiagnoses'. Self-report data suffers from reliability and validity concerns, since it collects highly sensitive information from individuals who are potentially still suffering under or committing abuse. In this way, self-report studies might have low response rates and exclude valuable information from the most vulnerable respondents. Caution is needed in making cross-country comparisons because there are slight differences across constituent countries regarding the definitions of maltreatment as well as data collected on children with different age range boundaries.

Administrative data shows that there has been a substantial increase in the number of children placed on child protection plans since 2010 in all four UK constituent countries. This could have been caused by the overhaul of the child protection system resulting from a number of high-profile cases concerning child fatalities due to maltreatment and child sexual exploitation. Neglect, emotional and physical abuse are the top three main reasons for placing children under child protection plans across UK countries. Children's gender does not seem to be a predicting factor of maltreatment but age does: rate of maltreatment declines as children get older. There has been a steady decline in infanticide across the UK since the 1960-1970s.

Self-report data relied mainly on the 2009 NSPCC study, on a random sample of households in the UK. This study showed that most abuse on children up to 17 years old is committed by a parent or guardian, while young adults (aged 18-24) suffer more at the hands of non-resident adults. Younger children are more likely to suffer neglect, emotional abuse and exposure to domestic violence, while adolescents are more likely to suffer peer victimisation, intimate partner abuse and exposure to community violence.

There has recently been a substantial increase in the number of children in younger age groups who have access to mobile phones, tablets and the internet. This exposes them to the threats of cyberbullying and exposure to inappropriate online content. The potential risk modern technology poses is mitigated, however, by its many advantages and by children's increasing awareness about how to use it safely.

Overall, the picture of the trends presented in this chapter is mixed. On the one hand, rates of child protection registrations and of recorded sexual offences against children have increased in the UK. On the other hand, there has been a long-term decline in violent deaths of children (at least in early and middle childhood), and there is evidence from self-report surveys of decreases in children's experiences of some forms of maltreatment. It is possible, as some commentators have suggested, that these contrasting trends could have occurred through an increased awareness and recognition of child maltreatment at the same time as a decline in children's experiences of maltreatment.

Chapter 10

[1] Although various forms of maltreatment may be criminal offences, children's experience of being a victim of crime in general is not explored in this chapter as this is covered in Chapter Twelve.

[2] See www.childwelfare.gov/topics/can/factors/contribute

ELEVEN

Childcare and early years

Christine Skinner

Key findings

- It is normal for three- and four-year-olds to attend some formal free early education provision.
- Family and child characteristics are the most important factors affecting child outcomes.
- Parenting skills and the 'home learning environment' are becoming increasingly important aspects of the evidence base.
- Targeted 'early interventions' in the 'early years of childhood' are on the increase – especially for the most disadvantaged children.
- There is a drive towards 'early intervention' in the early years of childhood that encompasses much more than childcare and early education provision.

Key trends

- Provision of childcare places is insufficient to meet the demands of working parents, whereas part-time early education for three- and four-year-olds is taken up nearly universally.
- The proportion of children attending different types of early education provider has been relatively stable over the last five years. Between 35% and 38% of three- and four-year-olds attended the private or voluntary sector, and around 55% attended the publicly maintained sector.
- The proportion of disadvantaged two-year-olds attending early education is on the increase, with England leading the way.
- The variety in the nature of provision and the differential ages at which children officially start school make comparisons of international trends very complex. It is not clear how investments in the UK compare to other countries.

Key sources

- Effective Provision of Pre-School Education (EPPE) (England, Wales and Northern Ireland) and Effective Pre-School, Primary and Secondary Education (EPPSE)

- OECD Study for Early Education and Development (SEED)
- 'An evaluation of a better start'
- Early Intervention Foundation (EIF)

Introduction

Since the last edition, policy-makers have become firmly convinced by the evidence that intervening in early childhood is a very good thing. The policy rhetoric is all about ensuring young children (aged 0-5) in the different countries of the UK have the 'best start in life', or a 'flying start' or a 'bright start' in life. Whether a best, flying or bright start, policies on childcare and early education across the UK continue to follow the twin aims of supporting parental employment and improving child development outcomes. These aims, however, can sit in contention and are often not disaggregated in political rhetoric, or in the discussions of research evidence, or in the design of new policy approaches.

Consequently, it is important to trace the policy story and the latest developments occurring in this fast-moving policy arena, as well as to relate them to the evidence base. While there are many policy challenges for the UK in terms of availability, affordability and quality of provision (and this is currently consuming a lot of political attention and resources), the focus here is on child outcomes. This chapter therefore explores the latest evidence on the impact of childcare and early education provision, and is divided into three sections: first, the policy background and challenges are outlined; second, the state of the existing evidence base on child development outcomes is described; and last, the drive towards intervening in the early years in a more goal-orientated way is discussed, in particular the work of the recently formed Early Intervention Foundation (EIF). This moves scrutiny of child outcomes beyond the potential effects of childcare and early education provision on child well-being, into a much broader and holistic exploration of the early years of childhood itself. Here the aim of early intervention into the early years of life is to improve children's well-becoming in adulthood and to increase social mobility, perhaps representing an emerging more explicit third strand to the policy aims surrounding childcare and early education provision.

Background

UK early years and childcare policy

Investment in childcare and early education provision is reportedly on the increase in the UK. According to the House of Lords' recent inquiry into childcare, the previous coalition government invested some £5.2 billion in 2014, and currently, under the newly elected Conservative government, expenditure is expected to rise to £6.4 billion per annum (House of Lords, 2015, p 6).[1] Yet between 2014–15 overall expenditure on children under five declined slightly, bucking the rising trend in the previous two to three years (see Figure 11.1). The expected increase in expenditure for 2015–16 relates mainly to changes in providing increases in tax-free support for working parents using childcare (see below).

The House of Lords' inquiry also involved detailed scrutiny of the expenditure figures. Comparatively, they report that the OECD data tended to show that the UK spent around 1.1% of GDP in 2010 on early education and childcare, reportedly more than most of the other countries (except for the majority of the Nordic countries). However, this is most likely an over-estimate as spending on school-aged children in the UK (between ages 5 and 6) may be included in these figures. Taking this and other factors into account, the Institute for Fiscal Studies reportedly estimated that the amount is somewhere nearer to 0.4–0.5% of GDP (House of Lords, 2015, p 27).

Figure 11.1: Expenditure on children under five years old, 2014/15 (£ million)

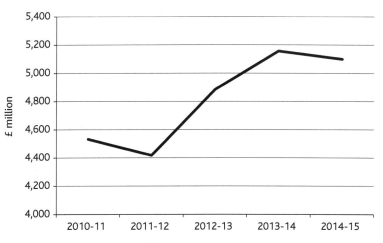

Source: HM Treasury (2015, Table 5.2)

Nevertheless, irrespective of expenditure, early education and childcare provision is now one of the key policy areas for the Conservative government (House of Commons Library, 2015), and was a key political battleground in the recent general election.

The incoming Conservative government hit the ground running. Within just weeks of taking office, they announced on 1 June the introduction of a new Childcare Bill and a ministerial Childcare Taskforce (Press Release, Prime Minister's Office, 1 June 2015). The Childcare Taskforce is one of many new 'implementation taskforces', and is headed up by Minister of State for Employment, Priti Patel. It will drive forward plans to double the amount of 'free childcare' to 30 hours per week for three- and four-year-olds in term time (in England and Wales), but only for those parents in paid work.[2] According to Ofsted (2015, p 4), this exemplifies an unprecedented level of political engagement in this policy area. Certainly, the latest plans follow on from the Childcare Payments Act passed in November 2014 under the previous coalition government. By the end of 2015, under this Act, childcare vouchers for working parents will be replaced with a more universal online tax-free childcare scheme. This will provide a top-up payment of £2 for every £8 spent on childcare, and is worth a maximum of £2,000 per annum per child. All four countries of the UK are covered, with the aim being to encourage low-income parents back into work. Thus, in terms of political rhetoric at least, policy is mainly focused on the first of the twin aims, to encourage parental employment.

As the Prime Minister David Cameron stated:

> That is exactly why we are pressing ahead with these reforms – so that not a moment is lost in getting on with the task – going further than ever before to help with childcare costs, helping hardworking families and giving people the opportunity to get into work. (Press Release, Prime Minister's Office, 1 June 2015)

Despite these plans, many policy challenges remain, however, including tackling the rising costs of provision resulting in parents paying as much as a quarter of their incomes on childcare (House of Commons Library, 2015;[3] Family and Childcare Trust, 2015b), the poor quality of care provided in some settings (Ofsted, 2015), the low skilled workforce, the complex funding formula that covers a mixed economy of providers, the gaps in provision with insufficient places for working parents and ineffective targeting on the most disadvantaged children who stand to gain the most from high quality provision. Only 40% of disadvantaged two-year-olds in England can access 15 hours per week of free early education (Family and Childcare Trust, 2015a). Many policy solutions are being sought, including the commissioning of a new government review on the cost of providing care in England (announced on 2 July 2015), and the implementation of a new 'Common Assessment Framework' by Ofsted in September 2015. The framework will bring together the inspection of different education, skills and early education settings. In addition, new childcare apprentices are planned which will upskill people to high levels and help to attract higher qualified workers into the sector (DfE, 2013). Most policy efforts are therefore aimed at improving the affordability, availability and quality of provision (4Children's Foundation Years, 2015). Yet, there are concerns that the sector does not have the capacity to meet the expansion required under these latest proposals.

Level of provision and take-up of childcare and early education

According to the most recent report by the Family and Childcare Trust (Butler and Rutter, 2015, p 2), just 43% of the local authorities in England and a paltry 18% in Wales have enough childcare places to meet the needs of working parents in 2015 (down from 46% and 50% in 2012). This is despite a duty being placed on local authorities in England and Wales under the Childcare Act 2006 to ensure that enough places were available to meet demand. This failing has led to the Family and Childcare Trust calling for a 'legal entitlement to childcare' to commence at the end of parental leave (Butler and Rutter, 2015, p 3). Similarly, in Scotland there are insufficient places despite the requirements placed on local authorities to have a strategic overview of childcare access under the 2008 'Early Years Framework' and the Children and Young People (Scotland) Act 2014. The Commission for Childcare Reform in Scotland report that just 15% of local authorities felt they had sufficient places to meet the demands of full-time working parents in 2015 (Commission for Childcare Reform Report, 2015, p 24). This compares to 23% of Scottish local authorities reporting sufficiency in 2014 (Rutter and Stocker, 2014). In Northern Ireland there is no legal requirement to meet demand, leaving them lagging behind the rest of the UK (Family and Childcare Trust, 2015a).

A different picture emerges, however, for the take-up of free early education places. In England it has become the norm, with 94% of all three-year-olds and 99% of four-year-olds attending in January 2015 (DfE, 2015n). Figure 11.2 shows attendance by sector: the majority of two- and three-year-olds were attending private and voluntary sector provision (95% and 61% respectively), whereas the majority of four-year-olds received early education within nursery or infant classes in primary schools in the state-maintained sector (74%), because the statistics include those four-year-olds who are almost of school age (five years old) and who are in reception classes in primary schools (DfE, 2015n, p 5). This difference across sectors is important because the quality of provision is higher in the maintained sector, which has a bearing on child development outcomes, as discussed in the next section. The trends seem pretty stable over time, however, with only a slight increase in take-up in the private and voluntary sectors, from 35% to 38% between 2011-15. There is a very slight decline of 2% in attendance in nursery classes in primary schools in the last five years. Early education provision and take-up follow similar patterns in Wales and Scotland, with the majority of three- and four-year-olds receiving free early education; however, there seems to be less flexibility in delivery in both countries in comparison to England,

Figure 11.2: Proportion of three- and four-year-old children benefiting from funded early education places by type of provider in England

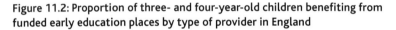

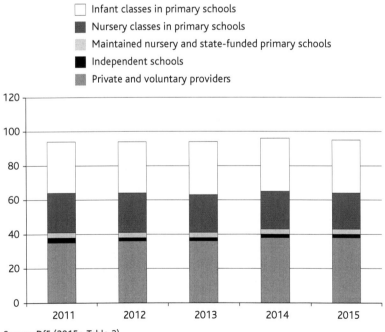

Source: DfE (2015n, Table 2)

which can provide it in bigger time lumps over a few days (House of Lords, 2015). In Wales, for example, 2.5 hours per day is typically offered over five days a week (Welsh Government, 2014a), whereas in Scotland, delivery is for slightly longer, typically 3 hours per day over five days (Kidner et al, 2014).

Formal early education provision is also on the increase across OECD countries, with the majority of children enrolling in some form of education before the age of five. Figure 11.3 shows this trend, comparing the rates between 2005 and 2010. The enrolment rates vary considerably, between 100% in France and 27% in Turkey, and there is a general trend across a majority of countries for slightly higher enrolments rates in 2010 compared to 2005 (OECD, 2013a).

The European Union Survey of Income and Living Conditions (EU-SILC) is an alternative source of comparative data. Figure 11.4 shows the proportion of children aged 3-5 in day care, pre-school or school both in full-time equivalent and head count terms. The UK is towards the bottom of this distribution, with 74% in care/education or 52% in the full-time equivalent. This indicates that care for this age group is much more commonly part-time than in most other EU countries.

In terms of targeted provision of free early education for two-year-olds, England introduced this for 20% of the most disadvantaged two-year-olds in September 2013 and extended it to 40% of the most disadvantaged in September 2014, resulting in 157,040 children taking up a place in 2015 (equating to 58% of those who were eligible) (DfE, 2015n). Targeting disadvantaged two-year-olds is a means to help close the 'attainment gap' in educational outcomes (House of Lords, 2015, p 6). Scotland is catching up with England and Wales, with eligibility widening in August 2015 to reach an estimated 27% of two-year-olds (Kidner et al, 2014). Northern Ireland's strategy is still emerging in comparison to the rest of the UK, and consequently statistical estimates are given for three-year-olds only. The estimates show that the majority of three-year-olds at least are receiving some free school early education (DoE [Northern Ireland], 2015).

In comparison, formal childcare usage in the EU for children up to the age of two (not necessarily targeted interventions aimed at the disadvantaged) shows wide variations in 2012. Figure 11.5 shows that nearly 70% of children have used some kind of formal childcare and/or early education provision in Denmark, and less than 10% were doing the same in the Czech Republic.

In sum, many of the policy challenges in the UK relate to the aim of aiding parental employment and dealing with supply and demand

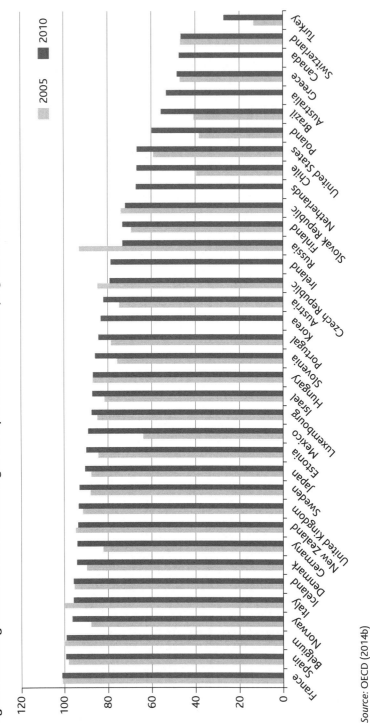

Figure 11.3: Average enrolment rate of children aged 3-5 in pre-school educational programmes, 2005 and 2010

Source: OECD (2014b)

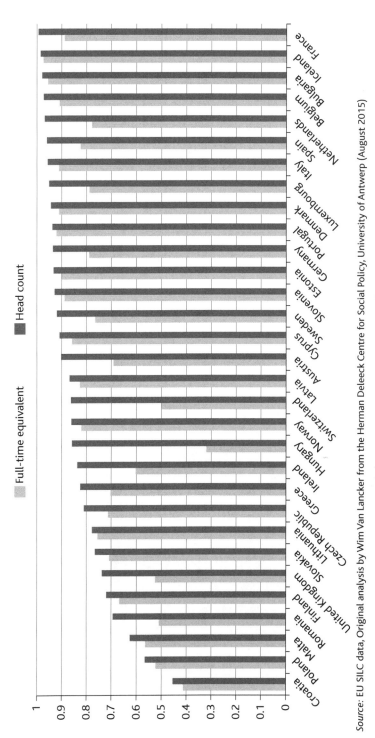

Figure 11.4: Proportion of children aged 3-5 in day care or pre-school or school, 2012

Full-time equivalent ▪ Head count

Source: EU SILC data, Original analysis by Wim Van Lancker from the Herman Deleeck Centre for Social Policy, University of Antwerp (August 2015)

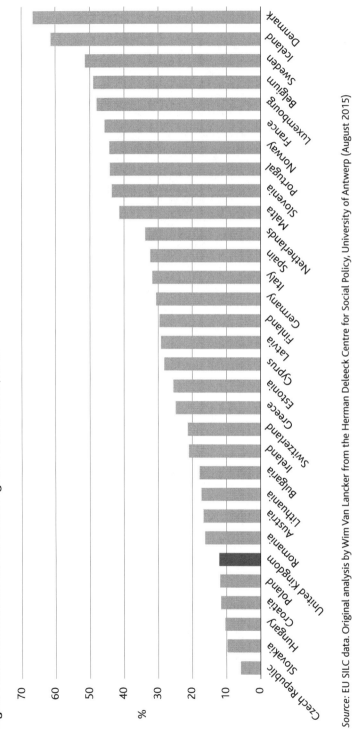

Figure 11.5: Formal childcare use for children aged 0-2 across the EU, 2012

Source: EU SILC data. Original analysis by Wim Van Lancker from the Herman Deleeck Centre for Social Policy, University of Antwerp (August 2015)

issues as well as quality standards. Provision of childcare places is insufficient to meet the demands of working parents, whereas part-time early education for three- and four-year-olds is taken up nearly universally. Targeted provision of early education for disadvantaged two-year-olds is on the increase, with England apparently leading the way on this. It is difficult, however, to get an accurate picture of the level of investment in the UK compared to other OECD countries. The variety in the nature of service provision and the differential ages at which children officially start school make data collection very complex, and it is difficult to compare like with like, similarly for the EU-SILC data describing the take-up of services for children under five. Regarding quality, this is inconsistent in the UK's mixed economy of provision. These are all important factors as they help set the context for the discussion that now follows on child development outcomes.

Child outcomes

Since the first book in this series was published in 2001, strong evidence has emerged showing that attendance in formal pre-school group provision can produce positive child development outcomes, that is, as long as it is good quality care (see Bradshaw, 2011; Skinner, 2011; Sylva et al, 2014; Taggart et al, 2015). The OECD confirms the positive value of early childhood education and care (ECEC) for child outcomes and for child well-becoming in adulthood. The OECD ECEC network states that the evidence shows 'the only way to dramatically decrease gaps in achievement later in life is to provide enriching learning experiences to children well before they enter school' (OECD, 2013b, p 4). Clearly, there is a strong UK and international consensus on the value of formal ECEC for producing good child development outcomes, based on what is believed to be a solid evidence base. For example, in the UK, the consensus is related especially to the robust findings from the series of longitudinal studies, Effective Pre-school, Primary and Secondary Education (EPPSE). These have been running for 17 years (from 1997-2014), and have been used extensively to justify policy interventions in the early years across three changes in government (under Labour, which set up the first ever National Childcare Strategy in 1998, to the Conservative-led coalition government, and now to the new Conservative administration that took office in May 2015). We turn now to explore the evidence base.

Effective Pre-school, Primary and Secondary Education experience studies

The EPPSE studies followed 3,000 children in England from ages 3-16 in four phases. A previous version of this chapter (Bradshaw, 2011) has reported these findings, and a recent up-to-date overview of the results across the 17 years is provided by Taggart et al (2015). To summarise here very briefly, the results showed that some experience of 'formal pre-school' in a group setting in the early years was better than none, especially in terms of attainment (Sylva et al, 2014; Taggart et al, 2015). The best form of attendance was frequent weekly visits of short duration, but also sustained over long periods of time – 2-3 years. Perhaps remarkably, the effects for attainment were still evident at age 16 on GCSE grades, although there was no longer any significant effect on social behavioural outcomes (unless attendance was at high-quality provision in the pre-school years). The EPPSE researchers consistently argue that there are greater gains to be had in outcomes for children from disadvantaged backgrounds, especially if they attend high quality pre-school for longer durations (2-3 years). This evidence provides a strong and convincing case for the potential of formal pre-school provision to narrow the attainment gap between children from disadvantaged families with poorly educated parents and more advantaged families with well-educated parents (with A-levels or above). A similar message comes from international bodies such as the OECD.

OECD

The OECD states: 'A growing body of research recognises that ECEC can improve children's cognitive abilities, and socio-emotional development, help create a foundation for life-long learning, make children's learning outcomes more equitable, reduce poverty and improve social mobility from generation to generation' (OECD, 2013a, p 2). They cite evidence from the third report of their 'Starting Strong' series (OECD, 2012a), and from their extensive analysis of OECD indicators in their 'Education at a Glance' series (2012b) as well as some results from a comparative analysis of PISA (Programme of International Student Assessment) data. However, the former two reports mainly analyse children's take-up and the quality of provision, whereas the PISA data (OECD, 2010) shows that attending an early education programme is strongly associated with better reading skills at age 15. But this relationship is strongest in countries where provision has certain quality features – such as high staff-child ratios, good duration of programmes and high public spending per child. The OECD argues therefore that countries need to pay attention to the quality of provision and not just the extent of provision.

Consequently, to drive up quality standards, the OECD have set up a framework to support curriculum development in ECEC programmes for children aged 0-8 (OECD, 2012a, 2013b). There is agreement, however, among the ECEC network members, that establishing a 'standards-based measurement of specific (academic) learning outcomes' for comparative analysis would be inappropriate, not least because children's rapid development in early childhood is highly variable by age, even when it is within normal parameters. Rather, their approach is to 'see assessment of young children being focused on assessment for learning which occurs on a daily basis by the professional educator working in partnership with the parent/ caregiver' (OECD, 2013b, p 10). To that end, the plan is for assessment to focus on what the child has learned using existing mechanisms and data already provided within countries. The challenge remains, however, of compensating for a lack of data on child development outcomes at the same time as dealing with tensions that occur between proponents who wish to measure child outcomes and those who want to monitor child development (OECD, 2012a, 'Challenge 4', p 1).

So where does that leave us? Do we know all we need to know about early education and childcare services and child outcomes? Certainly, the Department for Education (DfE) in the UK believed the EPPSE study represented a strong body of evidence proving the long-lasting positive effects of formal pre-school on child development, resulting in a growing political consensus that 'universal early education' is good for children (House of Lords, 2015, p 30; Brewer et al, 2014; Taggart et al, 2015). However, things are not quite as straightforward as they might seem. Remarkably, according to the Institute for Fiscal Studies (Brewer et al, 2014, p 172), 'we have stumbled a long way in the dark in this policy area'. What we lack to back up this consensus is the specific evidence on the effect of the latest service provision in the UK.

Limitations of the existing evidence base

There are a number of problems with the existing evidence base for evaluating current early years provision on child development outcomes. First, there are two elements in the UK – 'childcare' and 'early education'. According to Brewer et al (2014), these tend to be discussed interchangeably, but are different things. The former covers any type of non-parental care for 0- to 5-year-olds (be it from a one-hour crèche to an all-day nursery) and is usually paid for by parents (albeit with some government subsidies for low-income families). This provision mainly helps to support parental employment, whereas early education refers to a particular part-time educational curriculum, mainly for three- and four-year-olds paid for by government. It can be delivered by any 'qualified' service, for example, school nurseries, private day nurseries, childminders and so on, and is primarily aimed at improving child development outcomes (although it can also help support parental employment).

Second, these interwoven aspects of early education and childcare, often delivered together by the same provider, means that they are rarely disaggregated in policy discussions or in research findings, resulting in a lack of policy coherence (Brewer et al, 2014). This has been a longstanding issue (see Skinner, previous volumes (Bradshaw, 2011; Skinner, 2011)). The House of Lords inquiry into childcare in the UK (House of Lords, 2015) highlights just this problem. It notes that there are now three explicit policy aims: to enhance parental labour supply, to provide universal early education to improve child development outcomes for all children, and to target early education at the most disadvantaged to close the attainment gap. They also point out that there is a fourth more implicit aim, to reduce poverty. Importantly, the inquiry found that it is not clear what the aims of state intervention into the early years of childhood actually are, and moreover, the policy aims have competed with one other as different priorities were emphasised by different administrations, resulting in disparate and short-term approaches (House of Lords, 2015, p 20).

Third, while the EPPSE study showed positive outcomes arising from children having some form of formal pre-school experience compared to having none, it does not address the question of whether the current policy of offering early education for 15 hours a week is beneficial. In addition, although the EPPSE study was complex, multilayered and extensive, it followed children from only six local authority areas in England. This highlights some of the difficulties in gathering evidence on child outcomes in the UK as children experience highly variable service provision with different quality standards. For example, there are different qualification requirements and staff-child ratio standards depending on whether the early education setting is in the maintained public sector or the private voluntary sector (Blanden et al, 2014, p 8). If we combine the limitations of the UK evidence base with the lack of policy coherence, we know less about the actual benefits of the current early education policy than we might think, despite the political consensus. Brewer et al (2014) make exactly this point. Some new research evidence on pupil performance has recently emerged, however, and new studies have been commissioned by the DfE to tackle some of the evidence limitations.

Analysis of the National Pupil Database

Blanden et al (2014) conducted a detailed analysis of pupil performance in England using data from the National Pupil Database. They tried to gauge the impact of the availability of free early education services on pupil attainment at ages 5 (entry to school), 7 and 11. This was a complex undertaking as they explored the 'availability of free early education' provision on children's aggregate outcomes at local authority level as opposed to following individual children's experience of early education into the school years. What they did was follow the policy roll-out across time (from first implementation in 1999) as well as across local education authorities, and took snapshots of pupil attainment at the aggregate level, thereby modelling child outcomes as a function of free early education availability. They claimed to be the first to evaluate the 'causal effects' of this policy on outcomes.

Their results showed that early education availability for three-year-olds did produce better cognitive and non-cognitive outcomes at entry to school aged 5, the effects were much weaker, however, at age 7, and were not evident at all in the age 11 measurements. In terms of assessing differences in outcomes based on socioeconomic circumstances, they found only slight evidence that disadvantaged children gained more from improvements in access to early education than children from less deprived backgrounds. Their evidence is much weaker than that reported by EPPSE, although the studies are unalike as the former followed individual children's experiences. Even so, Blanden et al (2014) refer to the difficulty in assessing a causal link between pre-school attendance and future outcomes because enrolment depends on parental choice, and this is correlated with family and child characteristics confounding the impact. They argue that to really establish a causal effect would require a randomised experimental trial along the lines of the Perry Preschool project and the Abecedarian projects in the US. These were intensive targeted interventions that have frequently formed part of the body of international evidence advocating the positive impact of early years education on child development. Such an experimental approach is not appropriate to early education provision in the UK, however, because it is universal, and the majority of three- and four-year-olds already attend free early education.

Around the same time as the Blanden et al (2014) analysis, the DfE set out its research priorities for 'early education and childcare'. Gaps in the evidence base were identified relating to 'how to secure and sustain the best possible standards and the practice that makes the most difference to children's lives' (DfE, 2014d, p 7). Two new studies were therefore commissioned, in part as a response to rising concerns about whether the promised longer-term benefits of free early education are being produced and are cost-effective (Brewer et al, 2014; Speight et al, 2015, p 18). The first was an OECD international policy review of early years pedagogy. That report was provided in July 2015 (Wall, et al, 2015), and is not discussed here, other than to say that, comparatively, the pedagogic approach within England's Early Year's Foundation Stage curriculum was thought to be appropriate, suitably child-centred and well founded on research evidence. The second was the Study for Early Education and Development (SEED), now reported in detail below.

Study for Early Education and Development

SEED is a longitudinal study that will follow 8,000 two-year-olds from across England to the end of Key Stage 1 in primary school (ages 7-8). It began in October 2013 and is expected to finish in 2020. The main purpose of the study is to assess the effectiveness of free early education on attainment as well as the impact of the free provision for disadvantaged two-year-olds. In addition, it will explore how parenting and the 'home learning environment' interact with early education to affect child outcomes. It is being conducted by a large consortium of experts from the National Centre for Social Research (NatCen), the University of Oxford, 4Children and Frontier Economics. The first descriptive results, published in July 2015, form the baseline study that sets the scene for later impact analysis. Among other things, it reports on childcare usage up to age two, reasons for non-take-up of formal care, the home learning environment and child outcomes as well as the differences across all of these elements by children's socioeconomic background. Early results show that child outcomes at age two were worst for children from the most disadvantaged backgrounds, they had less language skills at age two, less positive behaviours and were less likely to take up formal care before age two and more likely to report limited availability of services in their area (Speight et al, 2015). Interestingly, however, the reasons for not using formal services were not that different across socioeconomic groups. Even so, 48% of the most disadvantaged families had used free childcare for two-year-olds. This concurs with the Office for Standards in Education (Ofsted) (responsible for the regulation and inspection of education and early years provision in England) using administrative data. They report that in July 2015, nearly half of all eligible disadvantaged two-year-olds in England were not taking up a free early education offer (Ofsted, 2015). Unlike other cohort studies, SEED is expected to provide a definitive answer to the specific question of how the current 'universal' early education provision affects child outcomes, especially for disadvantaged two-year-olds. The answers will take account of the variable quality and varying patterns of attendance across this mixed economy of provision involving the private, voluntary and maintained sectors. We will have to wait for the impact analysis in the coming years to find out the answers, although we do have other evidence on the effect of the home learning environment.

Home learning environment

As Dame Claire Tickell reminded us in her review of the Early Years Foundation Stage (EYFS), parents are still important (Tickell, 2011). Evidence – in particular from the EPPSE study – has shown that parents/primary caregivers and the home learning environment had the greatest influence on child development outcomes, but good quality early years services could compensate if the home learning environment was weak. This echoes with the conclusions drawn by Hansen and Hawkes (2009) in their analysis of early years' experience in the Millennium Cohort Study, that the differential effects of types of care (both formal and informal) on numerous child development outcomes are probably explained by the various ways in which children are 'cared for' (see the previous version of this book, Bradshaw, 2011). So, not surprisingly, informal parental care and high-quality formal care, in combination, improve child development outcomes. The home learning environment is particularly important, however, not least because free early education is provided for a maximum of 15 hours per week (currently), and the model of delivery varies widely, from 3 hours per day over five days or in lumps with full-time attendance across fewer days (depending on the provider from the voluntary, private or maintained sectors) (House of Lords, 2015, p 37).

Increasingly, an interest in factors shaping child development outcomes in the early years is becoming more focused on what parents do in the home learning environment. For example, both the All-Party Parliamentary Groups on Parents and Families and on Social Mobility conducted a joint inquiry into parenting and social mobility in 2015. They argued that 'parenting style' in the early years is 'the strongest factor' in shaping children's development, and that we need a National Parenting Programme to improve parenting skills in the 'early home learning environment' (National Childcare Trust, 2015, p 7). Simultaneously, a rapid review of the evidence on targeted 'parenting programmes' that aims to improve parent–child interaction in the home has also been conducted (Axford et al, 2015). This work is the first review of its kind, and was commissioned by the EIF (more information on the EIF is discussed below). It provides details on 32 case studies and is also accompanied by an online guidebook, providing details of all programmes and a scoring system indicating the quality of the evidence on programme outcomes.[4] The guidebook is aimed at supporting programme providers, policy-makers and practitioners to learn about 'what works' for children. There is also other new research underway that will help address the question of whether more targeted intensive interventions for disadvantaged children might prove better at reducing the gap in outcomes. This moves the discussion into exploring the idea of 'early intervention' in a much more holistic way than simply focusing on formal childcare and early education provision.

Early intervention

The 'early years' of childhood more broadly is falling under the scrutiny of policy-makers. It is seen as a fruitful period of life in which 'early intervention' offers opportunities to improve longer-term outcomes. Early intervention seems to be the new panacea (even if the multiple aims of early education and childcare policy remain incoherent), although like early education it, too, is said to help improve educational and health outcomes, break the cycle of disadvantage that leads to poor outcomes in adulthood (thereby breaking the cycle of inter-generational poverty) and to reduce inequalities for the most disadvantaged children and improve social mobility (House of Lords, 2015, p 6). According to analysis by the Institute of Education (Sylva et al, 2014) using the EPPSE study and GCSE scores, early intervention also promises to reduce state costs over the longer term. Sylva et al (2014, p 177) estimated the net present value of an individual's lifetime gross earnings resulting from attending pre-school. They cautiously predicted that if someone had some formal pre-school experience, they could benefit by as much as £26,788 compared to those who had no such experience. The Exchequer could also gain by as much as £11,000 per individual over their lifetime. If any of the assumptions by Sylva et al (2014) hold true, there is something to be gained over the longer term for intervening in early childhood, with a potential win–win scenario for individuals and the state.[5]

This focus on 'early intervention' takes us away from concentrating on universal provision of free early education services and childcare in the early years, and unlike that policy, the aims of early intervention are much clearer: to improve the future well-becoming of children in adulthood. To that end it is necessarily a cross-government responsibility involving more than just the DfE.

One example of broader early intervention in the early years involves Public Health for England (2014, p 18). They have designated the early years as one of their seven priority areas to improve the nation's health, with the goal of increasing the 'proportion of children ready to learn at two and ready for school at five'. This will be achieved by supporting local authorities to deliver their Healthy Child Programme for 0–5s. Yet, as Messenger and Molloy (2014, p 3) have noted: 'Local areas report that they are facing real challenges in bringing together the Healthy Child Programme (HCP), the work of Children's Centres and the Early Years Foundation Stage (EYFS) childcare and early education agendas.' The effective integration of institutional arrangements and services at a local level has therefore become increasingly important under an 'early intervention' agenda, as the close interconnection between the NHS and local authorities in the above example shows. Messenger and Molloy (2014, p 5) have provided practical examples of successful integrated working between health services and local authorities in intervening early in the early years. They evaluated the provision of 20 innovative early intervention places provided by the EIF, and have identified areas of 'good and promising practice across different dimensions of integration'.

Early intervention is therefore a more holistic approach to supporting children and their families, and has been strongly promoted. A new EIF was set up in 2013 involving a coalition of charities and organisations whose stated purpose is to 'lobby government' to help tackle the 'root causes of problems for children and young people' early on before they become 'embedded'. They want to drive a 'culture of change' to ensure families that need help can access it (Messenger and Molly, 2014, p 5). Since its inception, the EIF has successfully joined forces with the Social Mobility and Child Poverty Commission and the Cabinet Office to commission three research reports in 2014-15.

Feinstein (2015) provides a summary of all three reports, but the first of these is most relevant to this chapter (Goodman et al, 2015).

Goodman et al (2015) conducted an analysis of the British Cohort Study and Millennium Cohort Study to review how a range of social and emotional skills developed in childhood can contribute to good adult outcomes in terms of employment. From the British Cohort Study analysis they found that alongside having parents with professional occupations, having good emotional and social skills at age 10 could have positive effects on transmitting 'top job status' in adulthood at age 42. They built on this analysis using the Millennium Cohort Study to consider the level of social and emotional skill development in more recent cohorts of children from age 3-11. Interestingly, they found differences in level of skills by socioeconomic status emerging as early as three years of age and persisting to age 11. They argue that measuring social and emotional skills provides 'important signals' about likely outcomes in adulthood over and above measurements of cognitive abilities (2015, p 87). They are also keen to point out, however, that their evidence shows the risks associated with having poor skills – they are not causal effects that determine adult outcomes. Moreover, the observations of differences in skill levels cannot be easily isolated from the confounding effects of the characteristics of the child, the parents and the family. Thus, the research cannot explain *why* there is a gap between advantaged and disadvantaged children, or why that gap has widened for today's children in the Millennium Cohort Study compared to British Cohort Study children born in 1970. Nor can they say what the relative importance of genetic versus environmental factors might be (the latter being most amenable to policy intervention). The authors are convinced, however, that their findings make a strong case for early intervention in childhood, including in the early years, in order to find ways to improve skills development, to reduce the skills gap and to improve both outcomes in the here and now and in adulthood. New research, 'An evaluation of a better start', will attempt to build on this evidence further by closely scrutinising the environmental and spatial factors associated with targeted interventions at a local level (Axford and Barlow (no date 1, 2).

'An evaluation of a better start' is funded by the Big Lottery Fund that invested £215 million in 2014. This will deliver new preventative interventions for children from ages 0-3 across five areas in England, selected for their high levels of deprivation. The aim is to understand more about effective early intervention. To that end, collaborations across health, education and social care services are being supported in the five areas to encourage structural changes that will enable them to work with families at risk of poor outcomes in order to improve social, emotional, cognitive development and health outcomes. So far, two reports have been published, both by Axford and Barlow (no date 1, 2) from the Social Research Unit at Dartington. These form part of the evidence review, and also provide a methods framework for the 'place-based' interventions that will implement evidence-based programmes. The investment will last for 10 years. It is an ambitious undertaking, with evaluations being conducted by the Warwick Consortium that is made up of a large group of experts from a number of universities and independent research organisations.[6]

All this work on 'early intervention', alongside other evidence (Blanden et al, 2014; Brewer et al, 2014), builds strong cases for targeted interventions in the early years of childhood that go far beyond the provision of universal early education. Perhaps not surprisingly, the EIF and Social Mobility and Child Poverty Commission are powerful advocates of this approach. In the meantime, the new research project, SEED, will help provide definitive evidence on universal provision of free early education and the relationship with the home learning environment, and while the evidence is collected from families in England, it will feed into national policy-making via the DfE.

Conclusion

When this book series began in 2001, there was little UK-based evidence of the effects of formal childcare and early education on child development outcomes. The EPPSE project changed that, providing a robust longitudinal study demonstrating the lasting positive effects on child outcomes arising from attendance at some formal pre-school in the early years. It has had a strong policy impact (alongside international evidence from the Perry project in the US and others), and has been quoted extensively in policy documents and driven key policy decisions. Yet it is only more recently that policy-makers have stopped to question the impact of contemporary provision of free early education and childcare services on child outcomes. Consequently, a new longitudinal study, SEED, has now been commissioned. We await the results of SEED as well as the bigger area evaluations of 'a better start'. Given their longitudinal nature, their impact on policy developments at this stage is uncertain. Suffice to say, there is currently a strong drive for targeted early intervention as opposed to universal provision, at least, that is, if the policy aim is to improve child development outcomes.

Important questions for the evidence base of the future are therefore likely to be aligned more with the work of the EIF and 'a better start'; that is perhaps where the best evidence might be found of the factors that shape early years and childcare experience and their impact on child development outcomes. These will include evidence on parenting skills and the home learning environment as well as environmental factors such as living in disadvantaged areas, rather than simply children's experience of childcare and early education service provision.

Notes

[1] Childcare is a devolved matter in Scotland, Wales and Northern Ireland – the figures from the House of Lords inquiry relates to England only (2015, p 17).

[2] At the time of writing, the eligibility criteria identifying those in work is still being decided.

[3] This high relative cost is driven partly by government subsidies going directly to parents rather than to providers (see House of Commons Library, 2015).

[4] See www.eif.org.uk

[5] This holds true, notwithstanding the earlier criticism by Brewer et al (2014) that the evidence from EPPSE does not relate to current early education provision.

[6] See http://abetterstart.org.uk/evaluation-team/4

TWELVE

Children, crime and correction

Rachel Morris and Lisa O'Malley

Key statistics

- Adults commit the majority of crime, not young people.
- Boys commit most juvenile crime.
- Violence and theft are the most prevalent types of crime committed by children.
- Children of White ethnic origin commit most juvenile crime, although a disproportionate number of children from BAME (Black, Asian and minority ethnic) groups are arrested.
- The majority of young people are sentenced to community-based orders.
- There has been a sharp fall in the use of custodial sentences.
- The more entrenched a child gets in the youth justice system, the more likely they are to reoffend.

Key trends

- The proportion of children arrested (compared with adults) is falling.
- The number of children who are 'first time entrants' to the justice system is falling.
- The number of children who are being sentenced is falling.
- The use of custodial sentences has fallen dramatically, to the lowest numbers being in custody since 2002.
- Reoffending rates remain stubbornly high, with custodial sentences being the least successful in terms of reducing reoffending.

Key sources

- Ministry of Justice (MoJ)/Youth Justice Board (YJB) national statistics
- Police powers and procedures (national statistics)
- Crime Survey for England and Wales (CSEW)

Introduction

This chapter summarises trends and data about how much crime is committed by children in England and Wales, and the punishments that children receive through the youth justice system. It also explores evidence relating to reoffending among children and the risk factors associated with those young people who are convicted. The chapter focuses on administrative data collected by the police and youth offending teams across England and Wales while acknowledging the limitations of these sources, and the lack of survey data relating to the victimisation of children or up-to-date self-report statistics. The inclusion of trends and data relating to punishment provides a more complete picture of the experience of criminal justice by children than previous editions of this volume have been able to cover. This chapter covers the period up to March 2014 (the latest data available), updating those data that were reported in earlier editions (see Neale, 2006; O'Malley and Grace, 2011), and examining longer-term trends where appropriate.

Definitions and indicators

The available data is concerned with children aged between 10 and 17, reflecting the fact that most of the data comes from administrative sources that are concerned with formal criminal justice processes. A lack of knowledge about criminal behaviour among those under the age of 10 continues (see O'Malley and Grace, 2011). The chapter is also restricted to data relating to England and Wales, reflecting different criminal justice procedures in Scotland and separate data collection procedures in Northern Ireland.

Since the last edition (O'Malley and Grace, 2011), self-reported crime surveys have not been updated, although the Crime Survey for England and Wales (CSEW) (previously known as the British Crime Survey) has started to collect data relating to young people's experiences of crime (for the most recent data, see ONS, 2015e, pp 99-105[1]).

The definitions of crime that underpin the administrative data reported here are legalistic, and consequently may be criticised for reflecting a very particular and inflexible sense of 'crime'. Similarly, the data relating to punishments is underpinned by a specific set of instruments that are currently being used within the youth justice system – instruments that are frequently subject to change.

The chapter is organised as follows: the first section examines evidence relating to overall levels of crime committed by children before examining that relating to the arrest of children. We go on to examine trends in 'proven offences' which allows for a more detailed examination of specific age ranges, and includes data about ethnicity that is lacking from the police records of arrests. This edition includes an examination of trends in first time entrants to the youth justice system before going on to examine data relating to the punishment of children. It then explores trends in reoffending among children, and reviews the risk factors that have been associated with children who are convicted.

Overall levels of crime

In 2013/14 the police recorded 3.7 million offences, representing no change on the previous year (ONS, 2015e).[2] In contrast, figures from the CSEW continue to show falling crime levels, with 7.3 million crime incidents in 2013/14, down 14% from 2012/13 (ONS, 2015e). The differences in these figures is generally explained with reference to changes in police recording practices, which have been subject to increased scrutiny since 2010 (ONS, 2015e).

These overall reductions are reflected in arrest figures for children specifically. Figure 12.1 shows trends in arrests since 2002/03, which peaked in 2006/07, fell sharply for the following five years (to 2012/13), but are beginning to indicate a slowing down in reduction in the last 12 months.

However, this overall reduction belies continuing disproportionality in the arrest of young people. In 2013/14, 11% of arrests involved those aged 10-17 (see Figure 12.2). This compares with 77% for those aged 21 and over and 12% for those aged 18-20. Mid-year population estimates for 2013 show that 10- to 17-year-olds comprise 9% of the population (ONS, 2015e), but they account for 11% of those arrested. In 2008/09 the same comparison showed that young people comprised 11% of the population, but accounted for 19% of arrests. This may indicate positive trends in attitudes towards children's offending behaviour by authorities, but it remains the case that disproportionate numbers of young people continue to be arrested.

Types of crime committed by children

Table 12.1 shows that almost 113,000 children aged 10-17 were arrested for notifiable offences in 2013/14. Figure 12.3, based on Table

Figure 12.1: Trends in the arrests of young people aged 10-17 for notifiable offences, 2002/03-2013/14

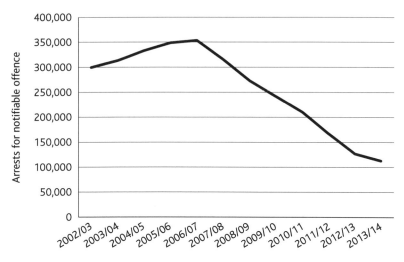

Source: MoJ and YJB (2015, Table 1.4)

Figure 12.2: Proportions of arrest by age, 2013/14

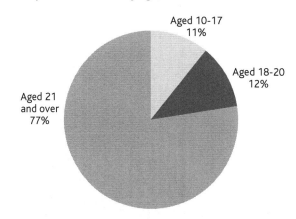

Source: Home Office (2015, Table A.01)

12.1, shows that the most prevalent offences were violence against the person (26%), theft and handling stolen goods (22%), which together account for almost half (48%) of all arrests in this age group. However, the vast majority of arrests for these offences continue to involve adults, who account for 91% of arrests for violence and 89% for theft and handling stolen goods.

Table 12.1: Numbers and percentage of people arrested for notifiable offences, by type of offence and age group, 2013/14

	Under 10		Aged 10-17		Aged 18-20		Aged 21+		Age unknown		All ages	
	N	%	N	%	N	%	N	%	N	%	N	%
Violence against the person	28	0.01	29,191	9	34,926	10	276,028	81	327	0.10	340,500	100
Theft and handling stolen goods	14	0.01	24,818	11	23,970	11	178,948	79	183	0.08	227,933	100
Criminal damage	18	0.02	13,533	18	10,461	14	52,907	69	64	0.08	76,983	100
Burglary	1	0.00	12,079	17	11,070	15	48,370	68	20	0.03	71,540	100
Other offences	1	0.00	11,274	8	15,790	11	114,416	81	193	0.14	141,674	100
Drug offences	1	0.00	10,423	10	15,634	15	79,241	75	65	0.06	105,364	100
Robbery	2	0.01	7,349	32	4,350	19	11,199	49	9	0.04	22,909	100
Sexual offences	5	0.01	3,401	10	3,148	9	27,160	80	46	0.14	33,760	100
Fraud and forgery	–	–	641	3	1,835	9	18,065	88	17	0.08	20,558	100
Total	70	0.01	112,709	11	121,184	12	806,334	77	924	0.09	1,041,221	100

Source: Home Office (2015)

Figure 12.3: Percentage of people arrested for notifiable offences, by type of offence and age group, 2013/14

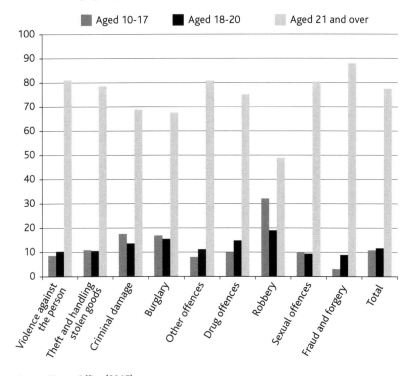

Source: Home Office (2015)

Comparing these data with those from 2009/10 (see Figure 12.4), we can see that the profile of the types of offence for which young people are arrested has remained static, with only minor changes in drug offences (an increase of 3 percentage points) and theft and handling stolen goods (a decrease of 3 percentage points) showing the biggest changes. Figure 12.5, however, shows more change in the proportion of children aged 10-17 who are arrested (compared to all other ages) for all offence types, with reductions in all categories. The most notable differences have occurred for robbery, for which young people accounted for 43% in 2009/10, down to 32% in 2013/14, and burglary, which has also seen a decrease of 10 percentage points in the period.

Overall, the data suggest that lower proportions of young people are being arrested compared with the adult population, but that the types of crimes they are arrested for are similar to previous patterns,

Figure 12.4: Proportion of notifiable offence types among 10- to 17-year-old arrestees, 2009/10 and 2013/14

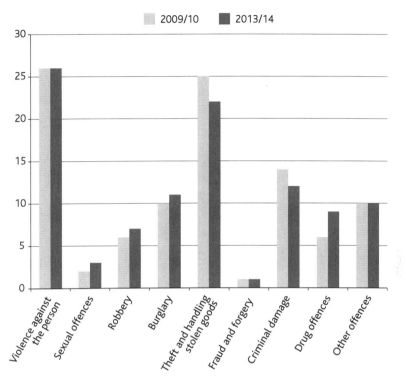

Source: Home Office (2015)

with violence and theft continuing to dominate children's offending behaviour.

Age and offending

Arrest data provides an insight into how young people's offending behaviour differs from that of adults, but to further interrogate differences in patterns of offending among 10- to 17-year-olds, the only data available relates to proven offences that are not comparable to arrest figures. Nonetheless, they provide some insight into the relative rates of offending across age groups.

Figure 12.6 shows trends in the number of proven offences by age since 2009/10, and reflects a similarly sharp decline as data for overall arrests, in this case falling from a total of 198,449 in 2009/10 to 90,769 in 2013/14. However, the decline is sharpest for older age groups

Figure 12.5: Proportion of arrests of 10- to 17-year-olds for notifiable offences, 2009/10 and 2013/14

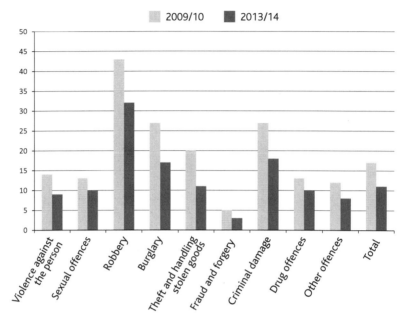

Source: Home Office (2015)

(from 108,625 to 52,883), and has shown signs of levelling off since 2012/13. Proven offences continue to follow age – highest among those aged 16-17 and lowest for those aged 10-11.

However, Table 12.2 shows that the proportion of offences committed across this age range has changed slightly between 2009/10 and 2013/14. In 2009/10, 55% of proven offences were among those aged 16-17 while in 2013/14 this had risen to 58%. The corresponding reductions are found among lower age groups, with 12- to 13-year-olds accounting for 8% of proven offences in 2013/14 compared with 10% in 2009/10.

Thus, despite overall patterns of decline in juvenile arrests and proven offences, the data points to some possible differences between specific age groups that we will return to in later sections.

Sex and offending

Data continues to highlight stark variations in offending behaviour between girls and boys (see Table 12.3), with the latter more likely to be arrested for all offence categories and disproportionately overall,

Figure 12.6: Trends in the number of proven offences, by age, 2010/11-2013/14

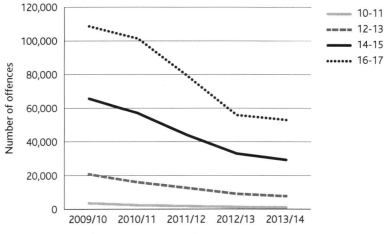

Source: MoJ and YJB (2012, 2013, 2014, 2015)

Table 12.2: Proportion of proven offences by age, 2009/10 and 2013/14

Age	2009/10	As % of all offences	2013/14	As % of all offences	Difference 2009/10-2013/14
10-11	3,475	2	999	1	−2,476
12-13	20,736	10	7,633	8	−13,103
14-15	65,613	33	29,254	32	−36,359
16-17	108,625	55	52,883	58	−55,742
All	198,449	100	90,769	100	−107,680

Source: MoJ and YJB (2012, 2015)

with notable variations in relation to sexual offences, where 38 times as many males as females were arrested, burglary (where males were arrested 13 times more frequently than females) and drug offences (11 times more males than females). Ratios are smaller for some offences, notably violence against the person, where boys are (just) three times more likely to be arrested than girls.

Arrest data reveals some differences in the rates of decline for boys and girls, as shown in Table 12.3, with girls experiencing an overall decline of 60% since 2009/10 and boys a 52% reduction. Some offence categories show notable differences such as robbery, where there has been a 55% reduction in arrests among girls and 46% for boys, and theft and handling stolen goods (72% reduction for girls and 53% reduction for boys).

Table 12.3: People aged 10-17 arrested for notifiable offence, by type of offence and sex, 2009/10 and 2013/14

Offence group	Males			Females			Ratio males to females	
	2009/10[b]	2013/14[a]	% point change	2009/10[b]	2013/14[a]	% point change	2009/10	2013/14
Violence against the person	47,577	21,702	-54	16,056	7,489	-53	3	3
Sexual offences	4,621	3,314	-28	122	87	-29	38	38
Robbery	12,462	6,687	-46	1,472	662	-55	8	10
Burglary	23,022	11,189	-51	1,946	890	-54	12	13
Theft and handling stolen goods	42,346	19,880	-53	17,534	4,938	-72	2	4
Fraud and forgery	1,071	465	-57	496	176	-65	2	3
Criminal damage	28,314	11,334	-60	4,960	2,199	-56	6	5
Drug offences	14,424	9,541	-34	1,252	882	-30	12	11
Other offences	19,866	9,461	-52	4,196	1,813	-57	5	5
Total	193,703	93,573	-52	48,034	19,136	-60	4	5

Sources: [a] Home Office (2015); [b] Povey et al (2011, Table 1b, p 15)

Ethnicity and proven offences

Arrest data for children is not available according to ethnic group, although the YJB continue to publish proven offences data by ethnicity.

Figures 12.7, 12.8 and 12.9 show the numbers of proven offences by ethnic groups (Figure 12.7), young Whites (Figure 12.8) and all Black, Asian and minority ethnic (BAME) groups (Figure 12.9). The data shows that proven offences have fallen across all ethnic groups since 2002/03 after rising to a peak in 2006/07. However, there are differences in the rates of these decreases, with BAME groups showing much less sharp reductions in the period, and evidence of increasing numbers of offences over the last 12 months (see Figure 12.7). Figure 12.7 indicates that the decline in proven offences for Asian and Black children has plateaued since 2012/13 and has risen for those of mixed ethnic origin. While some of these more fine-grained differences may reflect differences in counting/descriptive categories, the overall trends suggest that BAME groups are witnessing an increase in engagement with the youth justice system while their White counterparts continue to experience declining offences.

Figure 12.10 shows that in 2013/14 the proportion of proven offences among White children fell below 80% for the first time since 2002/03.

Administrative data pertaining to arrest and proven offences offers some insight into the prevalence of crime among young people and the offence categories they are most likely to be prosecuted for. However,

Figure 12.7: Trends in proven offences by ethnicity, 2010/11-2013-14

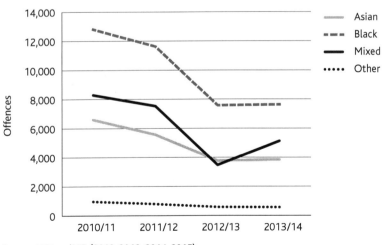

Source: MOJ and YJB (2012, 2013, 2014, 2015)

Figure 12.8: Trends in proven offences among White people aged 10-17, 2010/11-2013/14

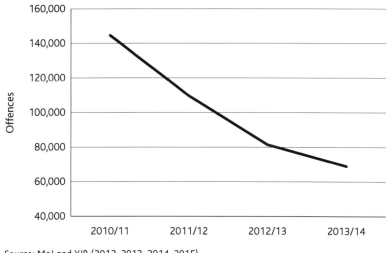

Source: MoJ and YJB (2012, 2013, 2014, 2015)

Figure 12.9: Proven offences among 10- to 17-year-olds for all BAME

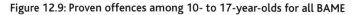

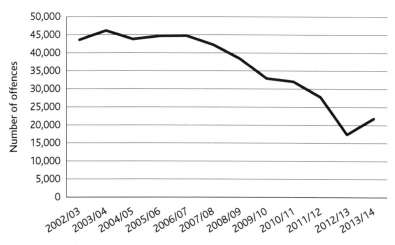

Source: MoJ and YJB (2012, 2013, 2014, 2015)

the limitations of this data are numerous – not least in relation to a lack of detail about the social characteristics of the young people who come into contact with the youth justice system. Police practices and changes in recording practices are often used to criticise the reliability of administrative data for estimating the amount of crime that takes place. On this basis it is likely that children commit more crime than

Figure 12.10: Proportion of proven offences among 10- to 17-year-olds by ethnicity

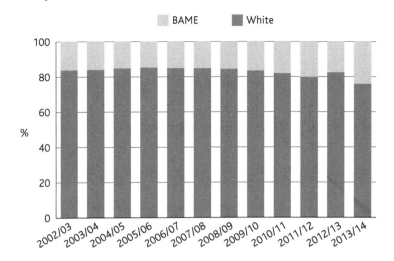

Source: MoJ and YJB (2012, 2013, 2014, 2015)

is reflected here, and the profile of the young people we are able to portray may reveal more about how the police deal with young people than the relative criminality of any particular age, sex or ethnic group.

First time entrants to the youth justice system

It has been a well-rehearsed argument among youth justice commentators since 1997 that the youth justice system can have an overall net widening effect, even when it is seeking to prevent crime among children and young people (Pitts, 2002; Smith, 2005; Goldson, 2010). Against the backdrop of widespread agreement that limiting exposure to the youth justice system would be beneficial, a series of government-led targets to reduce the number of first time entrants to the youth justice system were introduced in 2005.

Youth offending teams have been given responsibility for these reductions, and their overall success has been frequently reported (MoJ and YJB, 2012, 2013, 2014, 2015). Table 12.4 shows that in 2003/04 there were a total of 88,403 first time entrants to the youth justice system, of which almost 12,000 were aged 12 or under. By 2013/14 these figures had dropped to 22,393 and 1,450 respectively – an overall reduction of 75%. Some of the reduction has been explained with reference to police practices, including changes to police arrest targets from 2009 onwards (see, for example, MoJ and YJB, 2012, p 12) and

Table 12.4: Number of first time entrants by age, selected years

Age	2003/04	2006/07	2010/11	2013/14	% change 2003/04- 2013/14	% change 2010/11- 2013/14	% change 2012/13- 2013/14
10-12	11,968	15,755	4,252	1,450	−87.9	−65.9	−33.6
13	11,199	14,526	4,771	2,013	−82.0	−57.8	−24.5
14	15,273	20,369	7,490	3,335	−78.2	−55.5	−23.3
15	17,750	23,022	9,337	4,582	−74.2	−50.9	−22.3
16	16,536	20,094	9,873	5,267	−68.1	−46.7	−14.4
17	15,678	16,991	10,245	5,747	−63.3	−43.9	−15.7
Total (100%)	88,403	110,757	45,968	22,393	−74.7	−51.3	−20.2

Source: MoJ and YJB (2012, 2013, 2014, 2015)

the implementation of various initiatives that aim to divert young people from the youth justice system.

The overall picture appears to be very positive, but there are differences emerging within the 10-17 cohort that may signal divergent approaches, particularly in relation to specific age groups. Figure 12.11 shows the proportion of first time entrants from age groups 10-14 and 15-17, and highlights the fact that their age profile is changing – and is becoming older. The latter may be of concern if the trends are indicating that diversion schemes are less 'successful' with older age groups, which, in turn, may lead to further offending and, ultimately, entering the adult justice system.

Similar trends for boys and girls are shown in Table 12.5, where overall reductions have occurred for both groups, but the decline is more pronounced for girls (80% reduction since 2003/04 and 24% reduction in the previous year) than for boys (73% and 19% respectively).

Outcomes and punishments

Where prosecution proceeds, there are three tiers of sentencing available to magistrates and judges in the youth justice system (see Figure 12.12) – the Referral Order, the Youth Rehabilitation Order (YRO) and the Detention and Training Order (DTO) – and these will be the focus of the remainder of this chapter.

To provide some overall context, in 2013/14, there were 33,902 young people (aged 10-17) sentenced at criminal courts in England and Wales. The total number of young people sentenced fell by 23%

Figure 12.11: Proportion of first time entrants by age group, 2003/04-2013/14

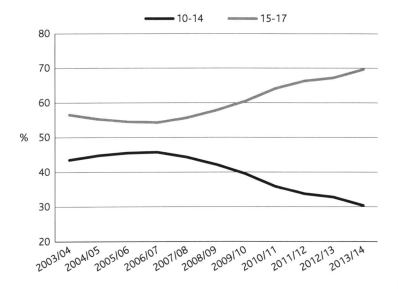

Source: MoJ and YJB (2012, 2013, 2014, 2015)

Table 12.5: Number of youth first time entrants to the criminal justice system by gender, selected years

Gender	2003/04	2006/07	2010/11	2013/14	% change 2003/04-2013/14	% change 2010/11-2013/14	% change 2012/13-2013/14
Male	63,225	75,803	32,881	17,136	−72.9	−47.9	−19.0
Female	25,081	34,597	12,856	5,035	−79.9	−60.8	−24.4
Unknown	98	357	231	222	126.5	−3.9	−4.3
Total 100%	88,403	110,757	45,968	22,393	−74.7	−51.3	−20.2

Source: MoJ and YJB (2012, 2013, 2014, 2015)

from 43,903 in 2012/13 (MoJ and YJB, 2015, p 33; see Figure 12.13 below). When examined by type of sentence:

- 2,226 young people were sentenced to immediate custodial sentences, with most (87 per cent) of these being DTOs
- 22,675 young people were sentenced to community sentences, including 9,767 YROs

Figure 12.12: Sentencing structure of the youth justice system in England and Wales

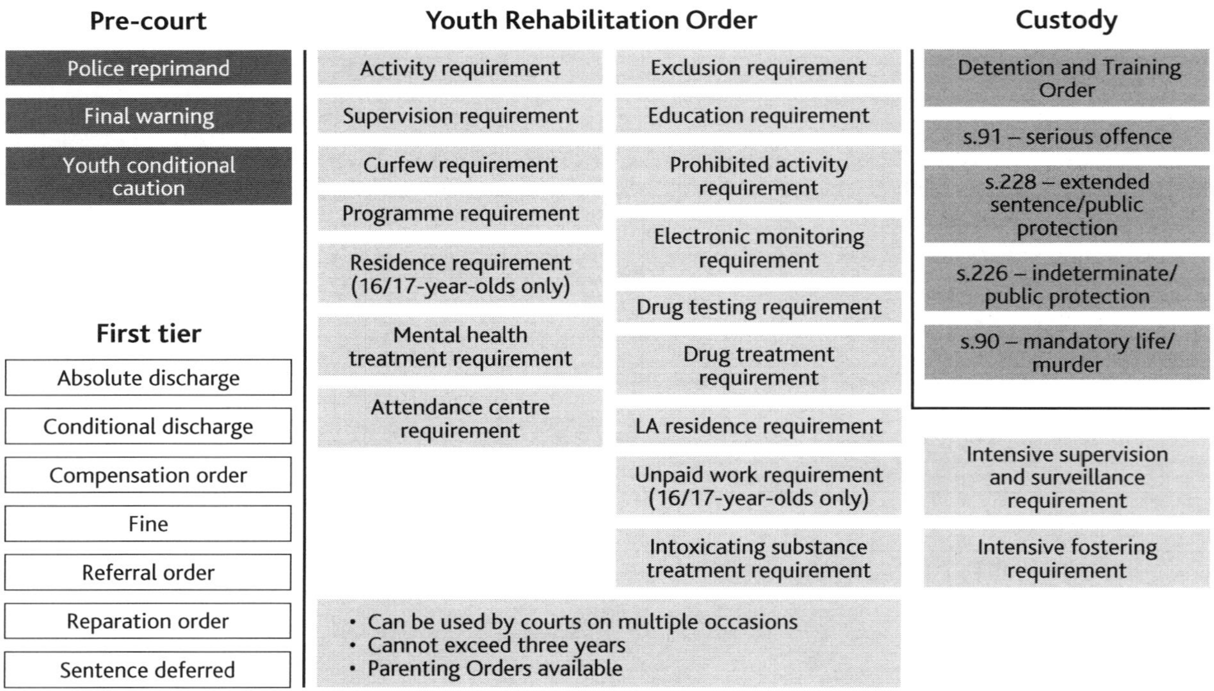

Pre-court	Youth Rehabilitation Order		Custody
Police reprimand	Activity requirement	Exclusion requirement	Detention and Training Order
Final warning	Supervision requirement	Education requirement	s.91 – serious offence
Youth conditional caution	Curfew requirement	Prohibited activity requirement	s.228 – extended sentence/public protection
	Programme requirement	Electronic monitoring requirement	s.226 – indeterminate/ public protection
	Residence requirement (16/17-year-olds only)	Drug testing requirement	s.90 – mandatory life/ murder
	Mental health treatment requirement	Drug treatment requirement	
	Attendance centre requirement	LA residence requirement	Intensive supervision and surveillance requirement
		Unpaid work requirement (16/17-year-olds only)	Intensive fostering requirement
		Intoxicating substance treatment requirement	
	• Can be used by courts on multiple occasions • Cannot exceed three years • Parenting Orders available		

First tier

- Absolute discharge
- Conditional discharge
- Compensation order
- Fine
- Referral order
- Reparation order
- Sentence deferred

Figure 12.13: Trends in the number of young people sentenced, 2002/03–2012/13

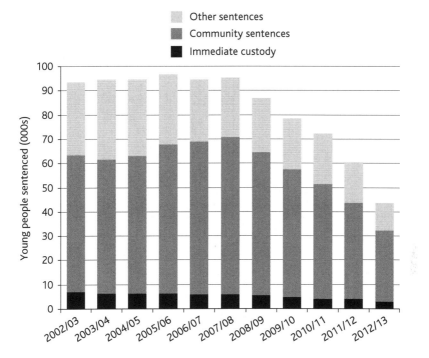

Source: MoJ and YJB (2015, p 35)

- 9,001 young people were sentenced to other types of sentences (these include discharges, fines and otherwise dealt with disposals).

Referral Order

The Referral Order was implemented on a national basis from April 2002. When a child appears in court for the first time and pleads guilty, the Referral Order is the mandatory disposal the court must apply. It is therefore the most frequently used sentencing option. It involves elements of restorative justice, with members of the community and the victim of the offence being involved in the young person's sentence. In 2009, the Referral Order became available for a second offence if the child had not had one previously, and it was also available as a second sentence in certain circumstances. The Legal Aid, Sentencing and Punishment of Offenders Act 2012 widened the use of the Referral Order further – while it remains the primary sentence for first conviction, it can now be imposed regardless of criminal history or if the child has previously received more than one Referral Order, the caveat that the child pleads guilty remains. Its use has seen a dramatic fall of 51% between 2003/04 and 2013/14, from 27,795 orders to 12,606 (see Figure 12.14). This fall can be arguably attributed to the increased use of out of court disposals as diversion from the formal youth justice system has increasingly become a priority for the YJB and youth offending teams. This is somewhat supported by the sharp decrease in the number of first time entrants (see above, MoJ and YJB, 2015, p 10).

Figure 12.14: Young people sentenced for all offences by three main types of sentence, 2003/04-2013/14

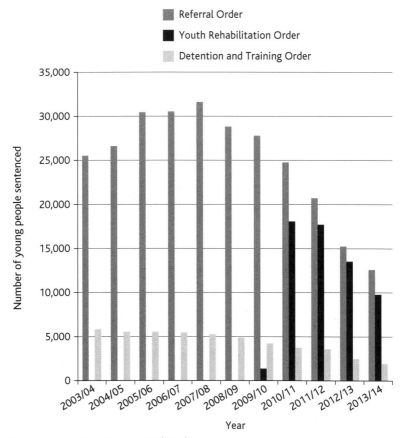

Source: Adapted From MoJ and YJB (2015)

Youth Rehabilitation Order

The YRO, introduced by Criminal Justice and Immigration Act 2008 replaced the previously existing nine community sentences with one community based order. There are 18 different requirements ranging from supervision to a programme requirement that can be attached to an YRO, and the court has a menu of different forms of intervention to choose from. As the YJB (2010b, p 9) states, 'the range of YRO requirements offers a community sentence which can be a viable and robust alternative to custody. If used effectively, the YRO should help reduce reoffending.' The YRO allows for, according to the YJB (2010b, p 9), youth offending teams to effectively manage resources and practitioners' time, an advantage when faced with a financial crisis which is resulting in serious public service financial cuts (see Travis, 2011). One of the most positive attributes of the new generic YRO is that it allows for the sentence to be tailor-made to suit the young person. For every section of Asset, the assessment tool used by practitioners in the youth justice system (YJB, 2006), there is a requirement that could be used to help reduce a young person's Asset score and therefore their risk of reoffending. It is stipulated in the guidance (YJB, 2010b) that one of the factors a court must consider before sentencing a young person to a YRO is the availability of the requirements at a local level, that is, there is no point in attaching a drug treatment requirement to the YRO if the youth offending team the young person will be supervised under does not have a drug worker or links to a drug intervention team, as they are essentially setting the young person up to fail. This is because should the young person be given this requirement, they will not be able to complete it, and are potentially faced with returning to court to be resentenced. While this is an extreme example, the possibility does exist, which is why it is important that the resources of youth offending teams are considered. MoJ and YJB (2015) statistics show that in 2013/14, 9,767 YROs were given to young people, and 1,772 of these YROs had one requirement attached to them. A further 2,124 had two requirements attached to them (see Table 12.6 below).

The data shows an increase in the number of YROs containing five or more requirements (from 4% in 2011/12 to 6% in 2013/14), potentially indicating that the YRO is being used as a higher-end community sentence in place of custodial sentencing. It does raise concerns, however, that ever more children are being subjected to increasingly complex orders. Of the 18 requirements, supervision has remained the most popular one throughout the past three years of the

Table 12.6: Distribution of YRO requirements from 2011/12 to 2013/14

Number of requirements	2011/12		2012/13		2013/14	
	Frequency	Share of total (%)	Frequency	Share of total (%)	Frequency	Share of total (%)
1	4,040	29	2,372	28	1,772	25
2	4,455	32	2,623	31	2,124	30
3	2,941	21	1,781	21	1,575	22
4	1,978	14	1,245	15	1,160	16
5 or more	541	4	470	5	453	6

Source: Adapted from MoJ and YJB (2013, 2014, 2015)

YRO being in use. The top eight requirements (see Table 12.7) that are recorded as being the most used over the last three years that the YRO has been available for are shown in Table 12.7 below.

It is of no surprise that supervision is significantly used more than any other requirement given that it is the only requirement that allows for direct one-to-one contact between a young person and their youth offending team practitioner. There are large differences in the requirements that are used, with the more unconventional and difficult ones to be monitored very rarely used, such as drug testing (used only 46 times in 2013/14), or the mental health treatment requirement (used only seven times in 2013/14). It is significant to note that there has been a progressive rise in the use of electronically monitored curfews for children and young people since 1998 when such a possibility was introduced. A total of 2,635 YROs in 2013/14 (14%) had a curfew attached to them, despite a curfew rarely being an appropriate sentence for a child since its primary purpose is generally punitive rather than rehabilitation (HM Inspectorate of Probation, 2012).

Table 12.7: Top eight YRO requirements used from 2010/11 to 2012/13

Requirement	2011/12	2012/13	2013/14
Supervision	11,991	7,375	6,297
Activity	5,145	3,287	3,108
Curfew	4,935	3,060	2,635
Electronic monitoring	3,426	2,350	2,222
Unpaid work	2,299	1,336	1,072
Programme	1,951	1,159	1,140
Attendance centre	1,432	823	581
Prohibited activity	400	283	303

Source: Adapted from MoJ and YJB (2012, 2013, 2014)

Custodial sentences

One of the most welcomed trends in relation to youth justice in England and Wales has been the reduction in the numbers of young people being incarcerated (see Figure 12.15). From a high of 3,029 children being incarcerated in 2002/03 this number has reduced to 1,239 in 2013/14, a fall of 56%. A significant milestone was reached in December 2014 when the number of children in youth custody fell below 1,000 for the first time since 2000 (MoJ and YJB, 2015).

The main custodial sentence used within the secure estate for children and young people is the DTO. This requires children to serve half their sentence in custody and the remaining half, under licence, in the community. Sentences can be given from a minimum of 4 months to a maximum of 24 months. Figure 12.16 illustrates the average numbers of days spent in custody for children on a DTO from 2009/10 to 2013/14; the average number of days decreased by six days (from 115 to 109) between 2012/13 and 2013/14, returning to the same level as in 2009/10.

The juvenile secure estate is made up of three types of institutions: secure children's homes, secure training centres and young offenders institutions (see Figure 12.17). Secure children's homes are the smallest institutions within the estate and have the highest staff-to-child ratio. They are the most expensive institutions, where the average cost of

Figure 12.15: Custody population for under-18s, 2002/03-2013/14

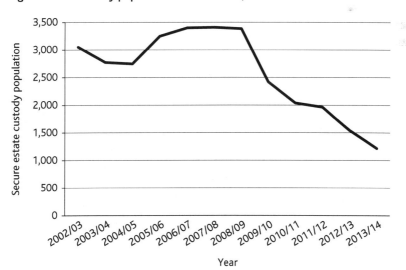

Source: Adapted from MoJ and YJB (2015)

Figure 12.16: Average days in custody for children on a DTO, 2009/10-2013/14

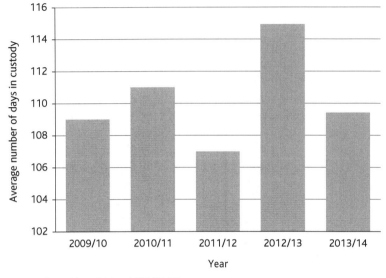

Source: Adapted from MoJ and YJB (2015)

one place is £209,000 per year. For this reason, they are used sparingly by the YJB that has the central responsibility of where to place children sentenced to custody in England and Wales.

Secure training centres are purpose-built, privately run centres for children that have a focus on education. There are three within England and they have a higher staff-to-child ratio than a young offenders institution, but not as high as a secure children's home. They have similarly high running costs as secure children's homes, at on average £187,000 per place per year.

The final institution that makes up the majority of the secure estate, both in terms of number of establishments and the number of children they hold, are young offenders institutions. These are usually managed by the Prison Service, and house 15- to 21-year-old young people, with usually the juveniles (15- to 17-year-olds) separate from the young adult offenders (18- to 21-year-olds). They have the lowest staff-to-child ratio of the institutions in the juvenile secure estate and are frequently cited as having the worse conditions (HMIP, 2014). They are, in comparison to the other two institutions, the cheapest type of accommodation to house children sentenced to custody, at only £60,000 per place per year on average.

Figure 12.17: Under-18 secure population by accommodation type, 2009/10-2013/14

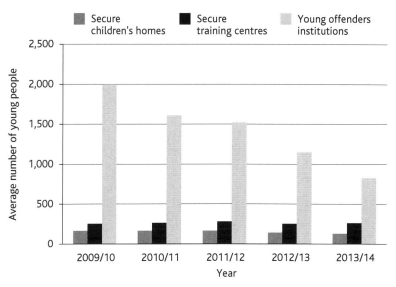

Source: Adapted from MoJ and YJB (2015)

Key issues in relation to the use of custody

As a consequence of the welcomed fall in the number of children being held in custody, there have been increased concerns raised that those who remain in custody have become increasingly disadvantaged.

Over-representation of BAME children in custody

The over-representation of BAME children within the youth justice system has been a consistent concern for many years (see, for example, Pitts, 1986; May et al, 2010). There is no starker point in the youth justice system where the over-representation becomes clearer then when looking at the number of children from BAME backgrounds in the custodial estate. While there are differences between ethnic groups (see Bateman, 2014, p 19), it is clear from the data that the overrepresentation increases with the severity of the intervention. As established earlier, the numbers of children in custody have dramatically fallen over the last few years, yet the number of White children in custody fell almost twice as fast as it did for BAME children (see Figure 12.18).

Figure 12.18: Numbers of young prisoners from different ethnic backgrounds in England and Wales, 2005/06-2014/15

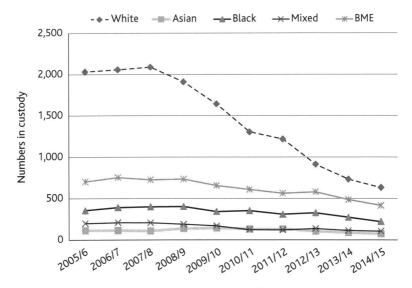

Source: Taken from Centre for Crime and Justice Studies (2015)

Research by the Centre for Crime and Justice Studies (2015) shows that when analysed further, the proportion of young White prisoners has fallen by around 20% since 2005/06, whereas the proportion of young Black prisoners has risen by 66%, and for Asian children it has gone up by 75%.

Children from BAME backgrounds make up only 25% of the offending population, they account for almost one in five of those receiving a custodial sentence and nearly one-third of those subject to long-term detention of two years or longer (Prison Reform Trust, 2014, p 46; MoJ and YJB, 2015). The House of Commons Home Affairs Committee (2007) conducted an inquiry into young Black people and the criminal justice system, concluding that social exclusion and disadvantage are the primary cause of over-representation in the youth justice system. If there has been a decrease in punitiveness, children and young people from BAME backgrounds have not experienced it.

Distance from home

The reductions in numbers have meant that the MoJ and YJB have decommissioned/closed several institutions within the secure estate, most recently Hindley Young Offenders Institute in the North of England, which was, prior to its closure, the largest youth prison in Europe. This means that it is increasingly likely that children will be placed further from home, family, friends and professionals who can provide support. As Figure 12.19 illustrates, those children who live in London made up 31% of the total number of children in custody in 2013/14, yet only a third of them were placed within London.

Over 30% of those children in custody were held more than 50 miles from their home, and 10% were held more than 100 miles from their home (Prison Reform Trust, 2014). This has a strong impact on the rehabilitation of a child, and perhaps goes some way to explain the high reoffending rate of those who have been in custody (see below).

Conditions within the secure estate

The United Nations (UN) Convention on the Rights of the Child (UN General Assembly, 1989), to which the UK is a signatory, requires that custody for children is used as a 'measure of last resort and for the shortest appropriate period of time' (UN General Assembly,

Figure 12.19: Custody population (under 18) by region of origin and region of establishment, 2013/14

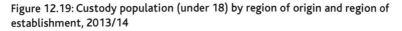

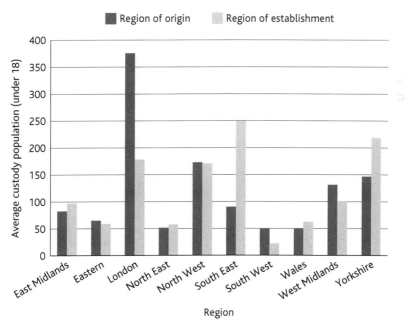

Source: Adapted from MoJ and YJB (2015)

1989, Article 37b). It is therefore positive news to see that the use of custody within England and Wales has fallen. However, there has been increased concern over recent years that the conditions that those children who are in custody experience have worsened, and that those who remain in custody are some of England and Wales' most vulnerable children. The MoJ and YJB collates data on four key areas in relation to child custody: use of restrictive physical intervention (RPIs) (restraint); incidents of self-harm; the number of assaults involving young people in custody; and the use of single separation (only in secure children's homes and secure training centres). Figure 12.20 shows the trends of three of these four key measures between 2009/10 and 2013/14.

Use of restrictive physical interventions (restraint)

According to the MoJ and YJB (2015, p 48), restraint, or restrictive physical intervention as it is now called, should only be used on young people as a last resort, ideally to prevent them from harming themselves and/or others. As Figure 12.20 shows, the number of RPIs per 100 young people increased by 39% from 2010/11 and 2013/14 (20.5 RPIs per 100 young people to 28.4 in 2013/14), and there was an increase of 19% compared to 2012/13 (from 23.8 RPIs per 100 young people to 28.4 in 2013/14) (MoJ and YJB, 2015, p 48). According to

Figure 12.20: Trends in the number of behaviour management incidents, 2009/10-2013/14

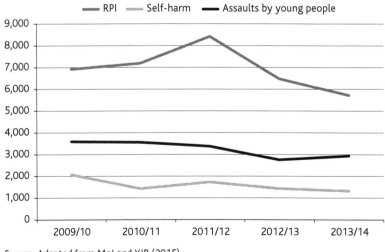

Source: Adapted from MoJ and YJB (2015)

official statistics, there were 120 RPIs involving injury to young people in 2013/14, and nearly all (98%) of these were classified as 'minor injuries' (MoJ and YJB, 2015, p 48). There were an average number of 476 RPIs per month in 2013/14 that involved 319 young people. According to Figure 12.21, those who are 15-18, male and of White ethnicity are restrained the most.

There has been a decline across all groups (see Figure 12.21) apart from in relation to females, where there has been a rise in the average number of restraints per month, from 37 in 2012/13 to 47 in 2013/14. Data also shows that those children placed in young offenders institutions are more likely to be restrained, with an average of 261 RPI incidents per month in 2013/14 in a young offenders institution in comparison to 98 (secure training centres) and 117 (secure children's homes) (MoJ and YJB, 2015).

Levels of self-harm

Self-harm in custody is defined as any act by which a young person deliberately harms him or herself irrespective of the method, intent or severity of the injury. There were 1,318 incidents of self-harm in 2013/14, down by 7% since 2010/11 and down by 8% since 2012/13 (MoJ and YJB, 2015, p 50). Statistics show (see Figure 12.22) that

Figure 12.21: RPIs by age group, gender and ethnicity, 2009/10-2013/14

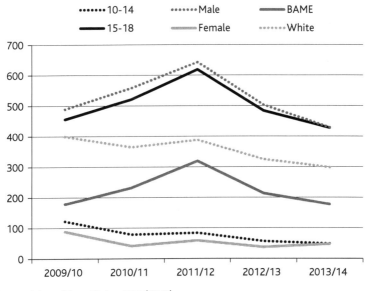

Source: Adapted from MoJ and YJB (2015)

Figure 12.22: Monthly average number of self-harm incidents for young people in custody, 2009/10-2013/14

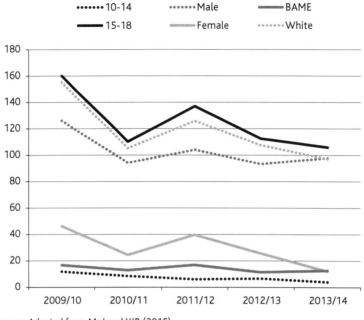

Source: Adapted from MoJ and YJB (2015)

in relation to self-harm, children who are male, from White ethnic backgrounds and aged 15-18 are more likely to self-harm while in custody.

Levels of violence in custody

The environment within a custodial institution can be a violent and disturbing place. In the context of the official statistics, assaults are defined as 'the intentional use of unnecessary force that results in physical contact with the victim. Physical contact can be by any part of the assailant's body or bodily fluid or the use or display of any weapon or missile. It is not necessary for the victim to suffer injury of any kind. Assaults of a sexual nature are included' (MoJ and YJB, 2015, p 51). There is, however, no breakdown provided in terms of the nature of an assault incident, which, as the definition indicates, can be wide-ranging. The victim can also be a member of staff within the custodial institution as well as another child.

There were 2,932 assaults involving children in custody in 2013/14, down by 18% since 2010/11 and up by 7% since 2012/13 (see Figure

12.23). There was an average of 244 assaults per month in 2013/14 involving an average of 209 children as perpetrators (MoJ and YJB, 2015, p 51). Figure 12.23 shows a breakdown of the monthly average number of assaults by key demographics, indicating that those children who are male, aged 15-18 and from White ethnic backgrounds are mostly likely to be involved in an assault incident in custody.

As previously indicated, there is no information publically available on the type and nature of the assaults, but there is information available on the severity of injuries that resulted from an assault. Figure 12.24 shows that while the majority of assaults result in minor injury that requires medical treatment, it is of concern in relation to the well-being of children that the number of assaults resulting in serious injury requiring medical treatment has risen from 23 in 2009/10 to 28 in 2013/14, albeit down from 46 in 2012/13 (MoJ and YJB, 2015).

Safety levels within the juvenile secure estate, particularly in relation to young offenders institutions, have been of increased political and social concern in recent years. The Chief Inspector of Prisons (HMIP, 2014, p 40), stated within his annual report, that 'there were fights and assaults in most establishments almost every day. Almost a third of boys overall told us they had felt unsafe in their establishment,

Figure 12.23: Monthly average number of assaults involving young people in custody, 2009/10-2013/14

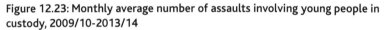

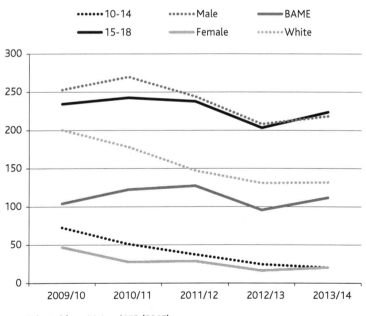

Source: Adapted from MoJ and YJB (2015)

Figure 12.24: Severity of injury resulting from assaults, 2009/10-2013/14

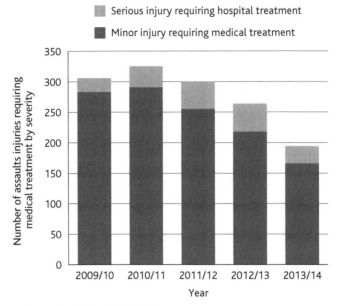

Source: Adapted from MoJ and YJB (2015)

and approximately one in 10 said they currently felt unsafe.' The report provides some illumination where the official statistics cannot, in relation to the nature of injuries sustained, which at one young offenders institution included 'broken bones, unconsciousness and multiple injuries, including black eyes, stab wounds and grazes' (HMIP, 2014, p 40).

Deaths in custody

The conditions within the secure estate show that it can be a volatile and unsafe place. Those in custody have been 'routinely disfigured by multiple and intersecting forms of social disadvantage' (Goldson and Coles, 2005, p 24). Placing children in custody is detrimental to their welfare and ineffective in terms of reducing their offending behaviour (see below). Arguably the most definitive way custody is harmful is that various young offenders institutions and secure training centres have been the places where children in the supposed 'care of the state' have died. Thirty-four children have died while in custody; 32 of those children committed suicide. However, the death of Gareth Myatt (aged 15) was caused by him being 'controlled and restrained', and the death of Chris Greenaway (aged 16) was ruled as homicide. The risk of suicide for incarcerated boys is 18 times higher than for those in the community (Jacobson et al, 2010). The first child who took his own life while 'in the care of the state' was Philip Knight (aged 15) in 1990, and since then there have been 31 more cases, the most recent being a unnamed boy (aged 15) who took his own life in 2015 while at Cookham Wood Young Offenders Institution (INQUEST, 2015).

Trends in reoffending

One of the three performance management targets that the government established as a measure of the work of the youth justice system involves reductions in the rate of reoffending by children. In comparison to considerable progress having been made in relation to the other two key performance management targets (to reduce the number of first time entrants and to reduce the use of custody; see MoJ, 2010, p 75), recidivism rates for children in the youth justice system have remained stubbornly high. The official statistics report on rates of proven reoffending for young people who were released from custody, received a non-custodial conviction at court, or received a caution, reprimand or warning between a set period, the most recent that are available being 1 April 2011 and 31 March 2012. According to the MoJ and YJB (2014, p 50), 'proven re-offending is defined as any offence committed in a one year follow-up period and receiving a court conviction, caution, reprimand or warning in the one year follow up.' In the 12 months ending March 2013, 52,648 young people were given a reprimand or warning, convicted at court (excluding immediate custodial sentences) or released from custody; these children form the reoffending cohort that has been analysed by the MoJ and YJB (2015, p 54). A total of 18,998 children out of 52,648 committed a proven reoffence within a year, which gives a one-year reoffending rate (measured using a binary rate, that is, a yes/no answer to who reoffended) of 36.1%, a rise of 0.6% in comparison to 2011/12 and 3.3% in comparison to 2008/09. Those children who did reoffend committed an average of three offences each, resulting in an average number of reoffences per offender (frequency rate) of 1.08. This is a sharp increase of 5.8% in comparison with 2011/12, which indicates that not only are children reoffending more, but on average they are also committing more offences when they do so. The evidence shows that there is significant variation between the type of sentence that a child receives and the likelihood of reoffending; the data makes clear that the more entrenched a young person becomes in the youth justice system, the more likely they are to reoffend (see Figure 12.25).

Figure 12.25: Proven reoffending data, by index disposal, March 2008-13

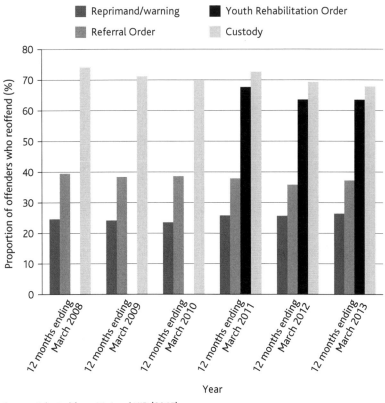

Source: Adapted from MoJ and YJB (2015)

Custodial sentences have the worst record in relation to reoffending, a 67.9% rate of reoffending in 2013/14 (MoJ and YJB, 2015), indicating that they are the least successful in terms of deterring and rehabilitating children from offending. Children who receive custodial sentences of between 6 and 12 months are significantly more likely to reoffend than a comparison group sentenced to a high-level community penalty (Bateman, 2014, p 34).

When looking at the data in terms of demographics (see Table 12.8 and Figure 12.26), it shows that the reoffending rate has increased for both male and females as well as for both age groups.

Figure 12.26 shows the proven reoffending data by gender and age over time (2008-13). It illustrates in a clear manner that after a peak in 2011, the reoffending rate has dropped, but is clearly on the rise again.

Reoffending rates differ based on the index offence of the young person, with those entering the cohort for sexual offences having a

Table 12.8: Proven reoffending data by gender and age, 2008-13

Proportion of offenders who reoffend by gender and age (%)	12 months ending March 2008	12 months ending March 2009	12 months ending March 2010	12 months ending March 2011	12 months ending March 2012	12 months ending March 2013
Male	36.3	36.6	37.3	39.2	38.4	38.6
Female	21.9	22.3	22.2	24.7	25.0	26.2
10-14	29.7	30.2	30.0	33.5	34.5	35.2
15-17	33.9	34.2	34.7	36.7	35.8	36.4

Source: Adapted from MoJ and YJB (2015)

Figure 12.26: Proven reoffending data by gender and age, 2008-13

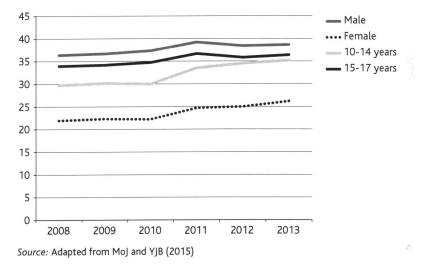

Source: Adapted from MoJ and YJB (2015)

reoffending rate of 15.0%, compared with those with robbery offences, which have a 41.5% reoffending rate (see Figure 12.27; MoJ and YJB, 2015, p 57).

There is a strong argument put forward by the YJB (2014, p 2) that while year on year the number in the reoffending cohort has fallen, showing some level of progress, those that remain within it are increasing in complexity, leaving a group of young people who are highly likely to be more entrenched in patterns of offending. The evidence would thus appear to support an approach to youth justice that maximises diversion from court and from custody, and promotes a strategy of minimum intervention within the court arena.

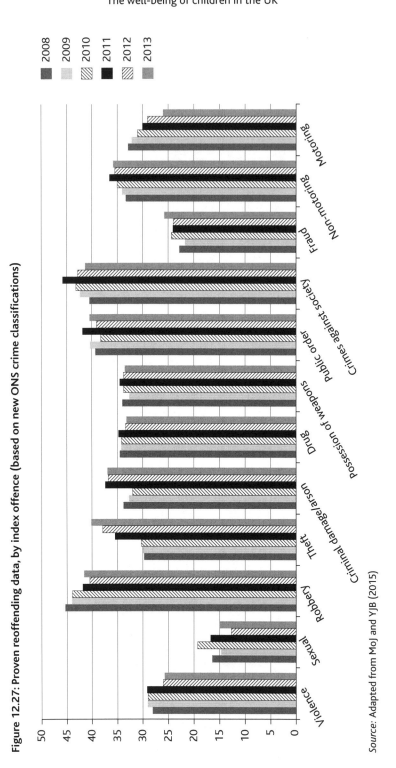

Figure 12.27: Proven reoffending data, by index offence (based on new ONS crime classifications)

Source: Adapted from MoJ and YJB (2015)

Risk factors for reoffending

Youth justice statistics 2010/11 (MoJ and YJB, 2012) reviewed the evidence relating to risk factors associated with one-year proven reoffending levels across 5,453 young people during the period 2008-09. The data are based on risk scores that derive from the risk assessment tool Asset, completed by youth offending team workers for all sentenced young people. Asset includes 12 components that cover factors that may be associated with offending (for details, see YJB, 2006). Young people are assessed across each component and given a score of between 0 (component presents no risk in relation to offending) to 4 (component presents substantial risk in relation to offending). A total score out of 64 is calculated, which forms the basis for categorising young people into one of three scaled approach bands that represent different levels of intervention: standard (those with total Asset scores of between 0 and 14), enhanced (score of 15-32) and intensive (33-64).

The study identified associations between risk factors and one-year proven reoffending as follows.

As the risk score band increased, so did the percentage of young people who reoffended (MoJ and YJB, 2012, p 50). Specifically, 29% of those in the standard category reoffended, 57% in the enhanced category and 79% in the intensive category (MoJ and YJB, 2012, p 52, chart 12.1). Moreover, 81% of those who had scores of between 2 and 4, across 11-12 risk factors, reoffended. These findings underline the complexity of needs among young people who are most likely to reoffend and who receive very high-risk assessment scores. However, the proportion of young people receiving the highest scores is relatively low (12% of the total sample), while the majority (54%) receive risk scores in the 'enhanced' band and around a third in the standard band (34%) (MoJ and YJB, 2012, p 52). Thus, a picture emerges of an increasing risk of reoffending associated with increasing complexity of need across a range of areas.

A higher percentage of those who had a moderate/substantial risk reoffended compared with those who had no risk (MoJ and YJB, 2012, p 50). Figure 12.28 shows the percentage of young people who reoffended across each Asset component, comparing those with no risk (score of 0) with those with a moderate/substantial risk (score of 2-4). Further analysis (see Wilson and Hinks, 2011) underlines the complexity of need among these young people, where half of the 12 asset components were found to be statistically significant predictors of proven one-year reoffending, as follows:

Figure 12.28: Percentage of young people who reoffended by risk assessment score

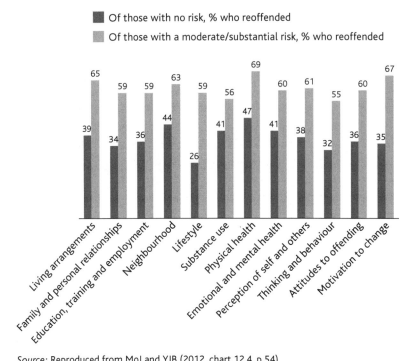

■ Of those with no risk, % who reoffended
■ Of those with a moderate/substantial risk, % who reoffended

Source: Reproduced from MoJ and YJB (2012, chart 12.4, p 54)

- lifestyle
- substance use
- motivation to change
- living arrangements
- family and personal relationships
- education, training and employment.

A range of criticisms have been levied at the Asset risk assessment tool, particularly in terms of the consistency of recording (Baker et al, 2005), and the selection and use of particular types of factors (Case and Haines, 2009). However, the results reported here do serve to highlight the complexity of needs experienced by young people who enter the youth justice system, and consequently their relative vulnerability. These levels of need raise questions about the appropriateness of contemporary punishment regimes for children who are, ultimately, exhibiting high levels of vulnerability.

Conclusion

The majority of data relating to children's offending behaviour continues to be dominated by official records collected by the police and youth offending teams (reported through the MoJ and YJB). To that end, our knowledge about those children who offend remains limited, particularly in relation to their key socioeconomic characteristics, including social class.

Data regarding age and sex are consistently available, but the various categories of offence used across different administrative agencies does not always assist in understanding the types of crimes that young people commit – particularly in broad categories around violence and theft. The lack of data made available relating to children's ethnicity, particularly in police records of arrests, also makes it difficult to determine more nuanced patterns of disproportionality that may occur within the criminal justice system.

In this edition attention has been paid to the range of punishments that children are subjected to once they enter the youth justice system, and similar data limitations exist around socioeconomic circumstances, ethnicity and classification of crime.

Overall, the data reviewed in this chapter indicates that while many children commit offences, the majority of crime is committed by adults, and the majority of serious crime is committed by adults. Furthermore, trends show reductions in the numbers of children who are arrested and therefore the numbers who are entering the youth justice system and/or receiving punishment.

While there is some positive news in terms of the reductions in the number of children who are entering the youth justice system, reoffending rates for those who do enter it remain high. It is significant that the data shows that the more a child progresses through the youth justice system, the more likely they are to reoffend with the higher tariff, more serious punishments such as the high intensity community sentences and custody having the worse records in terms of reducing a child's likelihood to reoffend.

It remains the case that risk assessment scores for those young people who are involved in the youth justice system reflect complexity of need and vulnerability across a wide range of indicators. This continues to raise questions about the criminalisation of (some) young people, and the decisions that are taken about how they are best punished.

Notes

[1] The CSEW data for young people is not reported here, but see O'Malley and Grace (2011) for earlier victim-related data.

[2] Most recent figures show a slight increase of 3% in police-recorded crime for the period to the end of March 2015 (ONS, 2015e).

THIRTEEN

Conclusion

Jonathan Bradshaw

This new edition of *The well-being of children in the UK* provides a more up-to-date picture of children's lives. The previous edition (published in 2011) contained data only up to 2010 – most of that was for the period before the start of the global economic crisis in 2008, and all of it was before the election of the coalition government in 2010 and the rolling out of austerity measures.

Now, in 2015, we are able to present a more modern picture and perhaps a picture that provides a more positive image of the impact of the Labour government during 1997-2010 and the beginnings of the impact of the coalition government during 2010-15.

We focus on two aspects of the evidence here: the comparative evidence and the evidence about trends.

What is the comparative evidence?

Is life good for children in the UK? One important piece of evidence is how they are doing in comparison with children elsewhere. Unless we know how we stand comparatively, we cannot know how good we could be – or even if we are better than we were.

Comparative evidence has been drawn on in the separate chapters of this book, and so a summary is presented here.

The UNICEF (2007) Innocenti Report Card no 7 had the UK at the bottom of 21 countries on overall well-being, and:

- 18th on material well-being
- 12th on health and safety
- 17th on education
- 21st on family and peer relations
- 21st on behaviour and risks
- 20th on subjective well-being.

The Bradshaw and Richardson (2009) comparisons of the EU29 countries ranked the UK 24th out of 29 countries on overall well-being, and:

- 24th on health
- 21st out of 28 on subjective well-being
- 15th out of 28 on relationships
- 24th out of 26 on material well-being
- 18th out of 28 on risk behaviour
- 22nd out of 27 on education
- 17th out of 26 on housing.

Although the OECD (2009a) did not produce a league table, it is easy to estimate one. The UK ranked 20th out of 30 OECD countries on overall well-being, and:

- 12th on material well-being
- 15th out 27 on housing and the environment
- 22nd on education
- 20th on health and safety
- 28th on risk behaviour
- 4th out of 25 on quality of school life.

The UNICEF Innocenti Report Card no 9 (2010a) is the first to attempt at an index of the *dispersion* of child well-being, exploring inequalities in three domains. Out of 24 countries, the UK was:

- 19th on material well-being inequality
- 13th on educational inequality
- 11th on health inequality.

Overall, the UK ranked 4th from the lowest group of countries out of five.

The UNICEF Innocenti Report Card no 11 (2013) ranked the UK 16th out of 29 countries overall (or 17th, if subjective well-being had been included). The UK was:

- 14th on material well-being
- 16th on health and safety
- 24th on education
- 15th on behaviours and risks
- 10th on housing and the environment

- 20th on subjective well-being (Bradshaw et al, 2013).

Although the number of countries was different and the domains, components and indicators were not consistent between the 2007 and 2013 report cards, the UK had made progress over the period. UNICEF (2013) concluded that taking a consistent set of countries with identical indicators over time, the UK had advanced from bottom (equal with the US) out of 21 countries to 16th out of 21 countries.

So the UK did better in the international league tables of child well-being in 2013 than it had done in 2007. But for a country with its level of GDP, it is under-performing, certainly compared with the rich Northern EU countries, and it is under-performing on most domains of well-being. Compared with other rich countries, the UK does consistently badly on:

- *Material well-being.* The UK relative child poverty rates are comparatively high, and although we do better using deprivation measures, we are still not very good and we do very badly indeed in the proportion of children in workless households.

- *Education.* Our pre-school enrolment rates are not good and our early years childcare is expensive. We are middling on achievement. In the PISA 2012 the UK does better at Science than Literacy and Maths. But our participation rates in post-statutory education are bad, and our NEET rates are middling.

- *Health.* We are middling on infant mortality, low birth weight as well as on immunisation rates. Children's self-assessed health is bad. We do comparatively badly on most health behaviours – diet, alcohol and drugs. We do above average on obesity, exercise and smoking. We do very badly on early sexual activity and teenage pregnancy. One health indicator that we do better on is childhood accidental death rates, which, in Europe, are most commonly caused by road traffic accidents. This is probably an achievement of policy – traffic calming and road safety education. But the niggling worry is that it is also the result of locking our children in at home, not letting them roam outside, with the knock-on effects on loneliness and obesity.

- *Housing.* We are doing quite well on children's housing conditions – for example, low overcrowding and good housing satisfaction. On the other hand, we are doing worse on environment problems, especially crime, violence and vandalism.

- *Subjective well-being.* We are low on life satisfaction and subjective health and middling on mental health, subjective education and relationships.

These results have been summarised in Table 13.1. Not all the domains have comparative indicators – in particular we are lacking comparative data on children and crime, children in care and the data on child maltreatment is not very satisfactory. A judgement has been made about whether the UK/Great Britain is comparatively good, middling or bad, depending on where it comes in an international league table of rich countries, using mainly the OECD Family database, PISA, HBSC and EU–SILC data. The comparator countries are not all the same. 'Good' means that the UK is in the top third of the distribution, 'middling' in the middle third, and 'bad' in the bottom third. Out of the 48 indicators, the UK is bad on 13, middling on 23 and good

Table 13.1: Comparative performance on child outcomes

	Comparative performance	Source
Material well-being		
Relative poverty BHC	Middling	EU-SILC (2013)
'Absolute' child poverty BHC	Middling	EU-SILC (2013)
Child poverty gaps	Good	EU-SILC (2013)
Material deprivation	Middling	EU-SILC (2013)
Persistent poverty BHC	Good	EU-SILC (2013)
Inequality	Bad	UNICEF (2010)
Health		
Stillbirths	Middling	Cousens et al (2011)
Infant mortality	Middling	World Development Indicators 2015
Child deaths	Middling	WHO mortality database (UNICEF, 2013)
Low birth weight	Middling	World Development Indicators 2015
Breastfeeding	Good	OECD Family database (2005)
Immunisation rates	Middling	OECD Family database (2010)
Self-assessed health	Bad	HBSC (Currie et al, 2012)
Obesity	Good	HBSC (Currie et al, 2012)
Sex	Bad	HBSC (Currie et al, 2012)
Diet	Middling	HBSC (Currie et al, 2012)
Alcohol	Bad	HBSC (Currie et al, 2012)
Smoking	Good	HBSC (Currie et al, 2012)
Drugs	Bad	HBSC (Currie et al, 2012)
Exercise	Good	HBSC (Currie et al, 2012)
Inequality	Middling	UNICEF (2010)

(continued)

Table 13.1: Comparative performance on child outcomes (continued)

	Comparative performance	Source
Subjective well-being and mental health		
Life satisfaction	Bad	HBSC (Currie et al, 2012)
Mental health	Middling	HBSC (Currie et al, 2012)
Suicide	Good	OECD Family database
Talking to mothers	Middling	HBSC (Currie et al, 2012)
Talking to fathers	Middling	HBSC (Currie et al, 2012)
School friends kind and helpful	Middling	HBSC (Currie et al, 2012)
Liking school	Middling	HBSC (Currie et al, 2012)
Subjective health	Bad	HBSC (Currie et al, 2012)
Education		
Literacy achievement	Middling	PISA (2012)
Maths achievement	Middling	PISA (2012)
Science achievement	Middling	PISA (2012)
Inequalities in achievement	Middling	UNICEF (2010)
Staying on rates	Bad	OECD Family database (2015a)
NEET	Middling	OECD Family database (2015a)
Housing		
Housing satisfaction	Good	EU-SILC (2013)
Living space	Good	EU-SILC (2013)
Inequality in living space	Bad	UNICEF (2010)
Environment	Good	EU-SILC (2013)
Child maltreatment		
Fighting	Good	HBSC (Currie et al, 2012)
Been bullied	Good	HBSC (Currie et al, 2012)
Bullying others	Middling	HBSC (Currie et al, 2012)
Children in care	–	
Crime	–	
Childcare		
Spending	Middling	OECD Family database (2015a)
Enrolment 0-3	Bad	EU-SILC
Enrolment 3-5	Bad	EU-SILC
Costs to parents	Bad	OECD Family database (2015a)
Staff/child ratios	Bad	OECD Family database (2015a)
Time and space	Middling	Children's Worlds survey

on 12. In the previous volume there were 42 indicators – 19 bad, 15 middling and 8 good. So the 'goods' have increased and the 'bads' have reduced, which indicates that we are doing better than before, but too often not as well as we could be doing.

What are the national trends?

While it is important to know how we are doing compared to other countries – not least to have a vision of how much better we can be – we also need to know whether we are moving in the right direction in terms of child well-being. Comparative data can be used for this purpose, but in practice it is more reliable to use national data.

So what are the trends in child well-being? These have been reviewed in more detail in previous chapters, and so the analysis here is extracted and summarised.

What we attempt to do is to establish a set of indicators across the domains of well-being that can be used to produce a composite summary. This is what was attempted in the *Opportunity for all* reports, now abandoned, and less formally in the Annex to the Department for Children, Schools and Families (DCSF) report (2007b). The period we are interested in is the period after about 2009, when the coalition government came to power and the recession began to bite. In Table 13.2 this is contrasted with the period from 1997 or the mid-1990s to 2010 – the Labour government's period in office.

In the period 1997-2010 there were 35 ticks, three Xs and 8 no clear trend. In the period since 2009, there are 27 ticks, 13 Xs and 8 no clear trend. So most indicators of child well-being have been getting better, but progress in child well-being is faltering.

The overall conclusion is that most elements of well-being have been getting better. It is important to remember that in many cases the improvement has started from a low base, and comparatively the UK could and should be doing much better.

The only available test of whether things are good for British children is whether they are doing as well as children in other similar countries, and the answer is that in too many domains they are not.

Recent context

Since 2008 the UK has been in recession, and in 2010 the coalition formed a new government.

The financial crisis in the UK was triggered by misguided investments in the US housing market. It was found that British banks had invested heavily in sub-prime housing loans in the US. As a result, two banks were nationalised and two others were bailed out and forced to merge. The problems of the banks led to a collapse in lending, which had knock-on effects in the manufacturing industry, housing demand, house building and general levels of investment.

Table 13.2: Trends in child well-being

	Labour period trend 1997-2010	After 2009 to latest	Source
Material well-being			
Relative poverty BHC	✓	✓	HBAI
'Absolute' child poverty BHC	✓	X	HBAI
Material deprivation	▪	✓	HBAI
Persistent poverty BHC	✓	▪	HBAI
Health			
Stillbirths	≈	✓	ONS
Infant mortality	✓	✓	ONS
Child deaths	✓	✓	ONS
Low birth weight	≈	≈	ONS
Breastfeeding	✓	✓	ONS
Immunisation rates	X	✓	DH
General health	✓	✓	HSE
Longstanding illness	✓	≈	HSE
Limiting longstanding illness	✓	✓	HSE
Diabetes	X	X	HSE
Asthma	≈	▪	HSE
Dental health	▪	✓	HSCIC
Injuries and accidents	✓	✓	DfT
Obesity	X	≈	HSCIC
Diet (fruit and veg)	✓	X	HSCIC
Alcohol	✓	✓	HSCIS
Smoking	✓	✓	HSCIC
Physical activity	▪	X	HSCIC
Drugs	✓	✓	CSEW
Subjective well-being and mental health			
Happiness overall	✓	X	BHPS
Mental health	✓	≈	ONS
Suicide	✓	X	ONS
Happiness with friends	✓	X	BHPS/US
Happiness with family	≈	≈	BHPS/US
Happiness with school work	✓	✓	BHPS/US
Happiness with appearance	≈	X	BHPS/US
Happiness with life	✓	X	BHPS/US
Happiness with school	▪	✓	BHPS/US

(continued)

Table 13.2: Trends in child well-being (continued)

	Labour period trend 1997-2010	After 2009 to latest	Source
Education			
Key Stage 2 attainment	✓	✓	DfE
5 GCSEs A-C	✓	✓	DfE
Level 2 qualifications	✓	✓	DfE
Staying on rates	✓	✓	DfE
Exclusions	≈	✓	DfE
NEET	≈	✓	DfE
Housing			
Homelessness	✓	X	CLG
Temporary accommodation	✓	X	CLG
House conditions	✓	✓	EHS/EHCS
Child maltreatment			
Fatal abuse	✓	≈	Home Office
Physical abuse	✓	X	NSPCC
Neglect	≈	X	NSPCC
Children in care			
Length of spells in care	▪	✓	DfE
Placement stability	✓	≈	DfE
Education attainment	✓	✓	DfE
Childcare			
Formal participation	✓	≈	DfE
Crime and drugs			
Proven offences	✓	✓	YJB
Arrests	✓	✓	YJB
Worry about crime	✓	▪	MORI

Note: ✓ =getting better, X=getting worse, ≈no clear trend, ▪=missing data

The Labour government's response to the developing recession was radically anti-cyclical. It spent huge amounts of money propping up the banks – the Bank of England made repeated cuts in interest rates and then, with the encouragement of the Treasury, began 'quantitative easing' – increasing the money supply. A host of fiscal and labour market measures supported this.

Under the Labour government there were no substantial cuts in benefits and services – in fact, expenditure had been sustained while revenue had fallen. Together with revenue going to support the banks, this resulted in a major increase in public sector borrowing. The UK had to wait a long time to see measures announced to deal with this deficit. And all parties were coy about the deficit in the May 2010 General Elections.

After the start of the recession in 2008, the relative and absolute child poverty rate continued to fall thanks to the Brown government maintaining the value of transfers. But after the coalition came to power in 2010 the picture changed. The deficit reduction strategy they adopted tried to achieve the bulk of saving by cuts in expenditure rather than tax increases. These cuts included the freezing of child benefit, cuts in the real value of working-age benefits and tax credits, limits to housing benefits in the private sector and the 'bedroom tax' in the public sector, and the localisation of Council Tax Benefits and the Social Fund. Useful benefits such as Educational Maintenance Allowances and the Health in Pregnancy Grant were abolished. Unemployment rose, and real earnings fell for six successive years. The price of essentials – food, fuel and private rents – increased more rapidly than general inflation. The Child Poverty Action Group (2014) estimated that the failure to uprate child benefit by inflation since 2010/11 has meant that it has lost over 15% of its value over this Parliament compared to its worth had it been uprated using RPI (retail prices index). In practical terms, this means a family with one child lost £543 of support over the five years, and a two-child family sustained losses of £900. The failure to uprate the child element of tax credits over the course of that Parliament resulted in reducing the real value by 8.5%. As a result, a family with one child will have lost £628 in the last five years, and a two-child family double this (£1,256).

Out-of-work benefit income as a proportion of the Minimum Income Standard has fallen to 57% (Hirsch, 2015). So low has Jobseeker's Allowance become that it appears that an increasing proportion of the population have just stopped bothering to claim.

The coalition promised fairness in its deficit reduction strategy, but we now know that it was particularly unfair to low-income families with children. There have now been a variety of analyses of the distributional consequences of austerity in the UK to date (Cribb et al, 2013; Office of the Children's Commissioner for England, 2013; Reed and Portes, 2014), and they all paint the same picture – low-income families with children have taken the biggest hit. The reason behind this pattern is that the real living standards of families with children have fallen as price inflation has exceeded income growth in every year for the six years up to 2014. This is partly the result of the freeze in child benefit and the uprating of working-age benefits and tax credits by only 1% over the last three years (offset in part by real increases in the personal tax allowance). In contrast, since 2010, pensioner incomes have been protected by the triple lock.[1] And the biggest cuts per capita in grants to local government were in the areas with the highest child poverty rates (Beatty and Fothergill, 2013). Universal Credit, the big reform of social security that might have mitigated some of this increase in poverty, if it had been implemented in 2013 as planned, is still mired in delay, and has now been undermined by cuts. It may still never emerge.

The consequences of this are that although the relative child poverty rate has not yet increased (because the 60% median income threshold fell and then remained static), the 'absolute' child poverty rate increased both before and after housing costs.

A report by the Social Mobility and Child Poverty Commission (2014) concluded that the Child Poverty Act targets could not be met, that it will be at least 2018 before falling average earnings are back to pre-recession level, and that by 2021 there will be 900,000 extra children in relative poverty. The Commission said then that the next government:

> … will have to adopt radical new approaches … if Britain is to avoid becoming a permanently divided society. Even a world beating performance on employment levels, hours and wages would not enable the child poverty targets to be hit given current public spending plans and the current design of the tax benefit system…. We have come to the reluctant conclusion that without radical changes to the tax and benefit system to boost the incomes of poor families, there is no realistic hope of the statutory child poverty targets being met in 2020. None of the main political parties have been willing to embrace such a change, nor to speak this uncomfortable truth. They are all guilty in our view of being less than frank with the public. They all seem content to will the ends without identifying the means. It is vital that the next government comes clean. (p 160)

Future context

After the long period of recession since the financial crisis began in 2008, the UK economy is now growing. Since the last quarter of negative growth in 2012, we have had nine successive quarters of positive growth in GDP – by 2.6% in the year up to the second quarter of 2015. The employment rate has been rising since late 2011 – to

73.5% in the January to March 2015 period. The unemployment rate has continued to fall, reaching 5.5%.

A new Conservative government was elected in 2015, and during the election committed itself to a further £12 billion cuts in social security spending. Most of these were announced in the Summer Budget on 8 July 2015 and included in a Welfare Reform and Work Bill. This includes:

- amending the Child Poverty Act 2010 by removing the duty on the Secretary of State to meet UK-wide targets and creating a new statutory duty to publish an annual report on children in workless households in England and on the educational attainment of children in England at the end of Key Stage 4;

- reforming and renaming the Social Mobility and Child Poverty Commission as the Social Mobility Commission. Reducing the level of the benefit cap to £20,000 for couples and lone parents and £13,400 for single claimants, apart from in Greater London, where it will be set at £23,000/£15,410 respectively;

- freezing the main rates of the majority of working-age benefits, certain elements of tax credits and child benefit for four years from April 2016;

- amending the manner for calculating the amount of Child Tax Credit payable to a claimant by limiting the number of children or qualifying young people in respect of whom the individual element of Child Tax Credit is payable to two;

- removing entitlement to the family element of Child Tax Credit unless a child or qualifying person is born on or before 6 April 2017, and creating a new disability element payable to claimants who are responsible for a disabled or severely disabled child or qualifying young person;

- restricting the number of children or qualifying young people in respect of whom the child element of Universal Credit is payable to two (with exceptions), and removing the higher rate of child element payable in respect of the first child or qualifying young people to creating a single flat rate;

- removing the work-related activity component in Employment and Support Allowance and the limited capability for work element in Universal Credit;

- increasing the work-related requirements imposed on Universal Credit claimants who are responsible carers of a child aged 2-4;

- reforming the payment of Support for Mortgage Interest from a benefit to a loan secured over the property of the claimant; and

- placing a requirement on local authorities and private registered providers to reduce social housing rents by 1% a year for four years from a frozen 2015/16 base line.

These cuts are to be partially offset by the introduction of a new increased National Minimum Wage (wrongly named as a National Living Wage). This will add a premium to the existing and prospective National Minimum Wage for those over 25 of £7.20 from April 2016 rising to £9 by 2020, pegged to 60% median earnings.

The distributional consequences of the Summer Budget are still being considered, but there is a useful analysis by the Institute for Fiscal Studies that shows that it is highly regressive (see Hood, 2015). It is also bound to damage children's well-being.

This is not a happy conclusion to this book. It behoves us all to redouble our efforts to monitor the well-being of children in the UK. They are, after all, our future.

Note

[1] Uprated by the best of movements in prices, earnings or 2.5%.

Bibliography

Abdallah, S., Main, G., Pople, L. and Rees, G. (2014) *Ways to well-being: Exploring the links between children's activities and their subjective well-being*, London: The Children's Society.

ADASS, ADCS and The Children's Society (2012) *Working together to support young carers and their families.* (www.youngcarer.com/sites/default/files/imce_user_files/PTP/mou_young_carers_2012.pdf).

Afifi, T.O., Taillieu, T., Cheung, K., Katz, L.Y., Tonmyr, L. and Sareen, J. (2015) 'Substantiated reports of child maltreatment from the Canadian incidence study of reported child abuse and neglect 2008: Examining child and household characteristics and child functional impairment', *Canadian Journal of Psychiatry, Revue Canadienne de Psychiatrie*, vol 60, no 7, p 315.

Anderson, H.R. (2005) 'Prevalence of asthma', *British Medical Journal*, vol 330, p 1037.

Arata, C.M., Langhinrichsen-Rohling, J., Bowers, D. and O'Brien, N. (2007) 'Differential correlates of multi-type maltreatment among urban youth', *Child Abuse & Neglect*, vol 31, no 4, pp 393-415.

Archambault, I., Janosz, M., Morizot, J. and Pagani, L. (2009) 'Adolescent behavioural, affective, and cognitive engagement in school: relationship to dropout', *The Journal of School Health*, vol 79, no 9, pp 408-15.

Asher, M.I., Montefort, S., Björkstén, B., Lai, C.K.W., Strachan, D.P., Weiland, S.K. and Williams, H. (2006) 'Worldwide time trends in the prevalence of symptoms of asthma, allergic rhinoconjunctivitis, and eczema in childhood: ISAAC phases one and three repeat multicountry cross-sectional surveys', *The Lancet*, vol 368, no 9537, pp 733-43.

Axford, N., Sonthalia, S., Wrigley, Z., Goodwin, A., Ohlson. C., Bjornstad, G., Barlow, J., Schrader-Mcmillan, A., Coad, J. and Toft, A. (2015) *The best start at home: what works to improve the quality of parent-child interactions from conception to age 5 years? A rapid review of interventions.* London: Early Intervention Foundation (www.eif.org.uk/wp-content/uploads/2015/03/The-Best-Start-at-Home-report.pdf, accessed 1.7.15).

Axford, N. and Barlow, J. (No Date, 1.) *The science within: What matters for child outcomes in the early years* (http://betterstart.dartington.org.uk/wp-content/uploads/2013/08/The-Science-Within.pdf, accessed 1.7.15)

Axford, N. and Barlow, J. (No Date, 2.) *Better evidence for a better start, what works: An overview of the best available evidence on giving children a better start* (https://dartington.org.uk/inc/uploads/What%20 works%20%20Overview.pdf, accessed 1.7.15).

Baker, K., Jones, S., Merrington, S. and Roberts, C. (2005) *Further development of Asset*, London: Youth Justice Board.

Barnes, M., Cullinane, C., Scott, S. and Silvester, H. (2013) *People living in bad housing – numbers and health impacts*, London: NatCen Social Research.

Barnes, M., Green, R. and Ross, A. (2011) *Understanding vulnerable young people: Analysis from the Longitudinal Study of Young People in England.* NatCen report for the DfE (DFE-RR118) (www.gov.uk/ government/publications/understanding-vulnerable-young-people-analysis-from-the-longitudinal-study-of-young-people-in-england, accessed on 10.08.2015).

Barnes, M., Lord, C. and Chanfreu, J. (2015) *Child poverty transitions: Exploring the routes into and out of child poverty, 2009-2012*, London: Department for Work and Pensions (www.gov.uk/government/ uploads/system/uploads/attachment_data/file/436482/rr900-child-poverty-transitions.pdf).

Barter, C., McCarry, M., Berridge, D. and Evans, K. (2009) *Partner exploitation and violence in teenage intimate relationships*, Bristol/London: University of Bristol/NSPCC (www.nspcc.org.uk/globalassets/ documents/research-reports/partner-exploitation-violence-teenage-intimate-relationships-report.pdf).

Bateman, T. (2014) 'Children in conflict with the law: An overview of trends and developments 2013', London: National Association for Youth Justice Briefing (http://thenayj.org.uk/wp-content/ uploads/2015/06/2013-Children_in_conflict_with_the_law_ briefing_Sep14.pdf).

Bazalgette, L., Rahilly, T. and Trevelyan, G. (2015) *Achieving emotional wellbeing for looked after children*, London: NSPCC.

Beardsmore, R. and Siegler, V. (2014) *Measuring national well-being: Exploring the well-being of children in the UK, 2014*, Newport: Office for National Statistics.

Beatty, C. and Fothergill, S. (2013) *Hitting the poorest places hardest: The local and regional impact of welfare reform*, Sheffield: Centre for Regional Economic and Social Research, Sheffield Hallam University (www. shu.ac.uk/research/cresr/sites/shu.ac.uk/files/hitting-poorest-places-hardest_0.pdf).

Beaumont, J. (2011) *Measuring national well-being: Discussion paper on domains and measures*, Newport: Office for National Statistics.

Belfort, M.B., Rifas-Shiman, S.L., Kleinman, K.P., Guthrie, L.B., Bellinger, D.C., Taveras, E.M., Gillman, M.W. and Oken, E. (2013) 'Infant feeding and childhood cognition at ages 3 and 7 years: effects of breastfeeding duration and exclusivity', *JAMA Pediatrics*, vol 167, no 9, pp 836-44.

Bellis, M.A., Lowey, H., Leckenby, N., Hughes, K. and Harrison, D. (2014) 'Adverse childhood experiences: retrospective study to determine their impact on adult health behaviours and health outcomes in a UK population', *Journal of Public Health*, vol 36, no 1, pp 81-91.

Ben-Arieh, A. (2007) 'The child indicators movement: past, present, and future', *Child Indicators Research*, vol 1, no 1, pp 3-16.

Ben-Arieh, A. (2010) 'Developing indicators for child well-being in a changing context', in C. McAuley and W. Rose (eds) *Child well-being: Understanding children's lives*, London: Jessica Kingsley Publishers, pp 129-42.

Berlin, M., Vinnerljung, B. and Hjern, A. (2011) 'School performance in primary school and psychosocial problems in young adulthood among care leavers from long term foster care', *Children and Youth Services Review*, vol 33, no 12, pp 2489-97.

Berridge, D. (1997) *Foster care: A research review*, London: The Stationery Office.

Berridge, D., Dance, C., Beecham, J. and Field, S. (2008) *Educating difficult adolescents: Effective education for children in public care or with emotional and behavioural difficulties*, London: Jessica Kingsley Publishers.

Better Regulation Task Force (2004) *The regulation of child employment*, London: Better Regulation Task Force.

Biehal, N., Clayden, J., Stein, M. and Wade, J. (1995) *Moving on: Young people and leaving care schemes*, London: British Association for Adoption and Fostering (BAAF).

Biehal, N., Ellison, N., Baker, C. and Sinclair, I. (2010) *Belonging and permanence: Outcomes in long-term foster care and adoption*, London: British Association for Adoption and Fostering (BAAF).

Bilson, A., Price, P. and Stanley, N. (2011) 'Developing employment opportunities for care leavers', *Children & Society*, vol 25, pp 382-93.

Blades, R., Hart, D., Lea J. and Willmott, N. (2011) *Care – A stepping stone to custody*, London: Prison Reform Trust.

Blanden, J. and Machin, S. (2007) *Recent changes in intergenerational mobility in Britain*, London: The Sutton Trust.

Blanden, J., Del Bono, E., Hansen, K., McNally, S. and Rabe, B. (2014) *Evaluating a demand-side approach to expanding free preschool education*, Essex: ISER, University of Essex (www.iser.essex.ac.uk/files/projects/the-effect-of-free-childcare-on-maternal-labour-supply-and-child-development/childoutcomes.pdf).

Blanden, J., Hansen, K. and Machin, S. (2010) 'The economic cost of growing up poor: Estimating the GDP loss associated with child poverty', *Fiscal Studies*, vol 31, no 3, pp 289-312.

Blum, R.W. and Nelson-Mmari, K. (2004) 'The health of young people in a global context', *Journal of Adolescent Health*, vol 35, pp 402-1.

Boyling, E., Wilson, M. and Wright, J. (2013) *PISA 2012: Highlights from Scotland's Results*. Scottish Government Social Research. (www.gov.scot/Publications/2013/12/4338/downloads, accessed on 06.08.2015).

Bowes, L., Wolke, D., Joinson, C., Lereya, S.T. and Lewis, G. (2014) 'Sibling bullying and risk of depression, anxiety, and self-harm: a prospective cohort study', *Pediatrics*, vol 134, no 4, e1032-e1039.

Bradshaw, J. (1990) *Child poverty and deprivation in the UK*, London: National Children's Bureau.

Bradshaw, J. (ed) (2001) *Poverty: The outcomes for children*, London: Family Policy Studies Centre.

Bradshaw, J. (ed) (2002) *The well-being of children in the UK*, London: Save the Children.

Bradshaw, J. (2011) *The well-being of children in the UK* (3rd edn), Bristol: Policy Press.

Bradshaw, J. (2013) *Consultation on child poverty*, PSE policy response working paper, No 8, Poverty and Social Exclusion in the UK (www.poverty.ac.uk).

Bradshaw, J. (2015) 'Child poverty and child well-being in international perspective', in E. Fernandez, A. Zeira, T. Vecchiato and C. Canali (eds) *Theoretical and empirical insights in child and family poverty: Cross national perspectives*, Springer: Dordrecht, pp 59-70.

Bradshaw, J. (nd) 'Programme for International Student Assessment (PISA) Results from PISA 2012: United Kingdom', *OECD Country Note* (www.oecd.org/unitedkingdom/PISA-2012-results-UK.pdf).

Bradshaw, J. and Chzhen, Y. (2009) 'Lone parent families in comparative perspective', Paper for the 'One parent families in the family diversity context' Conference, University of Barcelona.

Bradshaw, J. and Keung, L. (2011) 'Trends in child subjective well-being in the UK', *Journal of Children's Services*, vol 6, no 1, pp 4-17.

Bradshaw, J. and Mayhew, E. (eds) (2005) *The well-being of children in the UK*, London: Save the Children.

Bradshaw, J. and Mayhew, E. (2015) *Child poverty in the North East: A report for the North East Child Poverty Commission*, York: Social Policy Research Unit, University of York.

Bradshaw, J. and Richardson, D. (2009) 'An index of child well-being in Europe', *Child Indicators Research*, vol 2, no 3, p 319.

Bradshaw, J., Hoelscher, P. and Richardson, D. (2007a) 'An index of child well-being in the European Union 25', *Journal of Social Indicators Research*, vol 80, pp 133-77.

Bradshaw, J., Hoelscher, P. and Richardson, D. (2007b) *Comparing child well-being in OECD countries: Concepts and methods*, IWP 2006-03, Florence: UNICEF Innocenti Research Centre.

Bradshaw, J., Martorano, B. Natali, L. and de Neubourg, C. (2013) 'Children's subjective well-being in rich countries', *Child Indicators Research*, 6, 4, pp 619–35.

Bradshaw, J., Noble, M., Bloor, K., Huby, M., McLennan, D., Rhodes, D., Sinclair, I. and Wilkinson, K. (2009) 'A child well-being index at small area level in England', *Journal of Child Indicators Research*, vol 2, no 2, pp 201-19.

Bramley, G. and Watkins, D. (2008) *The public service costs of child poverty*, York: Joseph Rowntree Foundation.

Brandon, M., Bailey, S., Belderson, P. and Larsson, B. (2014) 'The role of neglect in child fatality and serious injury', *Child Abuse Review*, vol 23, no 4, pp 235-45.

Brandon, M., Sidebotham, P., Bailey, S., Belderson, P., Hawley, C., Ellis, C. and Megson, M. (2012) *New learning from serious case reviews: A two year report for 2009-2011*, London: Department for Education.

Brewer, M., Cattan, S. and Crawford, C. (2014) 'State support for early childhood education and care in England' in Emmerson, C., Johnson, P. and Miller, H. *IFS Green Budget 2014.* London: IFS. (www.ifs.org. uk/budgets/gb2014/gb2014_ch8.pdf, accessed 10.7.15).

Brooks, F., van der Sluijs, W., Klemera, E., Morgan, A., Magnusson, J., Gabhainn, S.N., Roberts, C., Smith, R. and Currie, C. (2009) *Young people's health in Great Britain and Ireland: Findings from the Health Behaviour in School-aged Children (HBSC) Survey, 2006*, Edinburgh: HBSC International Coordinating Centre, University of Edinburgh.

Buckingham, E.T. and Daniolos, P. (2013) 'Longitudinal outcomes for victims of child abuse', *Current Psychiatry Reports*, vol 15, no 2.

Bullock, R. and Gaehl, E. (2012) 'Children in care: A long-term follow up of criminality and mortality', *Children and Youth Services Review*, vol 34, no 9, pp 1947-55.

Burdette, H.L. and Whitaker, R.C. (2005) 'Resurrecting free play in young children: looking beyond fitness and fatness to attention, affiliation, and affect', *Archives of Pediatrics & Adolescent Medicine*, vol 159, pp 46-50.

Butchart, A., WHO (World Health Organization) and International Society for the Prevention of Child Abuse and Neglect (eds) (2006) *Preventing child maltreatment: A guide to taking action and generating evidence*, Geneva: WHO.

Busch-Geertsema, V., Benjaminsen, L., Filipovic Hrast, M. and Pleace, N. (2014) *Extent and profile of homelessness in European Member States*, Brussels: Feantsa.

Butler, A. and Rutter, J. (2015) *Access denied: A report on childcare sufficiency and market management in England and Wales*, London: Family and Childcare Trust.

Cabinet Office (2014) *Trends in risk behaviours and negative outcomes amongst children and young people*, London: Cabinet Office (www.gov.uk/government/uploads/system/uploads/attachment_data/file/452169/data_pack_risk_behaviours_and_negative_outcomes.pdf).

Cameron, C. (2000) *Resolving childhood trauma: A long-term study of abuse survivors*, Thousand Oaks, CA: Sage Publications.

Case, S. and Haines, K. (2009) *Understanding youth offending: Risk factor research, policy and practice*, Cullompton: Willan Publishing.

Causa, O. and Johansson, A. (2010) *Intergenerational social mobility in OECD countries*. OECD Economic Department. (www.oecd.org/eco/labour/49849281.pdf, accessed on 13.08.2015).

Cawson, P., Wattam, C., Brooker, S. and Kelly, G. (2000) *Child maltreatment in the UK: A study of the prevalence of child abuse and neglect*, London: NSPCC.

Caya, M.L. and Liem, J.H. (1998) 'The role of sibling support in high-conflict families', *American Journal of Orthopsychiatry*, vol 68, pp 327-33.

Centre for Crime and Justice Studies (2015) 'Sharp rise in proportion of young BME prisoners', 30 June, London: Centre for Crime and Justice Studies (www.crimeandjustice.org.uk/news/sharp-rise-proportion-young-bme-prisoners).

Centre for Social Justice (2014) *Finding their feet: Equipping care leavers to reach their potential*, London: Centre for Social Justice.

Cheung, R. (ed) (2012) *NHS atlas of variation in healthcare for children and young people*, NHS Right Care.

Child Poverty Action Group (2014) *Policy note 2: Uprating and the value of children's benefits* (www.cpag.org.uk/sites/default/files/CPAG-Uprating-childrens-benefits-policy-note-Dec-14.pdf).

Children's Rights Alliance for England (2015) *UK implementation of the UN Convention on the Rights of the Child: Civil society alternative report 2015 to the UN committee - England* (www.crae.org.uk/media/78665/crae_civil_society_report_to_un_web.pdf, accessed on 18.08.2015)

Christensen, P. and James, A. (eds) (2008) *Research with children: Perspectives and practices* (2nd edn), Abingdon: Routledge.

Chzen, Y. and Bradshaw, J. (2012) 'Lone parents, poverty and policy in the European Union', *Journal of European Social Policy*, 22.5.

Claes, E., Hooghe, M. and Reeskens, T. (2009) 'Truancy as contextualised and school related problem: A comparative multilevel analysis on Civic Knowledge among 14 year olds', *Educational Studies*, vol 35, no 2, pp 123-42.

Clapham, D., Mackie P., Orford, S., Buckley, K. and Thomas, I with Atherton, I. and McAnulty, U. (2012) *Housing options and solutions for young people in 2020*, London: Joseph Rowntree Foundation.

Clarke, A., Burgess, G., Morris, S. and Udagawa, C. (2015) *Estimating the scale of youth homelessness in the UK*, Cambridge: University of Cambridge.

CLG (Department for Communities and Local Government) (2006) *A decent home: Definition and guidance for implementation*, London: CLG.

CLG (2010a) *Local decisions: A fairer future for social housing*, London: CLG.

CLG (2010b) *English Housing Survey: Housing stock report, 2008*, London: CLG.

CLG (2010c) *English Housing Survey: Household report 2008-9*, London: CLG.

CLG (2015) *English Housing Survey 2013 to 2014: household report*, London: CLG.

Cockman, P., Dawson, L., Mathur, R. and Hull, S. (2011) 'Improving MMR vaccination rates: herd immunity is a realistic goal', *British Medical Journal*, vol 343.

Colechin, J. (2011) *Combating truancy: A family lives report* (www.familylives.org.uk/docs/family_lives_combating_truancy.pdf, accessed on 10.08.2015).

Coles, B., Hutton, S., Bradshaw, J., Craig, G. Godfrey, C. and Johnson, J. (2002) *Literature review of the cost of being 'not in education, employment or training' at age 16-18*, Research Report 347, Department for Education and Skills: Nottingham.

Coles, B., Godfrey, C., Keung, A., Parrott, S. and Bradshaw, J. (2010) *Estimating the lifetime cost of NEET: 16-18 year-olds not in education, employment or training*, York: University of York (http://php.york. ac.uk/inst/spru/pubs/ipp.php?id=1776).

Collishaw, S. (2015) 'Annual research review: Secular trends in child and adolescent mental health', *Journal of Child Psychology and Psychiatry*, vol 56, no 3, pp 370-93.

Collishaw, S., Maughan, B., Goodman, R. and Pickles, A. (2004) 'Time trends in adolescent mental health', *Journal of Child Psychological and Psychiatry*, vol 45, no 8, pp 1350-62.

Collishaw, S., Maughan, B., Natarajan, L. and Pickles, A. (2010) 'Trends in adolescent emotional problems in England: a comparison of two national cohorts twenty years apart: Twenty-year trends in emotional problems', *Journal of Child Psychology and Psychiatry*, vol 51, no 8, pp 885-94.

Collishaw, S., Gardner, F., Maughan, B., Scott, J. and Pickles, A. (2012) 'Do historical changes in parent–child relationships explain increases in youth conduct problems?', *Journal of Abnormal Child Psychology*, vol 40, no 1, pp 119-32.

Commission for Childcare Reform (2015) *Meeting Scotland's childcare challenge: The Report of The Commission for Childcare Reform June 2015*, Edinburgh: Children in Scotland (www.childreninscotland.org.uk/ sites/default/files/FinalChildcareCommissionReportJune2015.pdf, accessed 21.8.15).

Conway, L. and Morgan, D. (2001) *Injury prevention*, London: BMJ Books.

Cornia, G. and Danziger, S. (1997) *Child poverty and deprivation in the industrialised countries 1994-1995*, Oxford: Clarendon Press.

Costello, E.J., Copeland, W. and Angold, A. (2011) 'Trends in psychopathology across the adolescent years: what changes when children become adolescents, and when adolescents become adults?', *Journal of Child Psychology and Psychiatry*, vol 52, no 10, pp 1015-25.

Cousens, S., Blencowe, H., Stanton, C., Chou, D., Ahmed, S., Steinhardt, L., Creanga, A.A., Tunçalp, O., Balsara, Z.P., Gupta, S., Say, L., Lawn, J.E. (2011) 'National, regional, and worldwide estimates of stillbirth rates in 2009 with trends since 1995: a systematic analysis', *Lancet*, 16;377(9774), pp 1319-30.

Craine, N., Midgley, C., Zou, L., Evans, H., Whitaker, R. and Lyons, M. (2014) 'Elevated teenage conception risk amongst looked after children; a national audit', *Public Health*, vol 128, no 7, pp 668-70.

Crawford, C. Maccmillan, L. and Vignoles, A. (2015) *When and why do initially high attaining poor children fall behind?* Working Paper 20: Social Policy in a Cold Climate (http://sticerd.lse.ac.uk/dps/case/spcc/wp20.pdf, accessed on 13.08.2015).

Cribb, J., Hood, A., Joyce, R. and Phillips, D. (2013) *Living standards, poverty and inequality in the UK: 2013*, IFS report R81, London: Institute for Fiscal Studies (www.ifs.org.uk/comms/r81.pdf).

Currie, C., Zanotti, C., Morgan, A., Currie, D., de Looze, M., Roberts, C., Samdal, O., Smith, O.R.F. and Barnekow, V. (eds) (2012) *Social determinants of health and well-being among young people. Health Behaviour in School-aged Children (HBSC) study: International report from the 2009/2010 survey*, Health Policy for Children and Adolescents No 6, Copenhagen: WHO Regional Office for Europe.

Davies, C. and Ward, H. (2012) *Safeguarding children across services*, London: Jessica Kingsley Publishers.

Davies, P. (1999) *Learning and earning: The impact of paid employment on young people in full-time education*, London: Further Education Development Agency (www.eric.ed.gov/PDFS/ED439223.pdf).

DCLG (Department for Communities and Local Government) (2010a) *English Housing Survey: Housing stock report, 2008*, London: DCLG.

DCLG (2010b) *English Housing Survey: Household report 2008-9*, London: DCLG.

DCLG (2013a) Statistical data set: Dwelling condition and safety (Table DA3203 (SST3.4) Decent Homes – households, 2013). (www.gov.uk/government/statistical-data-sets/dwelling-condition-and-safety).

DCLG (2013b) *English Housing Survey: Home report, 2011*, London: DCLG.

DCLG (2015a) *English Housing Survey, 2013: Profile of English housing report*, London: DCLG.

DCLG (2015b) *English Housing Survey: Households: Annual report on England's households, 2013-14*, London: DCLG.

DCLG/Homes and Communities Agency (2015) *2010 to 2015 Government policy: Rented housing sector* (www.gov.uk/government/publications/2010-to-2015-government-policy-rented-housing-sector).

DCSF (Department for Children, Schools and Families) (2007a) *The children's plan: Building brighter futures*, Cm 7280, London: DCSF (www.dcsf.gov.uk/childrensplan/).

DCSF (2007b) *Children and young people today: Evidence to support the development of the Children's Plan*, London: DCSF (http://webarchive. nationalarchives.gov.uk/20130401151715/http://www.education. gov.uk/publications/eOrderingDownload/Childrenandyoung_ people_today.pdf).

DCSF (2007c) *Aiming high for young people: A Ten year strategy for positive activities* (webarchive.nationalarchives.gov.uk/20130401151715/ http://www.education.gov.uk/publications/standard/ publicationdetail/page1/PU214, accessed on 20.08.2015).

Dearden, C. and Becker, S. (2004) *Young carers in the UK: The 2004 report*, London: Carers UK (www.lboro.ac.uk/microsites/socialsciences/ ycrg/youngCarersDownload/YCReport2004%5B1%5D.pdf).

DfE (Department for Education) (2010) *Equalities Impact Assessment: Academies Bill.* (www.parliament.uk/documents/impact-assessments/ IA10-099.pdf, accessed on 23.07.2015).

DfE (2011) *Youth cohort study and longitudinal study of young people in England: the activities and experiences of 19-year-olds 2010* (www.gov. uk/government/statistics/youth-cohort-study-and-longitudinal- study-of-young-people-in-england-the-activities-and-experiences- of-19-year-olds-2010, accessed on 06.08.2015).

DfE (2013) *More great childcare, raising quality and giving parents more choice*, London: DfE (www.gov.uk/government/uploads/system/uploads/ attachment_data/file/219660/More_20Great_20Childcare_20v2. pdf, accessed 25.6.15).

DfE (2014a) *Statistical First Release: Participation in education, training, and employment, age 16 to 18* (www.gov.uk/government/statistics/ participation-in-education-training-and-employment-age-16-to-18, accessed on 04.08.2015).

DfE (2014b) *Achievement of 15-year-olds in England: PISA 2012 National Report* (www.gov.uk/government/publications/programme-for- international-student-assessment-pisa-2012-national-report-for- england, accessed on 21.07.2015).

DfE (2014c) *Statistical First Release: Special Educational Needs in England: January 2014.* SFR26/2014 (www.gov.uk/government/statistics/ special-educational-needs-in-england-january-2014, accessed on 12.08.2015).

DfE (2014d) *Early education and childcare: Research priorities and questions March 2014* (www.gov.uk/government/uploads/system/uploads/ attachment_data/file/288192/Early_education_and_childcare_ research_priorities_and_questions.pdf, accessed 10.8.15).

DfE (2015a) *Statistical First Release: National curriculum assessments at Key Stage 2 in England, 2014 (revised)*. Main text: SFR50/2014 (www.gov.uk/government/statistics/national-curriculum-assessments-at-key-stage-2-2014-revised).

DfE (2015b) Statistical First Release: National curriculum assessments at Key Stage 2 in England, 2014 (revised). National tables: SFR50/2014 (www.gov.uk/government/statistics/national-curriculum-assessments-at-key-stage-2-2014-revised, accessed on 21.07.2015.

DfE (2015c) Statistical First Release: Revised GCSE and equivalents results in England, 2013 to 2014. SFR02/2015 (www.gov.uk/government/statistics/revised-gcse-and-equivalent-results-in-england-2013-to-2014, accessed on 16.07.2015).

DfE (2015d) Statistical First Release: GCSE and equivalent attainment by pupil characteristics, 2013 to 2014 (Revised) (www.gov.uk/government/uploads/system/uploads/attachment_data/file/399005/SFR06_2015_Text.pdf, accessed on 16.07.2015).

DfE (2015e) Schools, pupils and their characteristics: January 2015. SFR16/2015 (www.gov.uk/government/statistics/schools-pupils-and-their-characteristics-january-2015, accessed on 12.08.2015).

DfE (2015f) Statistical First Release: A level and other level 3 results: 2013 to 2014 (revised). National table SFR03/2015. (www.gov.uk/government/statistics/a-level-and-other-level-3-results-2013-to-2014-revised, accessed on 30.07.2015).

DfE (2015g) Statistical First Release: Level 2 and 3 attainments by young people in England measured using matched administrative data: Attainment by age 19 in 2014. (www.gov.uk/government/statistics/level-2-and-3-attainment-by-young-people-aged-19-in-2014, accessed on 31.07.2015.

DfE (2015h) Statistical First Release: Participation in education, training and employment: age 16-18. Main text SFR19/2015. (www.gov.uk/government/statistics/participation-in-education-training-and-employment-age-16-to-18--2, accessed on 03.08.2015.

DfE (2015i) Pupil absence in schools in England: 2013-201. (www.gov.uk/government/statistics/pupil-absence-in-schools-in-england-2013-to-2014).

DfE (2015j) Statistical First Release: Permanent and fixed-period exclusions in England: 2013 to 2014. (www.gov.uk/government/statistics/permanent-and-fixed-period-exclusions-in-england-2013-to-2014, accessed on 10.08.2015).

DfE (2015k) Statistical First Release: Special educational needs in England: January 2015. SFR25/2015. (www.gov.uk/government/statistics/special-educational-needs-in-england-january-2015, accessed on 11.08.2015).

DfE (2015l) A guide to absence statistics. (www.gov.uk/government/publications/absence-statistics-guide, accessed on 17.08.2015).

DfE (2015m) A guide to exclusions statistics. (www.gov.uk/government/publications/exclusions-statistics-guide, accessed on 17.08.2015).

DfE (2015n) *Provision for children under 5 years of age: January 2015.* London: DfE (www.gov.uk/government/statistics/provision-for-children-under-5-years-of-age-january-2015, accessed 21.8.15)

DfE and DBIS (2014) *Review of vocational education: the Wolf report.* (www.gov.uk/government/publications/review-of-vocational-education-the-wolf-report, accessed on 16.07.2015).

DfE and DBIS (2015) NEET statistics quarterly brief: April to June 2015. NEET time series for England SFR:2015. (www.gov.uk/government/uploads/system/uploads/attachment_data/file/454421/NEET_harmonised_Supplementary_tables_National_timeseries_inc_Q2_2015.xlsx, accessed on 17.12.2015).

DfE, Cameron, D. and Morgan, N. (2015) Press release: Prime Minister announces landmark wave of free schools. 18 March 2015 (www.gov.uk/government/news/prime-minister-announces-landmark-wave-of-free-schools, accessed on 12.08.2015).

DfES (Department for Education and Skills) (2006) *Youth matters: Next steps*, London: DfES (http://webarchive.nationalarchives.gov.uk/20130401151715/http://www.education.gov.uk/publications/standard/publicationDetail/Page1/DFES-0261-2006).

DfT (2013) *Casualties involved in reported road accidents (RAS30)*, London: Dft (www.gov.uk/government/statistical-data-sets/ras30-reported-casualties-in-road-accidents).

DH and DCSF (2009) *Healthy lives and brighter future: The strategy for children and young people's health.* (http://webarchive.nationalarchives.gov.uk/+/www.dh.gov.uk/en/publicationsandstatistics/publications/publicationspolicyandguidance/DH_094400).

DHSSPS (Department of Health, Social Services and Public Safety) (2015) *Northern Ireland care leavers 2013/4*, National Statistics, Information Analysis Directorate, Belfast: DHSSPS.

Diener, E. (1984) 'Subjective well-being', *Psychological Bulletin*, vol 95, no 3, pp 542-75.

Dixon, J. (2008) 'Young people leaving care: health, well-being and outcomes', *Child & Family Social Work*, vol 13, no 2, pp 207-17.

Dixon, J. and Lee, J., with Stein, M., Guhirwa, H., Bowley, S. and Catch22 NCAS peer researchers (2015) *Corporate parenting for young people in care – Making the difference?*, London: Catch22.

Dixon, J. and Stein, M (2005) *Leaving care: Throughcare and aftercare in Scotland*, London: Jessica Kingsley Publishers.

Department of Education (DoE) (Northern Ireland) (2015) *Enrolments at schools and in funded pre-school education in NI, 2014/15* (www.deni. gov.uk/statistical_bulletin_-_february_15_final__24_06_15_.pdf, accessed 14.8.15).

Dunn, J. and Deater-Deckard, K. (2001) *Children's views of their changing families*, York: York Publishing Services for the Joseph Rowntree Foundation.

Dunn, J., Slomkowski, C. and Beardsall, L. (1994) 'Sibling relationships from the preschool period through middle childhood and early adolescence', *Developmental Psychology*, vol 30, pp 315-24.

DWP (Department for Work and Pensions) (2007) *Opportunity for all: Indicators update 2007*, October, London: DWP (www.bristol.ac.uk/ poverty/downloads/keyofficialdocuments/Opportunity%20for%20 All%202007.pdf)

DWP (2008) *UK national report on strategies for social protection and social inclusion 2008-2010*, London: DWP (www.dwp.gov.uk/docs/ uknationalstrategyreport12-9-08.pdf).

DWP (2014) *Households below average income: 1994/1995 to 2012/2013*, London: DWP (www.gov.uk/government/statistics/ householdsbelow-average-income-19941995-to-20122013).

DWP (2015) *Households below average income: 1994/1995 to 2013/2014*, London: DWP (www.gov.uk/government/statistics/households-below-average-income-19941995-to-20132014).

(EC) (European Commission) (2014) *EU-SILC data* (http:// ec.europa.eu/eurostat/statistics-explained/index.php/Housing_ conditions#Main_tables)

EC (2015) *Quality of life in Europe – facts and views – environment* (http:// ec.europa.eu/eurostat/statistics-explained/index.php/Quality_of_ life_in_Europe_-_facts_and_views_-_environment)

Ehtisham, S., Barrett, T.G. and Shaw, N.J. (2000) 'Type 2 diabetes mellitus in UK children – an emerging problem', *Diabetic Medicine*, vol 17, no 2, pp 867-71.

Ellonen, N., Kääriäinen, J., Lehti, M. and Aaltonen, M. (2015) 'Comparing trends in infanticides in 28 countries, 1960-2009', *Journal of Scandinavian Studies in Criminology and Crime Prevention*, pp 1-19.

EU Kids Online (2014) *EU Kids Online: findings, methods, recommendations*. London: LSE (http://eprints.lse.ac.uk/60512/, accessed on 14.12.2015).

EU-SILC (European Union Statistics on Income and Living Conditions) (2013) (http://ec.europa.eu/eurostat/data/database).

Evans, J., Macrory, I. and Randall, C. (2015) *Measuring national well-being: Life in the UK, 2015*, London: Office for National Statistics.

Family and Childcare Trust (2015a) *Election Fact Sheets*, London: Family and Childcare Trust (www.familyandchildcaretrust.org/election, accessed 7.7.15).

Family and Childcare Trust (2015b) *Annual Childcare Cost Survey*, London: Family and Childcare Trust.

Farmer, C. (2005) *2003 Home Office Citizenship Survey: Top-level findings from the Children's and Young People's Survey*, London: Home Office.

Farmer, E. and Wijedasa, D. (2013) 'The reunification of looked after children with their parents: What contributes to return stability?', *British Journal of Social Work*, vol 43, no 8, pp 1611-29.

Feinstein, L. (ed) (March 2015) *Social and emotional learning: Skills for life and work*, London: Early Intervention Foundation, Cabinet Office and Social Mobility and Child Poverty Commission (www.eif.org.uk/publications/social-and-emotional-learning-skills-for-life-and-work, accessed 1.7.15).

Fink, E., Patalay, P., Sharpe, H., Holley, S., Deighton J. and Wolpert, A. (2015) 'Mental health difficulties in early adolescence: A comparison of two cross-sectional studies in England from 2009 to 2014', *Journal of Adolescent Health*, vol 56, pp 502-507

Finkelhor, D., Ormrod, R.K. and Turner, H.A. (2009) 'Lifetime assessment of poly-victimization in a national sample of children and youth', *Child Abuse & Neglect*, vol 33, no 7, pp 403-11.

Finkelhor, D., Hamby, S.L., Ormrod, R. and Turner, H. (2005) 'The Juvenile Victimization Questionnaire: reliability, validity, and national norms', *Child Abuse & Neglect*, vol 29, no 4, pp 383-412.

Fitzpatrick, S., Pawson, H., Bramley, G. Wilcox, S. and Watts, B. (2015) *The homelessness monitor: England, 2015*, London: Crisis.

Fitzpatrick, S., Pleace, N., Stephens, M. and Quilgars, D. (2009) 'Introduction: An overview of homelessness in the UK', in S. Fitzpatrick, D. Quilgars and N. Pleace, *Homelessness in the UK: Problems and solutions*, Coventry: Chartered Institute of Housing, pp 1-20.

Ford, T., Vostanis, P., Meltzer, H. and Goodman, R. (2007) 'Psychiatric disorder among British children looked after by local authorities: comparison with children living in private households', *British Journal of Psychiatry*, vol 19, pp 319-25.

4Children's Foundation Years website (2015) *Entry requirements for Early Years Educator training* (www.foundationyears.org.uk/2014/03/news-from-government/, accessed 15.8.15).

Fuller, E. and Sanchez, M. (eds) (2010) *Smoking, drinking and drug use among young people in England 2009*, Leeds: NHS Information Centre for Health and Social Care (www.hscic.gov.uk/catalogue/PUB00384/smok-drin-drug-youn-peop-eng-2009-rep1.pdf).

Furedi, F. (2001) *Paranoid parenting: Abandon your anxieties and be a good parent*, London: Allen Lane.

General Lifestyle Survey 2008 (www.ons.gov.uk/ons/rel/ghs/general-lifestyle-survey/index.html).

Gill, T. (2007) *No fear: Growing up in a risk averse society*, London: Calouste Gulbenkian Foundation.

Gill, T. (2011) *Free range kids: why children need simple pleasures and everyday freedom, and what we can do about it.* Dairylea Simple Fun Report. Cheltenham: Dairylea (https://timrgill.files.wordpress.com/2011/07/dairylea-simple-fun-report-final.pdf, accessed on 16.08.2015).

Gill, T. (2014) *The Play Return: A review of the wider impact of play initiatives. Children's Play Policy Forum* (www.playscotland.org/who-we-are/playday/the-play-return-a-review-of-the-wider-impact-of-play-initiatives/the-play-return-a-review-of-the-wider-impact-of-play-initiatives-2/, accessed on 18.08.2015).

Gleave, J. (2009) *Children's time to play: A literature review*, London: National Children's Bureau (www.playday.org.uk/media/2640/children's_time_to_play___a_literature_review.pdf).

Gleave, J. and Cole-Hamilton, I. (2012) *A world without play: A literature review.* London: Play England.

Gobin, M., Verlander, N., Maurici, C., Bone, A. and Nardone, A. (2013) 'Do sexual health campaigns work? An outcome evaluation of a media campaign to increase chlamydia testing among young people aged 15–24 in England', *BMC Public Health*, vol 13, no 484 (www.biomedcentral.com/1471-2458/13/484).

Goddard, C. and Bedi, G. (2010) 'Intimate partner violence and child abuse: a child-centred perspective', *Child Abuse Review*, vol 19, no 1, pp 5-20.

Godfrey, C., Hutton, S., Bradshaw, J., Coles, B., Craig, G. and Johnson, J. (2002) *Estimating the cost of being 'not in education, employment or training' at age 16-18*, Research Report 346, Nottingham: Department for Education and Skills.

Goldson, B. (2010) 'The sleep of (criminological) reason: Knowledge-policy rupture and New Labour's youth justice legacy', *Criminology and Criminal Justice*, vol 10, no 2, pp 154-78.

Goldson, B. and Coles, D. (2005) *In the care of the state? Child deaths in penal custody*. London, INQUEST.

Goodman, A. and Goodman, R. (2012) 'Strengths and Difficulties Questionnaire scores and mental health in looked after children', *The British Journal of Psychiatry*, vol 200, no 5, pp 426-7.

Goodman, A., Joshi, H., Nasim, B., and Tyler. C. (2015) *Social and emotional skills in childhood and their long-term effects on adult life*. Early Intervention Foundation (www.eif.org.uk/wp-content/uploads/2015/03/EIF-Strand-1-Report-FINAL1.pdf, accessed 1.7.15).

Gordon, D. and Nandy, S. (2012) 'Measuring child poverty and deprivation', in A. Minujin and S. Nandy (eds) *Global child poverty and well-being*, Bristol: Policy Press, pp 57-101.

Goswami, H. (2014) 'Children's subjective well-being: socio-demographic characteristics and personality', *Child Indicators Research*, vol 7, no 1, pp 119-40.

GOV.UK (2015a) Child employment. (www.gov.uk/child-employment/restrictions-on-child-employment, accessed on 15.12.2015).

GOV.UK (2015b) Pupil premium: funding and accountability for schools. (www.gov.uk/pupil-premium-information-for-schools-and-alternative-provision-settings, accessed on 17.08.2015).

GOV.UK (2015c) Types of school. (www.gov.uk/types-of-school/academies, accessed on 22.07.2015).

Green, H., McGinnity, A., Meltzer, H., Ford, T. and Goodman, R. (2005) *Mental health of children and young people in Great Britain, 2004*, London: The Stationery Office (www.hscic.gov.uk/catalogue/PUB06116/ment-heal-chil-youn-peop-gb-2004-rep2.pdf).

Griggs, J. with Walker, R. (2008) *The costs of child poverty for individuals and society: A literature review*, York: Joseph Rowntree Foundation (www.jrf.org.uk/report/costs-child-poverty-individuals-and-society-literature-review).

Hansen, K. and Hawkes, D. (2009) 'Early childcare and child development', *Journal of Social Policy*, vol 38, no 2, pp 211-39.

Hansen, K. and Jones, M. (2010) 'Age 5 cognitive development in England', *Child Indicators Research*, vol 3, pp 105-26.

Hardelid, P., Davey, J., Dattani, N. and Gilbert, R. (2013) 'Child deaths due to injury in the four UK countries: A time trends study from 1980 to 2010', *PLOS ONE* (http://journals.plos.org/plosone/article?id=10.1371/journal.pone.0068323).

Hawthorne, J., Jessop, J., Pryor, J. and Richards, M. (2003) *Supporting children through family change: A review of interventions and services for children of divorcing and separating parents*, York: York Publishing Services for the Joseph Rowntree Foundation.

Hawton, K., Saunders, K.E. and O'Connor, R.C. (2012) 'Self-harm and suicide in adolescents', *The Lancet*, vol 379, no 9834, pp 2373-82.

Hayden, C. (2010) 'Offending behaviour in care: is children's residential care a "criminogenic" environment?', *Child & Family Social Work*, vol 15, no 4, pp 461-72.

Henry, K.L. and Thornberry, T.P. (2010) 'Truancy and escalation of substance use during adolescence', *Journal of Studies on Alcohol and Drugs*. vol 71, no 1, pp 115-24.

Higgins, D.J. and McCabe, M.P. (2001) 'Multiple forms of child abuse and neglect: Adult retrospective reports', *Aggression and Violent Behavior*, vol 6, no 6, pp 547-78.

Hill, L., Baker, C., Kelly, B. and Dowling, S. (2015) 'Being counted? Examining the prevalence of looked-after disabled children and young people across the UK', *Child & Family Social Work*.

Hills, J. (2015) *New research evidence on social mobility and educational attainment*. Part of the Social Policy in a Cold Climate research series. (http://sticerd.lse.ac.uk/dps/case/spcc/wp21.pdf, accessed on 13.08.2015).

Hirsch, D. (2008) *Estimating the costs of child poverty*, York: Joseph Rowntree Foundation (www.jrf.org.uk/publications/estimating-costs-child-poverty).

Hirsch, D. (2013) *An estimate of the cost of child poverty in 2013*, Loughborough: Centre for Research in Social Policy, Loughborough University (www.cpag.org.uk/sites/default/files/Cost%20of%20child%20poverty%20research%20update%20(2013).pdf).

Hirsch, D. (2015) *Minimum income standard for the UK* (www.onpes.gouv.fr/IMG/pdf/2015_JRF_mis-2015-full.pdf).

Hirsch, D. and Valadez, L. (2014) *Local indicators of child poverty – Developing a new technique for estimation*, Note, Loughborough: Centre for Research in Social Policy, Loughborough University, July (www.endchildpoverty.org.uk/images/ecp/paper_explaining_calculations_and_method_to_ECP.pdf).

HMIP (Her Majesty's Inspectorate of Prisons) (2014) *Annual report 2013-14*, London: The Stationery Office.

HM Inspectorate of Probation (2012) *It's complicated: The management of electronically monitored curfews*, London: The Stationery Office.

HM Treasury (2000) *2000 Spending Review: Public Service Agreements White Paper* (www.hm-treasury.gov.uk).

HM Treasury (2002) *2002 Spending Review: Public Service Agreements* (www.hm-treasury.gov.uk).

HM Treasury (2015) Public expenditure: Statistical analyses 2015, Cm 9122, London: HM Treasury (www.gov.uk/government/uploads/system/uploads/attachment_data/file/446716/50600_PESA_2015_PRINT.pdf).

Hobbs, S. and McKechnie, J. (1997) *Child employment in Britain: A social and psychological analysis*, Edinburgh: The Stationery Office.

Hobbs, S., McKechnie, J. and Anderson, S. (2007) 'Making child employment in Britain more visible', *Critical Social Policy*, vol 27, no 3, pp 415-25.

Holford, A. (2015) *The damage of part-time working on school girls' grades*. ISER working paper series 2015-16 (www.iser.essex.ac.uk/2015/03/26/the-damage-of-part-time-working-on-school-girls-grades, accessed on 21.08.2015).

Home Office (2010) *Recorded crime statistics 2002/03-2008/09* (http://rds.homeoffice.gov.uk/rds).

Home Office (2015) *Police powers and procedures England and Wales*, year ending 31 March 2014, London: TSO.

Homeless Link (2014) *Young and homeless, 2013*, London: Homeless Link.

Hood, A. (2015) *Benefit changes and distributional analysis*, London: Institute for Fiscal Studies (www.ifs.org.uk/uploads/publications/budgets/Budgets%202015/Summer/Hood_distributional_analysis.pdf).

House of Commons (2015) *16- to 18- year-old participation in education and training*. 31st Report of session 2014-15. London: The Stationery Office Limited.

House of Commons Committee of Public Accounts (2010) *Young people's sexual health: The National Chlamydia Screening Programme, Seventh Report of Session 2009–10*, HC 283, London: The Stationery Office (www.publications.parliament.uk/pa/cm200910/cmselect/cmpubacc/283/283.pdf).

House of Commons Home Affairs Committee (2007) *Young Black people and the criminal justice system*, London: The Stationery Office.

House of Commons Library (2015) *Key Issues for the 2015 Parliament*, HOC Library Briefing Paper. (www.parliament.uk/business/publications/research/key-issues-parliament-2015/social-protection/childcare/, accessed 25.6.15).

House of Lords (2015) Select Committee on Affordable Childcare Report of Session 2014–15 *Affordable Childcare*, London: TSO (www.publications.parliament.uk/pa/ld201415/ldselect/ldaffchild/117/117.pdf, accessed 21.8.15).

Howard, D. (2010) 'Cameron warns against funding cuts for child carers', BBC News, 16 November (www.bbc.co.uk/news/education-11764267).

HPA (Health Protection Agency) (2010a) *Notifications of infectious diseases (NOIDS), Reports* (www.hpa.org.uk/Topics/InfectiousDiseases/InfectionsAZ/NotificationsOfInfectiousDiseases/NOIDSReportsAndTables/).

HPA (2010b) *Sexually transmitted infections (STIs): Annual data tables* (www.hpa.org.uk/stiannualdatatables).

HSCIC (Health and Social Care Information Centre) (2006) *Health Survey for England 2004: The health of minority ethnic groups – headline tables*, Leeds: HSCIC (www.hscic.gov.uk/catalogue/PUB01209/heal-surv-hea-eth-min-hea-tab-eng-2004-rep.pdf).

HSCIC (2009) *Health Survey for England – 2008: Physical activity and fitness*, Leeds: HSCIC (www.hscic.gov.uk/pubs/hse08physicalactivity).

HSCIC (2012) *Infant Feeding Survey 2010*, Leeds: HSCIC (www.hscic.gov.uk/catalogue/PUB08694/Infant-Feeding-Survey-2010-Consolidated-Report.pdf).

HSCIC (2014a) *NHS immunisation statistics, England – 2013-14*, Leeds: HSCIC (www.hscic.gov.uk/catalogue/PUB14949).

HSCIC (2014b) *Health Survey for England – 2013, Trend tables*, Leeds: HSCIC (www.hscic.gov.uk/article/2021/Website-Search?productid=16572&q=children+trends&sort=Relevance&size=10&page=1&area=both#top).

HSCIC (2015a) *Hospital episode statistics, Admitted patient care, England – 2013-14*, Leeds: HSCIC (www.hscic.gov.uk/catalogue/PUB16719).

HSCIC (2015b) *Child Dental Health Survey 2013, England, Wales and Northern Ireland*, Leeds: HSCIC (www.hscic.gov.uk/catalogue/PUB17137).

IDF (International Diabetes Federation) (2014) *IDF diabetes atlas* (6th edn), Brussels: IDF (www.idf.org/sites/default/files/EN_6E_Atlas_Full_0.pdf).

INQUEST (2015) 'Deaths of young people and children in prison', London: INQUEST (www.inquest.org.uk/statistics/deaths-of-young-people-and-children-in-prison).

Ip, S., Chung, M., Raman, G., Chew, P., Magula, N., DeVine, D. et al (2007) *Breastfeeding and maternal and infant health outcomes in developed countries*, Evidence Report/Technology Assessment No 153, Boston, MA: Agency for Healthcare Research and Quality, US Department of Health and Human Services.

Ipsos-RSL & ONS (2003) *UK Time Use Survey 2000*. 3rd edn. UK Data Service. SN: 4504 (http://dx.doi.org/10.5255/UKDA-SN-4504-1).

ISC (Independent Schools Council) (2010) *Pupil numbers* (www.isc.co.uk/FactsFigures_PupilNumbers.htm).

Jackson, S. and Cameron, C. (2014) *Improving access to further and higher education for young people in public care*, London: Jessica Kingsley Publishers.

Jacobson, J., Bhardwa, B., Gyateng, T., Hunter, G. and Hough, M. (2010) *Punishing disadvantage. A profile of children in custody*, London: Prison Reform Trust.

Jones, R., Everson-Hock, E.S., Papaioannou, D., Guillaume, L., Goyder, E., Chilcott, J. et al (2011) 'Factors associated with outcomes for looked-after children and young people: a correlates review of the literature', *Child: Care, Health and Development*, vol 37, no 5, pp 613-22.

Jozwiak, G. (2014) 'Outdoor play under threat from local facilities and funding cull', *Children & Young People Now*, 7 January (www.cypnow.co.uk/cyp/analysis/1141332/outdoor-play-threat-local-facilities-funding-cull).

Jütte, S., Bentley, H., Miller, P. and Jetha, N. (2014) *How safe are our children?*, London: NSPCC.

Jütte, S., Bentley, H., Miller, P. and Jetha, N. (2015) *How safe are our children?*, London: NSPCC.

Kidner, C., Marsh, R. and Hudson, N. (2014) *Early learning and childcare*, Edinburgh: Scottish Parliament (www.scottish.parliament.uk/ResearchBriefingsAndFactsheets/S4/SB_14-26.pdf, accessed 10.8.15)

Kinney, H.C. and Thatch, B.T. (2009) 'The sudden infant death syndrome', *The New England Journal of Medicine*, vol 361, pp 795-805.

Klocke, A., Clair, A. and Bradshaw, J. (2014) 'International variation in child subjective well-being', *Child Indicators Research*, vol 7, pp 1-20.

Knies, G. (2011) 'Life satisfaction and material well-being of young people in the UK', in S.L. McFall and C. Garrington (eds) *Early findings from the first wave of the UK's household longitudinal study*, Colchester: Institute for Social and Economic Research, pp 15-22.

Knies, G. (2012) *Life satisfaction and material well-being of children in the UK*, Report no 2012-15, Colchester: Institute for Social and Economic Research, University of Essex.

Kramer, M.S., Aboud, F., Mironova, E., Vanilovich, I., Platt, R.W., Matush, L. et al (2008) 'Breastfeeding and child cognitive development: new evidence from a large randomized trial', *Archives of General Psychiatry*, vol 65, no 5, p 578.

Kumar, V. (1995) *Poverty and inequality in the UK: The effects on children*, London: National Children's Bureau.

Lacey, L. (2007) *Playday 2007 – Our streets too! Street play opinion poll summary*. Play England (www.playday.org.uk/media/.../street_play_opinion_poll_summary.doc, accessed on 18.08.2015).

Lai, C.K.W., Beasley, R., Crane, J., Foliaki, S., Shah, J. and Weiland, S. (2009) 'The ISAAC Phase Three Study Group. Global variation in the prevalence and severity of asthma symptoms: Phase Three of the International Study of Asthma and Allergies in Childhood (ISAAC)', *Thorax*, vol 64, pp 476-83.

Layard, R. (2005) *Happiness: Lessons from a new science*, London: Penguin.

Leen, E., Sorbring, E., Mawer, M., Holdsworth, E., Helsing, B. and Bowen, E. (2013) 'Prevalence, dynamic risk factors and the efficacy of primary interventions for adolescent dating violence: An international review', *Aggression and Violent Behavior*, vol 18, no 1, pp 159-74.

Lereya, S.T., Copeland, W.E., Costello, E.J. and Wolke, D. (2015) 'Adult mental health consequences of peer bullying and maltreatment in childhood: two cohorts in two countries', *The Lancet Psychiatry*, vol 2, no 6, pp 524-31.

Lester, S. and Russell, W. (2008) *Play for a change: Play, policy and practice: A review of contemporary perspectives*, London: Play England (www.playengland.org.uk/media/120519/play-for-a-change-summary.pdf).

Liabo, K., Gray, K. and Mulcahy, D. (2013a) 'A systematic review of interventions to support looked-after children in school: supporting looked-after children in school', *Child & Family Social Work*, vol 18, no 3, pp 341-53.

Liabo, K., Simon, A. and Nutt, J. (2013b) *Providing ICT for socially disadvantaged students: Technical paper*. CfBT Education Trust & SSRU (www.cfbt.com/en-GB/Research/Research-library/2013/r-beyond-the-digital-divide-2013, accessed on 20.08.2015).

Lichy, J. (2011) 'Internet user behaviour in France and Britain: exploring socio-spatial disparity among adolescents', *International Journal of Consumer Studies*, vol 35, 470-475.

Lilley, C., Ball, R. and Vernon, H. (2014) *The experiences of 11-16 year olds on social networking sites*, London: NSPCC.

Livingstone, S. (2007) 'From family television to bedroom culture: young people's media at home', in E. Devereux (ed) *Media studies: Key issues and debates*, London: Sage Publications (http://eprints.lse. ac.uk/2772).

Livingstone, S. and Smith, P.K. (2014) 'Annual research review: Harms experienced by child users of online and mobile technologies: the nature, prevalence and management of sexual and aggressive risks in the digital age', *Journal of Child Psychology and Psychiatry*, vol 55, no 6, pp 635-54.

Livingstone, S., Haddon, L., Gorzig, H. and Olafsson, K. (2011) *Final report, EU Kids Online II*, London: London School of Economics and Political Science/EU Kids Online Network.

Livingstone, S., Mascheroni, G., Olafsson, K. and Haddon, L. (2014) *Children's online risks and opportunities: Comparative findings from EU Kids Online and Net Children Go Mobile*, London: London School of Economics and Political Science.

Luke, N., Sinclair, I., Woolgar, M. and Sebba, J. (2014) *What works in preventing and treating poor mental health in looked after children?*, London: NSPCC.

Lupton, R. and Thomson, S. (2015) *The Coalition's record on schools: Policy, spending and outcomes 2010-2015*, London: CASE Working Paper 13, London School of Economics and Political Science (http:// sticerd.lse.ac.uk/dps/case/spcc/wp13.pdf).

Lupton, R., Burchardt, T., Fitzgerald, A., Hills, J., McKnight, A., Obolenskaya, P., Stewart, K., Thomson, S., Tunstall, R. and Vizard, P. (2015) *The Coalition's Social Policy Record: Policy, Spending and Outcomes 2010-2015*. Social Policy in a Cold Climate Research Report 4 (http://sticerd.lse.ac.uk/dps/case/spcc/RR04.pdf).

MacDorman, M.F., Mathews, T.J., Mohangoo, A.D. and Zeitlin, J. (2014) *International comparisons of infant mortality and related factors: United States and Europe, 2010*, National Vital Statistics Reports, vol 63, no 5, 24 September (www.cdc.gov/nchs/data/nvsr/nvsr63/ nvsr63_05.pdf).

Macfarlane, A., Stafford, M. and Moser, K. (2004) 'Social inequalities', in Office for National Statistics, *The health of children and young people*, London: Office for National Statistics.

Mackett, R., Banister, D., Batty, M., Einon, D., Brown, B., Gong, Y. et al (2007a) *Final report on 'Children's Activities, Perceptions and Behaviour in the Local Environment (CAPABLE)'*, London: University College London (www.casa.ucl.ac.uk/capableproject/download/CAPABLE_finalReport.pdf).

Mackett, R., Brown, B., Gong, Y., Kitazawa, K. and Paskinis, J. (2007b) *Setting children free: Children's independent movement in the local environment*, London: Centre for Advanced Spatial Analysis, University College London (http://eprints.ucl.ac.uk/3474/).

Macleod, S., Hart, R., Jeffes, J. and Wilkin, A. (2010) *The impact of the Baby Peter case on applications for care orders*, LGA Research Report, Slough: National Foundation for Educational Research (NFER).

Main, G. (2013) 'A child-derived material deprivation index', Unpublished PhD thesis, University of York.

Main, G. (2014) 'Child poverty and children's subjective well-being', *Child Indicators Research*, vol 7, no 3, pp 451-72.

Main, G. and Bradshaw, J. (2012) 'An index of child material deprivation', *Child Indicators Research*, vol 5, no 3, pp 503-21.

Main, G. and Bradshaw, J. (2014) 'Children's necessities: Trends over time in perceptions and ownership', *Journal of Poverty and Social Justice*, vol 23, no 3, pp 193-208.

Main, G. and Pople, L. (2011) *Missing out: A child-centred analysis of material deprivation and subjective well-being*, London: The Children's Society.

Marmot Review, The (2010) *Fair society, healthy lives, Strategic review of health inequalities in England post-2010* (www.instituteofhealthequity.org/projects/fair-society-healthy-lives-the-marmot-review).

Marsh, A., Gordon, D., Pantazis, C. and Heslop, P. (1999) *Home sweet home? The impact of poor housing on health*, Bristol: Policy Press.

Martin, A., Ford, T., Goodman, R., Meltzer, H. and Logan, S. (2014) 'Physical illness in looked-after children: a cross-sectional study', *Archives of Disease in Childhood*, vol 99, no 2, pp 103-7.

Matthews, H. (2001) *Children and community regeneration: Creating better neighbourhoods*, London: Save the Children.

Maughan, B., Collishaw, S., Meltzer, H. and Goodman, R. (2008) 'Recent trends in UK child and adolescent mental health', *Social Psychiatry and Psychiatric Epidemiology*, vol 43, no 4, pp 305-10.

May, T., Gyateng, T. and Hough, M. (2010) *Differential treatment in the youth justice system*, Equality and Human Rights Commission.

Mayhew, E. and Bradshaw, J. (2005) 'Mothers, babies and the risks of poverty', *Poverty*, vol 121, pp 13-16.

McAuley, C. and Rose, W. (eds) (2010) *Child well-being: Understanding children's lives*, London: Jessica Kingsley Publishers.

McGhee, K., Lerpiniere, J., Welch, V., Graham, P. and Harkin, B. (2014) *Throughcare and aftercare services in Scotland's local authorities, A national study*, Glasgow: Centre for Excellence for Looked After Children in Scotland (CELCIS).

McClung, M. and Gayle, V. (2010) 'Exploring the care effects of multiple factors on the educational achievement of children looked after at home and away from home: an investigation of two Scottish local authorities', *Child & Family Social Work*, vol 15, pp 409-31.

McKechnie, J. and Hobbs, S. (2001) 'Work and education: are they compatible for children and adolescents?', in P. Mizen, C. Pole and A. Bolton (eds) *Hidden hands: International perspectives on children's work and labour*, London: RoutledgeFalmer, pp 9-23.

McKechnie, J., Sandy Hobbs, S., Simpson, A., Howieson, C. and Semple, S. (2013) 'Protecting child employees: why the system doesn't work', *Youth & Policy*, no. 110, pp 66-87.

Meltzer H., Gatward, R., Goodman, R. and Ford, T. (2000) *Mental health of children and adolescents in Great Britain*, London: The Stationery Office.

Meltzer, H., Gatward, R., Corbin, T., Goodman, R. and Ford, T. (2003) *The mental health of young people looked after by local authorities in England*, London: Office for National Statistics.

Meltzer, H., Gatward, R., Corbin, T., Goodman, R. and Ford, T. (2004a) *The mental health of young people looked after by local authorities in Wales*, London: Office for National Statistics.

Meltzer, H., Gatward, R., Corbin, T., Goodman, R. and Ford, T. (2004b) *The mental health of young people looked after by local authorities in Scotland*, London: Office for National Statistics.

Mercer, C.H., Tanton, C., Prah, P., Erens, B., Sonnenberg, P., Clifton, S. et al (2013) 'Changes in sexual attitudes and lifestyles in Britain through the life course and over time: findings from the National Surveys of Sexual Attitudes and Lifestyles (Natsal)', *The Lancet*, vol 382, pp 1781-94.

Messenger, C. and Molloy, D. (2014) *Getting it right for families: A review of integrated systems and promising practice in the early years*, London: Early intervention Foundation (www.eif.org.uk/wp-content/uploads/2014/11/Executive-Summary.pdf, accessed 1.7.15).

Mhonda, J. (2007) *Reflections on childhood*, London: GfK Social Research.

Millard, B. and Flatley, J. (2010) *Experimental statistics on victimisation of children aged 10 to 15: Findings from the British Crime Survey for the year ending December 2009*, Home Office Bulletin 11/10, London: Home Office.

MoJ (Ministry of Justice) (2010) *Breaking the cycle: Effective punishment, rehabilitation and sentencing of offenders*, London: HM Stationery Office.

MoJ and Youth Justice Board (YJB) (2012) *Youth justice statistics – 2010/11, England and Wales, Statistics Bulletin*, London: National Statistics (www.gov.uk/government/uploads/system/uploads/attachment_data/file/279892/yjb-statistics-10-11.pdf).

MoJ and YJB (2013) *Youth justice annual statistics: 2011 to 2012*, London: National Statistics (www.gov.uk/government/statistics/youth-justice-statistics-2011-12).

MoJ and YJB (2014) *Youth justice annual statistics 2012/13, England and Wales, Statistics Bulletin*, London: National Statistics (www.gov.uk/government/uploads/system/uploads/attachment_data/file/399379/youth-justice-annual-stats-13-14.pdf).

MoJ and YJB (2015) *Youth justice statistics 2013/14, England and Wales, Statistics Bulletin*, London: National Statistics (www.gov.uk/government/uploads/system/uploads/attachment_data/file/399379/youth-justice-annual-stats-13-14.pdf).

Mooney, A., Oliver, C. and Smith, M. (2009) *Impact of family breakdown on children's well-being: Evidence review*, DCSF Research Report RR113, London: Department for Children, Schools and Families.

Munro, E. (2011) *The Munro Review of child protection: Final report: A child-centred system*, London: Department for Education.

Munro, E., Taylor, J.S. and Bradbury-Jones, C. (2014) 'Understanding the causal pathways to child maltreatment: Implications for health and social care policy and practice', *Child Abuse Review*, vol 23, no 1, pp 61-74.

Munro, E., Lushey, C., National Care Advisory Service, Maskell-Graham, D. and Ward, H. with Holmes, L. (2012) *Evaluation of the Staying Put: 18+ Family Placement Programme Pilot: Final Report*, London: Department for Education.

NAO (National Audit Office) (2014) *Children in care: Report by the Comptroller and Auditor General*, London: NAO.

NAO (2015) *Care leavers' transitions to adulthood*, London: NAO.

NatCen (National Centre for Social Research) (2009) *Profiling London's rough sleepers: A longitudinal analysis of CHAIN data*, London: Broadway/NatCen.

National Childcare Trust (2015 March) *The Parliamentary Inquiry into parenting and social mobility: Enhancing parenting support across the UK*, London: National childcare Trust (www.fatherhoodinstitute.org/wp-content/uploads/2015/03/Parliamentary_Inquiry_into_Parenting_and_Social_Mobility_-_Final_Report.pdf, accessed 10.7.15).

Natural England (2013) *Monitor of Engagement with the Natural Environment: The national survey on people and the natural environment: Annual report from the 2012-2013 survey* (NECR122), London: Natural England.

Neale, J. (2006) 'Children, crime and illegal drug use', in J. Bradshaw (ed) *The well-being of children in the UK* (2nd edn), London: Save the Children, pp 239-61.

New Scientist (2015) 'Unfounded vaccine myths harm measles herd immunity', 10 February (www.newscientist.com/article/dn26946-unfounded-vaccine-myths-harm-measles-herd-immunity/).

Nicoll, A., Ellimna, D. and Begg, N.T. (1989) 'Immunisation: causes of failure and strategies and tactics for success', *British Medical Journal*, vol 299, pp 808-12.

O'Brien, M., Jones, D., Sloan, D. and Rustin, M. (2000) 'Children's independent spatial mobility in the urban public realm', *Childhood*, vol 7, no 3, pp 253-77.

O'Malley, L. and Grace, S. (2011) 'Children, crime and illegal drug use', in J. Bradshaw (ed) *The well-being of children in the UK* (3rd edn), Bristol: Policy Press, pp 235-61.

O'Sullivan, A. and Westerman, R. (2007) 'Closing the gap: investigating the barriers to educational achievement for looked-after children', *Adoption & Fostering*, vol 31, no 1, pp 13-20.

ODPM (Office of the Deputy Prime Minister) (2002) *Homelessness code of guidance for local authorities*, London: ODPM.

OECD (Organisation for Economic Co-operation and Development) (2005) Family database. (www.oecd.org/els/family/database.htm).

OECD (2009) *Doing better for children*, Paris: OECD.

OECD (2010) Family database. (http://www.oecd.org/els/family/database.htm).

OECD (2010) *PISA 2009 Results: Equity in learning opportunities and outcomes (Volume II), PISA*, Paris: OECD Publishing.

OECD (2012a) *Starting strong III: A quality toolbox for early childhood education and care*, OECD Publishing. (www.oecd.org/edu/school/startingstrongiiiaqualitytoolboxforececadvancingdatacollectionresearchandmonitoring.htm, accessed 10.8.15).

OECD (2012b) *Education at a glance 2012: OECD indicators*, Paris: OECD Publishing. (www.oecd.org/edu/EAG%202012_e-book_EN_200912.pdf, accessed 14.8.15).

OECD (2013a) *PISA 2012 results: Ready to learn: Students' engagement, drive and self-beliefs, volume III*, Paris: OECD Publishing.

OECD (2013b) *Education indicators in focus – 2013*, Paris: OECD Publishing. (www.oecd.org/ education/skills-beyond-school/EDIF11.pdf, accessed 14.8.15)

OECD (2013c) *Outcomes on early learning and development framework and considerations on the development of early learning and development*, Directorate For Education And Skills Education Policy Committee, Network on Early Childhood Education and Care (www.oecd.org/officialdocuments/publicdisplaydocumentpdf/?cote=EDU/EDPC/ECEC(2013)8/REV1&docLanguage=En, accessed 12.8.15).

OECD (2014a) *PISA 2012 results in focus: What 15-year-olds know and what they can do with what they know.* (www.oecd.org/pisa/keyfindings/pisa-2012-results-overview.pdf, accessed on 06.08.2015).

OECD (2014b) *Family Database 'PF3.2: Enrolment in childcare and pre-schools'* (www.oecd.org/els/soc/PF3_2_Enrolment_in_childcare_and_preschools.pdf, accessed 14.8.15).

OECD (2015a) Family database (www.oecd.org/els/family/database.htm).

OECD (2015b) *PISA 2012 results: UK (revised).* (www.oecd.org/pisa/keyfindings/PISA%202012%20UK%20revised%20scores_for%20web_May15.xlsx, accessed on 07.08.2015).

OECD (2015c), *Youth not in education or employment (NEET) (indicator).* doi: 10.1787/72d1033a-en (accessed on 05.08. 2015)

Ofcom (2014) *Children and parents: Media use and attitudes report*, London: Ofcom.

Office of the Children's Commissioner (2013) *A Child Rights Impact Assessment of Budget Decisions: including the 2013 Budget, and the cumulative impact of tax-benefit reforms and reductions in spending on public services 2010–2015* (www.childrenscommissioner.gov.uk/content/publications/content_676).

Ofsted (2015) *The report of Her Majesty's Chief Inspector of Education, Children's Services and Skills 2015: Early years*, Manchester: OFSTED (www.gov.uk/government/uploads/system/uploads/attachment_data/file/445730/Early_years_report_2015.pdf, accessed 13.8.15)

ONS (Office for National Statistics) (1998) *Key health statistics from general practice 1996*, Series MB6 No 1, London: ONS.

ONS (2003) *Census 2001: National report for England and Wales*, Newport: ONS.

ONS (2008) *Non-resident parental contact, 2007/8*, Omnibus Survey Report No 38, Newport: ONS.

ONS (2010a) *Child mortality statistics* (www.statistics.gov.uk/downloads/theme health/child-mortality/Table1.xls and www.statistics.gov.uk/downloads/theme_health/child-mortality/Table2.xls).

ONS (2010b) *Infant and perinatal mortality in England and Wales by social and biological factors 2009*, Statistical Bulletin (www.ons.gov.uk/ons/rel/child-health/infant-and-perinatal-mortality-in-england-and-wales-by-social-and-biological-factors/2009/statistical-bulletin.html).

ONS (2013a) *National population projections, 2012-based projections*, Newport: ONS (www.ons.gov.uk/ons/publications/re-reference-tables.html?edition=tcm%3A77-318453).

ONS (2013b) *Conceptions in England and Wales, 2013, Key findings*, Newport: ONS (www.ons.gov.uk/ons/rel/vsob1/conception-statistics--england-and-wales/2013/stb-conceptions-in-england-and-wales-2013.html).

ONS (2013c) *Statistical Bulletin: Internet Access – Households and Individuals, 2013* (www.ons.gov.uk/ons/rel/rdit2/internet-access--households-and-individuals/2013/stb-ia-2013.html, accessed on 18.08.2015).

ONS (2013d) 2011 Census, Detailed Characteristics for Local Authorities in England and Wales (www.ons.gov.uk/ons/rel/census/2011-census/detailed-characteristics-for-local-authorities-in-england-and-wales/index.html).

ONS (2014a) *Measuring national well-being – Exploring the well-being of children in the UK, 2014*, Newport: ONS (www.ons.gov.uk/ons/rel/wellbeing/measuring-national-well-being/exploring-the-well-being-of-children-in-the-uk--2014/rpt-measuring-national-wellbeing-children-uk-2014.html).

ONS (2014b) *Population estimates for UK, England and Wales, Scotland and Northern Ireland, Mid-2013*, Newport: ONS (www.ons.gov.uk/ons/publications/re-reference-tables.html?edition=tcm%3A77-322718).

ONS (2014c) 'Chapter 3: Fertility, 2012-based NPP reference volume', Newport: ONS (www.ons.gov.uk/ons/rel/npp/national-population-projections/2012-based-reference-volume--series-pp2/fertility.html#tab-Distribution-of-Completed-Family-Size).

ONS (2014d) *Dependent children usually resident in England and Wales with a parental second address, 2011* (www.ons.gov.uk/ons/rel/census/2011-census/origin-destination-statistics-on-second-residences-and-workplace-for-merged-local-authorities-and-middle-layer-super-output-areas--msoas--in-england-and-wales/rpt---dependent-children.html, accessed on 13.08.2015).

ONS (2015a) *Child mortality statistics: Childhood, infant and perinatal, 2013*, Newport: ONS (www.ons.gov.uk/ons/rel/vsob1/child-mortality-statistics--childhood--infant-and-perinatal/2013/index.html).

ONS (2015b) *Large increase in 20- to 34-year-olds living with parents since 1996*, Newport: ONS (www.ons.gov.uk/ons/rel/family-demography/young-adults-living-with-parents/2013/sty-young-adults.html?format=print).

ONS (2015c) *Families and households, 2014.* Statistical Bulletin (www.ons.gov.uk/ons/dcp171778_393133.pdf)

ONS (2015d) 'Chapter 2: Violent Crime and Sexual Offences – Homicide', Newport: ONS (www.ons.gov.uk/ons/rel/crime-stats/crime-statistics/focus-on-violent-crime-and-sexual-offences--2013-14/rpt-chapter-2.html).

ONS (2015e) *Crime in England and Wales: Year ending March 2015*, London: TSO.

ONS (nd) *Conception and fertility rates*, Newport: ONS (www.ons.gov.uk).

Parke, R.D. and Buriel, R. (1998) 'Socialisation in the family: ethnic and ecological perspectives', in W. Damon (series ed) and N. Eisenberg (vol ed) *Handbook of child psychology, Vol 3: Social, emotional and personality development* (5th edn), New York: John Wiley & Sons, pp 463-552.

Parry-Langdon, N. (ed) (2008) *Three years on: Survey of the development and emotional well-being of children and young people*, Newport: Office for National Statistics.

Patterson, C.C., Gyürüs, E., Rosenbauer, J., Cinek, O., Neu, A., Schober, E. et al (2012) 'Trends in childhood type 1 diabetes incidence in Europe during 1989-2008: evidence of non-uniformity over time in rates of increase', *Diabetologia*, vol 55, no 8, pp 2142-7.

Patterson, G.R. (1986) 'The contribution of siblings to training for fighting: a microsocial analysis', in D. Olweus, J. Block and M. Radke-Yarrow (eds) *Development of anti-social and pro-social behaviour*, New York: Academic Press, pp 235-61.

Pearce, A., Li, L., Abbas, J., Ferguson, B., Graham, H. and Law, C. (2012) 'Does the home environment influence inequalities in unintentional injury in early childhood? Findings from the UK Millennium Cohort Study', *J Epidemiol Community Health*, vol 66, no 2, pp 181-88.

Pitts, J. (1986) 'Black young people and juvenile crime: some unanswered questions', in R. Matthews and J. Young (eds) *Confronting crime*, London: Sage, pp 118-44.

Pitts, J. (2002) 'The end of an era', in J. Muncie, G. Hughes and E. McLaughlin (eds) *Youth justice: Critical readings*, London: Sage, pp 413–24.

Play England (2009) 'Playday 2009 opinion poll summary', London: Play England (www.playday.org.uk/media/2634/playday_2009_opinion_poll_summary.pdf).

Pleace, N. (2000) 'The new consensus, the old consensus and the provision of services for people sleeping rough', *Housing Studies*, vol 15, no 4, pp 581-94.

Pleace, N. (2015) *Trends and strategies in European homelessness*, Brussels: Feantsa.

Pleace, N., Fitzpatrick, S., Johnsen, S., Quilgars, D. and Sanderson, D. (2008) *Statutory homelessness in England: The experiences of families and 16-17 year olds*, London: Department for Communities and Local Government.

Policy for Play (2011) Outgoing Play England director accuses coalition of "betraying a generation of children". Media release on 8 November 2011 (http://policyforplay.com/2011/11/08/outgoing-play-england-chief-accuses-coalition-of-betraying-a-generation-of-children-and-calls-for-new-government-action-on-play/, accessed on 18.08.2015).

Pople, L., Rees, G., Main, G. and Bradshaw, J. (2015) *The Good Childhood Report 2015*, The Children's Society and the University of York (www.childrenssociety.org.uk/sites/default/files/TheGoodChildhoodReport2015.pdf).

Povey, D., Mulchandani, R., Hand, T. and Panesar, L. (2011) *Police powers and procedures, England and Wales, 2009/10*, HOSB 07/11, London: Home Office.

Press release, Prime Minister's Office (2015) *Government brings forward plans to double free childcare for working families*. (www.gov.uk/government/news/government-brings-forward-plans-to-double-free-childcare-for-working-families, accessed 2.8.15).

Povey et al (2011) Povey, D., Mulchandani, R., Hand, T. and Panesar, L. (2011) *Police powers and procedures, England and Wales, 2009/10*, HOSB 07/11, London: Home Office.

Prison Reform Trust (2014) *Bromley Briefings Prison Factfile, Autumn 2014*, London: Prison Reform Trust.

Pritchard, C. and Williams, R. (2009) 'Does social work make a difference? A controlled study of former "looked-after children" and "excluded-from-school" adolescents now men aged 16-24 subsequent offences, being victims of crime and suicide', *Journal of Social Work*, vol 9, no 3, pp 285-307.

Pritchard, C. and Williams, R. (2010) 'Comparing Possible "Child-Abuse-Related-Deaths" in England and Wales with the Major Developed Countries 1974-2006: Signs of Progress?', *British Journal of Social Work*, vol 40, no 6, pp 1700–18 (http://doi.org/10.1093/bjsw/bcp089).

Public Health for England (2014) *From evidence into action: Opportunities to protect and improve the nation's health*, London: PHE (www.gov.uk/government/uploads/system/uploads/attachment_data/file/366852/PHE_Priorities.pdf, accessed 1.7.15).

Quigley, M.A., Kelly, Y.J. and Sacker, A. (2007) 'Breastfeeding and hospitalization for diarrheal and respiratory infection in the United Kingdom Millennium Cohort Study', *Pediatrics*, vol 119, no 4, e837.

Quilgars, D. (2011) 'Housing and the environment for children', in Bradshaw, J. (ed) *The well-being of children in the UK*, Bristol: Policy Press.

Quilgars, D., Fitzpatrick, S. and Pleace, N. (2011) *Ending youth homelessness: Possibilities, challenges and practical solutions*, London: Centrepoint.

Quilgars, D., Johnsen, S. and Pleace, N. (2008) *Youth homelessness in the UK: A decade of progress?*, York: Joseph Rowntree Foundation.

Radford, L., Corral, S., Bradley, C. and Fisher, H.L. (2013) 'The prevalence and impact of child maltreatment and other types of victimization in the UK: Findings from a population survey of caregivers, children and young people and young adults', *Child Abuse & Neglect*, vol 37, no 10, pp 801-13.

Radford, L., Corral, S., Bradley, C., Fisher, H., Bassett, C., Howat, N. and Collishaw, S. (2011) *Child abuse and neglect in the UK today*, London: NSPCC (http://clok.uclan.ac.uk/6022/).

Ravens-Sieberer, U., Erhart, M., Torsheim, T., Hetland, J., Freeman, J., Danielson, M. et al (2008) 'An international scoring system for self-reported health complaints in adolescents', *The European Journal of Public Health*, vol 18, no 3, pp 294-9.

RCPCH (Royal College of Paediatrics and Child Health) (2015) *National paediatric diabetes audit report 2013-2014*, London: RCPCH (www.rcpch.ac.uk/).

Reed, H. and Portes, J. (2014) *Cumulative impact assessment*, Research report no 94, Equality and Human Rights Commission.

Rees, G. and Bradshaw J. (2016: forthcoming) Exploring variation in the subjective well-being of children aged 11 in the UK. An analysis using data reported by parents and by children.

Rees, G. and Main, G. (eds) (2015) *Children's views on their lives and well-being in 15 countries: A report on the Children's Worlds survey, 2013-14*, York: Children's Worlds Project (ISCWeB).

Rees, G., Goswami, H. and Bradshaw, J. (2010) *Developing an index of children's subjective well-being in England*, London: The Children's Society.

Rees, G., Main G. and Bradshaw, J. (2015) *Children's Worlds national report: England* (www.isciweb.org/_Uploads/dbsAttachedFiles/England_NationalReport_Final.pdf).

Rees, G., Pople, L. and Goswami, H. (2011) *Links between family economic factors and children's subjective well-being: Initial findings from wave 2 and wave 3 quarterly surveys*, London: The Children's Society.

Rees, G., Bradshaw, J., Goswami, H. and Keung, A. (2010) *Understanding children's well-being: A national survey of young people's well-being*, London: The Children's Society.

Rees, P. (2013) 'The mental health, emotional literacy, cognitive ability, literacy attainment and "resilience" of "looked after children": A multidimensional, multiple-rater population based study', *British Journal of Clinical Psychology*, vol 52, no 2, pp 183-98.

Rendall, M. (2003) 'How important are intergenerational cycles of teenage motherhood in England and Wales? A comparison with France', *Population Trends 111*, Spring.

Richardus, J.H., Graafmans, W.C., Verloove-Vanhorick, S.P. and Mackenbach, J.P. (2003) 'Differences in perinatal mortality and suboptimal care between 10 European regions results of an international audit', *BJOG: An International Journal of Obstetrics and Gynaecology*, vol 110 pp 97-105.

Ridge, T. (2002) *Childhood poverty and social exclusion*, Bristol: Policy Press.

Riggio, H.R. (1999) 'Personality and social skill differences between adults with and without siblings', *Journal of Psychology*, vol 133, pp 514-22.

Robson, K. (2009) 'Changes in family structure and the well-being of British children: evidence from a fifteen-year panel study', *Child Indicators Research*, vol 3, no 1, pp 65-83.

Rock, S., Michelson, D., Thomson, S. and Day, C. (2015) 'Understanding foster placement instability for looked after children: A systematic review and narrative synthesis of quantitative and qualitative evidence', *British Journal of Social Work*, vol 45, no 1, pp 177-203.

Rodgers, B. and Pryor, J. (1998) *Divorce and separation: The outcomes for children*, York: York Publishing Services for the Joseph Rowntree Foundation.

Ross Anderson, H., Gupta, R., Strachan, D.P. and Limb, E.S. et al (2007) '50 years of asthma: UK trends from 1955 to 2004', *Thorax*, vol 62, pp 85-90 (http://thorax.bmj.com/content/62/1/85.full).

Rugg, J. (2010) 'Young people and housing: The need for a new policy agenda', *Viewpoint*, York: Joseph Rowntree Foundation.

Rugg, J. and Quilgars, D. (2015) 'Young people and housing: a review of the present policy and practice landscape', *Youth and Policy Special Edition: The Next Five Years: Prospects for young people*, No 114, May, pp 5-16 (www.youthandpolicy.org/wp-content/uploads/2015/04/rugg-quilgars-young-people-and-housing1.pdf).

Rutter, J. and Stocker, K. (2014) *The 2014 Scottish Childcare Report*, London: Family and Childcare Trust (www.fct.bigmallet.co.uk/sites/default/files/files/The_2014_Scottish_Childcare_Report_FINAL.pdf, accessed 10.8.15).

Schepman, K., Collishaw, S., Gardner, F., Maughan, B., Scott, J. and Pickles, A. (2011) 'Do changes in parent mental health explain trends in youth emotional problems?', *Social Science & Medicine*, vol 73, no 2, pp 293-300.

Schoeppe, S., Duncan, M.J., Badland, H.M., Alley, S., Williams, S., Amanda L. Rebar, A.L. and Vandelanotte, C. (2015) 'Socio-demographic factors and neighbourhood social cohesion influence adults' willingness to grant children greater independent mobility: a cross-sectional study', *BMC Public Health*, vol 15, no 690 (doi: 10.1186/s12889-015-2053-2, accessed on 17.08.2015).

Schofield, G., Biggart, L., Ward, E. and Larsson, B. (2015) 'Looked after children and offending: An exploration of risk, resilience and the role of social cognition', *Children and Youth Services Review*, vol 51, pp 125-33.

Scholes, S. (2014) 'Children's smoking and exposure to others' smoke', *HSE*, vol 1, chapter 9 (www.hscic.gov.uk/catalogue/PUB16076/HSE2013-Ch9-chi-smok-exp.pdf).

SCIE (Social Care Institute for Excellence) (2005) *The health and well-being of young carers*, SCIE Research Briefing 11, London: SCIE (www.scie.org.uk/publications/briefings/briefing11/index.asp).

Scottish Government (2013) Attendance and absence 2012/13 (www.gov.scot/Topics/Statistics/Browse/School-Education/AttendanceAbsenceDatasets/attab2013, accessed on 10.08.2015).

The Scottish Government (2014a) *National Guidance for Child Protection in Scotland, 2014*. Edinburgh: The Scottish Government.

Scottish Government (2014b) Summary statistics for schools in Scotland: Exclusions (www.gov.scot/Publications/2013/12/4199/20, accessed on 10.08.2015).

Scottish Government (2015a) Pupil Census Supplementary Data. (www.gov.scot/Topics/Statistics/Browse/School-Education/dspupcensus, accessed on 12.08.2015).

Scottish Government (2015b) High Level Summary of Statistics Trend Last update: December 2014: Additional Support Needs (www.gov.scot/Topics/Statistics/Browse/School-Education/dspupcensus, accessed on 12.08.2015).

Sefton, T. (2004) *A fair share of the wealth: Public spending on children in England*, CASEreport 25, London: STICERD, London School of Economics and Political Science.

Sellers, R., Maughan, B., Pickles, A., Thapar, A. and Collishaw, S. (2015) 'Trends in parent- and teacher-rated emotional, conduct and ADHD problems and their impact in prepubertal children in Great Britain: 1999-2008', *Journal of Child Psychology and Psychiatry*, vol 56, no 1, pp 49-57.

Sempik J., Ward, H. and Darker, I. (2008) 'Emotional and behavioural difficulties of children and young people at entry into care', *Clinical Child Psychology and Psychiatry*, vol 13, no 2, pp 221-33.

Shaw, M. (2004) 'Housing and public health', *Annual review of public health, 2004*, 25, pp 397-418.

Sidebotham, P., Atkins, B. and Hutton, J.L. (2012) 'Changes in rates of violent child deaths in England and Wales between 1974 and 2008: an analysis of national mortality data', *Archives of Disease in Childhood*, vol 97, no 3, pp 193-9.

Sidebotham, P., Bailey, S., Belderson, P. and Brandon, M. (2011a) 'Fatal child maltreatment in England, 2005-2009', *Child Abuse & Neglect*, vol 35, no 4, pp 299-306.

Sidebotham, P., Brandon, M., Bailey, S., Belderson, P. and Hawley, C. (2011b) *Serious and fatal child maltreatment: Setting serious case review data in context with other data on violent and maltreatment-related deaths in 2009-10*, Research Report DFE-RR167, London: Department for Education (http://dera.ioe.ac.uk/13695/1/DFE-RR167.pdf).

Sinclair, I., Baker, C., Lee, J. and Gibbs, I. (2007) *The pursuit of permanence: A study of the English care system*, London: Jessica Kingsley Publishers.

Skinner, C. (2011) 'Childcare and early years' in Bradshaw, J. (ed) *The Well-being of children in the UK* (3rd edn), Bristol: Policy Press, pp 213-34.

Smith, R. (2005) 'Welfare versus justice – Again!', *Youth Justice*, vol 5, no 3, pp 3-16.

Social Exclusion Unit (1999) *Teenage pregnancy*, Cm 4342, London: The Stationery Office.

Social Mobility and Child Poverty Commission (2014) *State of the nation 2014 report*, 20 October, London (www.gov.uk/government/publications/state-of-the-nation-2014-report).

Speight, S., Maisey, R., Chanfreau, J., Haywood, A., Lord, C. and David Hussey (2015) *Study of Early Education and Development Baseline survey of families Research Report*, London: NatCen (www.foundationyears.org.uk/files/2015/07/SEED-Baseline-survey.pdf, accessed 10.7.15)

Stack, N. and McKechnie, J. (2002) 'Working children', in B. Goldson, M. Lavalette and J. McKechnie (2002) *Children, welfare and the state*, London: Sage, pp 87-101.

Stein, M. (2009) *Quality matters in children's services: Messages from research*, London: Jessica Kingsley Publishers.

Stein, M. (2012) *Young people leaving care: Supporting pathways to adulthood*, London: Jessica Kingsley Publishers.

Stein, M. and Morris, M. (2010) *Increasing the numbers of care leavers in 'settled, safe' accommodation: Vulnerable children*, Knowledge Review 3, London: C4EO.

Stith, S.M., Liu, T., Davies, L.C., Boykin, E.L., Alder, M.C., Harris, J.M. et al (2009) 'Risk factors in child maltreatment: A meta-analytic review of the literature', *Aggression and Violent Behavior*, vol 14, no 1, pp 13-29.

Stocker, C. and Dunn, J. (1990) 'Sibling relationships in childhood: links with friendships and peer relationships', *British Journal of Developmental Psychology*, vol 8, pp 227-44.

Sutton, L. (2008) 'The state of play: disadvantage, play and children's well-being', *Social Policy & Society*, vol 7, no 4, pp 537-49.

Sweeting, H., Young, R. and West, P. (2009) 'GHQ increases among Scottish 15 year olds 1987-2006', *Social Psychiatry and Psychiatric Epidemiology*, vol 44, pp 579-86.

Sweeting, H., West, P., Young, R. and Der, G. (2010) 'Can we explain increases in young people's psychological distress over time?', *Social Science & Medicine*, vol 71, no 10, pp 1819–30.

Sylva, K., Melhuish, E., Sammons, P., Siraj, I., Taggart, B. with Smees, R., Toth, K., Welcomme, W. and Hollingworth, K. (2014) *Students' educational and developmental outcomes at age 16, Effective Pre-school, Primary and Secondary Education (EPPSE 3–16) Project, Research Brief* (September 2014) London: Department for Education (www.gov.uk/government/uploads/system/uploads/attachment_data/file/351496/RR354_-_Students__educational_and_developmental_outcomes_at_age_16.pdf, accessed 10.8.15).

Tabberer S (2002) 'Teenage pregnancy and teenage motherhood', in J. Bradshaw (ed) *The well-being of children in the UK*, London/York: Save the Children/University of York.

Taggart, B., Sylva, K., Melhuish, E., Sammons, P. and Siraj, I. (2015) *Effective pre-school, primary and secondary education project (EPPSE 3-16+) How pre-school influences children and young people's attainment and developmental outcomes over time: Research Brief June 2015*, London: Department for Education (www.gov.uk/government/uploads/system/uploads/attachment_data/file/435429/RB455_Effective_pre-school_primary_and_secondary_education_project.pdf, accessed 10.8.15).

The Children's Society (2006) *A good childhood? A question for our times*, London: The Children's Society.

The Children's Society (2011) *The good childhood report 2011*, London: The Children's Society.

The Children's Society (2012) *The good childhood report 2012*, London: The Children's Society.

The Children's Society (2013) *The good childhood report 2013*, London: The Children's Society.

The Children's Society (2013b) *Hidden from view: the experiences of young carers in England* (www.childrenssociety.org.uk/sites/default/files/tcs/hidden_from_view_-_final.pdf, accessed on 15.12.2015)

The Children's Society (2014) *The good childhood report 2014*, London: The Children's Society.

The Children's Society (2015) *The good childhood report 2015*, London: The Children's Society (www.childrenssociety.org.uk/sites/default/files/TheGoodChildhoodReport2015.pdf).

Tickell. C. (2011) The Early Years: Foundations for life, health and learning: Independent Report on the Early Years Foundation Stage to Her Majesty's Government (www3.hants.gov.uk/the_tickell_review_the_early_years_foundations_for_life__health_and_learning.pdf, accessed 10.7.15).

Tilbury, C., Creed, P., Buys, N. and Meegan, C. (2011) 'The school to work transition for young people in state care: perspectives from young people, carers and professionals', *Child and Family Social Work*, vol 16, pp 345-52.

Tippett, N. and Wolke, D. (2014) 'Aggression between siblings: Associations with the home environment and peer bullying', *Aggressive Behavior*, vol 41, no 1, pp 14-24.

Towner, E. (2002) 'The prevention of childhood injury. Background Paper prepared for the Accidental Injury Task Force', in Department of Health, *Preventing accidental injury: Priorities for action*, Report to the Chief Medical Officer of the Accidental Injury Taskforce, London: Department of Health.

Travis, A. (2011) 'Public sector cuts: rise in youth crime feared as key teams are reduced', *The Guardian Online*, 25 March (www.guardian.co.uk/society/2011/mar/25/public-sector-cuts-youth-crime).

Tromans, N., Natamba, E. and Jefferies, J. (2009) 'Have women born outside the UK driven the rise in UK births since 2001?', *Population Trends 136*, pp 28-42.

Tunstall, R., Bevan, M., Bradshaw, J., Croucher, K., Duffy, S., Hunter, C., Jones, A., Rugg, J., Wallace, A., and Wilcox, S. (2013) *The links between housing and poverty*, York: Joseph Rowntree Foundation.

UN (United Nations) (1989) *Convention on the Rights of the Child*, New York: UN.

UNICEF (1979) *The state of the world's children*, Geneva: UNICEF.

UNICEF (2001) *A league table of teenage births in rich nations*, Innocenti Report Card no 3, Florence: UNICEF Innocenti Research Centre.

UNICEF (2007) *Child poverty in perspective: An overview of child well-being in high income countries*, Innocenti Report Card no 7, Florence: UNICEF Innocenti Research Centre.

UNICEF (2010a) *The children left behind: A league table of inequality in child well-being in the world's richest countries*, Innocenti Report Card no 9, Florence: UNICEF Innocenti Research Centre.

UNICEF (2013) *Child well-being in rich countries: A comparative overview*, Innocenti Report Card no 11, Florence: UNICEF Office of Research.

UNICEF (2014) *Children of the recession: The impact of the economic crisis on child well-being in rich countries*, Innocenti Report Card no 12, Florence: UNICEF Office of Research.

UN General Assembly (1989) *The United Nations Convention on the Rights of the Child*, New York: UN.

Uprichard, E. (2008) 'Children as beings and becomings: children, childhood and temporality', *Children and Society*, vol 22, no 4, pp 303-13.

Värnik, A., Kõlves, K., Allik, J., Arensman, E., Aromaa, E. et al (2009) 'Gender issues in suicide rates, trends and methods among youths aged 15-24 in 15 European countries', *Journal of Affective Disorders*, vol 113, pp 216-26.

Verhulst, F. (2015) 'Commentary: Physical health outcomes and health care have improved so much, so why is child mental health getting worse? Or is it? A commentary on Collishaw (2015)', *Journal of Child Psychology and Psychiatry*, vol 56, no 3, pp 394-6.

VOYPIC (2014) *Our life in care, VOYPIC'S third CASI survey of the views and experiences of children and young people in care*, Belfast: VOYPIC.

Wade, J. and Dixon, J. (2006) 'Making a home, finding a job: investigating early housing and employment outcomes for young people leaving care', *Child & Family Social Work*, vol 11, no 3, pp 199-208.

Wade, A. and Smart, C. (2002) *Facing family change: Children's circumstances, strategies and resources*, York: York Publishing Services for the Joseph Rowntree Foundation.

Wade, J., Biehal, N., Farrelly, N. and Sinclair, I. (2010) *Maltreated children in the looked after system: A comparison of outcomes for those who go home and those who do not*, Research Brief DFE-RBX-10-06, London: Department for Education.

Wall, S., Litjends, I. and Taguma, M. (2015) *Pedagogy in early childhood education and care (ECEC): An international comparative study of approaches and policies*, London: DfE (www.oecd.org/education/early-childhood-education-and-care-pedagogy-review-england.pdf, accessed 11.8.15).

Weightman, A., Morgan, H., Shepherd, M., Kitcher, H. Roberts, C. and Dunstan, F. (2012) 'Social inequality and infant health in the UK: systematic review and meta-analyses', *British Medical Journal*, vol 2, issue 3.

Welsh Assembly Government (2014b) *Exclusions from schools.* (http://gov.wales/statistics-and-research/exclusions-schools/?lang=en).

Welsh Assembly Government (2015a) *Examination achievements of pupils aged 15 by local authority* (https://statswales.wales.gov.uk/v/v1h, accessed on 30.07.2015).

Welsh Assembly Government (2015b) *Examination achievements of pupils aged 17 by year* (https://statswales.wales.gov.uk/Catalogue/Education-and-Skills/Schools-and-Teachers/Examinations-and-Assessments/Advanced-Level-and-Equivalent/ExaminationAchievementsOfPupilsAged17-by-Year, accessed on 30.07.2015).

Welsh Assembly Government (2015c) *Absenteeism by pupils of compulsory school age in primary schools by school type and year* (https://statswales.wales.gov.uk/Catalogue/Education-and-Skills/Schools-and-Teachers/Absenteeism/absenteeismbypupilsofcompulsoryschoolageinprimaryschools-by-schooltype-year, accessed on 10.08.2015).

Welsh Assembly Government (2015d) *Absenteeism by pupils of compulsory school age in secondary schools by school type and year* (https://statswales.wales.gov.uk/Catalogue/Education-and-Skills/Schools-and-Teachers/Absenteeism/absenteeismbypupilsofcompulsoryschoolageinsecondaryschools-by-schooltype-year, accessed on 10.08.2015).

Welsh Assembly Government (2015e) *Pupils by local authority, region and age group* (https://statswales.wales.gov.uk/Catalogue/Education-and-Skills/Schools-and-Teachers/Schools-Census/Pupil-Level-Annual-School-Census/Pupils/pupils-by-localauthorityregion-agegroup, accessed on 12.08.2015).

Welsh Assembly Government (2015f) *Pupils with special educational needs by local authority, region and type of provision* (https://statswales.wales.gov.uk/Catalogue/Education-and-Skills/Schools-and-Teachers/Schools-Census/Pupil-Level-Annual-School-Census/Special-Educational-Needs/pupilssen-by-localauthorityregion-provision, accessed on 12.08.2015).

Welsh Government (2014a) *Flying Start Summary Statistics 2013-2014*, Cardiff: Welsh Government.

Welsh Government (2014b) *A review of the comparability of statistics of children looked after by local authorities in the different countries of the United Kingdom*, Cardiff: Knowledge and Analytical Services, Welsh Government.

Wheater, R., Ager, R., Burge, B. and Sizmur, J. (2013a) *Achievement of 15-year-olds in England: PISA 2012 National Report*. Slough: NFER (www.nfer.ac.uk/publications/PQUK01/PQUK01_home.cfm, accessed on 07.08.2015).

Wheater, R., Ager, R., Burge, B. and Sizmur, J. (2013b) *Achievement of 15-year-olds in Wales: PISA 2012 National Report*. Slough: NFER (www.nfer.ac.uk/publications/PQUK02/PQUK02_home.cfm, accessed on 07.08.2015).

Wheater, R. Ager, R., Burge, B. & Sizmur, J (2013c) *Student achievement in Northern Ireland: Results in mathematics, science, and reading among 15-year-olds from the OECD PISA 2012 Study*. Slough: NFER (www.nfer.ac.uk/publications/PQUK03/PQUK03_home.cfm, accessed on 07.08.2015).

WHO (World Health Organization) (1999) *Report of the consultation on child abuse prevention*, 9-31 March, Geneva: WHO.

WHO (2002) *The World Health Organization's infant feeding recommendation*, Geneva: WHO (www.who.int/nutrition/topics/infantfeeding_recommendation/en/).

Wilcox, S. Perry, J. and Williams, P. (2015) *UK housing review 2015*, Coventry: Chartered Institute of Housing (www.york.ac.uk/res/ukhr/).

Wilkinson, R.G. and Pickett, K. (2009) *The spirit level: Why more equal societies almost always do better*, London: Allen Lane.

Wilson, B. (2010) 'Children with a non-resident parent', *Population Trends 140*, pp 53-81.

Wilson, B. and Stuchbury, R. (2010) 'Do partnerships last? Comparing marriage and cohabitation using longitudinal census data', *Population Trends*, no 139, pp 37-63.

Wilson, E. and Hinks, S. (2011) *Assessing the predictive validity of the Asset youth risk assessment tool using the Juvenile Cohort Study (JCS)*, Ministry of Justice Research Series 10/11, London: Ministry of Justice.

Wilson, V., Malcolm, H., Edward, S. and Davidson, J. (2008) '"Bunking off": the impact of truancy on pupils and teachers', *British Educational Research Journal*, vol 34, no 1, pp 1-17.

Wolfe, I., Macfarlane, A., Donkin, A., Marmot, M. and Viner, R. (2014) *Why children die: Death in infants, children, and young people in the UK, Part A*, London: Royal College of Paediatrics and Child Health, National Children's Bureau and British Association for Child and Adolescent Public Health, May (www.ncb.org.uk/media/1130496/rcpch_ncb_may_2014_-_why_children_die__part_a.pdf).

Wolfe, I., Thompson, M., Gill, P., Tamburlini, G., Blair, M., van den Bruel, A. et al (2013) 'Health services for children in western Europe', *The Lancet*, vol 381, no 9873, pp 1224-34.

Wolke, D., Copeland, W.E., Angold, A. and Costello, E.J. (2013) 'Impact of bullying in childhood on adult health, wealth, crime, and social outcomes', *Psychological Science*, vol 24, no 10, pp 1958–70.

YJB (2006) *Asset profile guidance*, London: YJB.

YJB (2010a) *Youth Justice Board annual workload data 2008/9, England and Wales*, London: Youth Justice Board and Ministry of Justice (www.yjb.gov.uk/).

YJB (2010b) *The Youth Rehabilitation Order and other Provisions of the Criminal Justice and Immigration Act 2008: Practice guidance for Youth Offending Teams*, London: YJB.

YJB (2014) *Reoffending: Developing a local understanding. Guidance for YOT Management Boards arising from the YJB Reoffending Project Findings*, London: YJB.

Youngblade, L.M. and Dunn, J. (1995) 'Individual differences in children's pretend play with mother and sibling: links to relationships and understanding of other people's feelings and beliefs', *Child Development*, vol 66, pp 1472-92.

Young-Hyman, D., Tanofsky-Kraff, M., Yanovski, S.Z., Keil, M., Cohen, M.L., Peyrot, M. and Yanovski, J.A. (2006) 'Psychological status and weight-related distress in overweight or at-risk-for-overweight children', *Obesity*, vol 14, no 12, pp 2249-58.

Index

Page references for figures and tables are given in *italics*; those for notes are followed by n

Y